COLUMBIA UNIVERSITY PRESS   New York

THE MERCHANT'S TALE

Asia Perspectives

Weatherhead East Asian Institute, Columbia University

SIMON PARTNER

THE MERCHANT'S TALE

YOKOHAMA AND THE TRANSFORMATION OF JAPAN

Columbia University Press
Publishers Since 1893
New York   Chichester, West Sussex
cup.columbia.edu

Cataloging-in-Publication Data available from the Library of Congress
ISBN 978-0-231-18292-8 (cloth)
ISBN 978-0-231-54446-7 (electronic)

Columbia University Press books are printed on permanent
and durable acid-free paper.
Printed in the United States of America

Cover image: Shinohara Family, March 1872. Studio photograph, Yokohama.
Courtesy of Shinohara Yukio.

Cover design: Chang Jae Lee

To Shima

CONTENTS

TABLES AND ILLUSTRATIONS

NOTES ON THE TEXT

JAPANESE FAMILY NAMES ARE WRITTEN BEFORE GIVEN NAMES throughout this text, except in the cases of a few Japanese (such as Joseph Heco, who was a naturalized American citizen) who used the Western name order.

In the 1860s, Japanese date conventions varied considerably from the Gregorian calendar. It was customary to measure years by era name, with new eras being declared periodically for a variety of reasons. The period covered by this book includes the Ansei era (1854–1859), the Man'en era (1860), the Bunkyū era (1861–1863), the Genji era (1864), the Keiō era (1865–1867), and the Meiji era (1868–1912). Moreover, although the Japanese used a twelve-month calendar, the Japanese months did not align with the Gregorian equivalents. In general, the Japanese calendar was about a month behind. Thus, for example, the twenty-first of the sixth month of the Ansei era was July 20, 1859, in the Gregorian calendar. In this book, I use the Gregorian calendar in principle, but in many cases for the sake of clarity I also provide the Japanese equivalent.

Throughout this book, unless otherwise stated, "dollars" (or $) refers to Mexican silver dollars, the trade currency prevalent in nineteenth-century East Asia. I have tried, where possible, to give Western equivalents to Japanese monetary values as well as weights and measures. In the case of money, I give the Mexican dollar equivalent value in the year in which the event took place and not a twenty-first-century monetary equivalent.

ACKNOWLEDGMENTS

THIS HAS BEEN AN EXTRAORDINARILY PLEASANT AND REWARDING project, made all the more so by the many individuals, groups, and institutions that have helped and supported me along the way.

In North Carolina, I benefited tremendously from the support and input of the Triangle Center for Japanese Studies community. I received a great deal of material support from Duke University's Asian/Pacific Studies Institute (APSI), which financed several trips to Japan, as well as from Duke's Global Asia Initiative. Thanks to Global Asia director Prasenjit Duara, and thanks always to APSI associate director Yan Li and her wonderful staff for all they do for our Asian studies community. My thanks also to Kris Troost, David Ambaras, Morgan Pitelka, Gennifer Weisenfeld, Meg McKean, Gunther Peck, and Jan Bardsley. Thanks also to Beth Berry, who was visiting at the National Humanities Center during a crucial period of my project's gestation.

I was fortunate to be invited to present my work as part of Harvard University's Reischauer Institute of Japanese Studies Japan Forum series. My warm thanks to Ian Miller for the invitation and to Ian, David Howell, Bill Johnston, Franziska Seraphim, and the amazing graduate students of Harvard's Japanese history program for all their thoughtful and helpful responses. Thanks also to Stacie Matsumoto for impeccable administrative support.

In 2015–2016, I and my project moved to Heidelberg for a year with the research cluster "Asia and Europe in a Global Context." I was extremely fortunate to receive a Humboldt Research Award for my stay in Germany. The Alexander von Humboldt Foundation was a marvelous sponsor and went out of its way to connect me to a vibrant network of fellows and alumni, including memorable conferences in Bamberg and Berlin. Particular thanks to Jörn Leonhard and Christina Fleck. Thanks also to Carol Gluck, Andrew Gordon, and Sebastian Conrad for supporting my Humboldt application. At Heidelberg, my deepest thanks go to Harald Fuess for sponsoring my stay in Germany, applying to the Humboldt Foundation on my behalf, and sharing many discussion hours on topics related to the East Asian treaty ports. It was my good fortune that Harald is one of the world's greatest experts on this subject, and his support and friendship were enormous contributors to my project. Among other things, during my stay Harald organized a global conference on the Meiji Restoration and co-organized with me an international workshop on the East Asian treaty ports. I presented my work at both events and benefited greatly from the input of a veritable pantheon of deeply informed scholars.

Heidelberg contains an extraordinary community of Asian studies scholars, and I was fortunate to receive helpful feedback from many of them. Particular thanks to Melanie Trede, Monica Juneja, and Barbara Mittler. Monica and Melanie were enormously helpful and supportive as I took some tentative steps into the world of visual studies. Together, they arranged for me to present my work both at the research cluster and at the Heidelberger Kunstverein (my thanks also to Kunstverein director Susanne Weiss for making that possible). Barbara invited me to participate (together with Lee Ju-Ling of Tokyo University) in a special session devoted to the body in nineteenth-century East Asia, where I was able to develop my thoughts on changing bodies in the Yokohama treaty port. Special thanks also to my office mate, Steve Ivings, who was always ready with helpful feedback and congenial company; Christina Pietsch for first-class administrative support; Joachim Kurtz; Martin Krämer; Anna Andreeva; Shupin Lang; Mio Wakita; and Pablo Blitstein.

While in Europe, I was also invited to present in a number of other locations, all of which were helpful to me as I developed my project. My thanks to Martin Dusinberre and the participants in the Geschichtskontor workshop at the University of Zurich; Dominic Sachsenmeier at the University of Göttingen; Wolfram Manzenreiter at the University of Vienna; and Rotem Kowner at the University of Haifa.

In Japan, special thanks to Shinohara Yukio. Thanks also to the staff at the Yamanashi Kenritsu Hakubutsukan and the Yokohama Kaikō Shiryōkan, with a particular thank-you to Hirano Masahiro. Thanks also to Kanehyō Masaki for many years of friendship and for sharing his deep knowledge of Yokohama.

Thanks also to Dani Botsman, Carson Holloway, Kären Wigen, Mark Ravina, Mark Metzler, and Rob Hellyer. Thanks to Emily Partner for efficient scanning services, and special thanks to Fabian Drixler, who spent too much of his valuable time helping me sort through contextual and grammatical problems in my archival sources.

Throughout the book I have made liberal use of diary entries by Francis Hall, an American merchant who lived in Yokohama from 1859 to 1866. I am most grateful to Fred Notehelfer for editing this extraordinary resource and making it available to the public.

As the book moved into the publication stage, I benefited from several informed and helpful readings (including by three anonymous outside readers) and feedback from the editorial staff of Columbia University Press. Particular thanks to Jennifer Crewe, who took the project on and shepherded it through its many stages; Ross Yelsey; and Jonathan Fiedler. Thanks also to Reed Malcolm, who is always ready with helpful and impartial advice. A special thank-you to Gabriel Gordon-Hall, who read the entire manuscript during the revision stage and gave invaluable feedback. And thanks always to Carol Gluck, who was there at day one and has helped me at every stage of my career in Japanese studies.

Finally, deep thanks to Shima Enomoto for unwavering support of my career and much practical assistance with translation and interpretation of difficult texts.

INTRODUCTION

IN APRIL 1859, A JAPANESE FARMER TRAVELED TO THE SHOGUNAL
capital, Edo (now Tokyo), to seek permission to begin a new life. Shinohara
Chūemon (1809–1891) was fifty years old. He shared the hereditary headman's position in his village. He had a large and comfortable home, a wife
and at least six living children, a dense network of lifelong friends, and deep
business ties with fellow villagers from his own and surrounding communities. He was, in other words, established and privileged in his village environment. By contrast, the new life he sought for himself was a giant leap into
the unknown. Chūemon left his village of Higashi-Aburakawa in what is
now Yamanashi prefecture (three to five days' walk from Edo) in order to
apply to the shogunal authorities for a building lot in the brand-new international port town of Yokohama, scheduled to open in July, as well as for a license to trade with the foreigners who were expected to take up residence
there. Once granted permission, he would have to build his business from
scratch, in a town that did not yet exist, in premises that he would have to
construct, to trade with a group of people who were not yet present, whose

language and customs were unknown, and whose arrival in Japan was the subject of violent controversy. Why take such a chance on an uncertain and precarious future?

While much of this book is devoted to exploring Chūemon's motives and experiences, the simple answer is opportunity. In the opening of the new port, Chūemon saw a unique opportunity to create wealth and prosperity for himself and indeed for his entire community. In the years that followed, thousands of others, Japanese and foreign, privileged and marginal, men and women, merchants, artisans, artists, and tradesmen, poured into Yokohama in search of that same opportunity, swelling the population of the town from a few hundred in 1859 to more than thirty thousand by the mid-1860s. This book is a portrait of Chūemon and his experiences in Yokohama; of others who, like him, came to Yokohama in search of opportunity; and of the city of Yokohama itself during this first turbulent and dramatic decade.

With its window onto Japan's intriguing and hitherto inaccessible heartland, its silk merchants and curio shops, its exotic foreign settlement, and its glamorous entertainment district, Yokohama was a magnet for Japanese and foreigner alike from the moment it opened for trade on July 1, 1859. During the course of the following decade, the town experienced unprecedented economic and population growth. It became one of Japan's premier destinations for domestic tourism. It was a center for the study and acquisition of new technologies, new lifestyles, new knowledge of art, science, politics, and commerce, and new ways of understanding the world. And it became a byword for exoticism, glamour, and prosperity. But it was also a lightning rod for domestic opposition to the shogunate's foreign policy. It was a favorite target of radical antiforeign idealists. It was the scene of dramatic murders. It was the location of tense showdowns between the shogunal authorities and the foreign community (on at least one occasion, more than half the population fled in the expectation of a massacre). And it was a classic site of gunboat diplomacy, crowded at times with aggressive foreign warships and military garrisons.

Yokohama also played an important, and little-studied, role in the broader social, political, and economic transformations of the 1860s and beyond. The decade was a period of extraordinary transition in Japan's dramatic modern history. It witnessed the agonizing struggle of the Tokugawa shogunate to deal with threats at home and abroad; the revolution and civil war that finally overthrew the shogunal regime; the consolidation of power in the hands of a new, untested government of young reformers from outsider clans; and the initiation of what was to be a massive program of reform, industrialization, and technological transformation that over the following decades was to launch Japan into the ranks of the world's great military and imperialist powers. What was the relationship between Japan's first and largest port under the new regime of treaty-based commerce and the vast transformations of Japan in the 1860s and beyond?

My first aim in this book is to tell a story. I have always been fascinated by the narratives of ordinary people's lives and by their relationship to the great events that are the usual stuff of history books. In Shinohara Chūemon as he embarked on his adventure in the new and contentious port of Yokohama at the turn of what would prove to be a revolutionary decade, I felt I had found a worthy protagonist. But as I explored Chūemon's life and experiences and the wider story of his community, I came to understand just how transformative the new treaty port of Yokohama had been in the lives of ordinary people in Japan and even globally. Moreover, the catalyst of those transformations was not (for the most part at least) the weighty policy decisions of elite actors but the vibrant commercial culture of the treaty port itself.

Much of the impact of Yokohama can be tied to Japan's sudden and disruptive connection to global markets. In the Kantō region and beyond, the production of silk, cotton, and tea grew rapidly in response to foreign demand, bringing new wealth to merchants in both Yokohama and the rural hinterland, as well as to the small-scale farmers who produced the raw materials for these products. On the other hand the price rises, commodity shortages, supply-chain disruptions, and political upheavals caused in whole or in part by the activities of the new port resulted also in widespread suffering as villagers and townsmen were mobilized and taxed to support military campaigns, impoverished by runaway inflation, or sidelined by rapid shifts in demand. The second half of the 1860s saw an unprecedented increase in protests in both towns and villages as impoverished and debt-ridden farmers and artisans resorted to time-honored traditions of "smashing" (uchikowashi) as an outlet for their feelings of helplessness.

But the ripples cast out by the new international port also extended far beyond the economic sphere. The new port and its global communities contributed to profound transformations in Japanese society and culture and extended even as far as global cultural and material flows. They include the disruption of existing hierarchies, as the town's radically new business practices rewarded flexible and entrepreneurial risk takers, raising them into the ranks of a new merchant elite while freezing out the conservative merchant houses of the Edo establishment. They include a subtle reorientation of both space and time, as Japanese merchants and even rural peasant producers became dependent on global market opportunities (and vulnerable to global disruptions) and as the need to exploit information advantages created a technological imperative for greater speed of communication. They include the transformation of local and regional identities, as Japanese people came to grips with the idea of a Japanese "nation" and its potential place in global political, military, and racial hierarchies. And they include the negotiation of Japan's national identity and even its "brand" image in the global marketplace. They include the transformation of physical space, both in the reconfiguration of Japanese urban landscapes and in the transformations of Japanese bodies in response to new laws and customs relating to clothing, hairstyles, food, and public hygiene. And they include global transformations—such as the sudden and pervasive wave of *japonisme* with its profound effects on Euro-American aesthetics—in response to the insertion of Japanese material and visual culture into global flows.

The key mechanism of most of these transformations was not the reformist policies of the Meiji government (which came to power in 1868 but which began its concerted reform program only in the 1870s), but rather it was the commercial culture of the treaty port, which affected Japan's economy and society as soon as the port opened in 1859 and which continued to work its transformative effects through the 1860s and beyond. Yokohama was a melting pot of goods, ideas, visual images and verbal representations, physical interactions, architectural and sartorial display, and technological importation, almost all of which were mediated by the port's vibrant commercial culture. The profit-seeking agents of change were not just the merchants trading in cotton shirting, kelp, silk thread, or agar-agar. They included the writers, Japanese and foreign, who aimed to profit from domestic and global curiosity about Yokohama, Japan, and the world. They included the producers of cartoons, prints, photographs, and other visual media that contributed to new domestic and global understandings of "Japan" and its place in the world. They included performers who circulated new images of Japanese physical prowess throughout the world. They included craftsmen and artisans who made exquisite products for foreign collectors, contributing to a growing appreciation for Japan's manufacturing skills and design aesthetic. They included tailors, launderers, barbers, cooks, butchers, and countless other petty tradesmen and women who came to Yokohama in search of opportunity and who contributed to the transformation of Japanese lifestyles. And they included servants, coolies, prostitutes, and entertainers, who, through their physical interactions with the global communities of Yokohama, contributed to the complex transformations of Japanese bodily practice during the 1860s and beyond.

Most newcomers to Yokohama came in search of economic opportunity. Virtually every space in the town's Japanese and foreign settlements, on its waterfront, and in its licensed entertainment and brothel district was dedicated to commerce in one form or another, and just about everything in Yokohama was for sale. It was out of this mundane venality as much as the modernizing idealism of government leaders that the seeds of social, cultural, and economic change were planted. Each of the participants in this marketplace may have felt relatively powerless to affect the course of events, but collectively they were the agents of extraordinary change.

This book focuses as much as possible on the mundane actors in Yokohama's daily life: merchants, tradesmen, artists, performers, laborers, and entertainers. In particular, the book focuses on the experiences of one man, Shinohara Chūemon, and his family. Why Chūemon in particular? The simple answer is that a record of his life has survived. The records of ordinary people are hard to recover at the best of times, and the archival records of Yokohama have suffered from repeated destruction in devastating fires, the massive 1923 earthquake that leveled the city, and the appalling bombings of World War II. Chūemon left behind a remarkable personal archive that includes a collection of 367 letters written between 1859 and 1873, most of them from Chūemon to his eldest son, Shōjirō. Thanks to the care and attention of his descendants, this archive has survived down to the present day. Currently the manuscript archive is housed in the Yamanashi Prefectural Museum, while the letters were transcribed and published back in the 1950s. This archival record represents a unique window into the daily life of Yokohama's Japanese merchant community in the 1860s.

Chūemon is a richly rewarding subject in all sorts of ways. His personal experiences and daily life reveal a man of rare enterprise and determination. During the course of his decade and more in Yokohama he experienced devastating setbacks that might have made a lesser man give up and return to his comfortable home in the provinces. But Chūemon persevered, and eventually he prospered. The story of his prosperity reveals a great deal about the conditions for success in Yokohama's competitive commercial marketplace. Chūemon also teaches us much about the relationships between the Yokohama marketplace and the provinces that fed Yokohama with its export goods (and sometimes purchased its import goods). To follow the story of Chūemon is to follow not only Yokohama's growth and development but also its relationship to the rural hinterland of the Kantō region and beyond. Chūemon was not physically present in his home province during most of the period covered in this book, but his son Shōjirō remained in their ancestral home, managing the family farm and the family's village responsibilities while also helping his father with his business activities. Kōshū (the Edo-era name for what is today Yamanashi prefecture) had a history of growing commercial ties with the shogunal capital of Edo. In this book, I show how the economy of Kōshū was pulled into the orbit of the new commercial center of Yokohama, with sometimes radical effects on its social and political structures.

There are many gaps in Chūemon's record and many areas in which his experiences did not (based on the available archive) intersect with the larger stories of Yokohama's first decade. On these occasions, I have not hesitated to move away from Chūemon's life in order to present a wider portrait of the Yokohama community. The book's narrative, while loosely organized around a chronological account of Chūemon's life in Yokohama, goes back and forth in scale and focus between the granular microhistory of Chūemon's record and the larger history of the town and its varied communities. To that end, I have drawn on the archival records of many other participants in Yokohama's Japanese and foreign communities, including shogunal officials, foreign merchants and diplomats, soldiers and sailors, authors and commentators, illustrators and artists, doctors and educators.

This book, then, is a double portrait of two remarkable actors: the irrepressible Shinohara Chūemon and the bustling new international port town of Yokohama. I hope that the one informs the other and that, when taken together, these portraits will help illuminate the mechanisms of social transformation in Japan during the Meiji Restoration and highlight the importance of transformative space in the study of social and economic change.

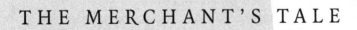

THE MERCHANT'S TALE

FIGURE 1.1 The route from Kōshū to Edo and Yokohama. *Map prepared by author*

1 OUT OF THIN AIR (1859–1860)

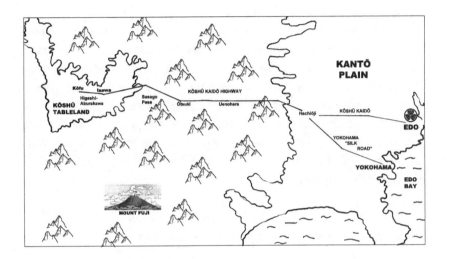

ON THE KŌSHŪ HIGHWAY

If we could travel back in time to April 3, 1859, we might see two travelers walking briskly along the Kōshū Kaidō highway absorbed in animated conversation. They are carrying packages strapped to their backs, wrapped in large pieces of indigo cloth knotted at the chest and waist. They wear conical hats to ward off sun and rain, and, like most travelers on the road, they wear simple straw sandals on their feet. Their cotton robes are hitched above the knees for ease of movement and to protect them from the mud of the road; their legs are tightly wrapped in cotton leggings.

Woodblock prints of Japan's five major highways (the Tōkaidō, Nakasendō, Nikkō Kaidō, Kōshū Kaidō, and Ōshū Kaidō) allow us to imagine the appearance and surroundings of these travelers. On either side of the wide, well-swept dirt road farmers are busy puddling rice fields in preparation for the spring planting, pruning their fruit trees and mulberry bushes, or pulling heavy wooden plowshares through the fallow wheat and cotton fields. The road is lined in some places with mature pine trees, in others with wooden stalls offering goods and refreshments to the passersby: a cup of tea poured over rice and sucked down sitting on a low wooden bench, straw sandals at a few *mon* for the pair, a bag of dried fruits, or a handful of roasted chestnuts. In the distance on all sides is a ring of mountains, those in the foreground green with tea and mulberry fields, the high mountains behind still white with snow. To the south, towering over them all like a god in the land of giants is the massive white cone of Mount Fuji.

Our travelers' names are Gorōemon and Chūemon. The suffix "-emon" was originally a marker of rank reserved for the court aristocracy in Kyoto, but over time the urban and rural classes appropriated it, and by now it was in common use among farmers, merchants, and townsmen. The same is true of the travelers' shaved heads and topknots: they were originally the style of the warrior class but are now almost universal—the exceptions being monks and the very poor—differing only in the degree of grooming. Well-tended men like Chūemon have their hair dressed once or twice a week, shaving their scalp smooth and oiling their hair before fastening it in a tight knot on the crown.

These men are not young. Chūemon is fifty, a considerable age for an era in which the average life expectancy is still in the thirties. "Compared

FIGURE 1.2 Keisai Eisen, *Kōnosu*, from the series Sixty-Nine Stations of the Kiso Kaidō (ca. 1835–1840). *Courtesy of Richard Kruml, http://www.japaneseprints-london.com/*

with the world of the Buddhas, a man's fifty years are but a dream."[1] But Chūemon is still very much in the flow of life. His deeply tanned face is a little lined, a little weather-beaten. But it is a handsome face, delicate featured with a small upturned nose, high cheekbones, and large, well-shaped ears. He is a trim, spare man, with fine, long-fingered hands. His age and his self-confidence give him a certain dignity, in spite of his simple traveling clothes.

For farmers like Chūemon, this is a busy time of year. The spring silkworm-rearing season is about to begin, cotton and wheat are going into the ground, and the paddies must be prepared for the May rice planting. The slack season is in the winter, a time when people who can afford it go on trips to hot springs or to visit relatives in Edo.

But Chūemon is leaving his son to manage the farm. He has an important mission that requires his presence elsewhere. Chūemon, a provincial farmer from the mountain-ringed province of Kōshū, is on his way to Edo, the capital of the Tokugawa shoguns, to request permission to open a shop in a town that does not yet exist, to begin trading with foreigners who might never arrive, in a language he does not understand or speak, and in commodities for which there is no proven demand.

Who is this man, and what has set him off on this surprising mission?

Chūemon's village, Higashi-Aburakawa, was one of hundreds that sprawled across the Kōshū tableland, a small but heavily populated and strategically important region in the mountains west of the shogunal capital. Although the region is surrounded by mountains, it offers benign conditions for agriculture. At an elevation of only a thousand feet, its soil is enriched by the volcanic minerals and abundant water resources of the turbulent mountains. Encircled as it was, it trapped sunshine and heat, giving it a longer growing season than most regions and lending it to the cultivation of warm-weather crops such as fruit and cotton. Kōshū was also one of the leading silk-producing districts in Japan. "What did you receive as souvenirs from Kōshū?" went a local folk song, "Striped silk and dried grapes."[2]

In the 1850s, the villages in the western part of the tableland, including Higashi-Aburakawa, specialized in cotton, while those to the east grew mulberry for silkworm cultivation. Fruit cultivation, including grapes, apples, persimmons, pomegranates, peaches, and pears, was carried out in specialized clusters of villages. Kōshū's famous grapes, for example, were grown in villages near the highway post station of Katsunuma.[3] In addition, farmers grew a variety of other commercial crops, including tobacco, nuts, and vegetables, as well as rice, grains, and vegetables for home consumption.

This land had close ties to Edo and to the shogunate. Until the sixteenth century Kōshū was the stronghold of the powerful Takeda family, whose most famous leader, Takeda Shingen, was a contender for national hegemony. However, in 1575 Shingen's son Katsuyori was crushed by Oda Nobunaga and Tokugawa Ieyasu, and since the turn of the seventeenth century the Tokugawa family had ruled Kōshū province. In spite of its violent beginning, their rule was for the most part benevolent. As a directly controlled territory of the Tokugawa shogunate, Kōshū was governed by three *daikan*, or governors. The Isawa *daikan* had jurisdiction over the area surrounding Kōfu, which included Higashi-Aburakawa.

Higashi-Aburakawa was a village of forty families, situated in the crook of two rivers, the Fuefuki and its tributary, the Aburakawa. The entire village was no more than one hundred acres in extent. Like much of the Kōfu basin, the district was prone to flooding when the snows melted and the rainy season came in early summer. Even in the 1950s, Chūemon's great-great-grandson Shinohara Yukio recalls having had to paddle to school in a boat when the roads were inundated. But the rivers also brought abundant irrigation and the promise of fertile soil and good crops.

This was perhaps the kind of community that Francis Hall had in mind when he wrote in 1865 of the prosperous villages of the Edo hinterland, villages where "there were no signs but those of peaceful industry and content, each hamlet to all intents a little republic by itself, knowing little and caring less for the outside world; to whom a change of rulers or revolution in the State would have no significance as great as the death of their own *nanooshi* or headman—people who know no oppression because they feel none, whose lives have fewer disturbing elements, perhaps, than any other people on whom the sun in its daily revolution falls."[4]

But appearances could be deceptive. In Higashi-Aburakawa, as in most villages of the Kantō and surrounding areas, the benefits of the land were hardly shared by all. In Higashi-Aburakawa, seven families controlled 72 percent of all the village's agricultural production, while twenty-six families had between them just 12 percent. Unable to feed themselves from their land, these marginal families survived by hiring themselves out for day labor, sending their children into service, and finding whatever employment they could to feed those they could not send away. The most prosperous families, on the other hand, had enough to live a comfortable life, to educate their children, to travel, to experiment with new agricultural methods, or invest in new business opportunities. These were the families that Chūemon grew up with: the Okamura family, who were Chūemon's in-laws (he had married the daughter of Okamura Kanpei); the Komazawa family, whose heir, Buzaemon, was one of Chūemon's closest friends and collaborators; and the wealthy Yamashita family, whose heir, Matsujirō, was to be one of Chūemon's close business associates.

Chūemon's own family, the Shinohara, was not the wealthiest in the village. Their five acres of land put them in the ranks of the haves, but at least four other families had greater holdings. But their landholdings and associated business activities did lend them status as a part of the local elite—the gōnō class, that group of wealthy farmers who were to play such an influential role in the political and economic life of Japan for the rest of the nineteenth century. As a member of this class, Chūemon had political obligations and privileges: his family was one of the designated nanushi (headmen) of the village. This hereditary position rotated in Higashi-Aburakawa between families, and the Shinoharas usually took the position in alternate years. Chūemon's membership in the gōnō class also made him a part of a densely connected network of men of similar background throughout the region. These were men whose ties transcended village boundaries. As a class they socialized, they intermarried, they studied together and implemented agricultural and other reforms, and together they invested their surplus capital in an increasingly vigorous regional network of commercial enterprise.

Although firmly grounded in agriculture, the economy of the Kōshū region had become highly commercialized over the past century. The region's agricultural abundance, its position on the periphery of the Kantō Plain, and its long-standing ties to the shogunal administration all made it a natural supplier to the rapidly growing consumer market in Edo. After the devastating wars of the sixteenth century, Edo had become the political center of the regime of the Tokugawa family of shoguns. As a political measure, all Japan's daimyo—feudal lords—were required to reside in Edo in alternate years, and their wives and children were required to live there permanently. This concentration of Japan's wealthiest barons and their samurai retainers generated growing demand for the artisans and commercial houses that supplied their needs. By the mid-eighteenth century, Edo was among the biggest cities in the world, with a population of more than one million and a vibrant urban consumer culture.

Kōshū supplied Edo and the regional centers that grew up around it with agricultural staples such as rice and wheat, as well as with specialty products like grapes, tobacco, cotton, and silk. By the mid-nineteenth century, most farmers with access to mulberry gained extra income by cultivating silkworms. Some would add a little extra value at home by unspooling the cocoons and reeling silk thread. Some even produced woven silk cloth. Many sold their cocoons to the commercial houses of Kōfu and other local towns, where an industry had grown up spinning and weaving silk and cotton. The final product was shipped down the Kōshū highway to the silk market in Hachiōji on the Kantō Plain or directly to one of the licensed silk wholesalers in Edo. As a result of these developments, many farming families made more income from cash crops like cotton, tobacco, and silk than from their traditional farming activities. Some, like the Shinohara, became quite wealthy in the process.

Chūemon's family landholdings would not on their own have been enough to finance an affluent lifestyle. Five acres were enough to feed a family comfortably but not to produce a surplus for travel, education, and investment. That came from the family's specialized activities in the production and trading of commercial crops. While a little more than half the family's land was devoted to rice production, much of the rest was planted in cotton. The Shinoharas' annual family income in 1858 was twenty-five ryō. The value of the ryō is hard to pin down in contemporary equivalents because of the disparity in available goods and services, but based on the wages of a skilled artisan then and now, the Bank of Japan equates it to three hundred thousand yen (about US$3,000) in today's money: not wealth but enough for a family self-sufficient in food and housing to buy a few of the good things in life.[5] This money could not have come from the sale of produce grown on the family land alone: the balance must have come from trade. Like many regional producers, Chūemon clearly supplemented his income by trading in local cash-based commodities such as cotton and silk. Chūemon was as much a part of the merchant as the farming community.

In fact, Chūemon's background was much more varied than the designation "farmer" would suggest. He was born a second son, and as a young man he had lived for several years in Edo. According to family lore, Yasutarō (Chūemon's childhood name) came to the attention of the local shogunal superintendent—the Isawa daikan—who recommended him for a trainee position in the Edo bureaucracy. Yasutarō went to work in the Kinza, the department responsible for the minting of coinage and the management of its circulation. Yasutarō did well in his job, and he was singled out for advancement by the head of the Kinza, Gotō Sanemon. Gotō is said to have taken a special interest in Yasutarō, and he would undoubtedly have furthered Yasutarō's career had circumstances not forced the young man to abandon his life in Edo.[6]

Those circumstances point to the unpredictability of life and the strange turns it can take. In 1830 Yasutarō's father, Kinzaemon, died, and Yasutarō's older brother became head of the family, changing his own name to Kinzaemon. In spite of having had two wives, Yasutarō's brother Kinzaemon had no children of his own. In the mid-1830s Kinzaemon's own health started failing. In light of this crisis, Yasutarō was urgently recalled to Kōshū, and at the beginning of 1835 he was adopted by his older brother. Yasutarō was now heir to the Shinohara family. Six months later Kinzaemon died, and Yasutarō, who was himself recently married with a newborn son, became family head. It was at this point that he changed his name to Chūemon.

By the time that our story opens, then, Chūemon was a man who had everything to lose. In this peaceful and abundant agricultural region, he was a member of the prosperous elite. He had a large and comfortable home; he had land and crops; he had storehouses full of produce; he had an honorable position as headman of his village; he had a wife and children (the youngest six, the oldest twenty-four); he had a dense network of friends and business associates; he was physically healthy; he was respected and liked; and he was secure in his place within a centuries-old social order. Experienced, energetic, and optimistic, he was an asset to the community in which his identity was so deeply rooted. What was it, then, that prompted him to leave all this behind?

Perhaps his experiences in Edo, and in particular with the commercial economy, made Chūemon open in 1859 to returning to the world of business and commerce. Perhaps he was bored with farming. Perhaps he felt it was time to pass the baton to his eldest son but did not yet feel ready to fully retire. Perhaps he was stirred by a sense of adventure as he imagined the possibilities that trade with the outside world might represent. Or perhaps he went to serve his community: it is clear from their early correspondence that Chūemon, Gorōemon, and their network of local friends, relatives, and investors saw their new venture as a form of partnership—a "Kōshū Products Company" (Kōshū Sanbutsu Kaisho) that would market the produce of the Kōshū region and benefit local producers.[7] Indeed, in their application for a plot of land in Yokohama, Chūemon and Gorōemon stated that "although we are farmers, we have been desiring for some time to become merchants, selling the products of our farming. Already the products of Kōshū are sold in every part of the country, and we would like to sell some of these same products [in Yokohama]."[8] It is clear that Chūemon and Gorōemon wanted to portray themselves as representatives first and foremost of their home province, Kōshū.

But if their mission was deeply embedded in a sense of loyalty to their community, it also reflected their own personalities and outlook. Chūemon's willingness to leave behind so much that was familiar and comfortable and to sink so much of his personal and financial capital into a venture in an unknown and wholly speculative new space indicates an unusual sense of optimism and adventurousness. This entrepreneurial spirit was, perhaps, the chief factor that set Chūemon off on the Kōshū highway on that April morning. As we will see, he was a resourceful and committed businessman who was driven by a perpetual optimism that great opportunities were out there, like ripe Kōshū grapes waiting to be grasped and plucked.

Japan's Reluctant Embrace

Chūemon's goal on that journey of April 1859 was to apply for a license to open a shop in the new port town of Yokohama. The creation of Yokohama marked the culmination of a six-year drama, starting with the arrival of Commodore Matthew Perry off Japanese shores in July 1853. Perry's mission was to put an end to Japan's reclusive foreign policy, which since the seventeenth century had limited officially sanctioned trade to an enclave in Nagasaki in the far southwest of Japan, inhabited by small colonies of Dutch and Chinese merchants. Under that policy Christianity was strictly banned, the shogunate eschewed diplomatic relations beyond a few sporadic exchanges with Korea, foreign visitors except for the regulated communities in Nagasaki were prohibited, Japanese were forbidden to build ocean-going ships, and overseas travel by Japanese subjects was banned. In practice, the shogunate turned a blind eye to a considerable volume of unofficial trade: the Satsuma domain in southwestern Japan imported goods from the Ryukyu Islands; the island domain of Tsushima acted as both trading partner and informal diplomatic intermediary with Korea; and the Matsumae domain in the far north traded with Ainu and other native peoples for furs, seafood, and medicines. But from the perspective of most Western governments, Japan was a closed country that rejected the international system of trade and diplomacy and even at times flouted the basic norms of international hospitality, such as offering succor to ships in distress.

During the first decades of the nineteenth century, Japan's position of isolation came under threat from several directions. Russia was rapidly expanding its empire into Siberia, and by the 1830s its ships were nosing into northern regions such as Ezo (including what is now Hokkaido) that were only partially integrated into the Tokugawa power structure. There was a distinct threat that Russia might lay claim to these regions. At the same time, Great Britain and France were aggressively expanding their imperial reach into East and Southeast Asia. China's humiliation in the Opium War of 1839–1842 launched the start of the treaty port system, by which Chinese ports became semicolonial enclaves in which the foreigners claimed special privileges beyond the reach of Chinese law. As if these developments weren't enough, the United States was completing its western expansion with the acquisition of California from Mexico in 1848 and the gold rush of the early 1850s. From this point on, the United States saw itself as having a vital interest in Pacific affairs.

In this environment, Commodore Perry led a U.S. naval fleet to Japan in 1853. Perry's message was simple: all we want is a treaty of friendship and safe harbor for our whaling vessels; America is a peaceful, nonimperial power and will be a good friend to Japan; and if you don't sign an agreement with us, you will have to reckon with the naval might of the aggressive European imperialist powers. Nevertheless, naval strength was an important part of Perry's calculation too. Ostentatiously, he brought his fleet within firing range of the massed wooden buildings of the city of Edo. If he had wanted to, he could have burned the city down. He wanted the Japanese to know that.

Intimidated by Perry's naval power and persuaded in part by his arguments, the shogunal authorities decided they had no choice but to enter into treaty relations with the United States. When Perry returned to Japan in early 1854, a signing ceremony was held in a rustic location along the shoreline near Edo. Its name was Yokohama.

As many in Japan had feared, the Treaty of Kanagawa (named for the nearest administrative center to Yokohama) turned out to be the thin end of a wedge that would ultimately force open Japan's restricted system of international relations and trade. In 1858 America's first ambassador to Japan, Townsend Harris, persuaded a reluctant shogunal government to sign a further agreement, a Treaty of Amity and Commerce, that would greatly expand the scope of Japan's foreign relations. Harris persuaded the shogunal authorities that Japan's eventual opening up to foreign trade was inevitable. He pointed to the example of China, where a second Opium War was leading toward another humiliation for the Qing dynasty. And, like Perry, he asked the Japanese authorities if they would prefer to enter into voluntary trade relations with a friendly America or involuntary trade relations with an aggressive Britain, which might foist opium on the Japanese people or even threaten them with colonial subjugation. The principal ministers of the shogunal government (the group of men known as the rōjū), led by Hotta Masayoshi, concluded that Japan had little choice in the matter since "our national strength has declined, our military preparations are inadequate, and we are in no position to eject the foreigners by means of war . . . not to enter into friendly relations entails war and not to wage war entails entering into friendly relations; there is no other way."[9] Indeed, Hotta argued that Japan's only real chance of overcoming the foreign threat was "to stake everything on the present opportunity, to conclude friendly alliances, to send ships to foreign countries everywhere and conduct trade, to copy the foreigners where they are at their best and so repair our own shortcomings, to foster our national strength and complete our armaments, and so gradually subject the foreigners to our influence until in the end . . . our hegemony is acknowledged throughout the globe."[10]

Hotta appointed Iwase Tadanao, a highly intelligent and farsighted career official, to lead the negotiations with Harris. While he was wary of the destabilizing impact of a foreign presence in Japan, Iwase clearly recognized the potential benefits of international trade, and indeed he went against many of his colleagues in arguing that Japan should agree to open a port in or near Edo. Iwase argued that the economic stimulus of trade might help the shogunate's finances (which were in a chronically parlous state), and technology flowing into the country from abroad would arrive first in Edo and not near the domains of potentially hostile daimyo. Iwase was particularly aware of the relative power of Osaka, which was still Japan's major commercial center—in part because it captured the economic benefit of the Dutch and Chinese trade in Nagasaki. If Osaka were also to benefit from trade under the new treaty, then Iwase warned that "first Edo and then the rest of the country will wither, and only Osaka will prosper."[11] Iwase felt that opening a new port for trade near Edo might help shift Japan's center of economic gravity more toward the shogun's power base in the east.[12] Iwase argued, "Only by bringing the wealth of the country to our doorsteps can we police the country and provide benefit for eternity. A rich country and a strong military must be the basis of our policy."[13]

The treaty that was finally signed on July 29, 1858, designated Kanagawa as one of three ports that would immediately open to foreign trade. The others were Hakodate at the southern tip of Hokkaido and Nagasaki in the far west. Hakodate was in fact already open as a part of the Perry treaty of 1854—though only for the resupply of foreign ships, not for trade; and Nagasaki had been a center of international trade throughout the Tokugawa era. So although all three ports would be covered by the new provisions of the treaty, the opening of Kanagawa was its most significant feature. Although the initial treaty was with the United States, the "most favored nation" clause of the treaty meant that Japan was soon forced to enter into similar treaties with Great Britain, Russia, France, and the Netherlands.

Kanagawa was a busy post station on the Tōkaidō highway, located only fifteen miles from the center of Edo. The shogunal authorities hoped that it was close enough to Edo to satisfy the foreigners but far enough away not to pose a direct threat—particularly since foreigners other than diplomatic staff would be expressly forbidden from visiting Edo: while the treaty permitted foreigners to travel a distance of up to ten ri (about twenty-four miles) from Kanagawa in every other direction, their right was limited to the western bank of the Rokugō (now the Tama) River in the direction of Edo, a distance of only seven and a half miles.

The new chief minister, Ii Naosuke, delegated five officials to act as commissioners of foreign affairs (gaikoku bugyō) and instructed them to come up with a detailed plan for the opening of the port. Iwase Tadanao, who had been an early proponent of locating a port near Edo, was one of these commissioners. Although Iwase was in favor of the economic benefits that foreign trade might bring to the shogunate, he shared the concerns of many government officials (including his boss, Ii Naosuke) that the foreign presence might undermine shogunal authority and destabilize Japanese society. Therefore, he favored isolating the foreigners in a controllable environment. To that end, Iwase proposed developing the farming and fishing community of Yokohama into a new port town and accommodating the foreigners there rather than in the center of Kanagawa.

Yokohama was located on the other side of the bay from Kanagawa and surrounded by marshes. With skillful management, the Japanese would be able to keep the foreigners confined to this gilded cage. To the foreigners, the location offered some real benefits. Unlike Kanagawa, Yokohama was only thinly populated, with farming and fishing villages, and it had ample space for residential development. The water off the shore of Yokohama was also much deeper than that along the Kanagawa shoreline. Large ships would be able to dock close to the shore, making the management of cargo easier for the foreign merchants. If the foreigners complained that Kanagawa and not Yokohama was the port specified in the treaty, the commissioners could argue that Yokohama was a part of the Kanagawa administrative district, and therefore it was not at all in contravention of the treaty—after all, hadn't the Treaty of Kanagawa actually been signed in Yokohama?

In December 1858 and January 1859 the American envoy Townsend Harris made two trips from his base in Shimoda to Kanagawa to discuss the precise location of the port. In spite of all the commissioners' efforts to persuade him that Yokohama was a more desirable location than central Kanagawa, Harris stubbornly opposed the idea. He was afraid that the Japanese were trying to create another Dejima—the island off Nagasaki on which the Dutch had been effectively isolated and controlled for the past two hundred fifty years. This argument was not far from the truth. Indeed, one senior councillor explicitly argued that "in the new port the Westerners would be just as isolated and tightly controlled as at Nagasaki. This would give Japan time to build up its military defenses and eventually return to *sakoku no ryōhō* (the good policy of isolation)."[14]

In spite of Harris's resistance, Ii Naosuke appointed five men to the newly created position of Kanagawa commissioners and charged them with implementing this expensive gamble. The commissioners aimed to build a first-class international port facility, complete with residential districts for Japanese and foreigners, entertainment facilities, and a full-scale brothel quarter. They were determined to build the port on a substantial scale, in the hope that this would mollify the foreigners and reconcile them to the isolated location. They were, in effect, planning to conjure a new city out of the marshes surrounding a cluster of fishing villages. If they succeeded in winning the foreigners over, they would score a tactical victory, achieving their policy goals and satisfying their boss. If the foreigners rejected the new port and insisted on relocating to Kanagawa proper, then the commissioners would have an expensive ghost town on their hands.

The treaties called for the port to be opened on July 1, 1859. By the time the final decision was made to develop Yokohama, the commissioners had less than six months to build the town.

Their first step was to invite Japanese merchants to apply for building lots. A call for applications was issued on January 23, 1859. The call was directed at the larger Edo merchant houses—members of the *ton'ya* (wholesaler) guilds, who had long been the recipients of special privileges in exchange for their willingness to work in close cooperation with the government. In spite of the promise of foreign markets, these great trading houses were reluctant to invest in this unknown and uncertain location. The Edo manager of Mitsui—Japan's wealthiest merchant house and largest retailer— had to be summoned to Commissioner Mizuno Tadakuni's house several times before reluctantly agreeing to take the plunge.

The invitation was extended to the entire country on February 18, and it was to this call that Chūemon responded. The commissioners imagined a variety of merchants setting up shop in Yokohama, not all of whom would sell export products; retail shops were also needed to supply the Japanese and foreign communities with the necessities of daily life. The commissioners particularly wanted to encourage local families from the surrounding villages, some of whom had lost their fields to government requisitions.[15] In all, seventy-one merchants were approved to open businesses in Yokohama. Of these, thirty-four were from Edo, eighteen from Kanagawa and other neighboring communities, and only nineteen from more distant places.[16] Even assuming that the shogunate communicated the invitation only to the residents of directly administered or closely allied domains in the Edo hinterland, that represents a very small number from many significant commercial centers including Hachiōji, Odawara, Machida, and Maebashi, not to mention the great silk-producing areas of Shinshū and Ōshū. It is all the more surprising, then, that among the nineteen was an unknown farmer from Kōshū called Shinohara Chūemon.

The Kanagawa commissioners assigned lots in an area roughly twelve acres in extent. Merchants were responsible for grading the land and building their own premises. The lots in the Japanese town were arrayed over rice fields and marshland, between the Benten shrine and what had previously been Hongō village. The layout of the town was in five neighborhoods (chō) organized around two intersecting avenues, known at the time as Ō-dōri and Honchō-dōri. Each of these avenues was sixty feet wide, creating a very grand space, far removed from the image many Westerners might have had of the crowded alleyways of an Asian city. The Edo merchants were located closest to the shrine, which was a strange choice since, although this area had the largest lots and the lovely grounds of the shrine as a backdrop, it was also the furthest from the docks, the foreign settlement, and the government's administrative center.

Meanwhile, the commissioners themselves were responsible for constructing all the administrative buildings, including two large stone piers, a customs house and a town hall, roads and streets, a few residences to get the foreigners started, and of course their own headquarters and residences. The commissioners completed their master plan for construction of the port on March 26, 1859—at which point there were only three months to go until the official opening. For their own headquarters, the commissioners selected a site high up on Noge hill in Tobe village, across a small inlet from the main town beyond the Benten shrine. The commissioners deliberately located their headquarters far from the center of the town, partly to keep their activities secret from the foreigners but also because the hilly location afforded the sort

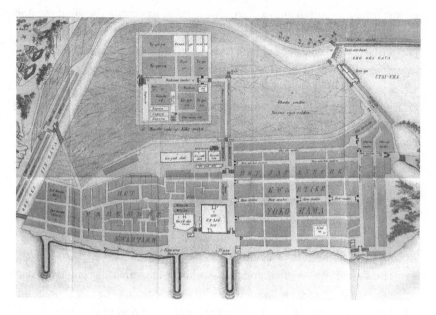

FIGURE 1.3 Map of Yokohama (ca. 1860). The Japanese quarter is on the right side, and the Benten shrine is the wooded area at right. The customs house and government buildings are in the center, and the foreign settlement is on the left. The brothel quarter is the moated area at the top. J. Hoffmann, "Yokohama, de nieuwe japansche haven en handelsplaats nabij Yedo," Bijdragen tot de taal-, land- en volkenkunde van Nederlandsch-Indië (August 1862): 415–32

of prominence traditionally claimed by the castles of feudal lords—indicating dominance of the surrounding districts. The piers and customs house were the centerpieces of their city plan—the latter was a large building located in the center of the port district, on the waterfront and between the two stone piers. The two-story building measured 1 chō (about 360 feet) on each side, for a total of 130,000 square feet. It was surrounded by a small moat and accessed by a huge wooden gate that was closed at night.[17] The commissioners administered the affairs of the entire Kanagawa region (which comprised the post station of Kanagawa and 206 other towns and villages) from their Tobe headquarters—including collection of the land tax (which they used to fund their operations), local village administration, road building and maintenance, and regional justice. Meanwhile, the commissioners handled the business of Yokohama and its trade at the customs house and surrounding offices. They also maintained a small office in the town of Kanagawa.[18]

The commissioners also built a new road connecting Yokohama to Kanagawa and beyond. In order to enter Yokohama, a traveler would have to cross one of two bridges, "Each . . . protected by a gate, shut at sunset, and by a guard-house, in which yakunin [officials] were always on duty to watch who entered or left the settlement, examine the luggage, bundles or parcels, and to see that they conveyed nothing contraband in or out."[19]

Even with all these preparations, one part of the plan remained to be implemented. The commissioners envisioned a community in which the foreigners would be able to fulfill all their needs—whether for food, souvenirs, entertainment, or sex—without ever having to leave Yokohama. In order to service the carnal desires of the foreigners, the government designated a marshy area outside the town of Yokohama as a brothel quarter.

Hitherto, foreigners residing in Japan had been able to purchase sexual services only under special dispensation from the government. In Nagasaki, Dutch merchants were not permitted into the town's houses of entertainment, but they were allowed to receive women on the island of Dejima where they lived. America's first consul, Townsend Harris, and his secretary, Henry Heusken, were assigned women (in the case of Harris, the famed Tōjin Okichi, who has since been the subject of many Japanese dramas, Kabuki plays, and films), but only as an exceptional policy and under the fiction that they were nurses to help the foreigners through times of sickness. Meanwhile, the diplomatic staff who took up residence in Edo were allowed to keep women, but in the guise of domestic servants.[20] Indeed, the idea of providing a special quarter to supply young Japanese women to the foreigners was deeply sensitive and might be seen as a humiliating concession.

However, the commissioners also recognized that by providing sexual services to foreigners, they would be able to exercise a measure of control. Based on their experiences in Hakodate and Shimoda (two ports that had been resupplying foreign ships since the mid-1850s), the commissioners recognized the danger of drunken sailors causing disturbances: "We have heard of repeated incidents in which foreign sailors, from their extreme boredom, enter the shops of merchants, steal liquor, and then go on a drunken rampage."[21] The commissioners reasoned that an officially monitored entertainment quarter would reduce unregulated contact between foreign sailors and the townspeople and prevent "major trouble arising from a trivial cause."[22]

The plan for the Yokohama entertainment district was to "open houses of prostitution on the same lines as those in [Edo's] Yoshiwara."[23] Like Edo's famous Yoshiwara licensed quarter, Yokohama's district would be separated from the residential areas of the town, it would be walled and guarded, and the brothel houses it contained would be strictly licensed and regulated. This was in contrast to nearby Kanagawa, where the prostitutes were located in teahouses lining the Tōkaidō highway in the town center.

The Kanagawa commissioners invited the brothel owners of Kanagawa and Shinagawa to apply for land grants on a twelve-acre site at a distance from the new town. As with the Edo merchants, the commissioners applied a mixture of incentive and arm-twisting to persuade the brothel owners to build the quarter at their own expense. The cost of construction was enormous: the designated area was in the middle of a marsh, which had to be drained before any construction could take place. Costs were so high that almost all the contractors pulled out before the project was completed. In the end only one man, a brothel owner from Shinagawa called Satō Sakichi, stayed to complete the project. Sakichi managed and financed the draining of the marsh, built the houses, and built a main gate and bridge, a moat, and an eleven-hundred-foot-long wooden causeway across the marsh to connect the district to the town of Yokohama.

The licensed quarter was still not ready at the beginning of July, when the port opened for foreign trade. As a temporary measure, the Kanagawa commissioners converted an unoccupied building in the foreign settlement to serve as a makeshift brothel.[24] On July 7, the commissioners issued a directive to the town leaders of Kanagawa and other well-known brothel districts along the highway: "We are asking all the restaurant owners and innkeepers to contribute women proportionate to their numbers so that we can complete this urgent task."[25] The leader of the association of Kanagawa brothel owners was instructed to "urgently recruit fifty women." However, according to one report, "the girls who were sent to Yokohama cried bitterly, and several of them fled" rather than be sent to service the sexual needs of the foreigners.[26] According to one diarist, "The prostitutes of Kanagawa were summoned to work in the brothels of Yokohama, but no one volunteered to move there. So they held a lottery and selected thirty women. They were all crying, and when it came time to go, they had to be forced into palanquins that were then roped shut."[27] When interviewed, one of the women lamented, "We do not plan to be prostitutes for our whole lives. In the coming years we hope to gain the status of wives. If we meet with harm at the hands of the foreigners, it will be a shame that will last our entire lives."[28]

In spite of coercion and resistance, delays, cost overloads, bureaucratic confusion, diplomatic disputes, and the last-minute nature of the construction program, the four major components of the Yokohama port town—the official buildings and infrastructure, the Japanese merchant quarter, the foreign settlement, and the licensed entertainment district—were all more or less ready for business by July 1.

Among the Japanese merchants racing to open their shops on time was Chūemon. He and his business partner, Gorōemon, received their lease on April 16. Their original plan had been to open a shop together, under joint ownership and management. To that end, they had planned to request a 21,000-square-foot (600 tsubo) lot. But the lease they ultimately received was for only 11,000 square feet (312.5 tsubo), on which they would build two separate shops and sublet land for a third shop. At some point along the way, Chūemon and Gorōemon had made the decision to operate independently of each other. Most likely this was because of financial considerations. Perhaps when it came right down to it, they were unable to work out an equitable ownership scheme for an operation that was jointly managed by two people but financed by a whole community. The legal framework of the joint stock company was not available to them, nor were the safeguards of a partnership agreement. The only model in widespread use was that of one-to-one loans and mortgages. In the end, this was the arrangement that they adopted.

Their ventures were nevertheless closely connected. Gorōemon and Chūemon continued collaborating throughout the following decade, and their relationship seems to have remained cordial. Their businesses were on the same lot, so they might have been seen from the outside as a single entity—especially since both proprietors called their shops by the same name, Kōshūya, or "House of Kōshū." The shops were of equal size: 3,600 square feet (102 tsubo). Each occupied 24 feet (4 ken) of frontage side by side on Honchō-dōri and stretched 150 feet (25 ken) to the back of the lot. The third shop on their lot, built by another Kōshū merchant, Gunnaiya Kōemon, was the same width but only 54 feet (9 ken) deep. The space behind Gunnaiya remained empty.[29]

It may seem strange to have had two shops with the same name sitting side by side. But the policy of the commissioners was to group merchants as much as possible by place of origin. There seems to have been an assumption that merchants from similar areas would collaborate as well as compete. On a map prepared by Mitsui in 1859, the three Kōshū shops are simply lumped together as "Kōshū merchants." The same applied to lots owned by merchants from Hodogaya, Kanagawa, Shinagawa, and Shibau.[30]

On April 26, 1859, Chūemon picked up the official lease documents for his property at the commissioners' office in Edo, and he set out for Kanagawa.

Soon after arriving, he wrote to a builder he knew in Kōshū and asked him to help with construction of his shop. "In Kanagawa there are no builders, and lumber is expensive, so I would like to have these materials prepared in Kawauchi in Kōshū and sent down by boat. Please talk to Shirōji and others at Kawauchi and discuss what supplies will be needed." Kawauchi was in a mountainous area on the edge of the Kōfu plain and was rich in timber and other natural resources.[31]

Chūemon succeeded in contracting with his builder, arranging for the shipment of construction materials down the Fuji River and around the Izu Peninsula to Yokohama, hiring local labor for the construction project (even when every other resident of Yokohama had a construction project under way), and completing his shop by June 1, 1859, in plenty of time for the opening of the port. Chūemon's building project seems to have gone quicker than most. The commissioners' office summoned all the Yokohama merchants for a conference on June 1 to scold those whose buildings remained unfinished. The only shops that were complete were Chūemon's Kōshūya and Mitsui's Echigoya. "Even though I was late in renting my land, I got to work quickly and made good progress with the construction, and so I was successful. Both of us received praise for this . . . Around sixty other [merchants] were scolded and sternly told to finish the construction as soon as possible."[32]

Chūemon hired a young man from his village named Yaemon as his assistant. For his initial stock of goods, Chūemon relied on two business partners, Matsujirō in Higashi-Aburakawa and Genzaemon from Kurokoma village, to get the word out that he was accepting produce on commission from Kōshū merchants. They sent him supplies of silk from the Gunnai region, cotton cloth, dried grapes, and tobacco.[33] On June 29, Chūemon wrote, "The foreign ships will arrive on the third of next month [July 2, 1859], and everyone has been told to try their utmost to prepare their goods by that time . . . We have been told by the commissioners not to despise the foreigners and to put our best goods on display."[34]

THE PORT OPENS

The new port of Yokohama opened for business on the stipulated date, July 1, 1859.

The Japanese were more or less ready, but the town could hardly be called lively. Only two foreign ships were in the port: one Dutch and one American. According to an early Japanese visitor, "The goods [for sale] were expensive and few transactions were taking place. The foreigners came to look at the goods, but they went back [to their ships] without buying anything. Moreover, Yokohama was a sad [looking] place . . . the construction was still not complete, and so the foreigners stayed away, going instead to stay in the temples of Kanagawa."[35] Another early report stated, "About 70 to 80 percent of the shops on Honchō-dōri are complete, but the others are still under construction."[36] Henry Holmes, captain of one of the first merchant ships to arrive in the new port, found "no pilot . . . no buoys to mark the proper channel, nor . . . any light to direct . . . I found no shipping or native craft in the place, nor were we boarded by any officials."[37] A Dutch merchant, "Cees" de Coningh, wrote,

> Upon our arrival, there was absolutely no trace of town or city to be discerned, no matter how close we came to the shore to drop anchor. The only preparation made for the arrival of foreigners was a large wooden building that the Japanese called their Interpreters' Office surrounded by a sextet of sheds, the whole encircled with palisades, and further beyond these sheds stood four little sentry boxes, which could best be compared to our waffle stalls. Otherwise, one could see nothing else nearby save for the cultivated fields between the lovely trees of the farmers' and fishermen's houses of the real village of Yokohama.[38]

The foreign quarter consisted of "a few dozen wooden bungalows with matching warehouses on nearby farmland from which the harvest had been completed; they were strewn chaotically across the uprooted turnip fields as if they had been shaken out of a box of children's toys." Beyond those, "wheat and turnips still lay on the ground of the terrain of the new foreign quarter."[39]

Sir Rutherford Alcock, the British envoy to Japan, formed a more favorable impression of Yokohama, which he visited soon after its opening:

> It was impossible not to be struck with the admirable and costly structures of granite which the Japanese had so rapidly raised, in a large broad pier running far into the bay, and a long flight of steps, at which twenty boats might land their passengers or cargoes at the same time. Immediately in front was a large official-looking building, which was pointed out as the custom-house, and thither we proceeded to find some of the officials and an interpreter. The gate gave entrance into a courtyard, paved with stones from the beach, and round the four sides were ranges of offices, some evidently still in the carpenters' hands.

To the southwest of the piers and customs house, out of a marsh by the edge of a deserted bay, a wave of the conjuror's wand had created a considerable and bustling settlement of Japanese merchants. A large wide street was bordered on both sides with handsome, well-built houses of timber and mud walls. But the occupants had evidently only that very morning been precipitated in; their goods were still for the greater part unpacked; while frantic efforts were being made by servants and porters, in a state of deliquescence, to make some sort of show of the salable contents.[40]

Alcock nevertheless found the shops full of "goods entirely selected to suit a foreigner's wants and tastes . . . lacquer, basket-work, porcelain and bronze, fancy silks and embroideries, spread out in every tempting form."[41] Alcock wanted to buy a pair of dogs—this seems to have been a popular purchase among early diplomats—and he looked for them in a street that specialized in livestock. Here he found goats, bears, deer, storks, and many other varieties of birds. Perhaps hearing of the foreign sailors' fascination with sea creatures, one enterprising craftsman had sewn together a preserved monkey's torso and a large fish tail to make a strikingly realistic mermaid, "as natural and lifelike as any dried mummy!"[42]

The American merchant Francis Hall, a keen observer and diarist who arrived in Yokohama in November 1859, described the shops as

under buildings of one and two stories, the fronts being open to the street. The goods were arranged on shelves or stood in boxes on a single platform or series of ascending platforms. The platform that constituted the main floor was spread with mats, fresh and clean. On the mats were squatted the sellers around a brazier of charcoal fire, smoking, talking, or drinking tea. Wherever I stopped, goods were freely shown and I was often invited to a cup of tea, or proffered some eatable like sweetmeats, cakes, or nuts . . . Each store had, as with us, its own class of merchandise. Silks and spices, goods, lacquered ware, porcelain, provisions, had each their own place.[43]

Commenting on the friendliness of the merchants, Hall nevertheless added that there was "an edict from Yedo prohibiting the Japanese to use the salutation "Ohio" [Good morning], except towards persons with whom they have business."[44] Indeed, in early July the Kanagawa commissioners had summoned village and township officials from throughout the treaty zone and given them a set of instructions on how to behave with the foreigners. Although salutations were not prohibited, the regulations did forbid Japanese from accepting any kind of gift or invitation from a foreigner, or from entering a foreigner's house unless it was essential for trading purposes.[45]

Contemporary Japanese guidebooks described the specializations of the different neighborhoods: Honchō Itchōme specialized in money changing, where "the clatter of the scales echoes throughout the district," while in Nichōme (where Chūemon's shop was located) "we come to the branch shop of the great Mitsui company." The main product of Nichōme was lacquerware, though there were also many silk merchants, pottery sellers, and tea shops. In Gochōme were shops selling lovely art objects including lacquer, lavish paintings decorated with gold and silver, and lacquered porcelain.

For the Japanese, the foreigners themselves were among the principal objects on display. They "come three and five at a time and walk around examining the wares of the merchants. In front of many of the shops are chairs placed for the foreigners to sit. Here they will sit with cigars in their mouths, and, striking a match, they will smoke them. The shop owners will bring piles of goods outside to show them. When the foreigner buys something, then the price is written down in a ledger, and the proprietor together with the foreigner must go to the customs house."

Because Honchō-dōri was wide, the foreigners liked to ride their horses there: "Husband and wife will ride together in a cart, and when they arrive at a place where they have business, he will pull on the reins and stop the horse, and they will do their shopping or whatever, and then get back in their cart and ride on . . . They will put down woolen rugs in the winter, while in the summer they use rush mats."[46]

Japanese observers were particularly struck by the accommodations the Yokohama merchants made to Western customs: "When it rains, the shops stand their tatami mats on their sides and put fresh straw on the floor. The foreigners walk inside in their boots, just as they do at home. And when the merchants of Honchō visit the foreigners in their houses, they, too, enter still wearing their straw sandals or wooden clogs."[47]

Japanese guidebooks also described the scenes around the customs house, where goods were unloaded and transactions took place:

The pier to the east is where the foreigners unload their vessels. It is a busy scene. Japanese and foreigners are all mixed up, with carts endlessly hauling off mountains of goods piled here and there and taking them to the trading houses of the foreigners, under the stern gaze of the

FIGURE 1.4 Foreigners shopping for lacquerware in Honchō Itchōme (ca. 1863). *Utagawa Sadahide, Yokohama kaikō kenbunshi (ca. 1863)*

guards. If there is any disturbance caused by either Japanese or foreigner, no one will be allowed to proceed . . . The pier to the left is for
the goods brought in by the Edo merchants. Tens of carts are coming
and going from here, the cries of the drivers echoing from the skies.[48]

Among the grandest of the Japanese shops was the Nakaiya, owned by
Kuroiwa Jūbei and opened in September 1859. The massive shop of twenty
thousand square feet was entirely roofed in copper, an extravagance that was
said to have outraged the shogunal officials, who were dealing with a major
financial crisis as they struggled to build a national defense against the foreign threat. Inside, the shop had an interior courtyard covered in netting, in
which exotic birds flew freely. The shop also featured a glass-walled aquar-
ium (glass was a novelty in Japan) and a floor-standing musical box.[49]

Although both Japanese and foreign merchants strove to offer tempting
products, they were handicapped by their limited knowledge of each other.
At first, Japanese merchants were more interested in selling export products
than in buying imported goods. Foreign merchants complained of weak demand and of the poverty of the Japanese merchants, who could not afford to

FIGURE 1.5 Utagawa Sadahide, *Complete Picture of the Great Harbor of Yokohama* (1859–1860). *Freer Gallery of Art and Arthur M. Sackler Gallery, Smithsonian Institution, Washington, D.C.: Gift of Ambassador and Mrs. William Leonhart*, S1998.52a-c

buy more than small samples. Even if they had the resources, most Japanese did not see much need for the goods on display in the foreign merchant houses. On seeing the near-naked coolies running through the streets of Yokohama, one early visitor dryly remarked, "It does not seem that there will be any great demand for Manchester cotton goods."[50]

Among the first foreign residents was William Keswick, a young Scotsman with the China-based trading firm of Jardine, Matheson. Keswick, twenty-five years old, was a junior member of the firm, but he was well connected. He was a great-nephew of company founder William Jardine and a grandson of William Jardine's sister and heir, Jean Johnstone. Keswick's father was a member of the company, and Keswick himself would become a partner in Jardine's in 1862 while still in his twenties and managing partner in 1874 (his descendants run the company to this day). An observer described the Keswick of 1859 as "still a young gentleman, with thin, reddish sideburns, a somewhat effeminate appearance, and lisping voice; yet a true diplomat who said all that he had to say with an ice-cold, deadened courtesy."[51] In a letter dated

July 21, 1859, Keswick wrote that business in the port was desultory. "There are now a fair number of Japanese merchants (shopkeepers) in the settlement, but they have as yet bought little or nothing, with the exception of a few trinkets from the Dutchmen. They have for sale isinglass, some of the better descriptions of seaweed, mushrooms etc. and raw silk, and silk piece goods."[52]

For a while at least, townsmen, foreigners, and villagers all lived side by side. Francis Hall described the still-remaining farming and fishing community of Yokohama as "a large village of brown cottages among which wind paths three to five feet broad . . . These streets and walks are very serpentine and bordered with evergreen hedges and bamboo polings all through the town . . . nothing could be more rural." Hall adds that the farmers of Yokohama were "very civil, inviting us into their houses, and set before us tea and hot sake." However, "I heard repeatedly the salutati]on of 'tojin,' and once 'tojin baka,' 'foreign or China fool.' "[53]

Not all the foreigners took up residence in Yokohama. The U.S. envoy Townsend Harris was so indignant at the creation of Yokohama (rather than using Kanagawa, as stipulated by the treaty) that he is said to have sworn never to set foot in the place.[54] Harris did his best to encourage Americans to take up residence with him in Kanagawa, even though there was virtually no accommodation for them. Although the merchants generally ignored him in favor of the comfort and convenience of Yokohama, a few missionaries—who wanted to be closer to the Japanese population—followed his advice. James Hepburn, with the American Presbyterian Mission, arrived on October 17, 1859, and, like all the other foreigners who chose to live in Kanagawa, he took up residence in a Buddhist temple. Such was the shortage of available housing that every single temple in Kanagawa had been rented out to the foreigners. "The people seem to take it very quietly indeed rather pleased, I should judge them—& the priests."[55] The rent for the temple was sixteen dollars a month, including the priest's residence. Hepburn and his wife remodeled the former into "a very comfortable dwelling house . . . containing some eight rooms, large & small." They sublet the priest's residence to another group of missionaries, from the Dutch Reformed Church. Since they brought very little with them from China, Hepburn had his furniture made by local craftsmen: "All they need is a model, their workmanship is good and they can make everything we want." He had, however, brought a Western-style heating stove from Shanghai, "and find it now indispensable."[56]

Commenting on the quality of life in Kanagawa, Hepburn wrote that he and his wife had "plenty to eat, such as fish, fowls, eggs, sweet potatoes, string-beans, turnips, radishes, rice of the best quality—carrots. We occasionally get a piece of fresh beef, mutton & veal from some kind Captain or our very kind Consul, and oysters too of excellent quality and large size from the market . . . milk and butter we have not." Margaret Ballagh, one of the Dutch Reformed missionaries who lived in the same compound, wrote that the vegetable seller would make the rounds, carrying (in November) "spinach, but not very tender; turnips, squashes and potatoes—both Irish and sweet," as well as chestnuts, walnuts, persimmons, oranges and grapes. "I select what I want and pay him with a few copper coins strung on a straw rope, and after thanking me by a low bow, making a deep inspiration at the same time, and passing the money up to his head and touching his forehead with it, he throws the string into his baskets, takes them up on each end of a pole and placing the pole across his shoulder, he trots off to another house." She bought fish in the same way and was able to send to Yokohama for "passable" beef. "We get a little pork occasionally, but the mutton is too expensive for us missionaries to look at." They made their own bread, grinding a mixture of local and imported flour using a stone pestle.[57]

The reason for the high prices and difficulty in obtaining meat products was the general absence of animal husbandry or butchering in Japan. Large animals like cattle and swine were expensive to rear, and butchering them was offensive to Japanese religious and cultural taboos against contact with death and blood (the main exceptions were mountain villages, some of which subsisted in part on wild game, and outcast communities that were designated to perform "unclean" tasks such as butchering). In Yokohama, meat such as beef and pork was supplied by visiting ships and a few enterprising foreigners who set up slaughterhouses and butchering facilities on the edge of the foreign settlement.

The Hepburns paid their two servants eight bu each per month, equivalent at the time to four dollars. Noting the relative economy of his household, Hepburn pointed out that "all other persons here, have either Chinese cooks & washermen, or English," and that "in Nagasaki two merchants send their clothes over to Shanghai to be laundered." Nevertheless, "we have found the price of marketing thus far higher than we expected, quite as high as it was at Amoy. I think we are imposed upon, and charged exorbitant prices . . . We pay as much for fish as we did in New York. Fruits are cheap." Most items of daily consumption were obtainable locally, but "they have no woolen goods that we have yet seen, and no tailors. We are much worse off in this respect than they are in China." Moreover, as one of the few foreign families living in Kanagawa proper, the Hepburns felt "certain that we are under constant surveillance, and all our movements and doings are reported to the rulers."[58]

Several visitors to Yokohama commented on one of its most notable features: its very visible brothel district. When the port opened in July, this was still in its temporary quarters in a residential block at the edge of the foreign quarter (later to reopen as the Yokohama Hotel). The prostitutes were moved to the new licensed quarter when it finally opened in November 1859. The district was given the name Miyozakichō. At the time of its opening, it consisted of six brothels occupying three semidetached residential buildings, as well as teahouses, geisha houses, and retail shops.[59] The Gankirō was the largest and grandest of the brothels. It was owned by Sakichi, the primary developer of the quarter. Sakichi was officially appointed the *nanushi*, or "headman," of the district, and he moved into a newly constructed district office adjacent to the brothels. From this office, he supervised the running of the quarter and took care of discipline and order among the residents.

The licensed quarter, as Francis Hall described it at the end of 1859, was "a small town of itself, and its buildings cover many acres in extent." The entrance was "through a massive gate just within which is a police station and ample police." The Gankirō was "a hundred and twenty five feet long by sixty broad, two stories in height. The lower story was divided into offices, reception rooms, and some bedrooms. Occupying a large quadrangle in the center was an artificial lake crossed by an elaborately furnished bridge . . . A wing connected with this lower story was set apart for Chinamen especially." On the ground floor was a "large apartment or sort of common living room, where twelve or fifteen girls were seated about on the mats, talking, smoking, painting their cheeks, whitening their necks, dressing their hair, and similar toilet devotions." At the entrance was a notice stating that "all noisy persons would be ejected." Another notice, in English and Dutch, listed the prices charged by the house. On the second floor was "a broad gallery around an open space looking upon the lake below. This gallery was divided into bedrooms of good size, fitted up with clean mats and handsome silk covered mattresses and comfortables . . . One large room was for a refreshment room and was fitted up with table, chairs, and lounges. The walls, and particularly the ceiling, were handsomely, though rather gorgeously, papered. There were seats in the same room for musicians."[60]

When the quarter officially opened, according to Rodolphe Lindau, "all the foreigners—the consuls among the very first—received a little package containing a porcelain cup, a paper fan and a strip of blue cloth . . . The fan pictured a bird's eye view of the establishment, and on the cloth appeared in English the statement, 'This place is designed for the pleasures of foreigners' . . . There was a great party at the Gankiro that lasted all night."[61]

The port town of Yokohama was established under treaties that were closely modeled on those that governed foreign concession areas in China such as Shanghai, Fuzhou, Guangzhou, Ningbo, and Xiamen. Many features of Yokohama would have been instantly recognizable to a habitué of the Chinese ports—for example, the substantial customs house that greeted inbound visitors, the large numbers of laborers and boatmen waiting at the docks, the hongs (foreign-merchant houses) with their godowns (warehouses), the waterfront bund with its emphasis on the needs and pleasures of the foreign community, and the enormous contrast between the spacious layout and (as foreigners started to build) Western-style buildings of the foreign settlement and the relatively crowded conditions of the "native quarter." Like the Chinese treaty ports, there were significant areas in which the Japanese government relinquished control, creating a semicolonial space within the foreign settlement. This semicolonial environment was most apparent in the system of extraterritoriality, which put foreign residents beyond the reach of Japanese law and empowered them to introduce their own systems of policing and control.[62] But it was also embodied in the built space of Yokohama, which gave foreigners immense spatial privilege and which was created entirely to serve their needs and desires.

Nevertheless, there were significant differences between Yokohama and the major Chinese treaty ports (though there was also considerable variation among the latter). Unlike the foreign concessions in Shanghai and other Chinese ports, Yokohama was planned and laid out entirely by the Japanese government, which retained a much higher degree of control over the urban environment of Yokohama than did the local governments in the Chinese ports. In Yokohama, for example, although there were several attempts to form an independent municipal council, the foreign community never succeeded in taking full control of its municipal affairs. In spite of widespread dissatisfaction and complaints by the foreign community, the shogunal government did a better job than the foreigners themselves of supplying essential services such as street maintenance, infrastructure improvements, drainage, and trash removal. Nor did the foreign community have the authority to mandate wholesale urban-planning initiatives such as harbor construction or the laying out of street plans (although the Japanese government did consult closely with the foreigners on such matters). Yokohama was indeed a planned city developed expressly for foreign residence; but the original planning was done entirely by Japanese administrators. Moreover, although the British, French, and Americans created their own police forces, augmented at times by military patrols, the Japanese retained overall control over security, in both the foreign settlement and the wider community. And in spite of initial plans to the contrary, the foreign settlement was never divided into national concessions under the control of competing foreign governments.

Thus, while the international concession in Shanghai became a haven for dissidents, Japanese subjects almost never had the opportunity to shelter from Japanese authority under the umbrella of extraterritorial privilege. The only exceptions were a tiny group of "overseas Japanese" (mostly castaways who had been educated in the United States, in some cases acquiring American citizenship) and a few servants and trading-house employees who were able to obtain a measure of informal protection when they got on the wrong side of the Japanese authorities. In fact, Japanese subjecthood was even more strictly enforced in Yokohama than in the residents' provincial places of origin: because of the unstable security situation as well the government's desire to control trade as much as possible, Japanese residents had to submit to strict systems of identification, registration, and monitoring.[63]

And although it was limited by the free-trade provisions of the treaty, the Japanese government was also able to assert greater control over the parameters of trade than its Chinese counterpart. For example, the import of opium was prohibited, as was the export of rice and other staples. The Japanese retained control over their customs house and the import duties it brought in. Travel within Japan by foreigners was prohibited, and trading could take place only within the treaty ports. A variety of bans on interactions between Japanese and foreigners also remained in effect, including the prohibition of overseas travel by Japanese (this was increasingly flouted, however) and the strict ban on Japanese practicing Christianity.

GETTING STARTED

Chūemon opened his store with high hopes. But he must have known that establishing a successful business in a new market like Yokohama would not be easy. Unlike the wealthy Edo merchants, he came with very little capital and limited contacts or government influence, and he had no experience of the foreigners he was hoping to deal with. Seen from the outside, at least, he surely fit one samurai official's description of the provincial Yokohama merchant: a man who dreamed of wealth "as though reaching for the clouds, or as though trees would turn into rice cakes."[64] Ernest Satow, a British diplomat who was resident in Yokohama in the early 1860s, commented that the Japanese merchant class were "adventurers, destitute of capital and ignorant of commerce."[65]

This description seems too harsh. Chūemon was certainly an experienced businessman, and even if he did dream of riches in the new port, his goals were not purely selfish: he also aimed to help his agricultural community back in Kōshū. But given his lack of capital, it is easy to see how he might have appeared to others—and why he had to struggle so to get his business started.

By the end of July, the port was well and truly open for business. "The construction in this town is something extraordinary. Large numbers of people are coming to view it. There are 11 ships here, decorated for their foreign travels. Japanese are arriving in great numbers to see the place."[66]

Business, however, was not getting off to such a good start. Chūemon explained to a group of eight business partners that the products they were

FIGURE 1.6 Utagawa Sadahide, *Picture of Newly Opened Port of Yokohama in Kanagawa* (1860). Chūemon's store is on the right, near the front of the picture. *Freer Gallery of Art and Arthur M. Sackler Gallery, Smithsonian Institution, Washington, D.C.: Gift of Ambassador and Mrs. William Leonhart, S1998.52a-c*

sending him, such as dried grapes, tobacco, pottery, and cotton, were not sell-ing. On the other hand, "The foreigners are buying large quantities of Seto ware [porcelain], lacquer, and *kanten* [agar-agar, a gelling agent made from seaweed] . . . There is also some demand for vegetables, fish, and chicken." Most of these were not products of the Kōshū region. Instead of trying to compete in these markets, Chūemon suggested it might be more profitable to buy goods from the foreigners for resale in the Kōshū market. To that end, he asked each business partner to contribute three *ryō* ($6). The letters do not indicate whether or not he succeeded in raising the fifty dollars or so that he was looking for to buy foreign goods, but even if he did, the foreign mer-chants would hardly have been overjoyed. A successful Shanghai merchant would have been looking for transactions in the thousands, or even tens of thousands, of dollars.[67]

Considering his disadvantages, Chūemon was actually quite successful in connecting with this exciting new market. But he also had an early lesson in its perils. Very soon after the port opened, Chūemon succeeded in selling on commission a consignment of silk from Hanbei of Ōno village to an En-glishman, James Barber. At the time, Barber was Keswick's assistant manager at Jardine, Matheson. Later, he was to start his own firm in Yokohama. He had a reputation for being a tough character.

On September 8, 1859, Chūemon wrote to his partners about a serious problem with the transaction:

> As I wrote the other day, I would like to sort out the business with the silk thread, but Barber is obstinate and I'm unable to make any prog-ress with him. I plan to take the matter to the town office, but it's by no means easy. Right now there need to be rules governing the exchange between Japanese and English farmers and merchants. However, I will certainly not lose in this. We must be reasonable and keep calm. You must go and talk to [Hanbei] and tell him to remain patient for a little longer.[68]

It appears that Chūemon had delivered a small shipment of silk to Barber (or to Barber's agent), for which he was expecting payment of some eighty *ryō* (about $160). For some unknown reason, Barber had failed to pay him.

Trade disputes between Japanese and foreign merchants were very com-mon, which is hardly surprising given the different business cultures of the two groups. Certainly, there were numerous opportunities for misunder-standing and miscommunication. The problem was exacerbated by the lack of any effective dispute-resolution mechanism. According to the extraterritoriality clauses of the trade treaties, foreign merchants could be sued only in a court of their own nationality. Quite apart from the linguistic complications, British law required the loser in such a case to pay the court costs for both parties. According to Yuki Honjo, only six cases were brought by Japanese merchants in the entire decade of the 1860s.[69] In practice, as we see in Chūemon's response, Japanese merchants saw their best hope in mediation by the Kanagawa commissioners. Similarly, foreign merchants had no ready recourse when they had a complaint against a Japanese merchant. There was an ad-hoc system for adjudication of foreign suits against Japanese subjects by a Japanese magistrate in the presence of a Western consul, but it seems to have operated almost exclusively for criminal cases. Only after 1874 did the newly established Kanagawa court (saibansho) begin to offer regular adjudication of disputes.[70] Until then it seems that, just as Chūemon took his complaint to the Kanagawa commissioners, so foreign merchants took their grievances to their diplomatic representatives in the hope of some redress. On April 1, 1864, for example, Samuel Gower of Jardine, Matheson wrote that he had placed a commercial dispute in the hands of British minister Sir Rutherford Alcock, who wanted to help, but "he does not seem sanguine of obtaining anything through the Japanese Government—unless it be the punishment of the man." Gower added, "I believe myself that the man . . . deserves punishment."[71]

There were numerous causes for complaint on both sides. As in the Barber case, Japanese merchants complained of the foreigners taking delivery of silk, whether a sample or a full shipment, and not paying for it. Typically, foreign merchants (or their Chinese managers) would examine samples of merchandise presented by Japanese sellers and agree on a price. The Japanese merchant would then have to deliver the full consignment of goods within a specified period, and, once delivered, the foreign merchant would inspect the goods in his company godown. Only when he was satisfied that the consignment fulfilled the contract would he pay the Japanese merchant.[72] A common accusation was that foreign merchants would deliberately wait until a ship arrived with news of foreign market conditions; if conditions were unfavorable, the merchant would reject the goods awaiting approval in his warehouse, on the ground that they had failed his inspection.

Other complaints centered on the Chinese compradors (business managers), employees of the China-based foreign merchant houses who operated more or less independently within their employers' houses of business. In most cases, the Japanese merchant was required to pay a commission, known as a "Chinese gift" (nankin shinjō), to the Chinese manager. Chinese managers were also accused of tampering with scales and a variety of other corrupt practices.[73]

The foreigners in turn complained of broken promises, silk deliveries of a lower quality than those promised in the samples, or Japanese merchants failing to deliver shipments at the agreed-upon price. William Keswick complained that "it is very disappointing that the Japanese have so very little respect for contracts and that we have no certain means of redress in cases of bad faith."[74] Ernest Satow offers a litany of dishonest practices on the part of Japanese merchants: "Foreigners made large advances to men of straw for the purchase of merchandise which was never delivered, or ordered manufactures from home on the account of men who, if the price fell, refused to accept the goods that would now bring them in only a loss. Raw silk was adulterated with sand or fastened with heavy paper ties, and every separate skein had to be carefully inspected before payment, while the tea could not be trusted to be as good as the sample."

As a result, "the conviction that Japanese was a synonym for dishonest trader became so firmly seated in the minds of foreigners that it was impossible for any friendly feeling to exist."[75] James Barber himself complained in a letter to his head office that "the dealers have no respect for their engagements."[76] Rutherford Alcock, the British envoy to Japan, called the Japanese merchants "among the most dishonest and tricky of Easterns."[77]

Unfortunately there is no record as to how or if Chūemon's dispute with Barber was resolved, but in any case Chūemon seems to have learned from his mistakes. There is only one other dispute with a foreigner recorded in the letters: in February 1864, he successfully negotiated the handover of an outstanding balance of a thousand dollars, presumably owed him by a foreign merchant in payment for a delivery of export goods, in a late-night negotiating session at the government offices.[78] By this time, it appears that the Japanese and foreign merchants had developed a functioning system of dispute resolution through the good offices of the Japanese authorities. In general, Chūemon seems to have developed excellent relationships with foreign merchant houses. In fact, he was much more likely to run into problems with his own government, which at times during the 1860s tried to restrict the volume of foreign trade, or even prevent it altogether.

More than business relations or regulation, it was the lack of capital that defined Chūemon's early years in business in Yokohama. From the beginning, his letters were filled with pleas to his son and business partners to advance him more money, to wait longer for payment of debts he owed them, and to

FIGURE 1.7 Picture of the American proprietor of number 33, Wenrīto (E. W. van Reed), on horseback inside his compound. *Utagawa Sadahide, Yokohama kaikō kenbunshi (ca. 1863)*

borrow money in Kōshū on his behalf. He lacked the capital to purchase an inventory of stock to sell from his shop, and, as we will see (chapter 2), he even lacked at times the money for his day-to-day expenses. And in this he was not alone. Among the provincial merchants who tried to establish themselves in Yokohama, lack of capital was the primary reason for business failure.

The capital shortage reflected the contradictions of the treaty port environment. The majority of the Japanese merchants were not capitalized on anything like the scale needed to fill the enormous foreign demand for silk, tea, and other export commodities. To give an example, a single packhorse load of silk thread purchased in the producing region cost from four hundred fifty ryō ($900) upward—many times Chūemon's entire income from the previous year.[79] Financing was available both in Yokohama and in Kōshū, but in Kōshū it was scarce and depended on personal relationships, while in Yokohama capital was relatively abundant but commanded very high interest rates exceeding 10 percent per month.[80] By contrast, foreign merchants were extremely well capitalized (though limited at times by their restricted access to Japanese currency) and could easily have extended credit to their Japanese suppliers.

However, the available legal mechanisms gave them almost no recourse if their Japanese debtor defaulted. They had nothing to rely on but trust, and that was in extremely short supply in the early years. In May 1860, William Keswick advanced a large sum to a Japanese merchant, Takasuya Seibei, whom Keswick was "satisfied . . . is to be trusted. He is a man of position and the most respectable merchant in Yokuhama [sic]."[81] However, Keswick's successor had to ask the British minister to demand Seibei's arrest for absconding with the money.[82]

Chūemon arrived in Yokohama with enough capital to get his trading license and lease a lot, but little more. He had virtually no money of his own, so he was dependent on his business partners and friends in Kōshū to advance him the funds to build his shop and purchase inventory. Even before opening, Chūemon was already begging his business associates to advance him more capital. In a letter dated April 18, 1859 (Ansei 6/3/16), he asked for a loan of twenty ryō: "If I can just raise this money, I foresee great profits in the future, so please, please lend me the money as requested."

This became the tone of many of Chūemon's letters for the next two years. When he was not begging his business partners to advance him funds, he was cajoling his son Shōjirō, who had remained in the village to carry on the family farming business, to raise money on his behalf.

On December 27, 1859 (Ansei 6/12/4), as the Japanese calendar year began to draw to a close, Chūemon faced the reality that he could not fulfill the traditional year-end settlement of debts. He wrote to his son, "I know that I need to send you money, but this winter I am extremely stuck for funds, and there is nothing I can do about it. Please discuss this with your mother, and also with Matsujirō and Jizaemon, and see if you can make some sort of plan. Also please go to Okamura and consult with him. You must also go to the village office, and also to Buheita of Higashi Takahashi village and consult with them. You must consult with vagrants and absolutely everyone."[83]

Chūemon had to deal with these issues in relative isolation. Although he had collaborators in Yokohama, his closest friends and business partners as well as his family were all back in Kōshū. Undoubtedly Chūemon missed his wife and children. His wife in particular was a close collaborator in Chūemon's business affairs, and he planned to bring her to Yokohama as soon as he was settled enough. Separated from his family by several days' walk, he worried about their health and well-being. In 1858–1859, Japan was swept by cholera and measles epidemics that many have linked directly to Japan's opening to foreign contact. Between them, they are thought to have killed as many as a hundred thousand Japanese. On September 22, 1859, Chūemon wrote to Shōjirō, "I hear that many people in the village have died of sickness, and this makes me a little worried about you. You must have faith and you must not be negligent."[84]

Chūemon's younger son Naotarō was more than eager to join his father in Yokohama. For a second son with no inheritance, the family's new venture in Yokohama represented an opportunity to escape from the straitjacket of village life. But Chūemon was concerned about Naotarō's immaturity and impatience: "Please tell him that while his father is away he must be especially patient. If he works hard at farming this year and is patient, then I will bring him to Kanagawa. Please tell him that he must certainly have patience."[85] Underlying Chūemon's encouragement was his evident worry about his younger son's character. In a letter dated August 6, Chūemon admonished Shōjirō to "tell [Naotarō] again and again that he must not be idle when I am away. And give him strict instructions not to go out and play at night."[86]

Although Chūemon missed his family and undoubtedly felt far from those he loved, in Yokohama he was literally swamped with travelers and merchants from Kōshū, who had come to try their luck selling produce to the foreigners and who looked to Chūemon for assistance and accommodation. "Every night forty or fifty or sixty people are staying here. They are bringing many packages with them, and there's nowhere to sleep. People are sleeping back-to-back in the entranceway."[87] Observing this situation, Chūemon saw a business opportunity if he could expand his premises to accommodate guests properly. Early in 1860 he wrote, "Many merchants are arriving from all over Japan, and there are no facilities for their accommodation. Many of them are high-class customers, and I would like to be able to accommodate them."[88] Chūemon would have to wait another eight years before he could realize his vision of opening an inn to accommodate the flood of visitors.

THE GOLD RUSH

The products offered for sale by Chūemon in these first months covered a wide range. The idea was to sell the products of Kōshū to the entire world. However, Chūemon quickly discovered that the foreigners were interested in only a small range of products. Foremost among these were silk and gold, neither of which Chūemon was easily able to provide. Silk was too expensive for Chūemon to purchase on his own account, and the sale of gold to foreigners was tightly controlled by the Japanese government.

In spite of the difficulties that foreigners had in obtaining gold, this was the commodity most in demand in 1859. The reason was the huge disparity between the gold-silver ratio in Japan and that in the rest of the world. In Japan, the nominal ratio was five to one. In the global market, it was fifteen to one. According to the trade treaties, foreign silver would be exchanged for Japanese one-*bu* silver coins on a weight-for-weight basis. Based on this agreement, one hundred Mexican silver dollars (the prevailing trade currency in East Asia) bought three hundred one-*bu* coins, which in turn bought as many as seventy-five gold *koban* coins (the *koban* was the standard gold coin, worth four silver *bu*) on the black market. A foreign merchant could ship those *koban* to Shanghai, sell them for three hundred Mexican dollars, and bring the silver back to Japan to make another purchase. With these easy profits in sight, the demand for Japanese gold was overwhelming.

The Japanese government argued in vain that its monetary system was not strictly based on gold or silver content but rather was a notional system in which coins were issued as tokens of value. In other words, the actual buying power of the one-*bu* silver coin was much higher than its silver content. The government even tried minting a new half-*bu* coin, especially for the foreign trade, with three times the silver content of the half *bu* circulating in the rest of Japan, to reflect its "true" value relative to gold. But this elicited protests from both foreign and Japanese merchants, and the new coin had to be abandoned.[89]

The British minister, Sir Rutherford Alcock, was sympathetic to the plight of the Japanese. In his memoir, he recalls a top Japanese official complaining that the opening of trade had brought Japan "nothing but expense. Everything is getting dearer and if this be the result of foreign trade at its first beginnings what will it be in its development?"[90] But Alcock and other foreign envoys were more concerned to preserve their rights under the treaties than to help the Japanese manage their consequences.

The export of currency—other than copper coins—was explicitly permitted by Japan's treaties with the foreign powers. Nevertheless, the shogunal government tightened its controls over the sale of gold to foreigners, threatening Japanese subjects with death if caught. It also tried to thwart the trade by severely restricting the issue of Japanese silver coins to foreigners—using the excuse that the currency was all needed for the reconstruction of the shogun's castle after a devastating fire. These policies were effective to some extent, but Japanese and foreign traders did their best to get around them, and the trade in gold coins continued. In practice, foreigners were willing to pay more than the legal value of the gold they purchased because of the high profits they could still get on the Shanghai market. On the other hand, Japanese black marketeers were willing to risk their lives selling gold coins because of the high prices the foreigners were willing to pay. As a result, in spite of the best efforts of the Japanese, possibly as much as sixteen million dollars' worth of Japanese gold (based on the global price) was exported to Shanghai in the first months after the opening of trade.[91]

Contemporary writers and subsequent historians have tended to blame the foreigners for this disruptive drain on the Japanese gold supply. It has been described as "a scandalous speculation . . . leaving many blots on the foreign name"; as an example of "bad faith" aimed at "illicit" gain; as "unscrupulous"; as creating "an amount of indignation and bitterness on the part of the Japanese as it will take years to allay"; and as "[draining] their treasury of native currency by false representations."[92] Indeed, like the opium trade in China, one could see it as typifying the exploitative and asymmetrical relations of trade under the East Asian treaty port system. There is a scholarly debate as to how obsessed the foreign merchants actually were with the gold and how detrimental the trade really was to the shogunal government or the Japanese economy.[93] But from the comments of early visitors to Yokohama it is clear that the gold trade was a huge lure to foreign merchants and adventurers, and that many did in fact make quick fortunes. At the same time, the upheavals in currency values that resulted from the foreign "gold rush" undoubtedly contributed to the destabilization of the Japanese financial system and ultimately brought hardship to millions of poor Japanese (discussed further in chapter 3).

John Brooke, an American naval captain who was stuck in Yokohama for several months after his first lieutenant ran their ship aground, witnessed the scramble for gold firsthand. In November, Brooke commented that "gold is abundant and there is a steady stream of it setting from the country . . . The Japanese government must be aware of the fact that gold is largely exported and I presume steps will soon be taken to check it."[94] Brooke declared himself "heartily tired of Yokohama. There is too much traffic, too much talking of cobans [koban]."[95]

Brooke's lieutenant—the same man who had grounded their ship and caused them to be marooned in Yokohama—did his very best to profit from their sojourn. As government officers, both Brooke and his lieutenant were given privileged access to Japanese silver coins. Brooke commented that "the Authorities allow so many [one-bu coins] for each person requiring the exchange. Lieut. Thorburn has been using my name by permission. I have often told him that I do not wish to change money, but he persistently requests it nearly every day."[96] In January, when their house was burned down in a fire, Thorburn confided to Brooke that he had been able to save his cash hoard of nine thousand dollars. Brooke commented rather sourly, "He has been fortunate then since his arrival here, for he was then in debt."[97]

Large-scale merchants like Jardine, Matheson were also trying to get their hands on gold coins, although their first preference was probably still to buy silk and other products.[98] On November 16, 1859, William Keswick asked his Shanghai office for two hundred fifty thousand dollars for the purchase of gold and silk. When he saw an opportunity to buy gold before these funds arrived, he was quite prepared to borrow at a 16 per cent rate in order to secure "a few hundred pieces."[99] On December 3, he wrote that "during the last two or three days I have not so much as seen even one Cobang. I very much fear from this . . . that the Authorities are really in possession of sufficient power to almost suppress the trade."[100] But a few days later, he was able to send onboard a Jardine ship a total of nine boxes of koban coins, under the accounts of six different Yokohama-based merchants. The total value was about thirty-five thousand dollars, and it appears that Jardine's was acting as exchange broker on their behalf.[101]

The American merchant Francis Hall reported meeting "a German Jew who will furnish one with kobangs."[102] The next day, Hall "obtained 50 kobangs of the Jew" before visiting a Japanese shop, in which "the old gentleman cautiously opened a drawer and brought out some kobangs. These I did not buy as he asked too much."[103] A few days later, Hall noted that "two or three shops have been closed by the authorities . . . for dealing in kobangs." And the following week Hall wrote that "all natives crossing the bridges into Yokohama are searched for kobangs."[104] Yet in spite of these threats and restrictions, on December 22, 1859, Hall was able to send his agent in Canton "120 kobangs and 75 quarters ditto."[105]

Cees de Coningh recalled in his memoir that since his house was in an isolated place, he was often visited by Japanese smugglers, who would illegally bring gold coins and gold dust into Yokohama. On one occasion, he was visited by a gang of three smugglers, men "with the most rascally faces I have ever seen"[106] They sold him a huge pile of gold dust that they had secreted about their bodies for four hundred bu ($200). De Coningh should have been alerted by the low price. When he had the "gold" sent to Shanghai for assay, he learned that it was in fact antimony, worth only $0.15 per pound.[107]

Although Chūemon was not directly affected by the Yokohama gold rush, the stagnation in trade caused by the unavailability to foreign merchants of Japanese currency—as well as their preference for using all the currency they could obtain to buy gold—surely reduced his prospects for doing business with them. However, in spite of these obstacles, Chūemon remained optimistic through the end of 1859. In addition to his abortive sale to Barber, surviving documents indicate at least five other sales of silk to foreigners during the second half of 1859.[108] And although Chūemon faced the New Year away from his family and unable to pay his debts, he continued to believe in the near-limitless potential of the Yokohama market.

The treaty port of Yokohama was created from conflict. A reluctant shogunal government accepted trade relations with the United States, Great Britain, and several other Western countries because it believed it had no other choice. The background to this reluctant embrace was an aggressive age of Western (including Russian) imperialism in Asia, fueled by technological development and the rapid opening of new routes to the Pacific. The subjection of large parts of Asia to European rule, and the humiliation of China in the two Opium Wars, were sobering reminders of Japan's precarious position.

But if the shogunal government was forced to accede to the main goal of the Western nations—trade conducted under the protection of extraterritorial privilege—it was successful in asserting a measure of control over the process. Under the guidance of Chief Minister Ii Naosuke, a group of senior administrators created a new town "out of thin air," a town that was expressly planned to manage and control Japan's relationship with its new foreign residents. Unlike many of the Chinese treaty ports, which were governed as colonial enclaves by powerful councils of foreign residents, Yokohama remained for the most part under the direct control of the shogunal administration. The planning, layout, construction, and day-to-day management of the town all remained in the hands of the Kanagawa commissioners. The plan they developed was designed to isolate the foreigners in a guarded location as far as possible from the mainstream of Japanese commercial and social activity. Japanese, foreigners, and the workers and prostitutes who served them—each group was allotted its own space, separated from the others and, wherever possible, closely supervised and controlled by the government. Key to the success of the project was the attractiveness of the town that the commissioners had created. Complete with grand government buildings, extensive commercial facilities, an excellent port, and lavish entertainment facilities, Yokohama was designed to be a place where both Japanese and foreigners would want to live.

In spite of the success of many of these measures, Yokohama was from the beginning a lightning rod of conflict, both for the Western powers that

occupied its foreign settlement and for domestic agitators determined to reverse the shogunate's humiliating submission to foreign demands. Indeed,
the conflict over the treaties and their implementation laid bare fissures in the
Japanese sociopolitical structure that were only to deepen in the decade that
followed—that called into question, indeed, the very notion of "Japan" as a
unitary state.

Yet even in the painful circumstances of its birth, Yokohama was understood by many to be a place of extraordinary opportunity. Its foreign residents
scrambled to take advantage of new trading opportunities and to profit from
the unintended consequences of ill-thought-out policies related to currency
and foreign exchange. In spite of the reluctance of many, and even the coercion
employed to bring them in the first place, Japanese merchants, laborers, entrepreneurs, and tourists soon flocked to the town in response to the opportunities it offered for wealth and pleasure.

Among those who responded to the call of Yokohama was Shinohara
Chūemon, a fifty-year-old man with no experience of foreigners or foreign
trade, with limited financial resources, and without the status or privilege of
the elite merchant houses of Edo. In order to move to Yokohama he left behind a comfortable life of local privilege, a position as political leader of his
village, and a rich network of family and friends in exchange for an uncertain
future as a small-scale merchant in a town that did not yet exist. What impulse was strong enough to uproot him from his comfortable place in the sun
and pull him to this new space of radical uncertainty? A part of the answer
lies in the enigma of individual personality—we can never truly understand
human motivation. What we can discern, though, are Chūemon's deep commitment to the well-developed commercial and human networks of the regional elite of Kōshū whom he aspired to represent; his sense of belonging
within the shogunal system that linked Yokohama and Kōshū; and the powerful lure of personal gain.

2 YEARS OF STRUGGLE (1860–1864)

NEIGHBORS

> The city was brilliant with ornament and spectacles . . . The whole population were in holiday dresses . . . as if a thousand rainbows had been shattered into four or five foot fragments and gone stalking about in curious pose, the robes of every imaginable hue.[1]

It was July 18, 1860, and the entire community of Yokohama had come together to enjoy an extravagant festival. Sitting on the mat of a Japanese shopkeeper, surrounded by smiling faces and plied with tea and snacks, Francis Hall watched as a procession of a dozen floats passed by, pulled by pairs of bullocks. Each float represented one of the neighborhoods of the Japanese town. Spellbound, Hall tried to interpret the twenty-five-foot-high individual tableaux atop each cart: a pine grove with waterfall, tiger and dragon; a colorful goddess "with long hair flowing down her neck and a gorgeous dress of brocade silks and gold silken tissues"; a man tossing his head and arms about "to represent a fox with a grotesque fox head adorned with a long beard"; and a "Nippon demi-god bearing aloft over his head an immense bell." Most intriguing to Hall was a "representation of the train of a daimio passing through the streets of Yedo [Edo]. The norimon [palanquin] was preceded by pike and standard bearers, armor bearers, weapon bearers who wound along with a peculiar slow and mock dignified step, for this scene was evidently a half caricature. The norimon instead of a Prince had another fox riding within who sat in dignified state. On each side of the norimon walked three men clad in female attire, their faces painted and colored like so many harlequins."

Indeed, bizarre scenes abounded: townsmen dressed as warriors with wooden swords and fan-bearing servants; "two, four, or more girls dressed as policemen and bearing in their hands the iron staff and rings of that office"; courtesans of the brothel quarter dressed in gorgeous finery, perched on the floats and acting out "a variety of plays, pantomimes, and dances"; and two men carrying penises "of colossal proportions" on their backs. As night fell, "the spectator was bewildered with the glare of light, the glittering of colors, the miming cars, the showy females in the house show, many graceful dances; it was a scene conjured up by a wizard's spell. All night long the revel lasted, there was no sleep." Hall found it "the gayest scene of popular festivity that it had ever been my lot to witness."

The Benten festival was a first-anniversary celebration for the town. The authorities, anxious to show off Yokohama's newfound prosperity and future potential (and also to impress their foreign guests), planned it on a grand scale. The festival was nominally a religious event, in honor of Benzaiten, the Buddhist-Shinto-Hindu syncretic deity of the Benten shrine (and, conveniently for the new town, one of the shichifukujin, or "seven deities of wealth"). In practice it was a lavish street party, raucous, brilliantly colored, and well lubricated with sake, which was "only less free than water."[2] The cost was said to be in excess of twenty thousand ryō ($40,000 in Mexican dollars), of which eighteen hundred ryō was donated by the shogun himself.[3]

Chūemon, his wife, and three of his sons were there. Naotarō had finally got his wish and moved to Yokohama to help his father in the shop. The younger boys, Seitarō and Katsusuke, had come to be with their mother. Happy to be reunited, the family was full of optimism about the future. For Chūemon and Naotarō, the festival symbolized the hope and glamour they attached to Yokohama. They had been building up excitement about the event for weeks, urging their family members and friends from Kōshū to join them and watch from Chūemon's storefront, in a prime position on Honchō-dōri and near one of the town's biggest intersections. Their street was brilliantly decorated, hung with brightly colored paper lanterns, the shop fronts covered in decorative paper and ornaments.

This was Chūemon's neighborhood, his home now. And as a proprietor of one of the first businesses to open, he had a respectable position as a leading member of the community. Chūemon and Naotarō could not watch the festival with their family because they had been deputed as parade marshals. Both were required to wear formal clothes—pleated *hakama* trousers and kimono with the family crest.[4] Since they did not own any such clothing, they had to have it specially made up.[5] That was not their only expense. A few days after the festival, Chūemon was presented with a bill for thirty-five *ryō* ($70) for his share of the festival costs. This was no small sum: as we will see, Chūemon was struggling to find even a few *ryō* in loans to invest in his fledgling business.

The entertainment was a splendid celebration of Yokohama's arrival on the national and global stage. Already the town was growing extraordinarily quickly, a magnet for merchants, adventurers, opportunists, transients, and migrants from all parts of the world. In Japan and abroad, Yokohama was coming to be known as a place where fortunes could be made, where the constraints of class and privilege could be thrown off, and anyone, if they were lucky, and clever, and hardworking enough, could make it big; a place where "one can see apprentices and coolies freely walking around the streets carrying large amounts of foreign silver."[6]

Chūemon was a core member of this community. The people in his immediate circle were the proprietors of the shops of Nichōme. Although they were all business owners, they were a diverse group. Chūemon himself was struggling to get his modest business on a firm footing. Right across the street from Chūemon was the Echigoya, the Yokohama branch of the Mitsuis, Japan's wealthiest merchant family. The grand two-story textile emporium and foreign-exchange broker had been built at an expense of almost four thousand *ryō*—twenty times Chūemon's own investment—with a wood-floored area with chairs for foreign buyers and a separate tatami-floored sales area for Japanese buyers.[7] The owner of the shop was Mitsui Hachirōemon, a distant and legendary figure who conducted his business from the family headquarters in Kyoto, sending runners up and down the two-hundred-fifty-mile highway (they made the journey in four days) to keep him informed. Chūemon was friends with Senjirō, the Echigoya's Yokohama branch manager.[8] At the other extreme was the Shibaya store two blocks down from Chūemon, which had been opened by a trio of villagers from nearby Shibau village, led by Tezuka Seigorō. Seigorō and his associates had built their eighteen-hundred-square-foot store at a cost of only thirty *ryō*.

The merchants of Nichōme were bound by the administrative system of the Edo shogunate, a system of which British diplomat Laurence Oliphant declared "the great principle . . . is the absolute extinction of individual freedom." The system worked by "a complicated machinery, so nicely balanced, that, as everybody watches everybody, so no individual can escape paying the penalty to society of any injury he may attempt to inflict upon it."[9] Certainly, this was a system in which every resident was assigned duties and obligations, with a high degree of oversight. The Kanagawa commissioners placed the headmen of Hodogaya and Yokohama villages in overall charge of the town's administration. Under them, at the head of every neighborhood was a *machi-nanushi*, or "neighborhood headman." The *nanushi* conducted their day-to-day business in the *chōkaisho* (town hall), a building in the administrative center of the town next to the customs house and under the supervision of the Kanagawa commissioners. The *nanushis'* responsibilities included communicating and enforcing the laws enacted by the commissioners; keeping an up-to-date register of all residents and their family members; ensuring that fire prevention and firefighting measures were in place; registering and approving financial and property transactions; rooting out bad elements in the neighborhood; mediating disputes; organizing the neighborhood's participation in festivals; and administering neighborhood funds.[10]

Below the level of the neighborhood headmen were the five-household groups (*goningumi*), which were responsible for the smooth operation of daily life in the neighborhood. They implemented fire and security checks, inspected houses and streets, and generally took joint responsibility for maintaining an orderly and law-abiding neighborhood. Fighting or disorderly conduct in the street or in any one house might result in the punishment of the whole neighborhood, on the principle that "he who neglected to prevent a crime when he could have is beyond doubt guilty of the same crime."[11]

Compared with Edo, which was administered by townsmen with relatively light supervision by the samurai class, in Yokohama the office of the Kanagawa commissioners was much more involved in day-to-day administration. Most merchants would encounter the samurai officials on a daily basis as the officials certified business transactions, inspected incoming shipments, mediated relationships with the foreign merchants, managed the town hall, and administered land transactions. The officials were particularly con cerned to manage contacts with foreigners. For example, Japanese in foreign employ were required to pay a monthly fee to help pay for "a man who kept a register of all foreigners' servants, their names, ages, where they came from, and other particulars of personal identity," an example in one foreigner's opinion of "the absolute knowledge this government endeavors to obtain of all its subjects, particularly those in foreign service."[12]

Chūemon was connected to this administrative and social web on several levels. As a merchant in the busy Nichōme district, he was an integral part of the local community. He participated in community events, and he contributed financially when called on, participating, for example, in an informal insurance network to compensate victims of fire and other disasters. Beginning in mid-1860, Chūemon also worked as a staff member in the town hall. This administrative position, which came with a nominal salary, involved a considerable commitment of time and effort. Chūemon was reluctant at first to take it on, not least because he was still one of the headmen of his home village in Kōshū. But "they told me that if I refused, my status in the community would suffer."[13] Once in the position, Chūemon took his duties seriously—indeed, with his previous bureaucratic experience he was a valuable member of the staff. Although we do not know the exact nature of his duties, one remarkable document that has survived in his family archive shows that in 1861 Chūemon performed a detailed survey of every merchant house in the five neighborhoods of Honchō. Chūemon's report recorded the names of the owner and manager, the land rent, the size of the buildings, the place of origin of the owner, any changes in or additions to the premises, and the trade items registered for that business. It remains today one of the most comprehensive sources of information on Yokohama's merchant community in the early 1860s.[14]

In addition to his role and responsibilities in the local and town communities, Chūemon also represented his home province of Kōshū. Chūemon's shop was a meeting place and even an overnight refuge for large numbers of visitors from Kōshū—mostly farmers and petty merchants hoping to sell consignments of silk, cotton, or other local commodities in the Yokohama marketplace. The flow of visitors from the provinces swelled the population of Yokohama, as did the rapid influx of petty shopkeepers, service workers, tea and sake shop proprietors, hawkers and street entertainers, porters and laborers, boatmen, beggars, prostitutes, and outcasts. Estimates of the Japanese population of Yokohama at the turn of the 1860s vary widely. Foreign consular estimates put it at three thousand, but Samuel Oliver, who visited Yokohama in 1861, estimated it as closer to twenty thousand. A Japanese guidebook

written around 1863 estimated there were ten thousand households in Yokohama, implying a population of thirty thousand or more.[15]

The bustling new port created enormous demand for manual labor. Porters were everywhere to be seen pushing heavily laden handcarts or carrying
loads suspended on each end of a pole. They were typically organized into informal groups, with a leader selected for his strength and charisma, who
contracted with employers on behalf of the group in exchange for a share in
the income. The groups operated like gangs, sometimes intimidating rivals
or taking part in public disturbances to protest rising prices or other difficulties.[16] According to Francis Hall, the Yokohama porters were "bare legged
fellows with ragged wrappers around their shoulders, a dirty set of vagabonds
as one could hope to see." In the summer months they worked naked except
for a cloth around their waists. They were "poor men who have no house, no
clothes, no family, who live by coolie jobs, drink sake, and gamble. The government furnishes them shelter, and if two or three hundred laborers are
wanted, you apply to the government and the government knows where to get
them."[17]

Slightly higher on the social scale, the skilled laborer might live "in his
room [with] no furnishings other than his bed, a little chest of unfinished
wood, the strictly necessary pieces of clothing, and some kitchen utensils. Of
course he has no servants, and he lives with his wife and two or three children quite well, on an income of twelve to fourteen itsebus a month [12–14
bu, $6–$7], including the house rent."[18] This class of laborer included carpenters, builders, gardeners, metalworkers, and the boatmen who rowed between the piers and the ships waiting to load and unload their cargo.

Boatmen also operated the ferry service between Yokohama and
Kanagawa, carrying passengers on their backs to the waiting boats during
low tide. The Japanese women would "throw their arms around the bearers'
necks, who throw their arms back under the fleshiest part of the riders' body
behind, and thus with her bare red legs hanging straight down (not astrad-
dle) the Japanese girl goes laughing to the ferryboat." Like many laboring
groups, the boatmen had a strong collective spirit. On feast days, they would
carry their boats through the streets "with loud demonstrations of joy"
and row out into the bay, "shouting, and flinging iron cash into the water for
good luck."[19]

At the bottom of the social scale were the outcasts and beggars. Outcasts
(known as eta or hinin) lived in designated areas on the edges of communities
throughout Japan. They were an essential part of the social and economic
functioning of Tokugawa-era society, performing a wide variety of reserved

tasks—often those involving contact with blood. Outcast status was hereditary, but it was possible to be cast into its ranks as punishment for a criminal
offense. In spite of the discrimination and limitations from which they suffered, the outcasts had found useful niches for themselves in society, and they
benefited from their monopoly over certain services. On April 21, 1860, Francis Hall visited a community of leather workers in a segregated hamlet outside Yokohama:

> The houses were in a thick cluster with no apparent regulation of streets.
> A few hides were stretched and drying in the sun. There was nothing
> about this quarter to indicate any special poverty except a number of
> houses that were underground. A cellar was dug and over it a straw roof
> placed with a paper window in the floor. In the quarter generally the
> people were as well clad and looked as prosperous as other parts of
> Kanagawa. Some of these leather dressers are said to grow rich in their
> proscribed traffic. Persecuted they truly are, being forbidden to marry
> without [outside] their own guild, or to enter the houses of others.

Beggars were highly visible on the nearby Tōkaidō highway, "a most de-
graded looking lot of outcasts. A few seemed beggars from disease, but the
most appeared to be professional beggars. They had a sinister expression of
countenance[,] their hair was cut short to about a half inch in length, their
clothing and whole appearance filthy beyond measure. Many boys were among
them." In addition, "travelling priests, shaven and shorn, followed the road
for alms."[20] The beggars were "very importunate throwing themselves across
our way and following after us." But unlike in the West, they were "never
teased in Japan and are seldom refused a mong [mon], or the 50th part of a
cent, the smallest of coins."[21]

However, beggars who attempted to solicit foreigners for money within
the Yokohama town limits were quickly ejected. John Black reports that in
the wake of a severe food shortage in 1867, poverty-stricken Japanese gathered
at the Yokohama docks, where large quantities of rice were being imported: "They would be seen at the landing-places, watching the unload-
ing of the cargo-boats, sweeping up the grain that might be shaken out
of the bags in handling them; and even following the kurumas, or trucks,
on which they were conveyed from the hatobas [piers] to the merchant's
godowns, to sweep up what might fall by the way." However, "the Governor of Kanagawa had the whole of them taken in hand by the police. From
that day to this [Black was writing in the late 1870s], with an exceptional

individual or two, the sight of the begging fraternity . . . is exceedingly rare."[22]

The streets of Yokohama were, however, crowded with peddlers selling "fancy goods, confectionery . . . dolls, figures of dogs, rabbits, cats, and other animals."[23] Some of the children's toys offered for sale were, as Francis Hall noted, "too indecent to describe. Every day convinces me more and more of what an utter want of modest[y] in some things pervades this people."[24] The peddlers tended to congregate around the shrines and other public gathering places: "Their wares were spread out on stands and lighted by paper lanterns suspended from bamboo poles. Children's toys, prints, and eatables were the principal wares offered for sale. There were oranges and dried persimmons, and sticky looking confectioneries, rice cakes, fish dipped in rice batter and fried in oil, crabs and prawns served up hot or cold, and tea and sake. There were miniature swords and boats for the children, dolls without clothes that could and could not cry, jumping jacks, sugar cats and wooden dogs and tiny houses and pictures of the great emperors."[25]

A contemporary Japanese guidebook described the sights and sounds of the Yokohama streets:

> There are countless carts coming and going, and the noise resounds in the heavens . . . At night, beside the gate, one can find peddlers of all sorts, selling sweets, tempura, sushi, *daifuku* [sweet rice cakes], *yakisoba* [fried noodles], and *dengaku* [miso-coated tofu]. There are also blind masseurs, impersonators, *gidayu* storytellers, and *jōruri* balladeers singing in high voices. Mixed with all these are the sounds of the merry-makers returning from Miyozaki in their palanquins, the clatter of wooden clogs, and the laughter of beautiful women as they walk together . . . Then there is the chanting of the pilgrim as he makes a trip to the licensed quarter on his way from Naritasan temple to Akihabarasan temple. And there is the cry of "Hi no yōjin!" ["Watch out for fire!"] of the town officers. Then there are night watchmen rattling their iron staffs. It is no different from Edo: as you try to sleep in your inn . . . the sounds of the blind masseurs, the cries of the *eta* house girls, the chatter of passing travelers all enter into your sleeping ears.[26]

Another book describes how "day and night, an unusual number of peepshows, mechanical contraptions, magic tricks, and street comics all ply their trades."[27]

No foreigner who visited Yokohama failed to mention the children, who must have been a prominent feature of the urban landscape: "The streets are full of them. They seem always to be merry and good natured. I have not seen a quarrel yet and rarely see a child crying." The children would gather in sunny spots and play with balls or spinning tops, many of the girls with baby brothers and sisters strapped to their backs. The boys loved to fly kites, whether decorated with "the hideous face of an ancient hero, or fabulous monster, or the pictured representative of just such a boy as themselves."[28] Foreigners often remarked on the harmony with which the children played: "graceful, dignified, and yielding to each other's wishes as so many little misses at home would hardly do." When offered a gift, they "not only awaited in quiet the division, showing no shade of greediness, but were rather pleased that all were to share alike."[29]

On holidays, the children would pour into the streets in their finest clothes, red ribbons in their black hair, cheeks bright, kimonos brilliantly colorful. The daughters of the samurai officials had "faces artificially whitened till not a vestige of the original color is left, with vermillion lips, hair in great shining coils of midnight, broad girdles gathered in buns behind half as large as themselves, and socks of spotless purity." As for the samurai boy, he would "strut . . . proudly in his new silk trousers and a gala robe such as his father wears and two swords tied to his side."[30]

Chūemon's youngest son, Katsusuke, was seven years old in 1860. It is not hard to imagine him playing with these children in the brightly decorated main street of Honchō Nichōme on a holiday afternoon. He would never have lacked for company, on the streets or in his home, which was usually full to bursting. For the thirty or forty Kōshū merchants who were sleeping on Chūemon's floor each night, Yokohama represented the hope of a profitable sale. For Chūemon, they brought news and familiar goods from home. Sometimes they brought letters from his family, and Chūemon often asked one of them to carry a letter back to Higashi-Aburakawa for him.

Every day, thousands of merchants and tourists poured into Yokohama. To the travelers on the Tōkaidō who turned off the main road to take a look at this famous new place, Yokohama offered gratification for their curiosity and a good story to tell their families back home. "From early in the morning till late at night the crowds will astonish the eye," wrote one observer. "Since we are living in such a fortunate era, it would truly be a shame not to see this place."[31] When Chūemon's in-laws came to pay him a visit and see the sights, he wrote, "I wanted to show them the foreigners' houses, but the crowds were so great, and everyone in such a hurry, that they just walked along the street and then hurriedly left for Edo . . . I'm so sorry that they went to so much trouble but saw so little."[32] So great was the crush of curious visitors that the government issued wooden tags to bona fide merchants who wanted to enter a foreigner's house or place of business. If they could not show an identity tag, they were liable to be rudely ejected from the premises. A contemporary travel guide described the house of Yokohama's wealthiest merchant, William Keswick of Jardine Matheson: "Outside the gate of this house congregate innumerable travelers who have come to see the foreigners of Yokohama and their houses . . . If someone sneaks in, there are black men and Chinese patrolling who will chase them off with sticks."[33]

Within a short space of time, a pioneer community was transformed into a teeming urban space, filled with all the diversity and restless energy of men, women, and children in search of entertainment and opportunity. People poured into the town from all parts of Japan and the world: some just to look, many to try their luck at gaining some small share of the town's reputed wealth and opportunity.

From the beginning, Yokohama was a global community. In spite of the government's efforts to separate Japanese and foreigners and control their interactions, the town depended on and prospered from those connections. Chūemon was no exception. Unfortunately, he offers little comment in his letters on his relations with the foreign community. He mentions a few by name, but for the most part the foreigners are lumped together as ijin (aliens). Chūemon refers several times to foreigners making the rounds of the Japanese traders in search of particular items, but he never specifies whether these are the British or American merchants themselves, or their Chinese intermediaries, or indeed their Japanese employees.

In fact, the foreign community that Chūemon would have encountered on any given day was extraordinarily diverse. The 135 registered foreign residents (in 1862) were a small section of a population that included not only merchants but also petty tradesmen, publicans, servants, artisans, sailors, and vagrants from Europe, the Americas, India, Southeast Asia, and China.[34]

Usually the foreigners were lured by the same impulse that brought Japanese people to Yokohama from far and wide: the desire for gain. Some were respected members of international merchant houses. Others were tradesmen or artisans in search of new opportunity, or missionaries in search of converts. Many were brawlers and adventurers, men who attracted epithets such as "lawless and dissolute," "a disgrace to Western civilization," and "the scum of the white race." They included "persistently drunk doctors, dissipated lawyers, absconding bankrupts, discharged officers, sottish ship captains—in short, all kinds of common characters that, just by the look of them, one would wish sent to the galleys or behind the bars of a prison."[35] Indeed, the life of the East Asian treaty ports was not for the fainthearted. Many of the residents of Yokohama had moved on from Shanghai or other Chinese ports, where they might have cut their teeth smuggling opium, and where they had seen their fellow countrymen decimated by epidemics. At the turn of the 1860s, China was suffering the convulsions of the Taiping Rebellion, combined with a severe cholera outbreak. Yokohama was thought to be a healthier place than Shanghai, but given the hostility of many Japanese to the foreign presence, here, too, the threat of violence always lurked in the background. It is not surprising, then, that Yokohama's foreign community quickly acquired a reputation for lawless and quarrelsome behavior.

Guns were common, hunting popular, and litigation rampant. In a notorious incident that combined all three, an English merchant named Michael Moss was arrested by a party of Japanese samurai officials with a dead goose in his hands. Hunting was prohibited by the Japanese authorities, and Moss had been caught red-handed. But he resisted arrest, and as he fought his captors his gun went off, hitting one of the Japanese guards. After Moss's release into British custody, the consul fined him a thousand dollars as a gesture of support for his Japanese colleagues (never mind that the consul was himself a keen hunter). On reviewing the case, British minister Sir Rutherford Alcock went even further, sentencing Moss to three months' imprisonment in the Hong Kong jail and permanently deporting him from Yokohama. Although Moss served only five days in jail, he launched a suit against Alcock for wrongful imprisonment and won two thousand dollars in compensatory damages.[36] Most lawsuits were pettier, such as that against American missionary Jonathan Goble, who shot the British vice-consul's dog from his bedroom window in front of the owner's eyes after the dog had strayed onto Goble's lot.[37] Perhaps, with this sort of incident taking place, it is not surprising that the British consul issued a decree against "the common practice of carrying fire-arms during the day and in the most ostentatious manner . . . There is something especially provocative and irritating in such ostentatious display of fire-arms, for men supposed to be following the avocations of merchants, which are or ought to be entirely peaceable . . . British subjects are hereby prohibited from so offending under penalty of fines and imprisonment." For good measure, the consul added, "Furious horse riding in the streets of Yokohama is a common practice among foreigners, and not only among them but among their Chinese servants . . . The undersigned can see no adequate justification for this."[38]

Of course, many members of the foreign community were known for their helpfulness and for the good works they did among the Japanese. James Hepburn, a doctor and American missionary, offered a free clinic for the Japanese in Kanagawa, and he published the first Japanese-English dictionary, which remained the standard work for the next hundred years. Hepburn opened an academy of Western sciences, and his wife opened a school. Duane Simmons, a Dutch Reform missionary and also a doctor, treated Japanese patients free of charge.

The fastest-growing section of the foreign population were the Chinese. At the outset, these were mostly the agents of European or American merchant houses—the so-called compradors—who handled many of the companies' dealings with the Japanese merchant community. Although few of the compradors would have spoken or understood Japanese, they did share a common culture with the Japanese, and they could communicate to some extent through the character-based writing system. The compradors working in the merchant houses managed many of the day-to-day activities of the business, including communications, assaying of goods and currency, customs procedures, bookkeeping, and the hiring of local labor. The chief compradors were important businessmen in their own right, bringing with them staffs of bookkeepers, accountants, inventory managers, cooks, and other servants.[39] Increasingly, foreigners also hired Japanese assistants (bantō) to take on many of the administrative duties of the firm. Japanese agents or employees were useful to foreign merchants not only as administrators but also as direct buyers of silk and tea in the producing regions, since neither European merchants nor their Chinese agents were allowed to travel outside the treaty limits. Nevertheless, the Chinese retained powerful influence within the foreign merchant houses, in spite of frequent complaints about their greedy or dishonest business dealings.[40]

The Chinese compradors in Yokohama fit into a broader diaspora that already had deep roots throughout Asia. In Japan, Chinese communities had been living in Nagasaki for some centuries. Chinese merchants might have preferred to come independently and operate their own trading operations, but since China did not have treaty relations with Japan, allying themselves with foreign merchants gave them a level of protection and security that they would not otherwise have had. Many of them, however, launched their own business activities once they had established themselves in Yokohama, and some became extremely wealthy importing Chinese products such as sugar and medicines.[41]

As the port grew, small-scale Chinese tradesmen also began arriving in Yokohama: tailors, printers, stationery suppliers, launderers, brick makers, silversmiths, barbers, furniture makers, and building contractors experienced in Western-style house construction. In 1862, a Chinese entrepreneur opened the first hotel in Yokohama aimed specifically at the growing Chinese market.[42]

English newspaper proprietor John Black, in his memoir of Yokohama in the 1860s, had little good to say about the Chinese: "The lower orders . . . flocked over in great numbers; the quarters of the foreign settlement that they quickly filled became an eye-sore from the filth in which they lived; and it was feared that it would become a hot-bed of disease and the source of some dire epidemic, unless some control were exercised over it." The Chinese were also "suspected of supplying the thieves who had latterly committed numerous depredations in the settlement; and they certainly had many gambling dens opened. So that they were very undesirable neighbours in a variety of ways."[43]

In 1865, there were fewer than six hundred Chinese registered with the Japanese authorities.[44] Most lived in a newly developed section in the southeast of Yokohama, behind the original foreign settlement—the area that was to become Yokohama's Chinatown. In addition, a significant number of undocumented Chinese undoubtedly slipped through the cracks of Japanese and foreign oversight. In an article of June 23, 1866, the Japan Times questioned the official statistics, pointing out that unemployed Chinese congregated nightly in two "low Chinese eating houses" and claiming that several recent robberies and thefts had been committed by Chinese drifters. Ishii Kanji estimates that of the thousand Chinese known to be resident in Yokohama in 1870, only thirty were compradors, sixty were servants or independent tradesmen, and the remaining nine hundred or so were "semiemployed day laborers."

At any given time, the majority of the foreigners in Yokohama would have been transients: sailors on shore leave, soldiers on short-term assignments, and a sprinkling of drifters, deserters, and vagrants. The sailors included merchant seamen who were temporary sojourners, in port for a few days and determined to have as much drink and sex as they could, and navy men who were stationed for longer periods. All of them, like sailors everywhere, were notorious for their drunkenness and rough behavior. Images of drunken foreigners were a favorite with illustrators of Yokohama street life,

FIGURE 2.1 Picture of the private room of the Chinese employees of a foreign merchant house in Yokohama. *Utagawa Sadahide, Yokohama kaikō kenbunshi (ca. 1863)*

and Ernest Satow wrote that "drunken" (*doronken*) was one of the few foreign words that almost all the residents of Yokohama knew.

Although the lives of the sailors are not well documented, we can get a hint as to their conditions from the consular court reports of the time. On any given day, the majority of the British court's cases dealt with drunken, and sometimes violent, sailors. For example, on April 3, 1866, the court recorded the following cases:

> Samuel Cook, a Seaman belonging to H.M.S Adventure, was charged by Constable Vollhardt, with being drunk and incapable in the public streets at 3 A.M. this morning. Prisoner in defence said, that he was not incapable, he had stowed a little liquor away and was slightly the worse for it, but was quite capable of taking care of himself without intruding upon the hospitality of the police for a night's lodging. The prisoner was dismissed after being admonished and warned never to be brought up again . . . George Whitston, who described himself as being an Assistant Military Steward aboard H.M.S. Adventure, was charged with being

FIGURE 2.2 Picture of drunken foreign sailors in Ō-dōri, Honchō Itchōme. *Utagawa Sada-hide, Yokohama kaikō kenbunshi (ca. 1863)*

drunk in the Main Street about 1 A.M. this morning, also with assault-ing a French police constable while in the execution of his duty . . . The prisoner in defence stated that he had taken a glass too much or he would not have behaved as he did. As a rule he was generally very quiet when in liquor; was very sorry for what occurred, but could not recollect anything about it. Fined $2 for being drunk and lying asleep in the streets, and $3 for the assault.[45]

Contingents of soldiers began arriving in Yokohama in 1863–1864. The British "China station" naval fleet, which arrived in January 1864, carried some six hundred sailors and Royal Marines, who were to remain in Yokohama on and off for the rest of the decade. In July 1864, they were augmented by almost six hundred men of the British Twentieth Light Infantry regiment. In August 1864 a further three hundred eighty men of the Sixty-Seventh Regiment arrived—most of them were South Asian sepoys.[46] Other British reinforce-ments came from the Ninth and Eleventh regiments, as well as detachments of artillery, engineers, and marines. While the British were much the biggest contingent, the French, Dutch, Russians, and Americans also brought military forces to Yokohama. By the middle of the 1860s, the military forces probably constituted the single largest segment of the foreign population, totaling as many as eighteen hundred men (as well as a few officers' wives). The sailors remained mainly on their ships, while the soldiers took up residence on "The Bluff," a hill directly adjacent to the foreign settlement. At first they were forced to live in tents, but eventually a small town grew up around them, including barracks, training grounds, rifle range, and riding circuit. Much of this infrastructure was built at Japanese expense.[47]

The soldiers and sailors were multiethnic and multiracial. They might have signed on in Boston, Liverpool, Calcutta, Charleston, Batavia, or Shanghai. Europeans also brought servants from their various colonies, adding to the racial diversity. Japanese observers found it hard to distinguish between African, Afro-American, Indian, and Javanese, generally lumping them all together as "blacks" (kuronbō). Japanese writers and illustrators had been depicting dark-skinned people throughout the Tokugawa era, as a part of the genre of exotic images of foreigners in Nagasaki.[48] From the perspective of commercially minded Japanese writers aiming to appeal to a curious readership, the multiracial community added greatly to the exotic aura of the new port town. The black men's "hair is curly like mustard, though their eyes are just the same color as ours. Among them are some very beautiful men. To look at, they are as lovely as the recently arrived Chinese women . . . [They] wash clothes in a tub with soap, just like women. They wrap red silk crepe around their heads, they wear yellow jackets and white trousers, and their faces are black. It's quite a sight!"[49]

Yokohama was also home to a number of foreign vagrants and beggars. John Black wrote that the community of foreign beggars, known locally as loafers, were

> far more importunate on Japanese than the Japanese poor had been with us. These men were generally seamen of intemperate habits, who, having got their discharge from their ships, soon spent the little money they had received from their captains, and instead of shipping again, and getting away as quickly as possible, wandered about the settlement for a time, getting any Jack ashore with whom they could foregather, to "stand a drink" or a meal at a grog-shop, until they became so well-known and so besotted in appearance that they were ashamed to show their faces any longer by day among their own countrymen. They

FIGURE 2.3 Scene of black people carrying fresh water. *Utagawa Sadahide, Yokohama kaikō kenbunshi (ca. 1863)*

would wander away among the country walks or sea-side villages, ever and anon begging a little rice from the kind-hearted natives, and to-wards evening making a descent upon the native settlement of Yoko-hama, or the adjoining Japanese village of Homura [Honmura], and levying blackmail upon the people.[50]

While Chūemon offers few clues as to the nature of his personal contacts with foreigners, there is ample documentation attesting to a wide range of relationships between the Japanese and foreign communities, from strictly business dealings, to personal friendships, to student-teacher relations, to en-mity and even murder. The most intimate relationships between foreigners and Japanese were with concubines, employees, and servants.

Japanese servants were readily available, although many of the more affluent merchants preferred to bring their personal staff with them from China or even England. Many foreigners seem to have formed close ties with their servants. Their biggest complaints were laziness and drunkenness. As one Japanese observer commented, it was "difficult to get a servant in Nippon that was good for anything that did not drink . . . All that are active and intelligent drink and all that do not drink are fools."[51]

Although for the most part the foreign community were appreciative of their Japanese servants, there were also accounts of bad behavior and even violence on both sides. Theft by Japanese servants was not uncommon. On May 26, 1866, the *Japan Times* wrote of a servant caught in the act who, on learning that he would be turned over to the Japanese authorities, tried to kill himself by slashing his own throat. According to the newspaper, "It is suspected that he has been convicted several times for crimes which he has committed, and thinking that he would suffer the full penalty of the law for this last offence, attempted to defeat the ends of justice by his self-destruction." Similarly, Francis Hall wrote of a missionary who had to protect his servant even though he had repeatedly stolen from his master, because "the Japanese have knowledge of his offence and are watching for him, [and] if they take him he will probably be executed."[52]

On the other hand, the Reverend Buckworth Bailey, rector of the English church in Yokohama, was said to have "whipped his servants and on one occasion put them in sacks to prevent them running away."[53] And in 1869, when an Englishman called Hoey was murdered, the Japanese who were arrested claimed that his killing was in retribution for a severe beating they had suffered at his hands.[54]

The most intimate relations were between foreign men and Japanese women. The Miyozaki brothel quarter was open to both Japanese and foreign men, with separate facilities for each ethnic group and social class. Although few writers or even diarists felt free to write honestly about their experiences, there are enough accounts surviving to indicate that it was a place of charm and hilarity as well as sexual pleasure. W. H. Poyntz describes a party at the Gankirō given for Sir Vincent King and the officers of his flagship in the early 1860s:

> The whole party assembled in a large room at the Gankirō at the entrance to which were boxes where the money was taken . . . Presently there entered about a dozen musume [girls], each with a musical instrument like a small banjo, who squatted on a raised dais and formed the orchestra; following them about twenty girls appeared, with a little more colour in their costumes than usual. The music struck up, and the young ladies attitudinized, pirouetted, and danced with considerable vivacity; some of them were very pretty, and all graceful. In company with the

FIGURE 2.4 Ochiai Yoshiiku, *Five Nations: Merrymaking at the Gankirō Tea House* (1860). *Chadbourne collection, Prints and Photographs Division, Library of Congress, LC-USZC4-8479-81*

instruments, singing and dancing went on at the same time; the former composed of apparently a single sentence over and over again, winding up at intervals with 'yah, yah, yah', jerked sharply out, at the expiration of which the dancers threw off a garment, till at last the greater part of their clothing was conspicuous by its absence, and the one who retained the most was the winner. It was a lively-spirited scene, and the officers of the flagship as well as ourselves much enjoyed it.[55]

While the Miyozaki quarter was clearly frequented as a place of entertainment by most of the foreign community (including the rapidly growing Chinese community), for sex most of the established foreign merchants preferred the more personal intimacy of an exclusive relationship. These relationships are almost never referred to by the foreigners themselves, even in their diaries and personal papers. But without a doubt many of these relationships were loving and deeply felt. Ernest Satow, for example, who was to become a distinguished diplomat and eventually British ambassador to Japan, remained close to his Japanese partner, Takeda Kane, throughout his life and supported and loved his two sons by her—without ever publicly acknowledging their relationship.[56] In other cases, the relations were more purely commercial: many of the foreigners selected women from the Miyozaki entertainment district and kept them for their exclusive use. As early as July 10, 1859, one of the brothel keepers, Zenjirō, submitted a request to lease two of his women, Kazeshima and Hatsukiku, to live in the foreign quarter for a fee of fifteen ryō (about $30) per month.[57] There were other cases in which women who were not from the licensed quarter were kept by foreigners.

No matter the circumstances, women who lived as the mistresses of foreigners were required to register as prostitutes with the Japanese authorities and pay a monthly fee of 1.5 ryō ($3) to Sakichi, the manager of the licensed quarter. If they came from a brothel, they would continue to be under contract to that institution, which would bill the foreigner a monthly fee for their services. A Detailed Account of Miyozaki (Miyozaki saikenki), published in 1865, lists the fees for the prostitutes of the Gankirō who became mistresses of foreigners as $50 per month, $25 per half month, or $5 per night. Other brothels charged only $25 per month and $2 per night. Sakichi's office charged the same $3 monthly fee regardless of the amount paid by the foreigner to the brothel.[58]

Women who consorted with foreigners were known by the derogatory term rashamen. The word means "sheep's wool." As a contemporary Japanese guidebook explains, "The origin of this name is that the foreigners carry with them across the ocean an animal called a sheep [rasha]. The character of this animal is to be very open and trusting with people. On the ship, when the sailors begin to burn with fleshly appetites, they are said to sometimes force themselves on these animals. For this reason, a person on whom the foreigners force themselves is known as a rashamen."[59] The derogatory name suggests the ambivalence and even contempt that Japanese men felt for women who served the sexual needs of foreign men. Of course, in most cases the women themselves had little or no choice in the matter. Some women did refuse to become the mistresses of foreign men. A prostitute called Kiyū, for example, was said to have killed herself rather than become the mistress of a foreigner: she subsequently became the subject of several popular dramas.[60] A report prepared by the Kanagawa commissioners' office in 1862 estimated that there were five hundred women servicing foreign men under the management of the Yokohama licensed quarter. Other estimates ranged as high as twenty-five hundred, with many of the women outside the purview of the official regulations. Given that the total resident population of foreigners including Chinese, Europeans, Americans, and their servants was probably no higher than five hundred in 1862, a large number of these women must have been serving the desires of transients, mainly sailors. According to a guidebook of 1862 called *Tales of Yokohama* (*Yokohamabanashi*), "What with the squealing of pigs [a favorite food of the foreign residents] and the crying of sheep [*rashamen*], Japan has come to an unimaginable state of things."[61]

One guidebook actually published a register of thirty-one *rashamen* and their foreign patrons, including the following:

Dutch consul "Bosubokusu" [Dirk de Graeff van Polesbroek], a *rashamen* called Chō
British consul "Kepitan Uisu" [Captain F. H. Vyse], a *rashamen* called Taka
No. 41, Dutch merchant "Batakui" [P. J. Batteke], a girl called Sekino
No. 70, Dutch merchant "Gabutaimen" [identity unknown], a girl called Kin[62]

Polesbroek's mistress is known to have been the twenty-one-year-old daughter of a Japanese merchant by the name of Bunkichi, who lived in Nichōme. Although she was already living with Polesbroek in his official residence in Chōenji temple in Kanagawa, once the new system was implemented, she was required to register with the Gankirō as one of its prostitutes, and she was billed to Polesbroek at the rate of fifteen *ryō* per month.[63]

While some writers expressed compassion for the fate of the *rashamen*, others expressed indignation at the women themselves and the foreign men who patronized them. One masterless samurai, Shimizu Seiichi, attacked and killed two British army officers in November 1864. Under interrogation, he justified his crime in part by referring to a visit he had made to a foreign merchant's house. Inside the house he had found a beautiful young Japanese woman: "She was richly dressed, as if she were the wife of an official: she greeted us with a friendly smile and did not appear to feel the shamefulness of her position. The servant addressed her with the greatest subserviency and asked permission of the hussy to show me the sleeping room and bath room of the master. When I returned to Yedo in the evening, I thought of all I had seen and my own misery."[64]

The women who worked in the Yokohama licensed quarter came mainly from the class of *meshimori onna*, or "teahouse girls." Most of them had been sold into prostitution because of the poverty of their families, who were landless villagers, manual laborers, or outcasts. Although little evidence has survived on the lives of these women, some information is available from surviving contracts of prostitutes in the teahouses along Japan's highways—the places from which most of the women in Miyozaki were brought. For example, in the case of a contract from 1848, a girl called Moto was sold by her father, Senjirō, to an innkeeper named Tōjirō for a four-year term as a prostitute. Senjirō gave as the reason for the sale that he was unable to pay his annual rice tax. The lump-sum payment was fifteen ryō, a relatively high sum (just a few years earlier, at the height of the Tenpō recession, girls were being sold for as little as two ryō). The entire amount was paid up front to Senjirō. Moto would have to work for the entire four years or her father would be sued as a debtor. Although Moto's age is not stated, surviving records from the same post station indicate that the majority of prostitutes were from eighteen to twenty-four, although some were as young as thirteen.[65] In another case, that of a peasant called Shigesaku who sold his twenty-five-year old wife, the contract even included a return clause: if the buyer was not satisfied with his purchase, he had the right to return her within twenty days for a full refund. Many such contracts also contained suicide clauses: if the girl or woman were to commit suicide for any reason, the seller was obliged to return the payment in full.[66]

One documented case of a Yokohama prostitute is that of Taki. Taki came from a respectable rural family, and at the age of twenty-two she made a good marriage, to a samurai in service to the Kii branch of the Tokugawa family. Taki's husband worked in the domain's Edo residence, and the couple lived there for seven years until, for unknown reasons, they divorced. When she returned to her village, she found her father gravely ill and the family sunk into debt. Forced to help her family, she consented to be sold to Tokubei in the Miyozaki licensed quarter. The following year, Taki was a victim of the great fire of November 1866.[67]

In 1867 William Willis, a doctor attached to the British legation, researched and wrote up a study on the sex trade in Yokohama and Japan more broadly.[68] Willis divided Japanese prostitutes into two classes: those who were bought at the age of six to ten and instructed in "such accomplishments and arts as it behoves them to acquire, such as playing music, making poetry, and writing letters, etc.," and those who were "picked up at different ages" below twenty-five. In either case, prostitutes were considered ready to start servicing men at the age of fifteen. The zengen, or "go-betweens" who arranged the purchase of prostitutes from their families, "are supposed to be respectable persons and their seal a guarantee that the transaction is a fair one and agreeable to the established custom of Japan."[69] According to Willis, the girl's consent was required in order for the transaction to be recognized as valid, "unless in the case of children where the parent seems to possess right of disposal." Consent might be given for a number of reasons, but the most common was the poverty of the girl's family. In Japan, Willis writes, "it not unfrequently [sic] happens that when a man is reduced to poverty his daughter or wife volunteers to sell herself for a term to a brothel, and such an act is looked upon as the highest evidence of filial or conjugal affection."[70] Given the circumstances of their sale and the extensive powers that brothel keepers had over the women they employed, their status amounted to little short of slavery. This was in stark contrast to the glamorous aura of beauty and lighthearted entertainment that the brothels strove to convey.

STUMBLING WITH TRADE

With so many people pouring in and so much national attention focused on Yokohama, it must have felt to Chūemon at times as though he had found his way to the center of the world. Now all he had to do was take advantage of the enormous opportunity that had opened up. By April of 1860 he had his family with him. His period of isolation was over, and his partners in Kōshū were waiting for him to start making money for them.

But how? Chūemon lacked the money to buy the product that the foreigners most wanted: silk thread. For a while, he clung to the idea of the "Kōshū Products Company" that would sell the varied produce of his region. But there were no buyers for grapes, tobacco, cotton cloth, or any of the other products on which they had pinned their hopes. What the foreigners wanted most was gold. And after that, silk and tea.

Forced to improvise, Chūemon began dabbling in a succession of low-value products, many of which were not from Kōshū at all. He scored one early success with eggs, which he was able to buy in Kōshū and resell at a small profit in Yokohama.[71] Chūemon also started trading in tea, buying small batches from growers around the Kantō Plain and peddling them to the foreign merchant houses.[72] He considered trying again with a small consignment of tobacco, but in the end he decided it was not worth it.[73] In January 1862 he submitted a sample of seaweed (kajime) to a foreigner. "If he buys, the deal will be for a total of 434 ryō." But there is no sign that this deal ever came to fruition.[74]

Chūemon also began trading Japanese products to the local Japanese community. In early 1861 he began buying dried sardines from Awa province (now Chiba prefecture), used by farmers in the Kantō area for fertilizer.[75] Chūemon also hoped to land a commission on a trade in Kōshū-made paper:

"Please tell Ichikawa's Tsujiya that if he wants to sell paper, he is welcome to come here. It seems he is planning to sell four thousand or five thousand ryō worth of merchandise, so even a 2 percent commission would be quite an amount."[76] These commission sales offered a basic livelihood to small-scale merchants like Chūemon. But if he was ever going to make real money, he would need to buy and sell on his own account, and preferably to the foreigners.

An inventory dated December 1861 listed all the trade products Chūemon had registered with the town hall during the course of the previous two years. They included seaweed, dried fish, cotton and silk cloth, tea, sundry imported goods, sweets, lacquer, medicine, vegetables, eggs, salted fish, cocoons, silk-worm eggs, tobacco, paper, cotton and silk thread, lumber, cabinetwork, soap for clothes, copper, wax, and foods aimed at foreign buyers. The picture that emerges from this list is of a sort of general store, with a mix of business with foreign buyers, the Kōshū market, and the local population. Meanwhile a merchant by the name of Mataemon who was subletting some of Chūemon's space was selling food to the foreign community, specifically chicken and other fresh meats—a detail that, put together with the dried fish and other food products, suggests that Chūemon's shop must have been quite a pungent place.[77]

One of the stranger items Chūemon dabbled in was animal bone. On August 29, 1861, he wrote, "A foreigner is buying horse bones. Top-quality bones are 3 bu [$1.50] for 100 kin [132 lbs.]." Chūemon mentioned that a daimyo in Edo was buying up available supplies in order to resell them to this foreigner. He asked his collaborators to send him a shipment if they could.[78] It is unclear what the foreign buyer might have planned to use them for: perhaps fertilizer. However, this venture did not go very far. On September 9, Chūemon wrote to his business partners, "The foreigner has left, so no one's buying them in Yo-kohama. The daimyo in Edo will still honor any commitments he had made, but after that he will stop. I will share any losses you have on this."[79]

Nothing that Chūemon tried his hand at really seemed to work. And in the meantime, the debts began to mount up. From the beginning, Chūemon's letters were filled with pleas to his son and business partners to advance him more money, to wait longer for payment of debts he owed them, and to bor-row money in Kōshū on his behalf. In the early months of 1860, Chūemon wrote repeatedly to Shōjirō asking him to raise money and send it to him: "Did you return to the village safely? Now, you need to let me know if you were able to raise the money I asked for. Even if you weren't able to raise it all, send what you can as soon as possible. Many customers are coming here, but I have no money for purchases or for transportation, so please send money as soon as you can."[80] Money was available for loan in Yokohama, but "on a loan of fifty ryō the monthly interest is from six to seven ryō, which you could hardly call a good deal. At home, even a so-called high interest rate is only 10 or 20 or at most 30 percent. Please understand this and borrow money even at a high rate."[81] So short of funds was he that Chūemon was forced to sublet the back half of his own shop: "I rented our work area [katte] with all its implements to Shirobei. I, Mother, Naotarō, Seitarō, and three others are all living in the front of the shop."[82]

It was customary for men of Chūemon's class to settle their debts twice a year, at the summer Bon holiday and at the New Year. When the Bon holiday approached in 1860, Chūemon faced the reality that he would once again be unable to repay his creditors. "I'm very sorry that I still can't send you money. I still haven't received the income from my tea sales." Chūemon was acutely aware that he needed to send gifts to his in-laws and the senior branch of his family, as expected at the Bon holiday, but "I haven't the money . . . I intend to send the goods as soon as I have the money."[83]

In the second half of 1860, things went from bad to worse. Chūemon's whole family fell sick with a severe skin disease that left them suppurating and bedridden. Chūemon identified the disease as hizen, or scabies: a parasitic mite that burrows into the skin causing irritating rashes. When left untreated, the mites can multiply into the millions, causing thick encrustations over the body. At best, the disease was disfiguring and socially disabling. At worst, especially if combined with other chronic conditions, it could be life threatening.

The disease hit Chūemon and his family as his expenses were relentlessly piling up. After a serious fire had destroyed many merchants' stocks in January, Chūemon had begun construction of a fireproof storage building, at a cost of seventy ryō. He needed a safe place to store his merchandise: he was holding much of it on commission, and if it was destroyed by fire, he would be held liable. But as the year went on and his entire family fell sick, he struggled more and more to make the payments. Meanwhile he had to find thirty-five ryō to cover his share of the cost of the July Benten festival described in the previous section. And he had to put food on the table.

In August, Chūemon was forced to pawn all his wife's kimonos just to pay the day-to-day bills.[84] This was the low point in his entire experience as a Yokohama merchant. In September, he wrote, "We are all losing our strength . . . I do realize that I have to work very hard on my end. However, I am suppurating with pus at present and really finding things difficult."[85]

Meanwhile, Chūemon's wife's illness was reaching a critical stage, to the point that he feared for her life. She was "vomiting everything and . . . is in pain both day and night." Chūemon summoned a doctor, who "mixed up some medicine for her, which had an immediate effect."[86] But now he had expensive medical bills to worry about on top of everything else.

In November, Chūemon's father-in-law became seriously ill in Edo. Etiquette prescribed that Chūemon should send a gift of money to help with expenses and, if the old man became worse, pay him a visit in person. But because of his sickness and his financial worries, Chūemon was unable to meet these obligations. "I am very concerned about the grave sickness of the old gentleman," he wrote apologetically.

> I understand that he will be leaving Edo shortly to return home, and I also understand that you want me to send some money, but, unfortunately, since the summer I have been sick and things have been difficult for me . . . There is really nothing I can say to excuse myself. I, too, would like to return home, but my wife has been very ill . . . even to the point that her life has been in danger . . . I, too, have broken out all over my hands and legs, and I have been unable to attend to my official duties but have been stuck at home lying next to my wife. Naotarō has also erupted all over his feet. The main thing, though, is to take care of my wife. I really want her to return home and was thinking of hiring a traveling chair to do so, but she has broken out all over her backside, so it would be impossible to sit. It is really extremely unfortunate.[87]

When the old man died a few days later, Chūemon wrote to express his bitter regret. "We very much wanted to return home to see his face one last time, but with my wife gravely ill we simply could not. I wrote to them, but I hope you will convey that message. Although we are grieving, [my wife] was gravely ill. Now at last her life is spared. But even if we were to set off now, it would be too late. There's really nothing we could have done." Chūemon added, "As for us, we have been taking medicinal baths since the twelfth, and we seem to be improving. Mother is able to eat two small rice balls at a time. We are unable to go to work in the town hall and remain stuck at home. I am conducting no trade, and I have no money. We are completely stuck as a result of these travails. I know I need to do something, but it is not going to happen immediately, and in the meantime I'm in a bad way."[88] Chūemon entered into some desultory negotiations to either sell or lease his shop, but no serious buyers came forward.

As the end of the year approached, Chūemon once again faced the prospect of being unable to settle his debts. Indeed, he urgently needed his son to borrow more money on his behalf. On December 1, 1860, he wrote,

> Your letter of the eighth [Man'en 1/10/8] did not mention whether you had succeeded in raising money. This is extremely important. You cannot abandon your father in this moment of trouble. No matter what other business people have, you must please send money. Our creditors will certainly not lose on their investment in this business. Please think about this carefully and help your gravely ill father in the nick of time . . . This winter the interest will be payable to our creditors in the village, and this is a grave worry. Here, too, I have had many worries since the spring. Trade has not gone well. All I am able to do is get a small commission on the sale of packages that people bring me, and with prices as low as they are in the current economy, there is no trade. My health problems have just made things worse . . . You must put your strength into it and come to your father's aid in his time of need![89]

Remarkably, in the midst of these troubles, Chūemon's mind could still turn to new business opportunities. As the days grew shorter and the nights colder, he had noticed the extremely high price of charcoal in Yokohama. Prices in general were high in Yokohama because of the strong demand for food and other supplies and the relative price insensitivity of the foreign community. In the case of charcoal, there was an additional stimulus from the enormous consumption of the foreigners. A contemporary description of the foreigners' lifestyles notes that "when winter comes around, they burn large amounts of charcoal or coal in each room, and the smoke exits the house through copper pipes that pass through holes in the roof or walls, without staining the ceilings or the walls in the least. It is as warm as though it were the third or fourth month [April or May in the Western calendar]."[90]

On December 16, 1860, Chūemon wrote to Shōjirō,

> In Yokohama the price of charcoal is above 400 mon [$0.08] for a 3-kan [25.5 lbs.] bag. In the Kawauchi region [of Kōshū] you can get a 6-kan bag for under 200 mon . . . It seems that Sadaemon in Minobu is the biggest charcoal trader in Kōshū. He sends charcoal to Edo all year long. I would

like you to use this man's price as a reference and talk to Nanbuya in Minobu, as well as others. I would like to send charcoal to Yokohama. If we can negotiate this successfully, then we can buy Minobu charcoal at 6 kan for 200 mon, add 200 mon for transportation, and then sell that same bag for more than 700 mon. That's the current price among townsmen. The foreigners pay even more.[91]

Of course, the problem was—as always—lack of funds. After four months of sickness and discomfort, Chūemon's skin disease had finally improved to the point where "I have been able to sit up for the past four or five days, and Naotarō is almost completely recovered. Seitarō has it on his hands, but he is still able to play on his own. Mother has been able to go to the bathroom on her own these past ten days, and she is eating a little better. At this point there is no worry at all for her life. As I mentioned, my real problem is money."[92] Chūemon was determined to put all his effort into raising money, come what may. "No matter how difficult it may be, you must succeed in raising some money on this occasion and send it to Yokohama. I have put my house and land up as security for a loan, but still I need you to send forty or fifty ryō. If we can just pull through this, we will be safe . . . The storehouse is now complete—it cost seventy ryō. Then there was the cost of the doctor and medicine and many other expenses. Hence we have come to this situation. Please consult well with our relations and send money."[93]

Shōjirō finally came through with some funds in mid-December. Chūemon wrote, "Your letter included an enclosure of thirty ryō, which I duly acknowledge. I have been waiting for it for some time, but since you did not send it, I assumed you were unable to raise the money at your end. I was at my wit's end and suffering from great mental stress. So now that I see that you were after all able to send it, I am so relieved."[94]

The combination of this money, plus the fifty ryō Chūemon had raised by mortgaging his shop, was enough to tide the family through the end of the year. In a remarkable testament to the power of entrepreneurial optimism, Chūemon then proceeded to mortgage everything else that he had—his outbuilding and his new storehouse—for an additional loan of forty ryō. With this money, he sent Naotarō off to Kōshū to negotiate the purchase of charcoal.

Chūemon's plan was an ambitious one. He wanted Naotarō to use the forty ryō as a down payment on a very large consignment—four hundred bags (about twenty thousand pounds)—of charcoal. Because of the enormous bulk of the charcoal, he planned to ship it by boat, down the Fuji River to Suruga

Bay, then by sea around the Izu Peninsula. He had done this successfully with the building supplies for his shop, and he anticipated a repeat of this experience. Chūemon was hoping that the shipment would arrive before the end of the Japanese calendar year (February 10, 1861, in the Gregorian calendar)—in time to sell it during the period of peak demand.

Naotarō set off for Kōshū in the middle of the eleventh month, giving him time to negotiate the purchase and arrange transportation of the shipment in time for it to reach Yokohama by the end of the year. Anxiously, Chūemon awaited news from his son. But no letter came, and as the end of the year approached, there was no sign of the charcoal. A worried Chūemon wrote to his older son Shōjirō: "I am wondering what has happened. Our partner in Kawauchi is very solid, and I don't think there are any other issues on our end."[95]

A week into the Japanese New Year, the goods had still not arrived, nor any word of their whereabouts. "Naotarō was supposed to have concluded a contract for this . . . Is this all on their side? Did they deceive Naotarō? I can't really believe that. We had a firm contract, and I had made a deposit. If they were lying to me, then it is a big waste of expenses. Or perhaps it is because the goods have been delayed at sea."[96] Two days later, Chūemon finally got a hint as to the nature of the problem. Naotarō and the seller had miscommunicated over the down payment, and in the meantime the seller had shipped his inventory to another customer. Rather than try to resolve the down payment issue and set up a new shipment, Naotarō had just turned around and gone back home to Higashi-Aburakawa. Chūemon was furious. "No matter what happens it's necessary to keep talking to them. For Naotarō to just go home and play shows a complete lack of responsibility with regard to money and a lack of feeling. This isn't just regular money. It is at a high rate of interest, and it is unacceptable for it to cost me even one day—or even half a day—of extra interest . . . No matter what happens we will make no profit from this."[97]

Chūemon gave Shōjirō strict instructions to confiscate the thirty-five ryō that Naotarō still had on his person and asked him to go personally to the seller in Minobu to try to resolve the problem. Shōjirō needed to persuade the seller to "send us large quantities, year-round, regardless of payment . . . and I will send the money as soon as the shipment arrives. There won't be any difficulty at all with that, so please make him understand and agree."[98]

A few weeks later, Shōjirō reported back to him that he had succeeded in negotiating a shipment of charcoal. Chūemon counted on its arrival to help dig himself out from the slump in his business. "If only the charcoal would arrive, then everything would go smoothly. I have been accepting goods from merchants on a commission basis, but I've been unable to sell those goods, so I'm left with no money."[99] Meanwhile, he continued to be overwhelmed by debts and obligations. In April, he was told he would have to contribute ten *ryō* toward the rebuilding of Edo Castle, which had burned in a disastrous fire in December of the previous year.[100]

On June 16, Chūemon finally got word that four hundred bags had arrived at the shipping agent's in Iwamoto village in Suruga. "But not a single bag has arrived in Yokohama. It is a huge loss to me. I am paying 2.2 *ryō* a month in interest, and I am really struggling to find the money. I am shortly going to refinance the loan at a lower rate, which will help."[101] Meanwhile, Naotarō had slunk back to Yokohama, hoping to make it up with his father. Unable to face Chūemon in person, he went to their neighbor, Goroemon, and asked him to intercede for him and beg Chūemon to forgive him. Chūemon, though, was unyielding. "Goroemon came to me with all sorts of apologies, but I refused to listen. I am disinheriting Naotarō."[102] After their recovery, Chūemon's wife and their son Seitarō had gone back to Kōshū (they would never return to Yokohama other than for brief visits), leaving Chūemon once again on his own.

On June 24, the first two hundred and fifty bags of charcoal finally arrived in Yokohama. At this point, Chūemon was not even clear how many bags his seller had shipped to him. Chūemon had made a down payment for four hundred, but apparently Shōjirō had done a good job persuading the seller that he should "send us large quantities, year-round, regardless of payment," and Shōjirō indicated there might be as many as fifteen hundred bags on the way. However, one disappointment followed another. Each bag turned out to contain only 4.5 *kan* (38 lbs.)—1.5 *kan* less than Chūemon had been expecting. Moreover, in the hot summer months there was little demand for charcoal, and the price had plummeted. "The cost has been much greater than anticipated . . . If the shipment turns out to be fifteen hundred bags, then I won't know what to do."[103]

By the beginning of August, seven hundred fifty bags had arrived. "I hope that prices will go up in the ninth month, and then perhaps I can redeem my losses."[104] Once again, Chūemon found himself unable to settle his debts by the Bon holiday. "I know people must be getting angry with me," he wrote to Shōjirō, "but please ask them to be patient a little longer . . . The thirteenth of this month August 18, 1861] was the deadline for the settlement of all accounts, whether official or private. But as usual I am out of funds."[105]

On September 9, 1861, at a low ebb, Chūemon wrote, "I have tried so many things, but none of them seem to work out. I feel that there must be something lacking in my spirit. Right now it's all I can do just to make a bare living.

I'd love to have some regular business that would earn a reliable living, but I have no spare hands here and no one who can work toward the future. If I even had a maid, then I could start earning a little extra."[106]

Perhaps it was his recognition of his inability to go it alone that persuaded Chūemon in the end to take Naotarō back. But he had one stipulation: Naotarō must get a wife. Chūemon asked two acquaintances in Edo to act as matchmakers.[107] They found a local girl, named Take, whose family came from Hoshikawa village near Yokohama. The ceremony took place without any fanfare, and by the end of 1861, Naotarō and his wife had moved in with Chūemon.[108]

As the Japanese calendar year drew to a close, Chūemon was once again forced to put off his creditors. "I will not be able to clear up all my debts before year's end. I am trying to either rent out or sell my shop, but that is not progressing, so I will not be able to settle my accounts this year . . . I keep trying at various things to make some money, but nothing seems to work out. Perhaps it's just the times we live in."[109]

"Expel the Barbarian!"

The times were, indeed, foreboding. In spite of the commercial promise of Yokohama, political clouds were gathering that were to further complicate Chūemon's life and help frustrate his dreams of prosperity.

The first hint of trouble to come was on August 25, 1859, just a few weeks after the opening of the port, when Chūemon reported to his son about a violent attack in the streets of Yokohama. "Three foreigners were murdered. One, a Russian, was killed instantly, while the other two were Americans, of whom one died at the ninth hour, and the other is still living. Most people are saying that the attackers were of the samurai class."[110] The unprovoked attack on a detachment of Russian sailors (all the victims were in fact Russian) marked the beginning of a concerted and escalating campaign of violence against foreigners and their supposed collaborators that terrorized the Yokohama community and ultimately destabilized the shogunate itself.

The antiforeign sentiment was indeed strongest among the samurai class, which saw the humiliation of the shogunate by the foreigners as a national outrage. Agitators could draw on a powerful intellectual tradition of nationalistic and antiforeign thought in Japan. Aizawa Seishisai of the Mito domain wrote in "New Theses" (1825) about the arrogance of the foreign powers but also the danger that Japan faced from them: "Today, the alien barbarians of the West . . . are dashing about across the seas, trampling other countries underfoot, and daring, with their squinting eyes and limping feet, to override the noble nations. What manner of arrogance is this!" Aizawa warned that the foreigners would try to beguile the Japanese with their technologies: "The weakness of some for novel gadgets and rare medicines, which delight the eye and enthrall the heart, have led many to admire foreign ways. If someday the treacherous foreigner should take advantage of this situation and lure ignorant people to his ways, our people will adopt such practices as eating dogs and sheep and wearing woolen clothing. And no one will be able to stop it."[111]

Motoori Norinaga, the eminent eighteenth-century founder of the Kokugaku (National Learning) school, drew attention to the centrality of the emperor in Japan's political and spiritual traditions:

> Our country's imperial line, which casts its light over this world, represents the descendants of the Heaven-Shining Goddess. And in accordance with that goddess's mandate . . . the imperial line is destined to rule the nation for eons until the end of time . . . That is the very basis of our Way . . . Foreign countries expound their own Ways, each as if its Way alone were true. But their dynastic lines, basic to their existence, do not continue, they change frequently and are quite corrupt. Thus one can surmise that in everything they say there are falsehoods and that there is no basis for them.[112]

These twin concepts of reverence for the emperor and resistance to the foreigners crystallized at the turn of the 1860s into the Sonnō Jōi (Revere the Emperor, Expel the Barbarian) movement. Although Mito was the early leader, the movement was to spread throughout Japan in the coming years. From the shogunal government's point of view, the danger of this thesis was that reverence for the emperor might also imply contempt for the shogun, who had arguably usurped power from the imperial line. Paradoxically, the emperor was a relative newcomer to the political scene. For many centuries, the emperor and his courtiers had been relegated to a ceremonial role while political affairs were conducted by the warrior class. Under the Tokugawa regime, the imperial line had been acknowledged but largely ignored while Edo consolidated its position as the nation's political center. Indeed, the early diplomatic missions to Japan, including that of Commodore Perry, assumed that the shogun was the sole and undisputed ruler of Japan and even styled him as "emperor." Now the Kyoto-based imperial dynasty was to reappear on the political stage, eventually coming to dominate Japanese political ideology.

The Mito warriors were deeply committed to the doctrine of direct action. Many believed that since the shogunal government was doing nothing to stop the foreigners, the Mito samurai would have to take matters into their own hands. In March 1860, a group of Mito samurai assassinated the shogunal chief minister, Ii Naosuke, in retribution for his vacillating policy toward the foreigners (as well as his persecution of their own daimyo). Many of them called for the destruction of the new foreign colony in Yokohama. Mito was widely blamed for the attack on the Russians, and in the months that followed it became a matter of common belief that samurai from Mito, with or without the blessing of their domain, were preparing a massed attack on Yokohama. It was assumed that in order to protect their daimyo, these men would relinquish their formal association with the Mito domain and become rōnin, or "masterless samurai." As the decade went on, the word rōnin would cover a wide range of activities, from selfless patriotism to outright banditry.

As a result of these attacks and rumors of attacks, a climate of fear quickly spread in Yokohama. The problems with security prompted British consul Howard Vyse to issue a notification—contradicting the orders of his predecessor—that "all British subjects will, for the future, go about always armed as much as possible for their own personal safety, as regards a revolver or any other deadly weapon they may be able to obtain; and the undersigned gives free permission to and hopes that all British subjects will give free use to the same, on any reasonable provocation, as regards the Japanese, whether official or non-official."[113]

Cees de Coningh vividly describes the fear that he and other foreign residents of Yokohama felt at the height of the hostility. When De Coningh went out for a drink with two Dutch merchants, "they each pulled a loaded revolver out from their belt and lay it on the table in front of them." The merchants explained, "God and our revolvers are the only things in which we can place our trust. We go to bed with the knowledge that we may be chopped up or burned in our own beds."[114]

It was widely assumed that the attackers would start their assault by setting fire to the town. So when a fire broke out on the night of January 3, 1860, and quickly spread, the foreigners gathered together "in a desperate defense so that we would not be helplessly cut down one by one," as De Coningh described.

> Not a single warship lay in the roadstead; but with the first outbreak
> of flames, the captains of the half-dozen merchant ships sent their
> sloops ashore with as many men as they could spare, so that in a

moment we were reinforced by almost six dozen sailors armed with swords and crowbars . . . We cast our gaze as far as we could by the light of the flames of our burning city, ready for anything, to see the murderers expected to show up any minute out of the darkness for the battle of life and death. In those moments we were completely indifferent to what burned away behind us because if there was an attack we would have to overcome it or die.[115]

The Japanese government was deeply concerned about the international repercussions of attacks on foreigners, and it took extraordinary measures to protect them. The Kanagawa commissioners had already installed sentry posts at all the bridges leading into Yokohama, as well as installing gates across the main streets that could be closed in an emergency. As the threat of attacks mounted, the commissioners increased the number of checkpoints; requisitioned two ships to guard the entrance to the harbor and stop and question incoming Japanese vessels; closed off minor roads that might have given access to the town; placed new guard posts on the Tōkaidō highway and stopped and questioned travelers there; and organized the Japanese townsmen into patrols, ordering them to beat drums if they saw anything suspicious, upon which all the gates of the town would be closed. Japanese entering the town were inspected, and anyone carrying a sword was required either to check it in at the sentry post or to register it and receive a tag, which he must return on his departure. The domains of Echizen and Matsuyama were charged with supplying the samurai forces to guard the town, but in addition the commissioners asked regional administrators from throughout the Kantō to send contingents of their police forces to patrol the town. The commissioners also recruited a force of three hundred fifty hired men, most of whom were local ruffians and members of outcast groups, placing them in guardhouses at strategic points throughout the town (including several in front of the houses of prominent foreigners). The Kantō police contingents were in turn charged with watching over these guards. The foreigners were anxious that the government should take all possible measures to protect them, but they were also understandably concerned that their "protectors" might end up being the ones who massacred them. The overall air of deep suspicion between shogunal officials and the foreign community tended to exacerbate the tensions.[116]

Chūemon might justifiably have been concerned for his own safety— merchants who did business with foreigners were also being targeted, and in an attack there was no telling who would be killed and who spared. But he was much more concerned about the confidence of his investors and business partners. He did not want them to think that the business they were investing in might be disrupted or even destroyed by violence. On January 13, 1861, Chūemon wrote, "I realize that in Kōshū this place has a great reputation as a depraved place. The other day there was a rumor that five hundred men of Mito were going to attack Yokohama, and the night guards were ordered to be extremely vigilant. But there is no truth to the story that Mito is dispatching its people to the Kantō area. So please don't be concerned."[117] And three weeks later, "Regarding Yokohama, I understand that it has a very bad reputation in Kōshū. However, there is nothing out of the ordinary here. Although there are rumors of Mito rōnin attacking us, there are no signs whatever of this happening. Indeed, in the [Japanese] New Year they are going to reclaim the Tadaya Shinden marshes and extend the town. You will have to see what prosperity is about to come to this town."[118]

In fact, the biggest threat to Chūemon during the early months of 1862 came not from aggressive samurai but from another, all-too-familiar foe. On May 8 Chūemon wrote to family and friends in his village,

> In the eighth hour of last night, a fire broke out in the public bathhouse of Tadachō Itchōme. There was a strong south wind, and by the morning [Honchō] Sanchōme and Nichōme [where Chūemon lived] were completely burned. Itchōme was unharmed. Our personal possessions were all saved, and the storehouse was also unharmed. None of us were hurt at all. At present we are sheltering in the rear quarters of a ginger merchant in Itchōme. You certainly don't need to worry. If you are worrying about whether or not you should come, you should not. I have fourteen or fifteen ryō in cash, so again you should set your mind at ease.[119]

No doubt Chūemon was doing his best in this letter to quell any alarm on the part of his son or their investors. To lose one's house and shop was a major disaster by any standards. Chūemon seems, however, to have recovered from the disaster quite quickly. He recognized his luck in losing only his building and not his possessions, nor the goods in his warehouse. He must have felt deeply grateful that he had had the prescience to build his fireproof storehouse the previous year. The community operated at times like this an informal insurance system. When disaster struck, residents of all the unaffected neighborhoods were expected to make substantial contributions to a fund to help the victims rebuild. In addition, Chūemon received gifts of money from friends, business partners, and relatives. On June 4 he was able to move into rebuilt premises, and on June 29, he asked Shōjirō to thank his business partners for their financial assistance.[120]

The political situation, meanwhile, continued to deteriorate. The Sonnō Jōi movement had by this time spread throughout Japan, stirring particular passions in the peripheral (but powerful) domains of Chōshū, Satsuma, and Tosa (Chōshū and Satsuma were both in the far west of Japan; Tosa was on Shikoku Island). In early 1862, samurai began flooding into Kyoto, determined to persuade the emperor himself to issue an edict of expulsion against the foreigners. On June 29, Chūemon commented on "a rumor that an order has been given to expel the foreigners. However, even if it is implemented, it will not be possible in less than three to five years. Moreover, the rumor that the rōnin followers of the daimyo have been gathering in Kyoto and that the emperor has issued an edict are also unfounded." Chūemon had to report, however, that "on the evening of the twenty-ninth of last month, at 8:00 P.M., at Tōzenji in Shinagawa, two foreigners were murdered. The murderers have not been apprehended."[121]

The same rumors were echoed by Francis Hall: "For several days past our ears have been full of rumors of disturbances in Japan, even so serious as their threatening revolution. The source of these rumors is wholly in the common people and it is difficult to ascertain what, if any, foundation they have." Among the rumors was one of a virtual coup d'état in Kyoto:

> We have rumors from Miako [Kyoto] that many ronins have concentrated there or in that vicinity, and demand so-called reforms to be instituted in the empire by the Mikado [emperor] . . . Great consternation is said to have been produced, multitudes fled into the country, the wealthy took away, or hid, their treasures, trade was suspended, crops were unsold, particularly tea just then coming to market, while the Mikado confers with his princes as to the state of affairs . . . The Governor of Osaca committed hara kiri, just why does not appear unless from the menaces of the ronins.[122]

There was a good deal of truth in these rumors. On May 21, 1862, some sixty proimperial loyalists met at the Teradaya Inn in Fushimi, near Kyoto, to plot a revolt aimed at seizing control of the Imperial Palace and bringing the emperor under their control. Most of the conspirators were samurai from Satsuma. At one point the group virtually kidnapped their own clan leader, Shimazu Hisamitsu, and forced him to Kyoto to lead their effort. Hisamitsu received a direct order from the emperor to disband the samurai group and make them disperse peacefully, and he attempted to carry it out. However, many resisted, and in the end several men were killed.

Meanwhile, closer to home, the rumor of an attack on foreigners was also true. Tōzenji was the site of the British legation in Edo, and after an attack the previous year, it was heavily guarded by several hundred Japanese guards as well as a detachment of British marines. But on the night of June 26, an assassin killed two British guards in a failed attempt to kill the British envoy, Colonel Neale. The assassin escaped, but he was identified and found wounded at his house, at which point he committed suicide. The assassin turned out to be one of the guard unit assigned to protect the British, a revelation that further deepened the foreigners' distrust of their hosts. As Francis Hall commented, "it certainly is an unpleasant reflection for any Minister resident at Yedo [Edo] that the guards sent to defend him may prove his most dangerous enemy."[123]

By this time, Japanese from the samurai and even the educated commoner classes were flocking to the Sonnō Jōi call for action. In later years, one Chōshū samurai reminisced, "At that time I should have thought it an act of the highest virtue, whatever were the consequences, to cut down a foreigner; and if more than one—so much the better."[124] Shibusawa Eiichi, who went on to become one of Meiji Japan's great business leaders (and a pioneer of Japan's Westernization), narrated in his autobiography how as a young man from a farmer-merchant family, he was determined to launch an attack on the foreigners. "Even supposing that the country had no choice but to accept the terms of the treaties, it would be better to fight first, meeting force with force, for only then could there be true amity between nations. What did it matter that the foreigners possessed huge gunboats and cannons? We had our samurai swords, we had honed our skills in the spirit of our ancestors, and we would cut them down, one by one, mercilessly."[125]

Fukuchi Gen'ichirō, a samurai official who was posted to Yokohama as an English interpreter, recalled that even the shogunal officials were provoked at times into hatred of the foreigners. He recalled his shock at seeing the Westerners walking onto the tatami floors of the official buildings, still in their boots and accompanied by their dogs.

> We officials grew indignant, some of us angrily declaring the barbarians' haughtiness and rudeness toward officials to be simply monstrous . . . But the foreign merchants also frothed in indignation. Prevented by the difficulties of language from fully understanding

commercial operations and suffering from indiscretions on the part of customs officials, they often reacted in anger. They protested vigorously against the constant procrastinations in negotiations. And they were not always unjustified in those protests. We did many things to invite their scorn. The only thing that kept matters from getting out of hand was the samurai spirit of the Japanese, the tendency of even lesser officials to bear the situation quietly and with dignity.[126]

Similarly, John Black recounts a conversation he had with a government official, recalling the mutual misunderstanding of the early days: "You know we didn't understand foreigners then so well we as do now. When we met them we knew that they had an uneasy feeling lest we should draw our swords; but we in like manner used to look out of the side of our eye as we passed, lest the foreigner should draw his revolver and shoot us." He goes on, "I assure you that I have seen foreigners take out their revolvers, perhaps only to shew that they had them, in a very menacing manner, and in a way that made me feel very uncomfortable at the time."[127]

In spite of all its precautions, the government could not prevent a series of attacks on foreigners, although almost none of them took place in Yokohama itself. The foreign legations in Edo came under sustained attack: in addition to two attacks on the British legation, the American minister's interpreter was cut down in the street, and the new British legation buildings were burned to the ground shortly before completion. There were also several attacks on the roads and highways around Yokohama, targeting foreigners traveling alone or in small groups. Chūemon reported on several of the murders in his letters to his son.

The most dramatic of these incidents, and the one with the most far-reaching consequences, took place on September 14, 1862. A party of four English friends rode out to the Tōkaidō highway in Kanagawa on their way to visit Kawasaki Taishi, a well-known temple. When they reached the highway, they found that a huge daimyo's procession was passing by—it was the train of Shimazu Hisamitsu (also known as Saburō), the regent of the Satsuma domain. The foreigners—three men and a woman—reined in their horses beside the road to watch the train pass. But the Satsuma samurai—who were virulently antiforeign—demanded that they dismount, and then threatened them. When one of the horses startled and moved toward the samurai, they drew their swords and attacked. One of the party, a Shanghai merchant called Charles Richardson who was visiting Yokohama, was killed. The others fled for their lives, with varying levels of injury.

The incident threw the entire community into a state of high alarm. On September 15, Chūemon sent a message by expedited delivery to inform his family: "At around six o'clock last night, all the foreigners living in Yokohama, together with their warships, proceeded to Kanagawa and prepared spears and guns to protest against the rough treatment by the Satsuma men." Chūemon reported that the Kanagawa commissioner had summoned the town's officials, and they had visited the Satsuma party at their lodgings in Hodogaya. "They have held discussions, but nothing has been settled. This affair will not end quickly and is causing great upset. As things stand I can't see any easy way to manage this problem."[128]

Indeed, many members of the foreign community wanted to launch an expedition to attack the Satsuma men—who were known to be staying in inns only a few miles from Yokohama—and exact retribution on the spot. They were overruled by their diplomatic representatives, who feared escalation into a broader conflict that might result in the wholesale massacre of the foreigners. But the British envoy subsequently submitted a series of demands for the arrest of the perpetrators, as well as compensation for the murdered man's family. The demands, and the threat of violence if they were not met, put intense pressure on the shogunate. In the eyes of many Japanese, the Satsuma samurai were heroic patriots who had undertaken an unpleasant job that the shogunate itself was unwilling to take on. If the shogunal government were now to cave in and pay the huge financial indemnity the British were demanding for Richardson's murder, then its prestige would only decline further.

Meanwhile, in Kyoto, an alliance of radical samurai and several restive members of the court aristocracy was gaining influence over the imperial court. In April 1863, they persuaded the emperor to demand that the shogun set a date for the expulsion of the foreigners and the final closing of the treaty ports. The emperor further demanded that the shogun present himself personally in Kyoto to inform the emperor of the date on which the expulsion would take place. The shogunal administrators, anxious to unite the country and worried about the growing power of dissenting daimyo, reluctantly consented. The shogun, Iemochi, set off on April 22, 1863, with an enormous train of retainers. It was the first time a shogun had made such a journey in more than two hundred years, and his submission was seen by many as a humiliating reversal (the long journey with twenty thousand retainers was also hugely costly for the shogunal government). On arriving in Kyoto, the shogun was pressed by the emperor and his courtiers to commit to a deadline for the expulsion of the foreigners. Reluctantly, the shogun vowed that he would expel the foreigners and enforce the closing of the ports by June 25, 1863.

By this point, many observers both within and outside Japan had come to the conclusion that the shogunate itself might (and perhaps should) collapse. Robert Fortune wrote in 1862,

> It is becoming clearer every day that the Government of the Tycoon [shogun], with whom we have made our treaties, is powerless to enforce those treaty rights. The feudal princes, with that curious personage the Mikado, or "Spiritual Emperor," are stronger than the Government at Yedo; and until a change takes place, resulting in the formation of a powerful Government either at Miaco [Kyoto] or Yedo, and the destruction of the feudal system, there will, I fear, be little security for the lives of our countrymen in this part of the world. How this is to be accomplished, whether by civil war or by the interference of foreign powers, is at present uncertain.[129]

The person of the "Mikado" (emperor) was indeed mysterious, to many Japanese as well as to foreigners. For centuries he had been a secluded figure removed from politics, living for the most part in genteel poverty in his austere compound in the ancient capital of Kyoto. But Fortune correctly prophesied the revolution and civil war that would, six years later, install the emperor in Edo as sole ruler of a unified Japan, leading shortly thereafter to the wholesale dismantling of the "feudal" system of class division and domainal power.

In spite of the tension, life in Yokohama went on. Given the proven prosperity of the Yokohama trade, and the relatively peaceful state of affairs in the port itself, it was hard for residents to believe that the community would actually be closed down. On December 5, 1862, Chūemon wrote, "I am certainly worried about how things will turn out in Yokohama. However, buildings keep going up here, and now they are completing construction of many new official buildings. The foreigners are also building many new houses. And you should see the liveliness of this place. Even the government officials are marveling at it. So there is really no cause at all for worry."[130] And a month later he added,

> Although the reputation of Yokohama is bad at the moment, you should not worry. Mitsui Hachirōemon is undertaking all sorts of new construction, and he is expanding his storehouses. If things here were really as bad as they say, then surely all this construction would not be taking place. I occasionally talk to Senjirō, the manager of the Mitsui

branch, and he assures me that everything is as normal. Nothing is changed, and there is really no cause for concern. I am making money a little at a time, and I am stouthearted.[131]

And indeed, Chūemon ended the second year of the Bunkyū era (1862) on a surprisingly optimistic note: "In the eighth month of this year, I leased an eighty-eight tsubo lot in the expanded Shibaichō district. I am now receiving two ryō per month rent on this property . . . On top of that I have the profits from my trading . . . So you should be extremely reassured . . . If we can prosper through trading here, our farming business at home will be on too small a scale . . . This winter, I will send you a roll of gold-embroidered cloth. It should be enough for eight and a half kimonos."[132]

The government in Edo was trying to deal with the foreign crisis amid intense confusion. The court in Kyoto was insisting that all the foreigners should be expelled from Japan, refusing to accept any compromise. Meanwhile, the foreigners threatened an attack in retaliation for the Richardson murder. In September 1862, the government abandoned its two-hundred-year-old policy of forcing daimyo to reside in Edo every other year while keeping their families as permanent hostages, asking the daimyo instead to concentrate on building up coastal defenses in their domains. Consequently, hundreds of daimyo with their families and tens of thousands of retainers left the capital, leaving Edo hollowed out and even further weakened.

The emptying of Edo was in stark contrast to the rapid growth and prosperity of Yokohama. Indeed, the two were directly related. The weakness of the shogunate stemmed from its inability to perform its historical function as military defender of Japan. Its failure to close the ports and the growing danger of foreign aggression fed agitation against the shogunate, which in turn forced it to make more concessions to its domestic critics. Among them was the shogunate's commitment—futile though it was—to close the ports and expel the "barbarians." If the shogunate had embraced foreign trade and participated more actively in the growing commercial prosperity of Yokohama, things might have worked out very differently. Instead, its hostility to foreigners and the trade that they brought hastened the decline of Edo and ultimately helped bring about the demise of the shogunate itself.

On March 9, 1863, anticipating the outbreak of war, the government developed a plan to evacuate the shogun's harem to Kōfu and to remove the Tokugawa family shrines at Ueno and Shiba into the mountains. Vassal samurai were ordered to move their families out of Edo, either to their allotted estates or to any safe place they could find. In April the government ordered all the remaining daimyo's wives and children to leave Edo and return home. The general populace began to panic at the possibility of a war, and people began hoarding goods, causing prices to shoot up. The government mobilized loyal daimyo, ordering them to prepare for the defense of Edo, and it ordered commoners to create firefighting units in anticipation of an attack.

On April 6, 1863, British envoy Colonel Neale announced a firm deadline—May 7—for huge indemnities to be paid by both the shogunate and Satsuma domain for the murder of Richardson. From the shogunate, Neale demanded £100,000 ($440,000), and from Satsuma, he demanded a further £25,000 ($112,000). During the month of April, powerful naval forces from England, France, and the Netherlands arrived in Yokohama. By the middle of April, to most residents of Edo and Yokohama, war between Japan and an alliance of foreign powers seemed all but inevitable.

In late April, as the crisis approached, Chūemon explained the situation:

> As I mentioned in my previous letter, there is talk of a war with the foreigners . . . Last year, when Shimazu Saburō was passing through Higashi Namamugi near Kanagawa, a foreigner was murdered. The foreigners demanded that if Shimazu Saburō does not hand over eight hundred thousand dollars, war will break out. Of course, he has not handed over even one mon. Indeed, there is not even any discussion of Saburō paying the money. He doesn't care what they do . . . England has told Japan that it must reply, and the Japanese officials are at a loss what to do.

It is striking that, rather than the foreign powers, Chūemon seems to hold the Satsuma clan and its leader, Shimazu Saburō, responsible for the unfolding disaster. His use of Saburō's given name without any of the honorifics normally used when referring to a great lord is remarkable, even in a private letter. Chūemon's dislike of Satsuma is palpable.

Chūemon ended his letter about the looming confrontation on a surprisingly patriotic note. "In this incident," he wrote, "truly Japan's martial prowess is to be feared. Truly, Japan is a first-rate power to be feared for ten thousand years by all the other nations of the world." This was, in fact, the first time in the surviving letters that Chūemon used the term "Japan" (Nippon). Previously, his references to his "country" (kuni) almost always referred to Kōshū. It is hard to say how aware Chūemon was of the broader currents of nationalism in Japan's political sphere. Given his education and widespread networks, it is hard to believe that he was not familiar with

National Learning ideology and the philosophies of imperial loyalism. But before emperor or nation, Chūemon's first loyalties were to his family, who depended on him for their livelihood, to his local community of Kōshū, and to the shogunate, which, for him, represented stability and security. There can be no doubt that the growing international confrontation gave Chūemon a stronger sense of Japanese identity—but it is probable that for Chūemon, being "Japanese" meant first and foremost being a loyal subject of the shogun. Chūemon's defiance of the foreigners was also tempered by his powerful belief in the beneficial wealth-creating opportunities that Yokohama offered. Indeed, Chūemon ended his letter with the reassuring admonition, "There is no need to fear: Yokohama will always be a safe place to live."[133]

Chūemon's confidence was not shared by the majority of the population. The looming confrontation threw both Edo and Yokohama into a state of panic. In Edo, wrote Chūemon, "it is said that a decision has been made to expel the foreigners on the thirteenth of this month [May 30, 1863]. The warriors are making fierce preparations . . . The women and children of the warriors have all returned to their fiefs, and those who have no fief have been sent to temples up to ten leagues away from Edo . . . The townsmen of Edo have nowhere to go. However, it is said that the owners of outbuildings in Kosuge and Ōji are asking high prices for them as places of evacuation."

Meanwhile in Yokohama, the May 7 deadline for payment of the indemnity for the Richardson murder approached, spreading panic through the community. Francis Hall wrote in his journal that "the native population are fleeing in the utmost haste . . . Scarcely a native merchant has the nerve to remain, but all offer their wares at any price they can get."[134] A French priest, Pierre Mounicou, wrote that "there is no food; only a few vegetables are still available and the European butchers have on hand no more than a two-day supply of meat. The merchants are hurriedly putting their goods aboard; hundreds of coolies are milling about the streets."[135] Those Japanese who had unsettled claims against the foreigners resorted to any means available to ensure payment before the expected outbreak of war. One merchant was abducted; another was "surrounded, thrown down, and beaten severely until his native servants interfered for his rescue." But in other cases, "servants left their masters robbing them as they went."[136]

The shogunal authorities were in complete disarray. The shogun himself was still in Kyoto, as were several of his chief advisers. The authorities in Edo begged for more time, and the British agreed to push the deadline into June. Meanwhile, the war of nerves continued. On May 31, six hundred French and British soldiers paraded in the customs house square. The next day the shogunate sent one thousand extra troops to Yokohama, ostensibly to protect the foreigners from the threat of activist samurai but causing many to fear that the government itself was planning a general massacre of the foreigners.[137]

Chūemon, however, stayed put through it all. On May 19 he wrote to his son that

> a market has sprung up for huts [outside the town], and people are bringing their emergency allocations of rice there. On the eleventh of last month, five hundred bales of rice were purchased at the town hall. In addition, many other necessities are being prepared . . . While we are keeping an eye on the military situation, we hope we can just live peacefully . . . Naotarō and his wife are working hard at their business and they are making a good living from it, so please be reassured, and tell Mother too. As for me, I am working without taking even half a day of rest. Everyone has fled, but we are prospering. We have sent our belongings to some relatives of Naotarō's wife, who live in Hoshikawa village, one and a half ri [3.7 miles] from Yokohama toward the Kōshū Kaidō. We are keeping here just our clothes, utensils, and other daily necessities. Inventory for our shop is arriving daily from Edo, and I have taken on two new workers."[138]

Finally, on June 20, 1863, the British chargé d'affaires, Colonel Neale, instructed the British naval fleet in Yokohama, led by Admiral Kuper, to get up steam in preparation for an attack on Edo. Kuper issued a proclamation to the foreign residents of Yokohama that he would wait eight days before attacking. During that time, "I think it necessary to recommend most strongly that all those of the community who have wives and families at Yokohama, should take the earliest opportunity of removing them, at any rate from the scene of danger, should they themselves determine upon awaiting the issue of events."[139]

The shogunal ministers, terrified at the prospect of an attack on Edo by British warships, finally recognized that they had no choice but to pay the enormous indemnity. Their fear was not misplaced. Given the limited state of Japan's coastal defenses, a single well-armed gunboat could have laid waste to the length of the Japanese coast. Most of Japan's great cities, with their flammable wooden buildings, were within shelling range of the coast.

On the night of June 24 a Japanese government steamer arrived in Yokohama with twenty chests of silver coins. As the *Illustrated London News* reported the event,

The authorities were exceedingly anxious to discharge their task at once, under the friendly shade of night; but Colonel Neale was firm, and next morning, before break of day, the sleepers of Yokohama were roused by the rattle of carts filled with dollars proceeding from the port towards the English Legation. Again the Japanese tried hard to induce Colonel Neale to accept the bulk as correct in amount and take it from them without further publicity; but this, too, was as firmly declined, and they had to count it out in the presence of the public and the laughing coolies.[140]

Ironically, the shogunate's humiliating and expensive stand-down came just one day before the date by which the shogun had committed to expel the foreigners and close the ports. After delivery of the money, the shogunal ministers formally presented the emperor's order that the foreigners should now leave Japan. When the foreign envoys reacted indignantly, the ministers apologized and quietly withdrew.

The next morning, as if to rub salt into the wound, the British forces— which had been building batteries in the hills above Yokohama to fortify it against a possible Japanese attack—mounted a grand parade in the streets of Yokohama, complete with artillery and a full marching band. The parade marched right up to the residence of the Kanagawa commissioners. The Illustrated London News gloated, "The weather was lovely and the music most inspiring. Ready and ingenious as ever, the Japanese had in a few hours spread abroad the report that our imposing visit to the Governor was for the express purpose of acknowledging the condescension of the Japanese Government in paying the compensation-money."[141]

A year earlier the British minister, Sir Rutherford Alcock, had told a shogunal officer in confidence that "Britain considered the Japan trade too small to be worth fighting for."[142] The confrontation in 1863, however, belied his statement. Later, Alcock was to justify Britain's actions on the ground that a clash between feudalism and Western commercial "civilization" was inevitable: "These two great forces, in their full development with conflicting aims and requirements were unfortunately destined to meet in this last home of feudalism."[143] Historians, however, have viewed the aggressive confrontation between Britain and Japan as a classic case of gunboat diplomacy.[144]

Throughout all this strife and high political drama, Chūemon remained stubbornly optimistic. He stayed in place when many others fled, and he continued to express his loyalty to and confidence in the shogunate. Even the debacle of the indemnity payment and the shogunate's humiliating stand-down failed to dent his optimism. The shogun returned to Edo on August 2, and Chūemon was convinced that now all would be well. "Nothing untoward has happened in Yokohama. There has been a change in the method of doing things, but it is based on ages past, so there is no need to worry."[145] Perhaps Chūemon was even heartened when the allied fleet, having been ready to attack Edo, turned around and instead steamed to Kagoshima, where on August 15 it sank three Satsuma steamships and shelled Kagoshima city.

A few weeks later, Chūemon wrote, "People are talking about Yokohama at present. They are saying that the Kantō daimyo are all at their stations ready to close the port. But that is nothing but a rumor. In Yokohama they are inviting bids for the construction of foreigners' houses as well as official buildings. If you saw that you would not think that the port would easily be closed."[146] And three weeks later, he added, "Here in Yokohama, they are beginning construction of a road to connect Kanagawa with Yokohama. It will all be reclaimed land. In the future, you won't need to take a boat—there will be a road all the way. They are also building a gun battery . . . There are all sorts of other construction projects going on, so please be reassured, everything is all right. However, there is major strife in Kyoto, and Edo has hardened its position. But I will write about that in another letter."[147]

FAMILY MATTERS

Throughout all his struggles, Chūemon continued to rely on his strong network of family members and close associates, who supported him in times of crisis and who shared many of his trials. Chūemon's son Shōjirō's participation in the business was crucial, since Shōjirō was not only a producer of many of the products that were to be so important to Chūemon's business—starting with cotton—but also the hub for Chūemon's network of local business relationships in Kōshū. It must have been extremely difficult for Shōjirō to manage his father's frequent—and often insistent—requests for him to initiate new shipments of goods, negotiate with creditors, dispatch buyers to distant parts of the region, and manage a variety of crisis situations while also running the family farm and raising his own family. Shōjirō also had to take care of his younger brother and sisters who remained in Kōshū. And he had to undertake burdensome duties as a village official, many of which he had taken over from Chūemon. It was a lot to ask of a young man still in his mid-twenties, but he seems to have undertaken this broad array of duties uncomplainingly and competently.

Chūemon's wife was also closely involved in the family business. After her return to Kōshū following her serious illness in Yokohama in 1860, she lived mostly in their home village, separated from her husband. But it is clear that she was fully engaged in business affairs. She was the manager of the family's silk-making activities, on which she was the acknowledged expert. But Chūemon also made sure that she was kept apprised of every detail of the family's business activities. Especially when a business problem involved delicate negotiations with relatives and other investors, Chūemon invariably told Shōjirō to consult carefully with his mother. The Okamura family seem to have been active investors in Chūemon's business enterprise, so it is possible that Chūemon's wife (who was from the Okamura family) was also a financial partner—though there is nothing in the correspondence to indicate this directly. In any case, Chūemon's wife was a trusted partner in his business affairs.

After his disastrous handling of the charcoal business, Chūemon's son Naotarō did his best to redeem himself in his father's eyes. He seems to have been the family's main contact person with the foreign trading houses, where, according to Chūemon, "Naotarō goes to sell our wares."[148] In January 1862, Naotarō was also given an administrative position in the newly created Merchants' Association (Shōhō Kaisho). The salary, twelve monme (about $0.35) a day, was small, but the family was expected to provide a representative, and perhaps after the charcoal affair, Chūemon was pleased to find an untaxing job for his son to do. From that point forward, Naotarō seems to have spent at least part of each day at the association.[149]

However, even with his new roles as sales agent, association functionary, and husband, Naotarō could not settle down. Perhaps, given the ill will between him and his father over the charcoal affair, he wanted to get away if he possibly could. And there is no doubt that Chūemon worried deeply about his son, who in his eyes was unable to succeed in anything. "Naotarō is very much a worry," he wrote to his oldest son. "I wish he could complete something successfully, no matter what." Chūemon added, as though to rub in the contrast, "I also worry about you working so hard."[150]

Throughout 1862 and into 1863, Naotarō continued to help his father in his business. He went on buying trips into the provinces in August and again in September of 1862. Chūemon had secured a fifteen-hundred-ryō investment from his partners in Kōshū to invest in the silk business.[151] Naotarō succeeded in purchasing silk at profitable rates, and for the first time since arriving in Yokohama, Chūemon and his family experienced a taste of success.

On October 1, Chūemon wrote for the first time of his plans to set his son up in his own business: "I would like to . . . build a shop, seven ken [forty-two feet] deep with three ken [eighteen feet] of frontage, including a reception room. I think the conditions are now right for this. I would like to sell socks [tabi] there, so please order them from Terake Kanpachi of Kōfu city . . . The socks won't sell unless they're dyed with indigo. He should make them in three sizes . . . He should send an assortment as soon as possible."[152]

For a while, the sock business took second place to other concerns, but in December 1862, Chūemon again started pressing Shōjirō to expedite the dispatch of sock samples to Yokohama: "I would like to start selling them as soon as possible. You need to ask Kanpachi to send me one ryō worth of samples as soon as possible. They should be indigo and include children's socks."[153]

The samples arrived a few days later, but the quality was not nearly good enough to sell in the competitive Yokohama market. They "are proving difficult to sell . . . Buyers for them are very scarce. Even those who do buy them, when they see the open seams, don't come back to buy again. If only the manufacture was of a good quality, then I would have no problem selling them, but these items are unsalable. Please return the previous order and take this letter to Kōfu and show it to them, and get a refund."[154] Instead, Chūemon asked his son to order several lengths of cloth to be sent to Yokohama. If the tailors of Kōfu couldn't give him what he needed, he would have Naotarō and his wife manufacture the socks themselves.

By May 1863, in the midst of the crisis over the closing of the port, Chūemon was able to report that "Naotarō and his wife are gradually working at their sock business and they seem to be getting better at it. Wherever they go they will be able to make a living from this, so please be reassured, and tell Mother, too."[155]

However, like so many affairs involving Naotarō, this business seems not to have had a happy ending. The correspondence is silent on the details, but in an undated letter from some time in 1863, Chūemon writes, "According to Naotarō's plan, we should have made three hundred ryō profit three times over. Clearly this was a miscalculation. I question whether there is any profit at all. Really that was a stupid plan . . . That fellow's imprudence is extremely upsetting. He's as stupid as can be. He needs to be reborn as a new person."[156]

After 1863 there is no more mention of socks, and Chūemon once again put Naotarō to work supporting his trading business.

Naotarō did manage to please his father in at least one thing. On July 17, 1864, his wife, Take, presented Chūemon with a granddaughter. Her name was Asa. Take was to have at least three more children. A son born on September 4, 1865, died soon after his birth ("all of us are feeling the blow").[157] But another son, Kōshirō, born in 1867, survived. An exceptional student, Kōshirō graduated from Tokyo Imperial University, though, sadly, he died in 1892 at the age of only twenty-five.[158]

During his early years in Yokohama, Chūemon experienced a variety of challenges that must have tried his faith in the vision that had lured him from a privileged and comfortable life in his small village in Kōshū. Some of these challenges were shared by many or even most of the Japanese merchants in Yokohama. The shortage of capital was a constant theme, harked on repeatedly by both Japanese and foreign observers. Even the largest and most reputable merchants lacked the huge financial resources needed to supply the foreigners' enormous demand for silk thread, tea, and a few other products. Small scale merchants like Chūemon struggled to finance even a minimal inventory. Meanwhile the deteriorating political situation, the constant threat of violence, and the alarming confrontations between shogunate and foreign powers made life insecure and frightening for the entire population of Yokohama. Other challenges—his family's battle with skin disease, his difficulties with his disaster-prone son Naotarō, and the fiasco with his charcoal venture—were unique to Chūemon's situation. We can see from his letters that there were times when Chūemon came close to giving up: "I keep trying at various things to make some money, but nothing seems to work out."

And yet, it is also possible to see why Chūemon held onto his faith. Yokohama represented a unique community in Japan, a new and powerful engine driven by the enormous motive force of the global market. Yokohama was a place where people congregated from every part of the world, almost all of them arriving in the hope of material gain. Watching the marshes being filled and the new buildings going up, Chūemon could already see a great city in the making.

The looming confrontation with the foreign powers over the enormous reparations demanded for the murder of a British citizen forced Chūemon to reassess his optimism, and tested his commitment to his vision. It took real courage for him to stay in Yokohama even as most of the Japanese population fled in the expectation of an outbreak of war. At the same time, the confrontation pushed Chūemon toward a stronger sense of national identity and even defiance. Unlike the Revere the Emperor, Expel the Barbarian movement, however, Chūemon never wavered in his loyalty to the shogunal regime which had offered him so much opportunity, nor in his underlying faith in the promise of Yokohama.

If the Japanese social and political order was cracking in front of Chūemon's eyes, he also saw in front of him the promise of a dazzling future, embodied by the emerging city of which he was a part. Although it was so new, Yokohama was vibrant with brilliant and exotic sights, with novelty and entertainment, with hope, enterprise, and glamor. Its streets rang with the clatter of hand-carts, the cries of hawkers and entertainers, the laughter of children, the drums and fifes of soldiers, the clapping of dancing-girls, and always, in the background, the tantalizing chink of silver. These were the sounds of opportunity.

3 PROSPERITY (1864–1866)

SUCCESS AT LAST

Although the payment of a £100,000 indemnity in June 1863 resolved the immediate crisis between the shogunate and its unwelcome guests, the imperial order to expel the foreigners remained in force. Having failed politically, the government turned to an economic strategy, attempting to cut off the flow of goods to the port. The commodity most desired by the foreigners was silk thread. Anxious to fulfill its pledge to close down the port, and worried also by the immense outflow of silk from Japan and the rapidly rising prices of silk and other commodities, the government began enforcing the Five Products Edo Circulation Law (Gohin Edo Mawashi Rei). This law required that all wholesale transactions in silk, grain, oil, wax, and clothing, including export transactions, be routed through one of the licensed wholesalers in Edo. The law had been created as early as 1860, with a view to preventing the Edo wholesalers (ton'ya), which enjoyed special privileges in exchange for paying extra taxes to the government, from being bypassed by the Yokohama trade. But in the face of strong foreign resistance to any restrictive measures, the government had not been able to enforce the law. Now, with relations between the shogunate and the foreigners already at a nadir, the shogunal authorities felt they had nothing more to lose. They ordered the law to be strictly observed. Direct silk shipments to Yokohama were forbidden, and merchants entering the port were searched to ensure compliance. At the same time, the government issued instructions to the Edo wholesalers to slow silk shipments to Yokohama, or even at times to halt them altogether. The government was able to use its choke hold on the Edo wholesale merchants to squeeze the Yokohama market dry.[1]

The shogunate's measures to choke off trade did little to appease the antiforeign samurai, who continued to wage a campaign of terror aimed at Japanese and foreign merchants as well as at the shogunal authorities themselves. Although they were themselves threatened, the authorities did their best to turn the mood of fear to their advantage. On October 31, Jardine, Matheson's new Yokohama manager, S. J. Gower, reported on a tense meeting in Edo at which the American minister and the Dutch consul were told by government representatives that

> the only possible way of averting a revolution was for all foreigners to leave and give up Yokohama and betake themselves to Nagasaki and Hakodadi where they might trade . . . As usual there are all sorts of rumors current, such as, that the Japanese intend to withdraw all their guards from about Yokohama, that several bands of armed men are collecting at different places with the intention of attacking [Yokohama], that if they can not get rid of us in any other way they will stop all supplies, etc., etc., in all of which I do not believe there is one word of truth. And it is also stated positively that the government has ordered ¾ of the silk worm eggs to be destroyed. But this also I doubt.[2]

In August, a Japanese silk merchant was murdered in Kanagawa and his head displayed on a pole with a notice stating that other merchants who traded with the foreigners would meet the same fate.[3] In September, six silk merchants were murdered in Kyoto and Osaka. The head of one of them, Yamatoya Ōhei, was stuck on a post at Sanjō Bridge in Kyoto, with a placard proclaiming that he and others like him "have trafficked in copper cash, silk, wax, oil, salt, tea, in fact in all the staples of the land, in articles necessary for the use of the people of the country" and "sold them to foreigners for their own gain. By so doing they have enhanced the price of all articles and all but themselves suffer. Many in the interior are pinched as in time of famine; families can no longer live in one place together; households are broken up and scattered; many have died from sheer want of food. On account of all this, we can no longer remain blind to the sufferings of the people."[4] A few days later, a list of twenty-four Yokohama merchants was posted on the door of the Kanagawa commissioners' headquarters, threatening a similar fate for them. And in December, eighteen Edo townsmen were murdered for their alleged dealings with foreigners—three of them merely for buying lumber that was to be used in the construction of a foreign house.[5] Gower wrote, "Trade is suffering from the present state of affairs. Many silk men, alarmed by the actual murder of some of the large merchants of Osaka and Edo and the proclamations that they will be similarly treated if they continue to trade with foreigners, are pulling down their houses and leaving the place."[6] The great Mitsui company, the largest textile merchant in Japan, ordered its Yokohama branch to stop trading in silk after the company manager in Edo was threatened with "divine retribution."[7] Gower estimated that by the end of 1863 a quarter of the Japanese shops in Yokohama had closed.[8]

In the meantime silk shipments into Yokohama slowed to a trickle. The only supplies coming through were those brought in under the seal of daimyo who felt free to flout the shogunal regulation. In August 1864, Chūemon wrote, "No silk whatsoever is coming into the port. Right now there is no trading taking place."[9] And the following month, "In Yokohama the enforcement is so strict that people are being arrested for trying to smuggle silk into the town [hidden] in shipments of cotton or tea."[10] And indeed at least one customs house official was ordered to commit suicide for abetting smugglers.[11] On July 14, 1864, William Keswick reported to his Shanghai office that the Yokohama customs house "is exercising its influence to apparently put a stop to business in Silk . . . How far the Authorities will go in their endeavour to obstruct trade it is impossible to say but I fear their interference . . . will reduce the export of Silk during this season."[12]

It must have taken a cool head and a great deal of courage and resolve to stay put in the midst of all these obstacles, threats, and acts of violence. Chūemon had already shown in the confrontation in May and June that he was not easily frightened, and in his letters in the latter part of 1863 and into 1864 he showed no sign of backing down from his confidence in Yokohama's bright future. And indeed, in the midst of all these difficulties and fears, an opportunity was developing in the Yokohama market that would play directly to Chūemon's strengths.

The American Civil War, which had begun in April 1861, upended the global cotton market. In an attempt to throttle the South's economy, the Northern navy blockaded the South's major ports, preventing the export of its major income-producing commodity. England's cotton mills imported 77 percent of their supplies from the American South. So severe was England's dependence on American cotton that the Confederate government had hoped Britain would join the war against the North. Many British mill owners did indeed support the Confederate cause and even flew Confederate flags in front of their factories. But the cotton mill workers supported the Union's fight against slavery and even wrote President Lincoln a collective letter of support. The British government remained neutral.[13]

Although English mills had considerable stockpiles of raw cotton at the beginning of the war, by the end of 1862 supplies were running out, and many mills were forced to cut back production or even close. The "cotton famine" in the English mill towns caused great hardship, to which the foreign merchant community in Yokohama responded by subscribing $2,160 (£558) to the Lancashire and Cheshire Operatives Relief Fund.[14] At the same time, seeing a commercial opportunity, European merchants in Yokohama began tapping Japan's domestic supplies of raw cotton. Ultimately, India, Egypt, and Brazil were to take over much of the productive capacity of the Southern states, but in the summer of 1863, any cotton-producing country saw immediate opportunities as the London market price skyrocketed from $0.10 a pound in 1860 to as much as $1.89 in 1863–1864.[15]

Chūemon first noticed this development near the end of 1862. In a letter dated October 1, he noted, "With regard to cotton, the price is going up rapidly . . . The foreigners have bought up between three hundred thousand and five hundred thousand kin [four hundred thousand to six hundred sixty thousand pounds], and deliveries are now in progress. Prices are going up in Edo, too, and they are sure to follow suit in Kōshū, so please take note."[16] Three weeks later, he asked Shōjirō to send him samples that he could show to the foreigners.[17]

Chūemon's response to the opportunity in cotton is the first indication of his growing global awareness. He did not specifically mention the American Civil War, nor the shortages of raw cotton in Manchester, but Chūemon was clearly aware of the importance of market movements originating far from Japan. This new awareness presaged a transformation in Chūemon's perceptions of time and space, as his mental map shifted from the politics and economics of the Kantō region to take on a new global perspective.

It was not until the cotton harvest was in in 1863 that Chūemon began to organize a concerted response to the opportunity. On November 15, 1863, Chūemon sent a letter to Higashi-Aburakawa by express messenger and marked "extremely urgent." In the letter, Chūemon told his son to sell any supplies he had of woven cotton, which was a domestic staple in which Chūemon's family had been trading for years. Instead, Shōjirō was to buy up all the raw cotton he could find. It was raw cotton that was in demand on the global market.[18]

In a detailed analysis, Chūemon calculated the potential profit from a shipment of raw cotton purchased at the prevailing prices in Kōshū. His analysis illustrates the complexity of the currency and measurement conversions that were needed to manage a transaction between Kōshū and Yokohama. Transactions in Kōshū were usually paid for in copper kan (equivalent to about 0.6 ryō). For bulk goods, quantities were denominated in packhorse loads, with one packhorse equivalent to 178 kin (about 235 lbs.). However, goods sold in the Yokohama market were denominated in piculs, with one picul equal to 100 kin (132 lbs.). For payment, the major commodity markets in Yokohama were denominated in Mexican dollars, which were valued by Japanese exchange brokers in silver monme (approximately 36 to the dollar). Finally, the entire tally of profit and loss had to be calculated in gold ryō, which was the notional unit of currency used by merchants and townsmen in the Kantō region. As Chūemon applied these calculations, "one horse load of cotton sells for 28 kan and 800 me. In Kōshū, the exchange rate for 1 ryō is 1 kan and 700 me, so the cost [per horse load] is 16 ryō 3 bu 3 shu. It would cost about 1 ryō to pack it and transport it to Yokohama, so the total would come to 17 ryō 3 bu 3 shu. Here in Yokohama, 100 kin is selling for $23 of Western silver. In dollars, 1 horse load would sell for $41.10 at 36 monme to the dollar. Our gross income would be 24 ryō 2 bu 3 shu. After deducting for packing and transportation, our net profit would be 6 ryō 3 bu [per horse load]."[19]

No matter the logistics, though, the opportunity was clear. In the following weeks, prices on the Yokohama market continued to soar. On November 22, Chūemon sold a large consignment of cotton—20 horse loads, or about 36 piculs (4,800 lbs.)—at $25 per picul, more than double the prevailing price in June.[20] And by late December in the Western calendar, the price had gone up to $33 per picul (equivalent to 34 ryō per horse load), while in Kōshū it was still possible to buy cotton for 23 ryō per horse load.[21]

This was exactly the kind of market opportunity Chūemon had been waiting for. Instead of waiting for Kōshū merchants to bring him goods to sell to foreigners for a 2 or 3 percent commission, Chūemon moved aggressively to exploit the wide gap between prices in his home province and the booming global market. By the end of 1863, he had dramatically expanded his buying activities, investing as much as six thousand ryō ($14,000) at a time in purchases of Kōshū cotton. This was an extraordinary transformation for a man who just two years earlier had pawned all his wife's kimonos just to pay the bills.

Chūemon could not have raised such sums of money on his own credit. Late in 1863, he developed a relationship with an Edo merchant named Kojikahara Jihei, who was willing to provide the financial capital for Chūemon's ventures.[22] In return, Chūemon could offer a deep network of business contacts in the cotton-producing region, as well as relationships with the foreign merchant houses that were the ultimate buyers of the product. In order to ensure access to the large amounts of cotton that he needed, Chūemon also developed a relationship with Matsudaya, a large cotton broker in Ichikawa town in Kōshū. In a typical example of the transactions that resulted from this three-way relationship, according to a letter dated November 22, 1863, Jihei provided 200 ryō ($467), and, with the help of Matsudaya, Chūemon purchased 20 horse loads of cotton. Chūemon sold this in Yokohama for $25 per picul, clearing a profit of 70 ryō ($163). After deducting expenses, the business partners split the final proceeds three ways. Chūemon called this process noriai—literally, "riding together" but perhaps better translated as "alliance capital."[23] As the business model proved itself to be effective, the size of the business partners' transactions increased dramatically. With Jihei's capital backing him, Chūemon was able to buy consignments as large as 300 horse loads (70,000 lbs.).[24]

Chūemon's partners were not limited to his wealthy Edo contacts. He continued to involve his network of business associates in Kōshū, bringing many of them into his deals with Kojikahara and others. In doing so, he was able to expand his capital base still further while also extending his deep network of rural contacts, many of whom were closely connected to the silk and cotton producers of the region.

The key to profits under Chūemon's model of alliance capital was to recirculate the available capital by buying as much and as often as possible. As he wrote to his son Shōjirō, "I am sending Naotarō out to buy cotton . . . It will be very profitable if I can repeat this transaction many times over . . . No matter how many times we [purchase], it will be to our profit."[25] Capital was a scarce commodity that had to be exploited as rapidly and aggressively as possible. With the same amount of capital, it was possible to make double the profits if the merchandise could be turned around twice as fast.

Indeed, because of the basic weakness of Chūemon's position as a small and undercapitalized merchant, he had to do his utmost to take advantage of those strengths that he had. In addition to his contact networks in Yokohama, Edo, and Kōshū, Chūemon's main strength was his access to information about the day-to-day movements of the Yokohama market. Chūemon was intensely conscious of the need for speed and secrecy in conveying this information, which he considered to be a crucial competitive advantage.

Chūemon repeatedly told his son Shōjirō to keep the contents of his letters secret, or to share information only with a few selected merchants. At times, he also instructed his son and business partners to deliberately spread misinformation. One conspicuous example was a plan to misinform the residents of Kōshū about the likely consequences of the Richardson murder in September 1862. In the wake of that crisis, Chūemon wrote to three of his business partners urging them to make the situation sound even worse than it actually was:

> It may be expedient to spread the word that there has been a complete halt to trade, and by this means spur a decline in prices in Kōshū . . . If necessary, I can write a separate letter that you can use to spread rumors. Right now it may be a good idea to sell all that you have purchased, and then once the prices have fallen, you can buy again. If you sell now, you may indeed suffer a loss, but if you use the letter I will send separately, then prices will collapse and you can perhaps profit by buying again. Please consider this, and I will abide by whatever decision you take . . . Please do not show this letter to anyone. Instead, you should repeatedly show the other letter that I will write . . . If you do it this way, the letter will be copied and circulated by the people of the Isawa post station, and its contents will become a topic of conversation.[26]

Once the cotton market began to take off, Chūemon also repeatedly told his associates to do their best to hide the news of rising prices in Yokohama: "Here cotton is selling for more than $18 per 100 kin, at 35.9 silver monme to the dollar. You must not talk about this to anyone. When you go to Ichikawa to order cotton to be sent here, you must say that the price of cotton is low. You should not mention that we are trying to buy as much as possible, and you should say that the price is falling."[27]

Of course, such a campaign of misinformation could be effective for only a limited time. Within a month or so, the foreigners' large-scale purchases became the talk of the province, and cotton that Chūemon had been able to buy for thirteen ryō a horse load in November shot up to twenty-three ryō by the end of the December 1863 and was at twenty-five ryō a week later.

Chūemon also relied increasingly on speed to preserve his information advantage. In his first few years in Yokohama, Chūemon had depended mostly on traveling merchants to deliver letters back and forth to Kōshū. As a result, it could take quite a while for a letter to arrive—a week to ten days in most cases, but sometimes much longer. One undated letter states that "your letter of the nineteenth of last month arrived on the twenty-third," which suggests an elapsed time of more than a month.[28] However, as he undertook larger transactions in which the timing of purchases was all-important, Chūemon began using the services of professional couriers (hikyaku), sometimes paying extra to ensure even speedier delivery.

Francis Hall described these couriers: "They travel fast, making the distance from Yokohama to Yedo, twenty miles, in three hours. They are nearly naked and carry their dispatch in a parcel tied on the end of a rod and borne over the shoulder, or in a wallet fastened by a cord around their necks . . . They wear cotton socks on their feet, the [highway] is free from loose stones and offers no inconvenience to such light shoeing."[29]

The delivery time from Yokohama to Kōshū using a hikyaku express service was three days. The regular hikyaku service departed three times a month, on fixed days. Since the messengers traveled only along the main highways, Chūemon would have to send his letter to Isawa—the closest post station to Higashi-Aburakawa—with instructions to forward it to Higashi-Aburakawa.[30] If Chūemon wanted to send an urgent message outside the regular delivery schedule, he had to pay for a special delivery, which could cost as much as three ryō for a single letter. Increasingly, Chūemon was willing to pay such high fees. His sense of urgency as he responded to global market opportunities reflects his growing awareness of information flows and the importance of information advantage. This awareness pushed merchants in the global marketplace to use every technique at their disposal to accelerate the flow of information and goods. If the telegraph and the railway had been available, Chūemon would surely have jumped at the chance to benefit from their speed and convenience. Chūemon's reorientation toward a global market and his focus on speed of transmission reflect a new relationship both to the spatial dynamics of the modern world trading system and to the temporal dynamic of ever-faster global transport and communication networks. These transformed relationships to space and time were soon to affect livelihoods throughout the Kantō region, from wealthy merchants to marginal farmers.

Chūemon's profits reflect the very high risk that he had to take on. From the time that Chūemon's agents (including his sons Naotarō and Shōjirō) purchased goods, Chūemon and his venture partners were out of pocket. They had to pay all the transportation costs and bear the risk of loss or spoilage before attempting to sell the product in Yokohama. They also bore all the market risk: if the price of the goods had declined during the days or weeks it took to buy them in the countryside and ship them to Yokohama, then Chūemon and his partners had to absorb the loss. This is another reason why Chūemon was so insistent on speed in all his communications as well as in the actual transportation of the merchandise. Of course, for the foreign merchants the risk was even greater: those shipping to Europe had to wait months to receive any return on their investment, with all the attendant risks of shipwreck, spoilage, and price changes during the interim.

In spite of the influx of capital from his wealthy business partners, Chūemon's transactions also remained highly leveraged. Chūemon's goal was to purchase cotton for as little up-front payment as possible, allowing him to maximize the use of his capital. Typically, he was able to buy cotton for an earnest-money payment of one to two ryō per horse load. On top of that he had to pay a little more than one ryō for transportation. So a one-hundred-ryō ($233) investment could potentially buy more than forty horse loads of cotton, with a market value in Yokohama of more than thirteen hundred ryō ($3,030). But the sellers demanded full payment within days of delivery, so it was crucial for Chūemon to turn the merchandise around and remit the proceeds back to the countryside.

Moreover, Chūemon remained substantially in debt to many of his creditors in and around Higashi-Aburakawa. Although the debts had in most cases been incurred much earlier, Chūemon preferred to use his available funds to buy more cotton rather than to pay debts. For example, on December 6, 1863, Chūemon wrote, "[For the rest of] this year I plan to invest fifty ryō. In the New Year, Naotarō will go further afield to make purchases. After deducting Jizaemon's share, I plan to throw all the rest back into the business. I will have to put off [some creditors], but they certainly won't lose by this. Please convey my apologies . . . If my creditors demand the money, please just tell them that I'm not doing well."[31] And once again, at year's end, when debtors traditionally settled all their accounts, Chūemon wrote to a group of villagers, "Unfortunately I am still unable to return home. Thank you so much for all the help you have given me this year. As you know, my biggest problem has been lack of funds, and I continue to be unable to pay my taxes and other debts. Next year I will come home and thank you in person."[32]

The patience of Chūemon's creditors in his home province is striking. It no doubt reflects Chūemon's personal standing in the region, but it also illustrates the profit-seeking dynamic of the rural capitalist system. By the mid-nineteenth century, commercial growth and the concentration of wealth had placed substantial capital surpluses in the hands of an emerging class of wealthy farmer-merchants—the gōnō. Surviving records indicate that many wealthy villagers operated local and regional money-lending businesses on a large scale. While some of these loans were to poorer villagers and tenant farmers, moneylenders generally preferred to lend money to wealthier, and more successful, farmers and farmer-merchants, who were in turn diversifying into new business ventures—even if those loans were sometimes riskier. For example, a detailed study of the Okada family of Oka village in the Kinai region indicates that although the family had many tenants farming Okada-owned land, the family's extensive money-lending operations were almost exclusively aimed at wealthier villagers and regional merchants. The loans extended over more than a dozen villages, and debtors included wealthy farmers, merchants, sake brewers, and the domainal administration. During the 1860s, loans averaged some six thousand ryō per year, with an average loan size of around one hundred thirty ryō.[33]

The expansion of lending in the village economy is a testament to the robust and growing commercial economy of rural areas in many parts of Japan.[34] But given the propensity of lenders to seek higher-growth and higher-return investments, lending on this scale inevitably involved a significant level of nonperforming and defaulted loans. During the period 1848–1854, for example, the Okada family was involved in forty-seven suits against debtors, with the amounts ranging from less than two ryō to more than three hundred ryō.[35] In a world in which audits and financial statements were unavailable, banks nonexistent, and the flow of information fragmentary, lenders had to rely on the quality of assets placed as security, and at times on personal trust. The high level of risk also helps explain the high interest rates that prevailed throughout most of Japan. In Chūemon's case, it seems that many of his debts were unsecured: his property in Higashi-Aburakawa would hardly have been enough to cover his extensive financial operations.

It certainly must have been troubling to his creditors that Chūemon was unable to pay his debts at the traditional year-end settlement time. The fact that they were willing to wait for repayment, and even to extend Chūemon additional credit, surely speaks to the opportunity they saw in his business venture, and to their personal faith in Chūemon himself. From the beginning, Chūemon saw his enterprise as a communal venture to improve the economy of his region. His goal was not just to get rich himself but to increase sales of Kōshū produce, for the benefit of his community. He hoped and expected that all the participants would benefit from the rising tide of prosperity driven by the Yokohama export market. And to some extent, his creditors and business associates must have agreed with him. Indeed, the available records suggest that the continued expansion of Chūemon's business through the 1860s brought in enough cash to keep his creditors happy, even if they were not always repaid on time.

As a result of his successes in cotton, by the end of 1863 Chūemon was able to enjoy a sense of prosperity that he had not experienced in a very long time. The previous year, his family had been almost entirely dependent on Naotarō's earnings from his work in the office of the Yokohama Merchants' Association, two ryō ($4.67) a month that Chūemon received from a real estate investment, and the small amount of money Naotarō and his wife made by producing tabi socks. Now Chūemon was dealing in thousands of ryō a month. At the end of the year, Chūemon shipped twenty-five cases of Okinawan straw, useful for packing bales of cotton, to Shōjirō, telling him that if he didn't have a use for it he could give it away to Hori Shōsuke of Ichikawa. This kind of generosity was unthinkable a year earlier.[36]

However, Chūemon's cotton business came to an abrupt end with the disastrous harvest of 1864. A destructive storm wiped out 60 percent of the cotton crop as well as 30 percent of the rice crop, causing widespread hardship in farming villages.[37] The scarcity of cotton pushed prices up to a point where they were no longer attractive to foreign traders, who anyway were finding alternative sources in China, India, and elsewhere.

Although the closing down of the cotton business deprived Chūemon of his most lucrative trading item, he remained highly optimistic. As a result of his success with cotton, he had gained a significant network of wealthy new business partners, including several in Edo, as well as a newfound self-confidence. Toward the end of 1864, he boasted to his son that he had done thirty thousand ryō ($70,000) worth of business—an extraordinary achievement for a man who, just five years earlier, had struggled to raise the first twenty ryō to open his shop.[38]

While the Japanese government was still pursuing a policy of restricting trade as much as possible, it was allowing a trickle of silk shipments to flow from Edo to Yokohama in order to avoid being accused of blatantly contravening the treaties.[39] In response to the Five Products law, Chūemon made an arrangement with an Edo silk wholesaler, Mokuya in the Kobunechō district of Edo. From this point on, he asked his business associates in Kōshū to send shipments of silk to Edo rather than to Yokohama. Mokuya would certify the goods and ship them on to Yokohama.[40] Chūemon himself moved to Edo in August of 1864, and he stayed there more or less continuously through the end of the year. Silk producers had been ramping up their production in response to the enormous demand from foreign buyers, and supplies were piling up in the warehouses of the Edo wholesalers, waiting for government permission to ship them on to Yokohama. No doubt Chūemon calculated that the government would have to either permit the sales or order the silk burned, which would cause untold hardship to producers.

And indeed in October 1864, after a strong intervention by the British and French ministers (supported once again by a fleet of warships in Edo Bay), the government abruptly abandoned its restrictions on silk shipments to Yokohama—although the law requiring them to go via Edo remained in place. As a result, in the final months of 1864 Yokohama was flooded with pent-up supplies of silk.

Since silk was such an expensive product, Chūemon was taking consignments on commission. Kōshū producers would ship supplies to Chūemon's account with Mokuya in Edo. Once Mokuya received permission to ship the goods to Yokohama, Chūemon handled their sale to foreign buyers. His cut was relatively small, so he needed to drum up as many shipments as possible. In the closing months of 1864 and into 1865, most of Chūemon's letters urge his son and business partners to send consignments of silk to Edo on commission. Chūemon himself remained busy enough that "if you have someone among your friends, I'd like them to come here to help me. Right now we have many merchants bringing goods on consignment, and I need help urgently. I will write to them separately, and if they are going to come, then they must meet with you and you must approve of them."[41]

Silk was a frustrating product to deal in. There was intense competition for limited supplies. The product was seasonal and not available at all times. The government was inclined to interfere in its distribution. And it was very expensive to purchase. Consequently, Chūemon was always on the lookout for lower-value products that he could invest in more directly. While in Edo, he took advantage of the local seafood market to buy a shipment of *surume* (dried squid) and ship it to Yokohama. Early in 1865, Chūemon began dealing in silk by-products, such as cocoon husks and silk thread leavings, for use as fertilizer. Although these products sold for only a tiny fraction of the price of silk thread, Chūemon was able to make higher profits by investing on his own account.[42]

In March 1865, Chūemon mentioned for the first time the prospects for selling silkworm eggs into the foreign market.[43] In the previous decade European silk producers had been devastated by the pébrine blight, which attacked silkworm larvae and made them unable to spin thread. Europe's silk production had been virtually wiped out, and there was strong demand from European (mostly French and Italian) buyers for Japanese silkworms, which were thought to be more resistant to the parasite.[44] At this point, the shogunal government still prohibited the export of silkworm eggs. Nevertheless, by mid-May Chūemon had committed to the trade: "As I mentioned in my last letter, I would definitely like to enter the egg business and succeed in it. I intend to send my people out to purchase eggs instead of silk. Please make sure that Hanjirō, Matsujirō, Shimosone, and Heiei don't talk about this to anyone else."[45] And indeed, in early June, the government responded to strong French pressure by lifting the ban on silkworm egg exports, and trade became possible.[46]

Chūemon's strategy, which he worked out with his local partners, was to turn Higashi-Aburakawa and surrounding villages into a manufacturing center for silkworm egg cards. This was a new venture. In the past villagers in the area had bred silkworms, sold cocoons, spun thread, and even woven cloth, but they had purchased their eggs from specialized producers. The preparation of silkworm eggs, carefully dried and mounted on sheets of cardboard, had long been concentrated in the Shindatsu district of Ōshū (now Fukushima prefecture) and the Ueda district of Shinshū province (now Nagano prefecture). Traders from these districts would either manufacture cards within their own families or represent groups of manufacturing families as they traveled through the silk-producing areas of Japan. They would sell their cards to small-scale cultivators, usually in the summer months, for a small down payment. They would not collect their final payment until six months later, when the farm families had cultivated silkworms from the eggs and sold their cocoons or thread. If the farmer's crop was poor, the egg traders would be paid less, so it was in their interest to propagate the best silkworm-rearing techniques. They did this by distributing manuals to their customers. The relationship was therefore long term and mutually dependent. That was the main reason why, in spite of enormous growth in the silkworm-rearing industry, the silkworm egg card business had stayed in the hands of a relatively small group of traders from well-defined producing areas.[47]

Now that there was an opportunity to sell egg cards to foreigners, the dynamics of the market fundamentally changed. Foreign buyers did not need loans or long-term support. Relationships were less important to them than a high-quality product, for which they would pay in full on delivery in Yokohama. Chūemon saw this opportunity early and responded to it.

Chūemon and his investor group formulated a plan to manufacture three thousand egg cards in Higashi-Aburakawa and another three thousand in the nearby town of Ichikawa. They contracted to buy a minimum of five thousand of the cards, for resale to the foreigners. Since the export price of a single card (which would contain thousands of eggs) was close to one ryō, this represented a very significant investment.[48] Chūemon also periodically sent his son cash so that Shōjirō could buy egg cards from other producers and traders in Kōshū and Shinshū. Chūemon's willingness to make a large up-front investment was based on his knowledge of the strong foreign demand for silkworm eggs. "The foreigners are saying they would like to buy a million cards; but I don't think there are that many in the whole of Japan. That is what they are saying about next year. At present I think we need to have large shipments coming in. I am sure I will be able to sell them."[49]

As with silk, the government planned to control the trade in silkworm eggs using a licensing system. Shipments to Yokohama had to be channeled through one of eleven licensed wholesalers in Yokohama, which would handle the sales to foreigners for a standardized commission of 11 percent. But in September 1865, Chūemon himself was granted official status as an egg card wholesaler, enabling him to participate in every stage of the production and marketing cycle from harvesting and mounting of the eggs, to wholesale purchases in the egg-producing regions, to shipment to Yokohama and direct sale to foreign buyers.

One issue that Chūemon faced in his plan to manufacture and sell Kōshū egg cards was the lack of name recognition for his region's produce. Akira Shimizu has shown how important branding was for a variety of products in the Tokugawa era, and how hard established players worked to develop a premium for their brand and to protect its exclusivity.[50] Although Kōshū was one of the top four silk-producing districts in Japan, it had no reputation for silkworm egg cards. Cards from Ōshū (which included Shindatsu) and Shinshū (including Ueda) had a high reputation; those from other provinces were an unknown quantity. On December 2, 1865, Chūemon suggested a plan to pass his Kōshū egg cards off as the produce of Ōshū by bribing a licensed Ōshū merchant. "I believe it is possible to rent a license [kansatsu] [from] . . . one of the Ōshū merchants . . . It might be a good idea to do that and sell at a high price. If you have one of these permits, then without a doubt you can travel freely on the road as the subordinate of one of the egg card merchants of Ōshū."[51]

TALES OF PLENTY

In spite of financial difficulties, management issues, antiforeign extremism, violent outbursts, political tension, and the government's attempts to squeeze trade in Yokohama, Chūemon rode on a wave of prosperity beginning in the mid-1860s. Although statistics for the period are very imperfect, total exports from Yokohama grew from roughly $2.7 million in 1861 to $10.6 million in 1863 and $17.5 million in 1865.[52] Beginning in 1863, Chūemon was able to participate in that growth, and during the course of the following year he underwent a transformation from penurious shopkeeper to prosperous international trader. It seemed that Chūemon's faith in Yokohama as a place not of fear and violence but of opportunity and wealth had been vindicated.

He was not alone in this belief. Both within Japan and globally, Yokohama was quickly gaining a reputation as "if not a land of oil olives and vineyards and flowing with milk and honey, at least a terrestrial paradise, where 'all but the spirit of man was divine.' "[53] Its reputation brought a flood of visitors and migrants to Yokohama, some just to look and admire, others to stay and try their luck at business and financial success. Francis Hall noted in his diary, "Our streets are daily thronged with travelers. Curiosity to see how we tojins live has brought them in such numbers to Yokohama."[54]

The town's growing fame was stoked by a vibrant media industry, transmitting information about the port in broadsheets, illustrated prints, travel and guidebooks, and public exhibitions. Within Japan, the opening of Yokohama stimulated an outpouring of colorful prints and guidebooks describing daily life in the port. Their emphasis was not on politics or violent confrontation but on the town's prosperity and its exotic scenes of daily life. Overseas, word quickly spread of the rapid growth of Yokohama, of the adventure and glamour of life in a country still ruled by feudal princes, and of the quick fortunes being made there. In the early years after the opening of the port, much of the international print media focused on political issues, including attacks on foreigners and rumblings of war between Western countries and the various domains of Japan. But the ships arriving in Shanghai, San Francisco, and ports around the world laden with silk, tea, and gold were undoubtedly carrying a different message—one that was, by the middle of the

1860s, being reinforced by a flood of printed materials on the exotic pleasures of life in Japan.

In an era of unprecedented mobility, anyone able to buy or work his way across the water could find his way to Japan. While Shanghai and other China ports had the most direct connections to the Japanese ports of Nagasaki and Yokohama, new routes were rapidly opening up, whether from Europe via the new railway link to Suez and the Arabian Sea (the canal, which was under construction, would open in 1869); from California, thronged with new settlers and adventurers from the goldfields (regular steamer service between San Francisco and Yokohama opened in 1867, and the American Transcontinental Railway was completed in 1869); or from Siberia, rapidly developing under Russian expansionist policies.

A brief but symbolic meeting that took place in September 1861 illustrates the global currents and connections that brought people from across the world together in Yokohama. Alexander von Siebold was a fifteen-year-old German who had grown up in Nagasaki and was one of the few truly bicultural Europeans in Japan. His father was the famous Japanologist Phillip Franz von Siebold, and Alexander had a half-sister, Kusumoto Ine, who was Japan's first female doctor of Western medicine. Alexander, who was in Edo with his father in 1861, records an evening he spent at the Yokohama Hotel, one of the prime watering holes for Yokohama's merchant community. At the hotel he met Mikhail Bakunin, the aristocratic Russian anarchist who had just escaped from detention in Siberia and found his way via Hakodate to Yokohama. Bakunin, a man of extraordinary charm and self-confidence, had talked his way out of house arrest more or less under the noses of the Russian authorities, and he was now on his way back to Europe to pursue his revolutionary cause. Also present in the lounge of the Yokohama Hotel was Wilhelm Heine, a German artist and radical who had fled Europe following his participation in the Dresden uprising of 1849. By an extraordinary coincidence, Bakunin and Heine were old friends and comrades-in-arms, having manned the barricades together in Dresden. After fleeing Germany, Heine had taken American citizenship and in 1853 had accompanied the Perry expedition to Japan as its official artist. Now he was on his way to the United States to join up on the Union side in the Civil War. A few days later, Bakunin was to accompany Heine on his passage to America. A third companion on that journey (and most likely also present at the encounter described by Siebold) was Joseph Heco (Hamada Hikozō), a Japanese who as a boy had been shipwrecked while on a sightseeing trip to Edo, swept across the Pacific, rescued by an American ship, and brought to San Francisco. After receiving an American education and taking U.S. citizenship, Heco had returned to Japan in 1859 and was now a businessman in Yokohama. Heco probably helped Bakunin make his way to San Francisco and on to New York in the midst of the Civil War. Bakunin, always a friend of the oppressed, was tempted to join Heine on the Union side in the battle against slavery. Instead, he found passage to Europe and went on to become one of the most famous and charismatic radicals of his era.[55]

Their encounter illustrates the liminal nature of Yokohama's urban environment. Four extraordinarily adventurous individuals were able to meet in the legal no-man's-land of the treaty port, protected by the extraterritorial provisions of the treaty as well as by the town's frontier mentality. They came from all corners of the earth and yet they were united by a multicultural outlook that transcended conventional notions of nationality. Neither fully Japanese nor under any other national aegis, Yokohama was a global space whose inhabitants—of whom there were a dozen transient sojourners for every longer-term resident—were united by a desire for adventure, new experiences, and financial gain. The Yokohama Hotel, incidentally, was a fitting setting for this encounter. A former brothel and a notorious hangout for adventurers and ne'er-do-wells, it was described by Ernest Satow in his diary as "a horribly noisy place, where people quarrel & fight, kick up rows till two & three in the morning, & what is worse let off firearms without caring where the bullets go to."[56]

Most new arrivals in Yokohama—Japanese and foreign—were a good deal less colorful. They were tourists, merchants, entrepreneurs, artisans, and shopkeepers who hoped to benefit from the town's vaunted prosperity—many of them people like Chūemon who dreamed of great new opportunities and who had the energy and restless drive to tear up their roots and try their luck in a new commercial space. Some failed and moved on. Others were persuaded by the same restlessness that had brought them to Yokohama to try once again for greener pastures. A few made large fortunes. Many more made a living, stayed, settled, and made of Yokohama a home for themselves and their families.[57]

Few of the new arrivals were able to hold on to a monopoly of any service: European, American, Chinese, and Japanese aspirants were quick to jump in and start up rival enterprises. In spite of the division of Yokohama's urban space into foreign and Japanese quarters, in reality the divisions were fluid, and among the tradesman and artisan classes especially, there were no enduring national boundaries around business advantage. The first Western-style clothes-making store, for example, was run by a Dutchman called P. J. Batteke, who arrived in 1860 together with a Chinese partner. They hired several

Japanese assistants, and one of them, Masuda Bunkichi, soon set up his own shop as a Western-style tailor. Before long, tailoring services were also being offered by Chinese immigrants. Best known is "Cockeye," who began advertising his services in 1864 and who was still in business in 1918. As we will see, Chūemon himself opened a tailor's shop in 1870.

Foreign women, meanwhile, could turn to Mrs. Pearson for dressmaking services. She opened the Yokohama branch of a Shanghai-based company in 1863, then started her own shop in 1866—by which time there were at least four other foreign dressmakers.[58] But before long Japanese clothes makers, too, were getting into the business. Among the first was Sawano Tatsugorō, a maker of Japanese-style tabi socks who had been trained in dressmaking by an American missionary in Kanagawa.[59]

A Japanese, Chūshichi of Aogiya, offered laundry services to the foreign community from the time of the port's opening. Watanabe Zenbei, a shopkeeper from Kumamoto who had previously worked in Nagasaki, opened his laundry service in the early 1860s. There was a stream running in front of the shop, and Watanabe put a large, round stone in the middle of it, which his workers used to beat the dirt out of foreigners' clothes. When the British Twentieth Regiment arrived, with hundreds of men in need of laundry services, Wakisawa Kinjirō received a contract to do all the regiment's washing. However, W. H. Smith, a retired army captain, still saw opportunity in 1865, when he opened the Yokohama Washing Establishment, managed by two Englishwomen. They guaranteed that clothes brought in by 8:00 A.M. would be ready by 5:00 P.M. (except on rainy days).[60]

The first Western-style hairdresser known to have set up shop in Yokohama was a man called Ferguson, who by March 1864 was operating a "Hair Dressing and Shaving Salon" in the Yokohama Hotel. By June 1864, there was also a French hairdresser working in Yokohama, a former employee of the Parisian Salon in Hong Kong.[61] While Europeans offered their services to the established foreign residents of Yokohama, the barbers to the sailors who passed through Yokohama were usually Japanese. According to the reminiscences of Ogura Torakichi, he, together with six or seven other Japanese-trained hairdressers, would go onboard the ships to offer their services. At first they used the traditional Japanese razor, but eventually they learned how to cut with scissors. By the end of the 1860s, they had their own salon in Yokohama, on the premises of a Chinese by the name of Ah Con.[62]

On March 4, 1865, T. S. Smith advertised his services as a "Sign Painter" in the Herald: "All orders neatly executed on reasonable terms." This was a specialized service, but there were many housepainters among the Chinese community—and some, such as Ah Why of number 81, took on Japanese apprentices. According to the recollections of Itō Chōgorō, his grandfather Kametarō started a painting business in Kanagawa, and Kametarō's son Kōtarō moved the business to Yokohama's Kaigan-dōri, where he purchased his imported paint from a Dutch shopkeeper.[63]

By the mid-1860s, there were at least three Swiss watchmakers operating in Yokohama, including James Favre-Brandt, from the famous watchmaking village of Le Locle. Favre-Brandt, who arrived in Japan at the age of twenty-two, set up a business importing guns, machinery, watches, and jewelry. He was soon joined by his brother Charles. The Favre-Brandts were said to have been a major supplier of French precision rifles to the Satsuma and Chōshū forces that defeated the shogunate in 1868. James married a Japanese and never returned to Switzerland.[64] In addition to selling personal watches, the Favre-Brandts also installed institutional clocks such as those at the town hall and post office. They trained several Japanese watchmakers, including Takeuchi Jisaburō and Mizuno Taichi, both of whom traveled to Switzerland to study at the Le Locle watchmaking school.[65]

Not everyone who arrived in Yokohama came in search of money. Many came to acquire some of the many forms of knowledge that were to be found there. English-language skills were to be a vital route to knowledge, success, and influence in the years that followed, and the schools run by Clara Hepburn and other missionaries were training grounds for many ambitious young Japanese. Hayashi Tadasu came to Yokohama in 1862 with his father, who sent him to Clara Hepburn's school to learn English. In 1866 Tadasu was selected by the shogunal government to travel to England for further study, and he went on to become a successful diplomat and eventual foreign minister of Japan. Tadasu's classmate with Clara Hepburn was his nephew Satō Momotarō. Momotarō went on to study in America, becoming a successful retailer and silk merchant in New York before returning to Japan to work for the Ministry of Finance.[66] Kishida Ginkō came to Yokohama to be cured of an eye complaint. After his successful treatment by James Hepburn, Ginkō stayed to help Hepburn produce the first Japanese-English dictionary. He studied English with Joseph Heco and helped Heco produce Japan's first Japanese-language newspaper, the Kaigai shinbun (Overseas news). After making a fortune selling an eye medicine based on Hepburn's treatment, Ginkō went on to become a journalist in Tokyo and a successful entrepreneur promoting Japanese-Chinese cultural exchange.[67] Other notable pupils of Clara Hepburn included future literary entrepreneur Hayashi Yūteki (founder of the Maruzen chain of bookstores); future prime minister Takahashi Korekiyo;

future head of the Mitsui conglomerate Masuda Takashi; and one of Japan's most famous doctors of the nineteenth century, Miyake Hiizu.[68]

Yokohama was also a magnet for artists, craftsmen, and entertainers. They came in response to the lure of new artistic media such as photography, to the excitement of learning new techniques, or to the exotic appeal of Japan as a place of unfamiliar visual wonders. Whatever the pull, they forged their careers in Yokohama's vibrant but competitive commercial culture, and they measured their success in dollars and ryō.

Charles Wirgman arrived in Yokohama in 1861 as a correspondent for the *Illustrated London News*. Wirgman was said to be "nearly bilingual in French and German, and fluent in Italian and Dutch. He knew Greek and Latin, was able to write in Spanish, Portuguese, and quote literary tags in Russian, Scottish, Gaelic and Arabic."[69] He quickly established himself as a prominent figure in the Yokohama community, well known for his offbeat humor and eccentricity. His friend Ernest Satow described him as wearing "wide blue cotton trousers, a loose yellow pongee jacket, no collar, and a conical hat of grey felt," all of which "gave rise to a grave discussion as to whether he was really an European, or only a Chinaman after all."[70] In addition to his work for the *Illustrated London News*, Wirgman founded, in 1862, a satirical magazine, the *Japan Punch*. The magazine, which was printed on woodblocks using Japanese techniques, lampooned the members of the small foreign community. Although Wirgman's cartoons could be sharp at times, the magazine became a treasured asset of the Yokohama foreign community, surviving until 1887. Wirgman was also known as a teacher of Japanese artists, some of whom became prominent in their own right. Best known among them was Goseda Yoshimatsu, whom Wirgman taught beginning in 1865, when Goseda was only twelve years old.[71] Goseda went on to become the first Japanese artist to exhibit in a Paris salon.

Wirgman's close friend and business partner was the photographer Felice Beato. A British citizen born in Corfu and raised in Venice, Beato was one of the earliest war photographers, traveling to Crimea in 1855 to photograph the Russo-British-Turkish conflict. He went on to cover the Indian Mutiny and the second Opium War in China, where a witness described him as "in great excitement, characterising [a] group [of dead soldiers] as 'beautiful,' and begging that it might not be interfered with until perpetuated by his photographic apparatus."[72] Beato used the wet collodion method, which allowed for great sharpness of image and multiple prints from a single negative while requiring only a short exposure time—as little as two seconds in an open-air setting and ten seconds in the studio. However, the negative plate had to be prepared on-site, used immediately, and developed while it was still damp. As a result, Beato carried with him a dark tent as well as the chemicals needed to develop negatives on the spot, in addition to a collection of large, fragile glass plates.[73]

Beato arrived in Yokohama in early 1863, and soon afterward he and Wirgman, whom he had met and collaborated with in China, opened a studio where they jointly exhibited their work. They also collaborated on work for the *Illustrated London News*—Beato taking photographs, from which Wirgman created drawings that he then sent to London to be engraved for the magazine. In July 1863, Wirgman wrote of the popularity of their studio: "My house is inundated with Japanese officers," who "come to see my sketches and my companion Signor B-'s photographs."[74] Wirgman offered sketches, watercolors, and oil paintings of Japanese scenes and people, while Beato sold photographs of Japanese daily life, landscapes and street scenes, as well as portraits and cartes de visite. Both Wirgman and Beato had strong journalistic instincts. Whenever possible, they traveled to the scene of dramatic incidents or military conflict and recorded the scenes firsthand. Like Wirgman, Beato worked closely with Japanese assistants, including Kusakabe Kinbei, who was to go on to become one of Japan's most prominent photographers. Beato also hired a number of Japanese artists, who carefully hand tinted Beato's black-and-white prints, creating exquisite and unique works of art that could be sold at a premium to foreign visitors and residents.

Many Japanese were also captivated by the medium of photography, and before long Beato had competition from several Japanese studios. Among the first was that of Shimooka Renjō, an artist who was drawn to photography when he saw a Dutch daguerreotype in Edo. In 1860 he found work in Yokohama as an assistant to the American merchant Raphael Schoyer. While living with Schoyer, Renjō formed a relationship with an American photographer, John Wilson, who lived in one of Schoyer's rental houses and had a part-time studio in Schoyer's shop. In January 1862 Wilson decided to leave Japan, and Renjō offered to take over his studio, including camera, chemicals, and furnishings. He paid Wilson by giving him a set of eighty-six canvas landscapes illustrating famous places and scenes of daily life in Japan, which he had been working on for the past year under the tutelage of Anna Schoyer, Raphael's wife. Each painting was approximately eight feet by twelve, and the entire collection could be combined into a gigantic panoramic scene, more than a thousand feet long.

Renjō struggled for six months to master the equipment he had purchased and the complex chemical processes involved in making high-quality prints. Wilson's failure to teach him properly was not unusual. Foreign photographers generally did not want Japanese to acquire the skills that might set them up as competitors. One confided that he trained each of his assistants in only a part of the photographic process, to head off their acquisition of competitive skills for as long as possible.[75] But by the end of 1862, Renjō had mastered the technique sufficiently to open his own studio on Benten-dōri, where, according to one Japanese guidebook, he was "able to offer much lower prices," even though "his method does not vary in the least from that of the foreigners."[76] Renjō was to thrive not only in his photographic business (he eventually owned three studios) but also in a variety of other business enterprises, including a part share in one of the first Japanese-owned horse-drawn carriage services. In 1872, Chūemon himself, together with three of his sons and two grandchildren, was to sit for a portrait by Renjō (see chapter 4).

Yokohama was also a magnet for performing artists, including actors, entertainers, acrobats, and circus performers. Visitors to Japan often commented on the traveling entertainers they encountered on street corners, squatting by the side of the highway, or in the precincts of temples and shrines. The acrobats were usually young children, "dressed in loose trousers and coat all in one garment" and sometimes wearing animal-head costumes. They performed to a drum or tambourine accompaniment, performing "the usual tumbling exploits of the circus, somersaults, etc."[77] Children also formed theatrical troupes. Francis Hall watched a performance by a children's troupe, commenting that their acting "was remarkably excellent. That of one little fellow, six and a half years old, was so extraordinary that he would at home have occupied the head of a bill poster in red letters as the 'infantile prodigy' and taken rank at once with the little Batemans."[78]

In addition to acrobatics, the extraordinary spinning-top performances foreigners witnessed also often drew comment, as did the "butterfly trick," in which a performer kept origami paper butterflies in the air through the gentle waving of a fan, "now wheeling and dipping towards it, now tripping along its edge, then hovering over it, as we may see a butterfly do over a flower on a fine summer's day, then in wantonness wheeling away, and again returning to alight, the wings quivering with nervous restlessness! One could have sworn it was a live creature."[79]

Several larger troupes of professional acrobats passed through Yokohama during the mid-1860s, in response to the town's rapid economic growth and its reputation as a door of opportunity. Unlike the street acrobats, who were generally recruited as orphaned children and who seldom rose above the class of beggar entertainers, the Hamaikari, Tetsuwari, Matsui, and Sumidagawa

FIGURE 3.1 Utagawa Yoshikazu, *Foreign Circus in Yokohama* (ca. 1864). *Chadbourne collection, Prints and Photographs Division, Library of Congress, LC-USZC4-10932*

troupes had established a reputation as high-class performers over several generations. The troupes could muster as many as thirty members, and they performed in cities all over Japan.[80]

When in Yokohama, the Japanese troupes encountered several of their foreign counterparts, who were quickly integrating the Japanese treaty ports into their global performance circuits. Among the most colorful was Richard Risley, a celebrated acrobat who was said to possess "a combination of every anatomical beauty of which the human form is capable."[81] Not only a powerful and graceful athlete, he was also a crack shot, master equestrian, ace billiard player, and master of many other sports that required extraordinary physical strength, agility, or reflexes. Risley was also an imaginative entrepreneur with a flair for publicity. He arrived in Yokohama on a world tour with a small traveling circus, but he stayed to run a riding school, manage a tavern, import and sell Chinese ice during the hot summer months, and import a herd of cows from America to create Yokohama's first dairy. As his friend the former theatrical performer and later newspaperman John Black wrote, "Had he been content to make [the dairy] his business, and stick steadily to it, he might long ere this have been a thoroughly independent man."[82]

Risley's entrepreneurial impulsiveness is typical of many Yokohama so-journers, driven by a restless urge to seek greener pastures or to move on from past failures. In Risley's case, his restless entrepreneurialism led him, in 1866, to stake everything he had on an ambitious plan to take a troupe of Japanese performers on a grand tour of the United States and Europe.

CREATING "JAPAN"

The popular perceptions of Yokohama in Japan and the rest of the world were mediated by an outpouring of books, articles, prints, and exhibitions that circulated both within Japan and around the world. From the book-shops of Edo to the exhibition halls of London's Crystal Palace, Yokohama—and, by extension, Japan itself—was on display. The vast majority of the Japan-related works being sold and displayed around the world originated in the commercial marketplace of Yokohama, where writers, artists, photog-raphers, and craftsmen sought to feed the global imagination with works of exquisite craftsmanship, exotic and erotic description, and rich and colorful imagery. Collectively, these globally circulating representations had a pro-found influence on perceptions of Japan and its place in the world. Indeed, they helped create understandings of "Japan" that remain with us to this day.

These influential representations were, in turn, a part of a wave of change that was by now sweeping into Japan through its opened ports and, within a few years, was to transform livelihoods as well as patterns of daily life through-out Japan, and even to influence global economic and cultural trends. Much of the rest of this book is an attempt to address these transformations and to assess the role of Yokohama, and even of individual actors like Chūemon, in the processes of change.

Japanese artists responded to the popular fascination with Japan's exotic new international port of Yokohama with an outpouring of wood-block prints, maps, guidebooks, and broadsheets. During the 1860s, as many two hundred and fifty thousand colorful woodblock prints illustrating scenes of Yokohama life were produced and sold in markets throughout Japan.[83] Whether he was aware of it or not, Chūemon was an actor in a very public performance.

The artists and writers portraying Yokohama to the Japanese public were not much interested in politics, nor in the controversies swirling around the decision to open the ports. They were entertainers, and they saw a market for scenes of daily life that played up the glamour and prosperity of this exotic place that was both a part of Japan and yet "would make one think oneself in the port at Washington in America, or London in England."[84] According to *Yokohama Tales: Flower of the Port (Yokohama kidan: Minato no hana)*, "Since trade has been permitted in our sacred country, all sorts of goods have been exchanged, both bought and sold, and for both purchases and sales the amount has been like nothing seen before in this country, with transactions amounting to ten, twenty, or even fifty thousand *ryō* per day; indeed there is no limit to the amount . . . The town is truly blessed to have achieved such prosperity before even five years have passed."[85]

In many cases, the Yokohama portrayed in the lavish and colorful prints was pure fantasy. Some artists never even visited Yokohama, drawing instead on existing printed sources such as imported foreign magazines or Japanese prints of life in the Dutch trading enclave in Nagasaki. And even in cases where the artists were physically present in Yokohama, their work often mixed actual observation with extrapolation and fantasy. Woodbock prints and illustrated books from the early 1860s invariably portrayed beautiful and glamorous foreign women in the streets of Yokohama, even though the actual number of European and American women in the town could be counted on one hand. By an even greater stretch of the imagination, Yokohama prints often showed foreign women, including those who appear to be the wives of merchants, consorting happily with Japanese courtesans from the brothel quarter, even playing games with them or accompanying them in musical duets. The result was an image of life in the port that Chūemon surely would not have recognized, even though he must have approved of the glamorous and prosperous image of the town that the prints and books conveyed.[86]

At least ten illustrated guidebooks to Yokohama were published during the 1860s—generally describing themselves as virtual guides for those unable to visit the town in person. *Unusual Stories of the Five Nations in Yokohama (Chinji gokakoku Yokohama hanashi)*, for example, was written "for women and children of distant provinces" and used "simple children's words while setting down my account of the actual things I have witnessed."[87] The typical format of the guidebooks was to take the reader on a "walking tour" of the town, visiting and describing the different neighborhoods along the way, with lavish details about the strange and exotic lives of the foreigners—Europeans, Americans, Chinese, Africans, Javanese, and others. *Flower of the Port* starts with a ferry ride out into the bay. From here,

the view from the water is truly incomparable. To the west, Mount Fuji is in full view. To the right are the mountains of Chichibu, Sagami, and

FIGURE 3.2 Foreigners visiting a brothel in Miyozakichō are surprised by the beauty of the interior and the elegance of the courtesan. *Kikuen Rōjin, Yokohama kidan: Minato no hana* (Kinkōdō Zō, *ca.* 1864)

Kōshū. To the left is Mount Amagi at Hakone. Nearby, Kamakura and Kanazawa are within arm's reach; and to the east, Mount Kanō and Mount Nokogiri in Bōsō are clearly visible. Right in front of one's eyes are the fishermen at work, and one can see the famous views of Kanagawa . . . To the west, there is a fine view of the foreign ships flying their blue, yellow, and red flags. Seeing the foreign houses in the distance one would not believe oneself in Japan.[88]

Japanese representations of Yokohama, whether in books or prints, tended to dwell on the same themes again and again: exotic sights and sounds; glamour and prosperity; intriguing customs; awe-inspiring technologies; and alluring foreign women, of whom it was said "one might well think they were angels descended from the heavens."[89] The guides typically included lavish descriptions of the Miyozaki brothel quarter, where "the lanterns coming and going at the main gate are more frequent than fireflies.

The cherry trees in the main street are so bright that they do battle with the courtesans . . . Morning or night, you can find Japanese and foreigners mixed together as they explore its delights. The courtesans in the street are gorgeously dressed, combining foreign and Japanese clothes as they please . . . If one can disport oneself even once in this quarter, one's spirit will soar to the heavens, and one will forget to return to one's home."[90]

The guidebooks dwelled at length on aspects of Yokohama life that Chūemon and his family may have quickly become used to but that most Japanese would have found both strange and fascinating: the daily routines of foreigners ("They get up at 5:30 and immediately enter the bath. The water is lukewarm, like water left to warm up in the sun. Moreover, there are some people who insist on bathing only in cold water, summer and winter"); foreign clothes ("They are always of black wool, which has an excellent texture, like that of leather. When it comes to the neatness of their appearance, they do not differ from the Japanese at all"); foreign houses ("They are built of cut stones, and the windows are of glass . . . When it gets dark, the covers are removed from the glass lamps, and the brightness is such that even a single hair is clearly visible"); foreign games such as billiards ("The strangeness of this practice is really a matter for surprise . . . They will bet one hundred, five hundred, or even one thousand dollars on the result");[91] the foreigners' love for their pets ("If by chance a dog should go missing, I believe the owner would search for it like a parent for his lost child, parting the undergrowth and calling its name");[92] and the foreigners' penchant for "walking throughout the city even when they have no business to transact. This is something that is unknown among our people."[93]

The guidebooks' authors were also fascinated by Western technology: steamships, clocks and watches, and photography in particular. The steamship, for example, "is powered by a wheel, and it will proceed even if there is no wind at all . . . It is hard to describe the perfection of its construction."[94] Pocket watches were fascinating not only for their elaborate construction ("The inner workings are very complicated: I could neither draw a picture of them nor adequately describe them in words") but also for their usefulness in daily life. "[The foreigners] will not be separated from them even for a short time . . . because of their convenience in daily life. For example, if you were to make an appointment for a meeting at a particular time on the next day, when that time comes around, you can be sure of coming home on time to await your guest. Your guest in turn will consult his watch and will be sure to be on time for the appointment."[95] As for photography, it "transfers through [a] mirror the exact and detailed shape—right down to the colors—of people,

FIGURE 3.3 Foreigners playing billiards. *Utagawa Sadahide*, Yokohama kaikō kenbunshi (*ca. 1863*)

or places, or landscapes." Imagine if, using this technology, "you could give a command to a painter while you were living and have an exact likeness made of yourself, which you could turn into a hanging scroll that you could pass down to your descendants—how close you would seem to them!"[96]

Although these representations deliberately played up the exotic and unusual aspects of life in Yokohama, they also had the effect of familiarizing Japanese readers and viewers with foreign lifestyles, foreign technologies, and foreign values. The commentary in the guidebooks was not always admiring. The author of *Flower of the Port*, for example, found that "the Westerners are without exception interested only in the study of the sciences. As for the pleasure that we Japanese take in elegance, taste, or beauty, I have as yet seen none of this."[97] While maintaining an overall tone of humorous observation, the guides made some sharp comments on many of the foreigners' habits, from the jealousy of their women ("ten times more so than Japanese women"),[98] to their permitting dogs inside their houses ("In the old days, there was a similar custom among the people of Ezo [Hokkaido], but now there is no such thing."),[99] to their practice of gruesome trades such as butchering: "All sorts of

FIGURE 3.4 Utagawa Sadahide, *Banquet at a Foreign Mercantile House in Yokohama* (1861). *Chadbourne collection, Prints and Photographs Division, Library of Congress, LC-USZC4-9989*

animals are being herded and beaten, screaming tremendously. There is a sound of iron chains rattling, and the lament of the birds penetrates the ear. Truly, this is what the birds' hell must be like."[100] Another favorite topic was the drunken sailors who were a daily sight in the port.

But even as they observed customs that would have seemed distasteful to many Japanese, the guidebooks seldom passed direct judgment. Meat eating, for example, "has been their everyday food since they were children so they do not dislike the custom."[101] There was so much that was novel about the foreign lifestyles on display in Yokohama, one has the sense that the authors preferred to suspend judgment even about habits that would be horrifying or disgusting to the average Japanese.

Indeed, even as they employed traditional techniques of glamorizing and exoticizing foreigners, the authors were conveying to their readers a radically different way of looking at the world that required the suspension of many preconceived ideas. For example, in a discussion of race one can see both criticism of the institution of slavery and at the same time a qualified acceptance of Western ideas of racial hierarchy:

> There are also many foreigners called blacks [kuronbō]. These people were born in Arabia, and the skin of both men and women is extremely black. One might compare them to a crow: they are black to the tips of their toes. They are by nature stupid, and their actions are close to those of animals. Previously, the Westerners treated them just like cows or horses, buying and selling them and using them as their slaves. Eventually, some of the more intelligent ones became extremely angry, saying, 'We are people of the world just like everyone else. Why, then, should we be bought and sold like cows and horses? We should be hired for a proper wage.' After that, they became servants in the normal fashion.[102]

One can sense here a probing of the conflicting views about race that were circulating in international society—the American Civil War was still raging at the time—and also perhaps an underlying insecurity about Japan's own place in that hierarchy. It was important for Japanese commentators to clearly distance themselves from races that were considered "by nature stupid" while at the same time refusing to condone a system of racial hierarchy that might in turn consign the Japanese to a lower rung on the perceived hierarchical ladder.

In addition to representations of foreign lifestyles and technology portrayed in the printed media, Yokohama was also a physical display case for foreign goods, lifestyles, ideas, and institutions. Imported textiles, machinery, and even steamships were prominently for sale in the harbor and the warehouses of the foreign merchants. Japanese buyers could bargain for silk-spinning equipment, cameras, beer and champagne, rifles (prohibited by treaty but a major trade item nonetheless), kerosene, sugar, medical implements, livestock, bricks and glass, and a host of other imported goods. Visitors to Yokohama also had the opportunity to observe Western institutions—such as hospitals, law courts, and military parades—firsthand.

As a merchant in Yokohama's international marketplace, Chūemon was an agent in the introduction of Western technologies and lifestyles into Japan, even though in his private life and political outlook he remained rather conservative. Chūemon was a middle-aged villager, a product of the Tokugawa political and social environment. There is no reason to think that he admired Western values, embraced foreign lifestyles, or shared the

apparent admiration of the guidebook authors for the habits and technologies of the foreigners' daily lives. In the letters, his main concern is not to
promote new ways of living but to emphasize the enormous commercial
opportunity represented by the Yokohama market. Nevertheless, Chūemon
occasionally discussed the prospects for selling imported Western products in his home province of Kōshū, and he and Naotarō actually tested the
market in a variety of imported goods—apparently with little success (these
ventures are taken up in chapter 4).[103] Chūemon was also interested in Western
machinery, discussing with some excitement the arrival of a shipment of
cotton-spinning machines in Yokohama. He also discussed the possibility
of purchasing rice-hulling machines capable of processing one thousand
bales of rice per day, concluding, however, that they were inappropriate for
Kōshū farmers, most of whom had no more than two acres of rice fields per
family.[104] Chūemon does not discuss the ways in which these foreign lifestyles and technologies affected his daily life, but he must surely have felt their
influence. He certainly became familiar with foreign textiles and clothing:
not only did he try selling them in Kōshū but, as we will see, he also eventually
tried his hand at setting up his own Western-style tailor shop in Yokohama.

   Even as Chūemon participated in the international marketplace and (at
times) helped spread foreign goods and ideas into his home province, we can
also—in spite of his innate conservatism—see him being shaped by the new
ideas circulating in Yokohama. This is most evident in his developing understanding of nationality and nationhood. Like most people in Japan's two-
hundred-plus domains, Chūemon identified first and foremost with his local
and regional communities. For the majority of people, this meant the village.
Villagers depended on one another for mutual assistance, labor cooperation,
communal water and other resource supplies, and contributions to the
payment of the village tax burden. While wealthier Japanese were remarkably
mobile by the mid-nineteenth century, probably most villagers had seldom if
ever been beyond their nearest provincial town. The decisions that were made
and the actions taken within the village community could mean the difference
between subsistence and destitution. Next to the village was the domainal
administration. Villagers paid their taxes to the domain, and the domainal
authorities held the power of life and death over them. The domainal lord
was the ruler to whom villagers and townsmen owed both tribute and loyalty,
and for most, their identity was closely tied to their domain and its ruling
family.

   Beyond his village of Higashi-Aburakawa, Chūemon belonged to Kōshū.
Kären Wigen has shown how the historical provinces of Japan, which were

meaningful administrative units in ancient times but had long since been replaced by feudal domains (of which there might be several in any one of Japan's sixty-six historical provinces), were reconstituted in the Tokugawa era as units of regional identity. This was based on imagination more than political reality (except in a few domains where the domain and the province were coterminous) and abetted by mapmakers and others who were promoting regional consciousness, often for economic reasons.[105] Certainly for Chūemon the province of Kōshū was the primary location of his identity beyond his village of Higashi-Aburakawa. The name of his shop was Kōshūya, he described himself as representing the products of Kōshū, he hosted and represented visiting merchants from Kōshū, and when in his letters he referred to his "country" (kuni), he almost always meant Kōshū.

It is much harder to assess how people like Chūemon understood the concept of "Japan." Mitani Hiroshi has written of a "protonation-state" arising in the eighteenth century as educated Japanese under the long and peaceful Tokugawa reign began to conceive of an "imagined community" of the Japanese nation through the influence of extensive domestic travel networks and the distribution of nationalistic publications.[106] Certainly, most people had some sense that they were not just domainal subjects but also "Japanese"— Nipponjin. Even villagers would have understood their connection to other Japanese through language, history, highways and commerce, sites of spiritual power and pilgrimage, and perhaps even through some concept of political unity. But "Japan" itself must have been a fuzzy notion. Did it mean loyalty to the emperor? Did it mean obligations beyond those demanded by regional feudal authorities? Did it mean common beliefs and symbols? While nationalist ideologies were gaining traction among the educated classes, it is hard to imagine that most villagers would have understood or cared much about the implications of a Japanese national identity.

Chūemon was a subject of a directly administered shogunal domain and he had lived in the shogunal capital, so for him, if "Japan" meant anything, it probably meant the realm of the shogun. Yet Chūemon's encounters with foreigners in Yokohama, and especially the political clashes of the early 1860s, must surely have pushed him to rethink his identity. In his letters, the foreigners remained ijin (aliens) until the very end of the decade, when he began to use the politer gaikokujin (foreigners). But as Chūemon became comfortable with the idea and also the reality of the ijin, he must have come to understand that the word had real meaning only when contrasted with an implied "us." And Chūemon's experiences in Yokohama must have made it starkly clear to him that the "us" was not "people of Kōshū" or even "subjects of the shogun" but "Nipponjin," or Japanese people. The evolving political crisis of the mid-1860s forced him to develop a new understanding of the meanings of "Japan" even as the social and political structures of his country were falling into chaos and collapse. It is no coincidence that Chūemon's first use in the surviving letters of the term "Nipponjin" came at the moment of greatest conflict with the West, as the shogunate braced for a massed attack by a foreign naval alliance (described in chapter 2).

We can see something similar happening in the guidebooks to Yokohama, which wrote of the foreigners as an exotic "other" in Japan's midst but which also portrayed an implied "Japaneseness" in contrast to that other. To be "Japanese" meant to be justifiably uncomfortable with the consumption of meat, drunken behavior, the enslavement of blacks, or the disregard for elegance and good taste; but it might also mean to be behind in technology, unadventurous, unable to afford the comforts that foreigners expected, unaware of time and punctuality, and to acknowledge the need to question long-held assumptions about food, clothing, medicine, or Japan's place in the world. Yokohama stimulated new concepts and understandings of the meanings of "Japan." This reformulation of national identity was a vital bridge to the new world of national unification and imperial loyalty that emerged from the overthrow of the shogunate in 1868.

Even more than Chūemon, his children must have become accustomed to foreign ways of living from relatively early in their lives. For Naotarō, who arrived in Yokohama at the age of twenty-two, and even more for his younger brother Katsusuke, who came to join his father at the age of seven, the international community of Yokohama with its varied lifestyles and global connections was a part of the fabric of their lives, which they probably more or less took for granted. They were the children of a new global era, for whom distinctions between "Japanese" and "Western," "traditional" and "modern" might have seemed a little quaint and outdated.

In the West, too, the outpouring of information and artifacts from Yokohama prompted new assessments of "Japan" and its meanings. There was a fascination with the mysterious, hidden country that was now reluctantly allowing its secrets to be pried open (at least, this was how many foreign commentators perceived it). At times it seemed that any visitor to the treaty port of Yokohama was required to write an account of his or her experiences. Some of these contributions were humble: Francis Hall, an American merchant, sent regular dispatches to his hometown newspaper, the *Elmira Gazette*. Others were more grandiose: Rutherford Alcock, English minister to Japan, wrote a wordy two-volume memoir, prompting one of his subordinates to lament that "he would have been a greater man if he had never written a book about a country which he did not understand."[107] In the earlier part of the 1860s, writers tended to focus on the dramatic murders of foreigners, the antiforeign sentiment in Japan, and the duplicitous dealings of Japanese officials, while illustrators showed scenes of official negotiations, Japanese government leaders, and violent scenes such as the foreign attacks on Kagoshima and Shimonoseki. But foreign readers also clamored for vivid descriptions of Japanese daily life and social mores.

Certain themes quickly became standard attributes of the Japanese as portrayed to Western audiences. They included alluring and exotic physical appearance, gorgeous clothing, medieval martial display, a casual lack of concern about public nudity, unawareness of time or the pressures of modern life, and unusual skills such as storytelling or paper folding. These attributes combined to create an exotic and sometimes erotic image. This would have been a familiar combination to foreign audiences. Many colonized regions were similarly exoticized and sexualized, in ways that tended to reinforce the audience's sense of the "otherness" and difference of the colonized peoples and of its own power and superiority over those peoples. In the case of Japan, there was particular interest because the country for so long had successfully prevented itself from being put on global display. Now, there was a sense that Japan could be "opened," "revealed," "bared," and indeed this was in many cases done with literal representations of naked Japanese.

Charles Wirgman was one of the most prolific commentators on Japan through his regular contributions to the influential *Illustrated London News*. Wirgman often used Yokohama as a model of "Japan" in miniature. In addition to political news and the occasional travelogue, when the opportunity arose, Wirgman submitted frequent sketches of daily life in words and pictures, based on scenes he observed in Yokohama. Such sketches might be a miscellany of seemingly unconnected details, as in a lithograph titled *The Storyteller (a Daily Scene) in Yokuhama* (sic) with its accompanying commentary: "He takes up his post on a table every afternoon, and recites to an admiring audience who stand and squat around him; sometimes he accompanies himself on the banjo, as I have shown . . . The men for the most part have their towels round their heads, and are not remarkable for pegtops or, in fact, any breeches at all. The girls are on their wooden pattens, and they seem to find no difficulty in running in them."

The lithograph illustrates some of the themes described: the near nakedness of many of the men, the towels around their heads, and the sense

FIGURE 3.5 Charles Wirgman, *The Storyteller (a Daily Scene) in Yokuhama* (sic). Illustrated London News, *August 10, 1861*

of timelessness as a leisurely audience gathers unhurriedly for the daily performance.[108]

Wirgman's partner, Felice Beato, contributed to the creation of an exotic and erotic image of Japan through his souvenir photography. His studio portraits were generally taken using paid models, and they might include images of women at the toilette, often partially clothed; naked porters and grooms, sometimes heavily tattooed; samurai in armor; and artisans such as carpenters or printmakers pursuing their craft. Already by the time the albums were produced, many of the customs they portrayed were falling into disuse. Warriors preferred guns to swords, and by the end of the 1860s, the wealthy preferred to travel by horse-drawn carriage or Japan's newest contribution to public transport, the rickshaw, rather than the palanquins portrayed in the images. Like his prints, which he fixed with chemicals to capture an unchanging image for decades to come, Beato and other artists were deliberately preserving and immobilizing a culture that already existed more in the artist's imagination than in the realities of daily life. These images of a "traditional" Japan helped create an imagined past that remains with us to this day.[109]

However, Beato also helped develop appreciation for Japan's highly developed artistic and craft traditions, as he used Japanese artists to turn each

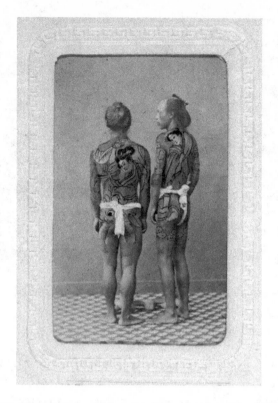

FIGURE 3.6   Felice Beato, Betto (groom), tattooed à la mode (ca. 1863–1867). *Prints and Photographs Division, Library of Congress, LC-USZC4-14496*

of his black-and-white prints into an individual work of art.[110] As the number of visitors to Yokohama increased in the later 1860s and beyond, Beato began concentrating on the production of souvenir photographic albums that combined hand-tinted photographic images, printed commentary, and gorgeous bindings in leather and lacquered wood. The artifacts that he produced were exquisite examples of Japanese craftsmanship, and they helped produce an image of Japan as a place of refined and sophisticated artistic sensibilities.

Japanese cultural entrepreneurs also participated in the creation of an exotic "Japan." In his Yokohama photographic studio, Shimooka Renjō catered to both Japanese and foreign customers. For the benefit of foreign customers, Renjō followed Beato's lead, hiring female models and photographing them in a variety of poses. Like Beato, he had many of his photographs hand tinted by Japanese artists. His friend Samuel Cocking recalled that "when [Renjō] first started in business, instead of receiving payment from his sitters he was obliged to reverse the operation and pay them to come, and has given as much as twelve shillings to a good-looking Japanese lady to have her portrait taken. But even this upside-down state of affairs answered his purpose very well in a commercial sense, as he used to sell copies of such to foreigners at three dollars each."[111]

This trend toward portraying exoticized and sometimes eroticized images of daily life in Japan mixing Western and Japanese artistic styles became a distinctive genre, centered in Yokohama and aimed at presenting a commodified image of Japan for sale to the outside world.

At the same time, however, Japanese photographers like Renjō were able to add their own inflections to the developing image of "Japan." Although Renjō catered to the foreign taste for the exotic and the erotic, he also used his art to reflect a more robust and assertive image of "Japan," one that might even have something to teach the rest of the world. Many of his portraits show Japanese people engaged in aesthetic practices such as flower arranging and the tea ceremony, while also incorporating into his work techniques derived from his training as a painter and lithographer. His promotion (both as artist and patron) of a variety of Japanese artistic traditions contributed to the rapid assimilation of Japanese artistic and aesthetic traditions in the European and American arts, which, beginning in the 1860s, were swept up in a wave of japonisme.[112]

Like Renjō's portraits, traveling exhibits of Japanese arts, crafts, and manufactures also showed a dual agenda of portraying a richly exotic "Japan" to feed the Western imagination and profiling the excellence of Japan's manufacturing and craft traditions—as well as, at times, highlighting Japan's rapid adaptation to new techniques.

Japanese art, crafts, literature, antiquities, and daily life were placed on display at galleries and exhibitions in cities in Europe and America. After the immense success of London's Crystal Palace exposition of 1851, international expositions became a regular feature of the European capitals: there were two major expositions during the 1860s, the Great International Exposition at London's Crystal Palace from May to November 1862 and the Exposition universelle d'art et d'industrie in Paris in 1867.

At the time of the Great International Exposition, London was experiencing a burst of Japan fever. More than a dozen books on Japan appeared during the course of the year, including Sir Rutherford Alcock's ponderous two-volume memoir of his stint as Britain's envoy to Japan. Meanwhile, the shogunate's first diplomatic mission to Europe arrived in London on April

FIGURE 3.7 Shimooka Renjō, *Woman with Pipe* (ca. 1865–1875). *Courtesy of Tom Burnett Collection, New York*

30, 1862. The members of the delegation lodged at Claridge's Hotel and visited the London Docks, the Tower of London, and Kew Gardens, as well as taking trips to Liverpool and Birmingham to inspect industrial and naval facilities.[113] During their visits they were photographed, drawn, lithographed, and painted: they were as much an object of display as the exhibits of Japanese arts and crafts that were springing up around London.

On May 22, John Wilson put Shimooka Renjō's massive collection of panoramic paintings on display at the London Polytechnic, advertising it as "Wilson's Grand Panorama, painted in oil, by Japanese Artists, on 9,000 feet [*sic*] of canvas, and showing with scrupulous fidelity the Costumes, Temples, Streets, Bridges, Scenery, and Rivers of the Japanese Empire. This unique and curious Panorama was painted secretly by native artists, who would, if discovered, have incurred the penalty of death, and it is exhibited Daily, at 1.30 and 5.30. Admission, 1s."[114] The *Illustrated London News* reported on the exhibit: "Japan, once a sealed book, is now unclasped, and we may freely inspect its treasures. It not only permits travellers to visit it, but has sent its Ambassadors to visit us. These are now amongst us, and may examine these pictures for themselves, and learn how vain were the State precautions that were taken to prevent such a result . . . The state of Japanese art is exemplified by the various pictures presented, which in that and other respects will prove highly instructive to European visitors."[115]

Although the Japanese representatives did not visit the "Grand Panorama" (and they would certainly not have wished any harm to the artist, since the images betrayed no state secrets, conveying in fact a desirable image of Japan as a peaceful, beautiful, and cultured nation), they did visit the Great International Exposition at the Crystal Palace. This lavish display of the diverse arts and manufactures of the nations of the world attracted six million visitors over the course of its six months. It was a showcase for national pride and national aspiration. While the shogunal government—still reluctant to engage in international relations—was not a formal participant in the exhibition, the British envoy, Sir Rutherford Alcock, had provided a large collection of Japanese artifacts from his personal collection. They included examples of Japanese crafts such as personal accessories, paper manufactures, porcelain, arms and armor, and printing, as well as samples of Japanese money, drugs, and medical implements.[116] Many of these would certainly have been purchased in the curio shops of Yokohama's Japanese quarter. In an admiring review, the London *Times* praised the exquisite craftsmanship of the miniature sculptures—probably netsuke (belt ornaments) and inro (containers for personal belongings)—while also commenting on their "comic genius." The objects of porcelain on display were "if anything, almost thinner than egg-shell. Even the renowned specimens of this china made at Worcester are mere earthenware compared to them." Similarly, the swords on display—which included one of the swords used in an assassination attempt on Alcock himself—were "of a most exquisite temper." And the Japanese skills in papermaking "have undoubtedly obtained an excellence and skill of which we in Europe know nothing."[117]

Five years later, the shogunate was an enthusiastic participant in the Paris exposition of 1867, sending a large consignment of arts, crafts, and manufactures there for the show. This exposition was on a colossal scale. Occupying a one-hundred-fifty-acre site in the Champs de Mars, it attracted fifteen million visitors during its six months of display. Now anxious to show itself as a worthy aspirant to join the community of modern nations, the Japanese government sent the younger brother of the shogun to represent Japan and to receive his education in France. But the shogunate's message was muddied by the fact that the domains of Satsuma and Hizen also submitted competing exhibits. While the shogunate was attempting to claim a position among the "civilized" powers that shared their industrial products at such events, the multiple exhibits vividly highlighted Japan's lack of national unity.

Nevertheless, the exhibits were hugely admired and they did much to enhance Japan's image both as a fascinating and exotic culture and as a center of manufacturing excellence and rapid modernization. The shogunal exhibit was housed in three specially built structures: models of Japanese merchant and artisan houses and a miniature reconstruction of a daimyo's palace. The houses were furnished to show the living conditions of their inhabitants, thus creating an ethnographic space where Japanese lives were placed on display. But the exhibit also highlighted the excellence of Japan's artistic and manufacturing traditions, its rich natural resources, and its rapid adoption of modern techniques. The collection included a large map of the city of Edo, examples of books and other printed media, an exhibition of paper work, extensive displays of Japanese silk production and manufacture, displays of raw materials such as iron, quartz, and bronze, and a wide variety of artworks: paintings on silk by famous Edo artists, watercolor portraits of young Japanese, miniature sculptures used for personal ornamentation, bronze vases decorated with birds and flowers, fine porcelains, and lacquered furniture. A notable feature of the exhibit was a display of four life-size models of Japanese samurai warriors, armed and mounted on horseback. While the models emphasized the warriors' medieval glamour, at the base of the display were two boxes of modern rifles, manufactured by Japanese craftsmen. Commenting on the modern weapons, the steamship-equipped navy and Western-trained army that the shogunate was creating, and the large number of Japanese coming to France and quickly adopting European lifestyles, the Revue des deux mondes concluded that "Japan seems, in a word, to have decided to put itself on an equal footing with the modern nations."[118] While it catered to the foreign desire for the exotic, the exhibition also helped spread an understanding of Japan as highly cultured, technically adept, and committed to rapid modernization. The exhibits of Japanese arts triggered a wave of interest among French painters and designers, helping launch the fad for japonisme that was to remain a deep influence in European art for the rest of the century.

Yet another route through which "Japan" was put on display was the highly visible tours of troupes of Japanese performing artists, particularly acrobats. Altogether at least three troupes set off in 1866, six in 1867, and many more in the following years.[119] Indeed, theater historian Mihara Aya sees the treaty ports of Yokohama and Nagasaki as having been quickly integrated into a "theatrical network of the Pacific Rim,"[120] a network that included Japanese artists performing overseas, foreign artists in Japan, and Japanese and foreign impresarios. Indeed, in the theatrical world, then as today, nationality was less important legally or culturally than as a construct employed in the service of a brand. The troupes emphasized their "Japaneseness," and they played up to the strong demand for exotic display. At the same time, they gained a reputation for extraordinary physical prowess and became the objects of admiration and even adulation among the theater-going public.

The Hamaikari troupe was one of the first to embark on an overseas tour—a tour that would take it across America and Europe and last more than two years. The troupe was sponsored and managed by the American impresario and entrepreneur Richard Risley. The budget for this ambitious venture was a hundred thousand dollars, an enormous sum that Risley raised together with three partners from the Yokohama foreign community.

Risley and the "Imperial Japanese Troupe" arrived in San Francisco in January 1866 and went on to Philadelphia, Washington, New York, London, Paris, Amsterdam, Lisbon, and Madrid. The tour was an extraordinary success, making international stars out of some of its young performers. Its performances were sold out for months on end, even when the troupe performed in some of the largest performance spaces in the world, including the massive Cirque Napoléon in Paris. A large part of its members' acclaim was owing to their skill in such unusual acts as top spinning and the butterfly trick, as well as their extraordinary acrobatic performances. But a part also came from their exoticism—their unusual clothing and grooming, their unfamiliar language, and their props and stage sets. As one reviewer put it, "The mere sight of these yellow men—with their shaven temples, slanted eyes, flat noses between two protruding cheekbones, and blue-black hair rolled in a top-knot on top of the skull—transports us into a world as eccentric as that of another planet."[121]

The most celebrated member of the troupe was the twelve-year-old Hamaikari Umekichi, who became a household name throughout America and Europe as "Little All Right." He acquired this name because, after completing his extraordinary feats of acrobatic skill and courage, he would throw his arms up in the air and shout, "All right!" This may at first have been the only English he knew, but his willingness to engage with the audience in their own language shows the child's cultural and linguistic flexibility. Umekichi was truly a child of Japan's international era, even as he was seen as a representation of all that was traditional and exotic in Japanese culture. In many ways he was a symbol of "Japan" as a cultural export—commercial, enterprising, and looking both forward and back as Japan sought its place in the international "comity of nations."[122]

A DARKENING WORLD

In Japan, the middle years of the 1860s brought increased political instability, widespread economic disruption, and unprecedented peasant protest as the Tokugawa political and social order began to fall apart. Rumors of attacks on Yokohama were a regular event through the last months of 1863 and into 1864, with the warriors of Mito usually held up as the most likely perpetrators. Mito was radically antiforeign and remained opposed to the policy of opening Japan to foreign trade. But it was also deeply divided, between those who remained loyal to the shogun and those who felt that the shogunate was as much to blame as the foreigners for Japan's troubles. By 1863, the domain was virtually in a state of civil war, as the more extreme antiforeign factions resorted to assassination and terror in order to overcome the resistance of the domain's supporters of the shogunate.

The political destabilization of Mito was accompanied by a general breakdown in law and order throughout the Kantō region. One village headman, Kojima Tamemasa, reported in his diary on ten murders in the surrounding area. In response, Kojima and other village heads raised militias, arming them with guns purchased in Edo, swords, spears, and, when nothing else was available, bamboo staves.[123] Although military affairs had traditionally been the domain of the samurai class, local administrators began surveying villagers to identify manpower and guns available in the event of an emergency. In Kōshū, every man between the ages of seventeen and fifty was considered eligible for militia service. In a country where farmers were prohibited from owning weapons, a surprising number were identified. In one district of 132 villages, 280 guns were registered as well as 1,236 able-bodied men.

In April 1864, around two hundred Mito samurai dedicated to the expulsion of foreigners and the closing of the ports gathered at Mount Tsukuba, just to the northeast of the Kantō Plain. Their stated goal was to march on

Yokohama and implement the order to expel the foreigners. As their numbers grew, they began terrorizing the local communities, which they forced to supply their needs. In June, they burned the provincial town of Tochigi. One group launched a bold raid on Sendagaya, on the outskirts of Edo, where they raided a shogunal ammunition store.

Chūemon was in Edo to witness the aftermath of this raid.

> I checked to see if the heads of the rōnin were exposed in Nihonbashi as you reported, but they were not. Perhaps they are at Ryōgoku Bridge. They are saying that the rōnin of Edo are now on their way to attack Yokohama . . . A force of two hundred guards with guns left Edo yesterday at the fifth hour and arrived here today at the fifth hour. In addition, the lords of Sakai and Aoyama have sent many men, who are gradually arriving. So we are in a very disturbed condition . . . It is said that the commanding general of the lord of Mito has asked why any dealing with foreigners is necessary. On the thirteenth at around the seventh hour, the lord of Mito and his household passed through Kanagawa. If they encountered any foreigners, his men were instructed to cut them down and expel all the foreigners . . . Some senior officials of the house of Mito have demanded that the foreigners should be expelled.

Chūemon took care to add that "here in the port everyone is behaving as normal, and trade is carrying on."[124]

In early July 1864, the shogunal government sent a force of almost four thousand men to Mount Tsukuba to crush the insurgents. During the second half of 1864, battles raged across the Mito domain, with the rebels even besieging their own daimyo's castle at one point. At the beginning of November the shogunal army, now numbering more than ten thousand, defeated the rebels at the battle of Nakaminato. But more than a thousand rebels escaped and began advancing on the Kantō. By the end of 1864, an army of eleven hundred well-armed men was advancing through the mountains, its numbers swelling along the way, and nobody knew if and when it would emerge at the gates of Yokohama.

Eventually it became clear that the goal of the rebels was not Yokohama but Kyoto, where they planned to plead their cause directly to the emperor. This was a relief for the residents of Yokohama, but it was alarming for the people of Kōshū, who now faced the possibility of the rebel army marching through their province. The shogunal authorities ordered domains and territories along all the possible routes to mobilize. The Kōshū authorities summoned the militias, sending some of the men to neighboring Shinshū to protect the crucial Nakasendō highway, with its direct line to Kyoto. Others were set to patrol regional highways. The Kōshū villagers who stayed home were on a state of high alert, with frequent false alarms. In Utada village, a farmer's maid accidentally pulled down the woodpile behind the house and screamed, prompting alarm bells to be rung throughout the region.[125]

At the beginning of January 1865, Chūemon commented on the unrest: "I understand that there are many reports of rōnin in Kōshū. We hear that all the officials have been mobilized. It sounds as though it is very turbulent. Certainly these are eventful times. I hope that there will be no interference with trade, but please consult with me at any time."[126]

In fact, the Mito warriors never entered Kōshū. Instead, they forged on through the mountains and descended on the Nakasendō in Shinshū. There, they were surrounded and defeated by a large shogunal army. More than two thousand rebel soldiers were imprisoned—virtually the entire force. Of those, almost five hundred were executed or died in prison. But even as the threat of the Mito rebels receded, the security situation in Kōshū remained turbulent. Unrest, poverty, and stretched resources combined to raise concerns about crime in a generally stable society. In October 1865, one of Chūemon's close business associates reported having his shop burgled and one hundred fifty egg cards stolen (the thief was later caught trying to sell the cards in Yokohama).[127] Some time later, Chūemon's own home in Higashi-Aburakawa was burgled, though the losses were minor. Chūemon, who had been frequently reminding his son to lock the doors at night, now exhorted him to "get a workman to strengthen the doors."[128]

On July 28, 1866, Chūemon reported yet another threat to the security of the Kantō region:

They are saying that large numbers of rōnin have assembled . . . near Hachiōji in Bushū, no one knows how many, and that they are pressing forward. They say that yesterday there was great destruction in Tokorozawa, and that they are steadily making their way to Yokohama. They say there are as many as three thousand of them. Information is coming in steadily. Here, the security is very strict. All the villagers nearby have armed themselves with bamboo spears as well as guns in order to defend themselves. What times we live in![129]

As it turned out, Chūemon was mistaken. He corrected himself a few days later:

> Regarding the reports of rōnin assembling in Hachiōji, it turns out that they are not warriors at all but peasants. Driven by distress, about eight hundred of them rioted in Hinonohara. Egawa Taroemon dispatched an army of villagers. They fired at the rioters, and three of them were killed. The rest all fled. About thirty of them were arrested. The matter has now been settled, and all the villages are under strict supervision. A force of guards is said to have left yesterday from Edo to Yokohama, with a hundred and fifty regular soldiers and many others. These are just rumors.[130]

The Hachiōji protest was a reflection of the enormous distress inflicted on many villagers by the turmoil of the 1860s. From the mid-1860s to the turn of the 1870s, almost three hundred and fifty peasant protests erupted throughout Japan—about five times the average rate of the preceding three centuries. The disturbances of this time were varied in cause and outcome. They ranged from relatively minor complaints about local abuses of power or wealth to organized, domain-wide insurgencies. Although the authorities generally dealt with peasant protesters firmly, often executing their ringleaders, there was also a great deal of sympathy for the plight of the protesting villagers and townsmen. They were, in many ways, the most helpless victims of the changes roiling the Japanese economy and politics, and they were for many the symbol of the damage caused by the opening of Japan.

The opening of Yokohama undoubtedly had far-reaching effects on the rural hinterland, though by no means were all of them negative. It is not easy, however, to separate the economic effects of the opening of Japan to foreign trade from the turbulence and disruption caused by accompanying political upheavals. In the Kōshū region, as in many other parts of Japan, merchants, farmers, and townsmen experienced both new economic opportunities and major challenges during the 1860s.

Overall, the Kōshū silk market increased as rapidly as expanding mulberry cultivation would allow. In response to the enormous foreign demand, shipments by the main Kōfu silk merchants increased 420 percent by volume between 1863 and 1868.[131] Cotton production and prices also rose in response to the global supply shortage of 1863–1864. Rising prices and expanded production brought sorely needed cash income to poor farmers, and local merchants were able to take advantage of unprecedented opportunities. Even here, though, the benefits of the opening to trade could be double-edged. In her detailed study of the Ina valley to the west of Kōshū, Kären Wigen has shown how the opening of Japan to international trade produced radical inversions of the regional economy, with previously prosperous centers of production falling into decline, while new centers oriented toward the silk trade with Yokohama became newly prosperous.[132] Similarly, in the Kōshū district, while some merchants became wealthy as a result of opportunities in the cotton and silk trades, others found themselves unable to keep up with the pace of change.

Chūemon is of course a Kōshū farmer-merchant who did well out of the new business opportunities. Other newly successful merchants included Wakao Ippei from Zaiketsuke village in the mountains west of Kōfu. In addition to profiting from the trade in silk thread and silkworm egg cards, Ippei also opened two silk-reeling factories in Kōfu, which together used as many as twenty-five silk-reeling machines (using a Japanese design originating in Maebashi), employing women to operate them. But other business owners were not so successful at adapting to the new opportunities and challenges of the international market. Of the established silk merchants in Kōfu at the turn of the 1860s, only one, Ōtaya Sahei, survived the decade. For the others, the speed of growth and the constant need for new sources of supply were too much to keep up with. Aggressive entrepreneurs were always ready to take their places. Cotton merchants, on the other hand, did well from the windfall of demand created by the American Civil War, and several of them used the capital they gained to expand into silk, further squeezing out the established players.[133]

Similarly, for the artisans and small-scale farmers of Kōshū the changing economic conditions brought opportunity for many, but also hardship. For those with access to mulberry and cotton, the flood of demand for silk thread and raw cotton brought cash income that could be used to pay taxes, improve land, or invest in agricultural expansion. The growth also brought wage income to farm laborers and factory girls. But the opening of Japan to foreign trade also brought a destabilizing inflation that hit hardest at those on fixed incomes outside the silk and cotton industries—artisans, laborers, and tenant farmers. Those people saw steep increases in the prices of essential commodities, without benefiting from equivalent income gains.

In Edo, from 1859 through 1867 rice increased in price by 270 percent, oil by 300 percent, paper by 240 percent, and sugar by 220 percent. Meanwhile, the wages of a carpenter increased during the same period by only 70 percent, while tatami-mat makers saw their wages increase by only 10 percent. Overall, artisan wages and incomes increased by no more than 50 percent on average.[134]

Undoubtedly the price increases were closely linked to the opening of Japan to foreign trade. The links were both direct and indirect, and it is hard to assess which was the more important. In 1860 the government issued a new gold *koban* coin, reducing its bullion level by almost two-thirds compared with the coin it replaced but retaining its exchange rate to the silver *ichibu* coin at the same four-to-one ratio. This reflected the drastic adjustment of Japan to the world market rate for gold, and it undoubtedly contributed to the destabilization of prices. On top of that, the enormous demand from the foreign merchants for silk, cotton, tea, and other agricultural and marine commodities created a rapid inflation in the prices of those commodities. Silk went up in price so quickly that the government feared Japanese people would no longer be able to afford it for their own use (though as a luxury product, this hardly affected the artisan and laboring classes). Inevitably, the price rises in these export commodities had a knock-on effect on prices in other parts of the economy. And a third factor in the inflation of the 1860s was the shogunal government's own insatiable money needs. The destabilization caused by the opening of Japan resulted in vastly increased military and security expenses for the shogunal government, which now found itself threatened from several sides, both domestically and internationally. The government responded by minting more and more money—particularly copper and iron coins—of a lower and lower quality. Since most artisans and laborers were paid in these same small-denomination coins, they found that their buying power was drastically reduced.[135]

The problem of monetary inflation was compounded by a series of poor harvests, notably in 1866. For most Japanese people, the price of food was the most important determinant of well-being. While prices overall climbed steadily through the first half of the 1860s, the rice shortages of the mid-1860s caused dramatic food-price increases and accompanying hardship. Mark Metzler has pointed out that the inflation of the 1860s and the food shortages of 1866–1867 also reflected global trends. The entire global trading system experienced steep commodity inflation in the middle years of the decade, exacerbated by severe weather events and culminating in a serious financial panic—a combination that prompted one British journal to call 1866 a year "of almost uniform disaster."[136] As a result of their new connections to global markets in silk, cotton, and tea, Japanese farmers and small-scale merchants were now vulnerable to events taking place thousands of miles away.

According to Francis Hall, in 1860 the typical unskilled laborer in Yoko-hama made roughly 400 copper *mon* ($0.08) per day. A skilled artisan might make as much 800 *mon*.[137] In 1860, 100 *mon* would buy 4.3 *gō* of rice (about 3.25 cups), or enough to feed an adult for a day. But by 1866, 100 *mon* would only buy 0.83 *gō* (only a little more than 1 cup)—only a fraction of the amount needed to support a working adult. For a family of four, 400 *mon* might have been enough for survival in 1860. By 1866, it meant starvation.[138]

Clearly, the inflation also fed antiforeign sentiment. Indeed, critics di-rectly linked the foreign trade to the suffering of villagers throughout Japan. Some of the activists who murdered Japanese merchants in retribution for dealing with foreigners justified their actions by referring to the price in-creases and shortages resulting from the large-scale export of "the staples of the land": "We can no longer remain blind to the sufferings of the people."[139] In December 1861, when it transpired that foreign merchants had been evad-ing the restriction on the export of staple foods by buying up flour (which was not explicitly covered in the treaties), Kanagawa commissioner Hori Toshi-hiro committed suicide in expiation.[140]

However, for the artisans and laborers of Kōshū, the political and social instability caused by the antiforeign campaigners compounded the hardship and misery. The political upheavals of the 1860s forced villagers to provide labor and defense services as well as financial contributions to the struggling shogunal government. Among other demands, Kōshū villagers were required to help manage the enormous increase in traffic on Japan's highways as aris-tocrats and feudal lords with their armed retainers moved about the country in response to political developments; they were forced to provide labor and defense services to ward off repeated threats; and they had to pay numerous extra taxes to help finance the shogunate's military campaigns. Meanwhile, the breakdown of law and order within the province added to the stress and insecurity of daily life.[141]

On June 10, 1865, Chūemon stood and watched as a vast procession of warriors and foot soldiers passed through the post stations of Hodogaya and Kanagawa. The shogun himself was leading an army west to subdue the recalcitrant domain of Chōshū. "From Yokohama, the officers ordered two hundred men to be sent to assist. I and five other local leaders went and supervised. Around twenty thousand men are passing through today and to-morrow, all day without ceasing. Altogether who knows exactly how many tens of thousands there are?. . . The amount requisitioned in Edo for this is said to be around two million *ryō* [$5.5 million]. I understand they are expecting requisitions in Kōshū, too."[142]

The enormously expensive expedition was to end in defeat and humiliation for the shogunate, ushering in a period of momentous political change culminating in the collapse of the two-hundred-fifty-year-old Tokugawa regime. In the meantime, the costs of the expedition were indeed borne by merchants, artisans, and farmers throughout the shogunal domains, including Kōshū. In the city of Kōfu, the merchant community was called on to provide almost 6,000 ryō ($16,400) for the campaign, allocated based on wealth. Altogether 1,400 or more people had to contribute, all the way down to humble shopkeepers. In the countryside, Hayashi village, a poor mountain hamlet with 27 households, was required to contribute 70 ryō ($191). Its normal annual tax was only 45 ryō ($122). The two wealthiest families paid 17 and 13 ryō, respectively, 4 families paid 5 ryō, 2 paid 3 ryō, while 8 families could pay only a quarter of a ryō ($0.70).[143]

The financial distress fractured the social bonds and security infrastructure that had kept Kōshū safe throughout the Tokugawa era. Wealthier families were forced to respond with handouts and loans. In 1864, when Kōfu's wealthiest merchants donated several hundred bales of rice in order to alleviate distress (and also to deflect anger away from themselves), almost five thousand people—about 40 percent of the entire population—lined up to receive food handouts. In 1867 in Nakahagiwara village a group of poor villagers staged a sit-in at the house of Heijiemon, a member of the village elite, asking him to lend them rice. In response, the wealthy villagers of Nakahagiwara donated a total of forty-one bales of grain to more than fifty needy villagers—five bales were donated personally by Heijiemon. The following month, the better-off villagers raised 108 ryō ($295) in cash to distribute to almost eighty needy villagers, in the form of gifts and loans. Similar dramas played out in villages across the region and indeed throughout Japan.[144] While silk merchants in the regions surrounding Yokohama prospered from the booming demand for silk thread and other products, the established textile industries of Kyoto and the Kansai region went into decline, their raw materials increasingly unaffordable and their finished product unable to compete with high-quality imports.[145]

Meanwhile, Edo itself was falling into a deeper and deeper slump. With the abandonment in 1862 of the alternate-attendance system that had required daimyo to maintain large households in Edo, a massive exodus of domainal samurai caused Edo's population to decline by almost one-quarter. The loss of more than half the city's samurai elite caused a severe depression—exacerbated by the price inflation of major commodities—among the merchants and artisans who had catered to them. The departure of the shogun and a large army of retainers in 1865 further hollowed out the city. For much of the rest of the decade, the shogun Iemochi and his successor, Yoshinobu, spent as much or more time in the Kyoto area as in Edo (Iemochi died in Osaka in August 1866). Meanwhile, Edo suffered from a progressive breakdown in law and order, starting with the depredations of antiforeign rōnin and culminating in the surrender of the city to antishogunal forces in July 1868. While it would be wrong to attribute Edo's decline entirely to the opening of Yokohama, there is a remarkable contrast between the steep decline in the fortunes of Edo and the rapid growth and prosperity of Yokohama. At least a part of this disparity was caused by the shogunate's forlorn commitment to close the treaty port and its consequent inability to share in the prosperity created by growing international trade.

The middle years of the 1860s were a time of great opportunity but also of great challenge and hardship for many. The very factor that created new possibilities for wealth and prosperity—the enormous demand for export products in the new treaty ports—was also deeply destabilizing for Japan's economy and political system. Shinohara Chūemon made his fortune in the midst of dramatic upheavals, including the threat of war between Japan and the Western powers; the very real possibility of the massacre of both Japanese and Western merchants in Yokohama; samurai unrest and widespread acts of terror, many of them targeting merchants like Chūemon; the fracturing of the two-hundred-fifty-year old "Pax Tokugawa" and the threat of civil war; and severe economic distress among large sections of the population.

At the center of many of these events was the rapidly growing city of Yokohama, the outlet that connected Japan to the global network of markets and commerce. While some blamed Yokohama and its foreign residents for the ills that were afflicting Japan, for many the wealth and prosperity of this city were a siren call, luring them from all parts of Japan and the world to share in the opportunities created by its rapid growth. A huge outpouring of printed materials and other media created alluring images of this exotic place, where strange customs, beautiful women, exciting new technologies, and new economic opportunities could all be enjoyed.

The processes of economic, cultural, technical, and human exchange that took place in Yokohama were also influential in creating new understandings of the world and of Japan's place in it. For many Japanese, this meant casting aside long-established preconceptions and prejudices and reconceiving the meanings of lifestyle, class, race, civilization, and indeed of "Japan" itself. In the West, too, a new "Japan" was being created through print media, photography, souvenirs, exhibitions, arts and crafts collections, and performances—many of them mediated by the commercial marketplace of Yokohama. The images of Japan were both crafted and commodified—exotic, erotic, and looking back to Japan's ancient traditions—but also exquisite, original, exhibiting extraordinary artistic and physical prowess and looking forward to Japan's new role as a rapidly modernizing society taking its place in the community of nations.

The middle years of the decade brought great prosperity for Chūemon. They also brought about a shift in his perception of his spatial and political identity. He started his sojourn in Yokohama as a subject of the shogun and a representative of his "country," Kōshū. But by the mid-1860s his business activities extended well beyond the boundaries of Kōshū as he adjusted to a new frame of reference that was both national and international. And while he remained loyal to the shogunate and no doubt abhorred the idea of revolution, it is also possible to see him reevaluating his identity and coming to understand what it might mean to be "Japanese." It would not be long indeed before Chūemon was called on to cast aside his old loyalties and take on a new identity as citizen and subject of a unified Japan and its new symbol, the emperor.

4 TRANSFORMATION (1866–1873)

Branching Out

Toward the end of 1866 Chūemon turned his attention to an ambitious project he had first mentioned two years earlier. In mid-1864, Chūemon had talked of raising ten thousand *ryō* and going to Ōshū (in northeastern Japan, now Fukushima prefecture) to investigate business possibilities there.[1] In October 1866, with business at home in a lull, Chūemon set off on the mountainous, one-hundred-forty-mile journey to distant Nanbu domain in the southern part of Ōshū. He left Naotarō in Yokohama and Shōjirō in Kōshū to take care of the business.

Chūemon's trip to northern Japan reflects his widening outlook and his developing national scope. Although he started out trading in Kōshū's agricultural produce, Chūemon's experiences in Yokohama brought him into contact with a much wider sphere of enterprise. Many of the major domains had offices in Yokohama, sometimes using their domainal privilege to bypass shogunal trade restrictions. Back in 1864, Chūemon hinted at a connection with

Nanbu when he mentioned a plan to sell four thousand cases of Nanbu silk in Yokohama (at a time when silk shipments were at a standstill because of government restrictions), from which "it may be possible to profit."[2] Now, Chūemon's access to large amounts of capital opened up new avenues of opportunity. Kōshū was no longer big enough to satisfy his ambition.

Nanbu was a major producer of silk and silkworm egg cards, but on this trip it was not silk but quartz that interested Chūemon. Quartz crystal was a product of the Kōshū mountains, and there was a developing industry in Kōfu making decorative items such as netsuke (belt ornaments), inro (containers for personal belongings), and sculptures for display in wealthy homes, as well as more practical items such as lenses for spectacles. Mount Kinpusen, on the border between Kōshū and Shinshū, was known to contain huge lodes of quartz, but the shogunate prohibited commercial mining, and the only available supplies were derived from small quantities dug up by farmers in the region.[3] Once before, in June 1865, Chūemon had asked his son to buy quartz in Kōshū and send it to Yokohama. Now, Chūemon had heard that the lord of Nanbu domain was open to relaxing the restrictions on mining in his territory. Quartz was not a significant export product—at no point in the 1860s is it listed in the top-ten export items—but the growing wealth of the Yokohama market must have persuaded Chūemon that there was opportunity in this luxury product.[4] In October 1866 he set off on the long road north, leaving his son at home to manage the business.

With Chūemon gone, Naotarō did his best to keep things going in Yokohama. There was little business in silk, but Naotarō asked his brother Shōjirō to buy up silk cocoon waste—"Don't worry too much about the quality—if you can get it for less than three hundred mon [$0.06] per kan [8 lbs.], any quality will do."[5] Naotarō also got quite excited about the possibilities for selling goji berries in the Yokohama market. On November 13 he wrote, "I want you to buy these very secretly . . . Please go around very urgently, and buy. If they are raw . . . please have them semidried, in boxes, and send them to me. I can sell top-quality dried berries for twenty to thirty dollars for sixteen kan [130 lbs.]. Unlike other products, these items are not abundant, so please do not talk to anyone about this . . . If you handle it badly, the price will go up. If anyone asks, tell them that you are buying them as gifts for children."[6]

In the midst of these scenes of peaceful enterprise, on November 26, Yokohama was struck by disaster. A fire broke out in the kitchen of a restaurant near the Miyozaki licensed quarter. There was a strong wind that day, and the fire spread more rapidly than anyone imagined possible. Within an hour, it had leveled almost half the town and killed dozens.

John Black, an eyewitness to the fire, wrote how it spread through the foreign settlement:

> The new American Consulate was now literally level with the ground, and reports flew around, that No. 1, the residence, offices, and godowns of Messrs. Jardine, Matheson & Co., had caught. In another few seconds it reached the whole settlement that the private residence of No. 2, Messrs. Walsh, Hall & Co., was on fire. Simultaneously with this, the whole range of the old Consular buildings—the French, Prussian, American and English, in which latter several gentlemen of the English Legation and Consulate were residing—were swept off like so much tinder. The wind increased almost to a typhoon: the sparks communicated with the old Japanese Custom house, and in almost as short a time as it takes to pen this tale of desolation, it was a thing of the past.

Black also described the total destruction of the brothel quarter: "With the exception of one or two fire-proof godowns, and the temple at the end, not a single stick was standing to mark the boundaries of dwellings. Unhappily, here was a terrible loss of life, no less than thirty five dead bodies having been found."[7] Black added that the British soldiers who were brought in to help fight the fire looted the houses they were supposed to be saving and quickly became "utterly and helplessly drunk."[8]

Ernest Satow described watching the fleeing prostitutes struggle to escape across the single bridge that spanned the moat surrounding the brothel quarter. "There were one or two boats available, but they were already overcrowded, and their occupants were so paralysed by fear that they never thought of landing and sending back the boats to take off others. I saw a few poor wretches plunge into the water in order to escape, but they failed to reach the nearer bank."[9] The foreign observers were unable in their commentaries and letters to write directly about what must surely have been weighing heaviest on their hearts: that most of the victims of the fire were women who had been virtually enslaved in the walled and moated town of Miyozaki for the purpose of serving the foreigners' own sexual desires.

By a miracle, the fire stopped just short of Chūemon's neighborhood, and his house and storage buildings were untouched. But, wrote Naotarō, "I will have to pay thirty ryō in consolation money, so I share in the loss. It is terrible for us all."[10]

In the midst of the desolation of the ruined town, Naotarō struggled to keep the family enterprise going. Chūemon had told them he would return by December 21, 1866 (Keiō 2/11/15), but no word came from him. With the end of the year approaching, Naotarō had to send gifts to the family and manage the year-end finances without his father's help. He needed to send money to Shōjirō for the year-end payment of their Kōshū debts, but once again "this year-end will be extremely difficult."[11]

Chūemon finally returned on January 27, 1867. In spite of the devastation he found on his return, he was euphoric. He recounted his adventures in a long letter to Shōjirō. "On the twenty-ninth [of the ninth month, November 6, 1866] I arrived at a place called Kōriyama, in the Nanbu domain of Ōshū. I traveled by horse." Chūemon requested permission to visit the quartz mines, and he was sent to a mountain called Wayama, sixty miles from Kōriyama.

> I identified one place here to investigate, and I spent 10 ryō digging a shaft 5 ken [30 feet] deep into the rocks. I brought about 800 me [7 lbs.] of different kinds of earth to the mine head, as well as 2 bales of fine powder. In order to assess the quality, I brought along Mr. Godakegane from Kōshū, as well as Jūsuke from Koseki village, and Yamahigashiya Shinpei from Yamagakechō in Kōriyama. We all worked fervently in pursuit of success regardless of the snow. We concluded that from this mountain we can make 5,000 ryō or possibly 10,000 ryō. I was told I should take a close look at Minami Shōzan and one other place next year, after the snow has melted. According to the private analysis of a member of the daimyo's family, that mountain has quartz, silver, and gold. Ever since the beginning of Japan, that mountain has been known as Treasure Mountain, and no one has been allowed to go there. However, in my case I was invited to a banquet, where the chief minister gave me written permission . . .
>
> I left Morioka on the 5th of this month and arrived in Edo on the 21st. Naotarō was there on business, so we met in Edo. Along the road I traveled in a kago [palanquin] with a hibachi [porcelain stove], so I didn't feel cold at all. My body stayed healthy, and I am eating well, so no need to worry. At the sea near Morioka I bought 15,000 pieces of dried squid, at 450 pieces for 1 ryō . . . Even after all the expenses I think the total cost may be 45 ryō, and I believe I can sell it in Edo for 90 ryō. With this news, please put your hearts at rest and look forward to a prosperous new year.[12]

Travel on horseback and by palanquin was a privilege reserved for the wealthy. Chūemon had clearly come into his own as a member of the new merchant elite. He added, "We were unharmed by the fire here in Yokohama. This is a matter for congratulation, and we can greet the coming year with our hearts at peace."[13] Chūemon's optimism is understandable given his growing prosperity and the bright prospects for his new venture. And indeed, his business continued to grow through much of 1867. Nothing could have prepared him for the extraordinary turmoil with which the year would end.

REVOLUTION

In mid-1867, after a period of declining prices, Chūemon's business dealing in silkworm egg cards began to boom again. In spite of financial constraints and market uncertainties, Chūemon was determined to profit from this market. On May 5, he wrote to his son, "No matter what happens, this year I plan to undertake trade in egg cards. If possible, please let me know how many egg cards we could expect each village to produce."[14] A month later, he reported, "Everyone is making profits at this time . . . Prices are on the rise, likely to go up to around three bu [$2] each. We need to put our effort into this."[15]

Once again, Chūemon planned for his own family, as well as other silk-making families in Higashi-Aburakawa and neighboring villages, to manufacture egg cards that he would sell in Yokohama. But "preparing the cards requires great care, and [the foreigners] want only those of top quality . . . If they are poorly made, they will be difficult to sell . . . They must be thickly spread but not too crowded. They must not have any holes in them. You must put all your effort into making them carefully. If you can make them well, then at present I can sell them for one ryō and one or two bu [$3.30–$4] . . . The foreigners are secretly asking me to supply them, so sales are likely to be extremely good . . . The money is in front of our eyes."[16]

Chūemon added, "Yesterday a group of five or six Italians arrived to buy egg cards. It is not yet known how many they want to buy, but some people are talking about a price of one ryō per card."[17] This is the only direct reference in Chūemon's letters to the cause of the boom in egg cards—namely, strong demand from European silk-producing countries struck by the silkworm blight.

By the end of June, Chūemon was riding the crest of a sudden boom in the egg card market. "At present the foreigners are visiting here wanting to enter into contracts. Even if we don't make a contract, they are saying, 'Please don't sell to anyone else, I will buy as many as you can offer.' They are coming daily to enter into these discussions."[18] A few days later, Naotarō wrote to his brother to "please make top quality if you want to ensure good sales. I understand that people are selling cards in the villages all around. If the cards are good quality, then you should contract to buy them at three bu [$2] or up to three bu two shu [$2.35], paying a deposit now and the rest on the last day of the seventh month. And send them to me. Please go around the villages and make sure no one else buys the top-quality cards."[19]

Once again, Chūemon was concerned that the cards should not be identified with Kōshū, which was still considered a second-class producing area. In response to requests from the foreigners for better identification and quality control, the regional government had been requiring producers to add the Kōshū seal to their packages, but "Kōshū eggs should not be identified officially this year. I have informed the officials of my opinion . . . It should be enough to have an inspection stamp. If we add the Kōshū name, the foreigners will look down on our egg cards. Please explain this to all concerned. Already last year when they attached the Kōshū name, our traders all lost money." The following year, Chūemon actually instructed his son to cut off the inspection stamp so that the cards' origin would not be visible.[20]

By late July, Kōshū egg cards were selling for more than one ryō per card, while top-quality cards from name-brand regions like Ōshū were selling for as much as three ryō ($8) per card.[21] "I believe the price will remain firm, so if Buzaemon keeps buying, I should be able to sell at one ryō one bu. Please also ask Gorōemon and Chūkichi to buy thick cards as soon as possible and send them here . . . I know I keep saying it, but unless they're good and thick, they won't sell. Even if you have to pay a little more, please buy good quality. If you are short of funds, you must buy on terms, paying by the last day of the seventh month. If you need money urgently, I can get it to you within five days of receiving the goods here."[22] In other words, in spite of his prosperity, Chūemon still did not have enough capital to finance large-scale purchases on his own account, without resorting to credit.

In the second half of 1867, Chūemon's business was flourishing as he traded in a variety of products. Top-quality egg cards were selling for more than two ryō, and Chūemon was able to sell as many as he could get his hands on. "Right now eggs are what the foreigners want the most . . . At present there are many buyers, so even inferior product is selling."[23] But Chūemon was also dealing in tea, silk thread, cocoon shells, seafood, and charcoal. He had recently purchased a new building lot in the Ōtachō district, and he had spent two hundred ryō ($530) developing the property. He planned to sell the lease and invest the profit in his business.[24] In August

1867, he wrote to his son, "Right now market conditions [in Kōshū] are difficult. It's hard to tell if you will profit or lose . . . If you have extra money, you
should not keep it uselessly at home. You should give it to me, as I am using it
profitably."[25]

At this time, Chūemon's wife was staying in Kōshū with their children.
Shōjirō was running the affairs of the family in Kōshū, and at about this time,
Chūemon made him official head of the Shinohara family (in 1868, Shōjirō was
to change his name to Chūemon). Seitarō was working on the family farm,
taking responsibility for the agricultural side of the business. Naotarō, his
wife, daughter, and their newborn baby were living with Chūemon in Yokohama. And Chūemon's youngest son, Katsusuke (age fourteen), was being
schooled for a fee of two *ryō* per month in Edo, where (Chūemon comments
rather proudly) "he is said to be the leader of evil pleasures."[26] In March 1867,
Chūemon was delighted to hear that his wife had negotiated the betrothal of
their daughter Fuki. She was to marry Okamura Kanemon, making her the
third member of Chūemon's immediate family to marry into the Okamura
family (both Chūemon's and Shōjirō's wives were Okamuras).[27]

Throughout 1867, Chūemon's irrepressible optimism seemed to be justified. His decision to invest heavily in silkworm egg cards was paying off
handsomely; he was trading successfully in a variety of other products; the
threat of attack by hostile *rōnin* had receded; the shogunate was no longer
interfering with trade; and Chūemon's family were all doing well. There was
nothing in the air to warn him of the turmoil and near disaster that were
about to overwhelm Chūemon personally, nor of the revolution that was to
bring the world he knew to a sudden and irrevocable end.

The first hint came on November 9, 1867. Chūemon wrote, in a brief message, "I have to go to the city commissioner's office [*machibugyōsho*] in Edo,
but you shouldn't worry. However, it will take a good deal of time." Chūemon
clarified the situation in a letter to three of his creditors on November 19:

> The Mitsui branch in Yokohama has lost one hundred thirty thousand
> *ryō* [$350,000] of the government funds deposited there. The manager,
> Kōmura Senjirō, as well as one other has been jailed. Thirteen people
> of Yokohama who had borrowed that money [these included Chūemon]
> were summoned by a letter of the ninth of this month from the Edo city
> commissioner's office to appear there on the twelfth. We were ques-
> tioned about the amount of the loans. The officials suspect that the
> loans were made improperly, which is why those two individuals were
> jailed for misconduct. Those summoned were ordered to return the

borrowed money immediately . . . Already one person called Nakaya Tō-suke has been thrown in jail. The rest of us were required to submit a full accounting of the affair. Upon presentation of these accounts, the officials inspected our statements, and now they have demanded that any merchants with whom we did business should provide an accounting of transactions involving these official funds . . . The money I was supposed to receive from these transactions is now frozen. While the books are being inspected, I must request a delay and ask for your patience. At present I have no money on hand. Depending on the decision of the officials, I may be treated the same as Tōsuke. Now I am just at a loss. I know that you need your money returned. But if you insist too much, that would negate all your kindness to this point. If you insist on repayment, please allow me to extend the date, and I will be able to settle all these matters. I am out of funds, and I am the object of a severe investigation.[28]

According to the Mitsui company history, the loss was the result of mismanagement rather than fraud. During the course of the previous decade, Mitsui's Edo and Yokohama branches had been given a large new portfolio of responsibilities by the shogunal government, including management of the shogunate's foreign exchange accounts and financial management of the Yokosuka Shipyard, which was under construction with French technical support. Most of the managers in the Edo branch had experience only in textile retailing, and they were unable to develop an effective system of bookkeeping, especially since the money entrusted to Mitsui moved frequently between the Edo and Yokohama branches, which were managed independently of each other. Moreover, there was little oversight of the branch managers, who seem to have thought they had permission to invest government funds in speculative loans and investments. The top management of Mitsui in Kyoto became aware of the shortfall as early as mid-1866, and they immediately recognized the threat that it represented. If the government were to call in the funds that it had on deposit with Mitsui, the entire enterprise was in danger of going bankrupt. Mitsui sent a senior executive to Edo to try to sort out the muddle, but all he could do was confirm the shortfall. Out of two hundred thousand ryō and forty thousand dollars of government funds under Mitsui management, only ninety thousand ryō and twenty-five thousand dollars could be physically accounted for. The rest had been lent to Yokohama merchants by the branch's managers. While the merchants might have been able to repay the loans in time, none of them had the funds for immediate repayment.

A portion of the government funds had also been lost in foreign-exchange speculation.[29]

Now that the scandal had been exposed, Chūemon, a prosperous Yokohama merchant who wanted nothing more than to be wealthy, respected and admired, was suddenly facing the terrifying prospect of being thrown into jail.

Then, just four days later, Chūemon sent word of more ominous events. The political world was descending into chaos. A year earlier, Chūemon had reported in passing on the death of the shogun, Iemochi, the appointment of Tokugawa Yoshinobu as the fifteenth shogun, and the withdrawal of the shogunal army from its campaign against Chōshū in western Japan. He did not mention that the campaign had been an unmitigated disaster, costing the shogunate millions of ryō and resulting in its humiliating defeat at the hands of Chōshū's samurai-commoner army. Nor in the following months did his letters touch on Japan's deteriorating political situation. Indeed, up to this point Chūemon had only really shown any interest in national or international politics when Yokohama was directly threatened. To some extent, this reflects the attitude of many commoners—that the affairs of "those on high" did not concern them. Chūemon was concerned mostly with making money within his own sphere.

But Chūemon could not ignore the reports of civil war in the Kyoto area, nor the rumors that a showdown was imminent between the new shogun and the hostile forces surrounding the imperial court. The shogun, Tokugawa Yoshinobu, was an energetic reformer who was determined to unify the country around its most pressing need: to develop a national government capable of resisting foreign aggression. With time, he might have succeeded in persuading the domains to accept his leadership. But in the aftermath of the failed shogunal campaign against Chōshū, the two western domains of Satsuma and Chōshū had already formed a secret alliance, dedicated to the overthrow of the Tokugawa. On November 9, 1867, the young Emperor Meiji, who had recently ascended to the throne, was persuaded by courtiers sympathetic to Satsuma and Chōshū to call for the shogun's arrest.

News of the events in Kyoto reached Chūemon two weeks later:

There are rumors here that Nijō Castle [in Kyoto] has been burned to the ground and that rōnin have flooded into Osaka Castle. Also that Lord Itakura [Itakura Katsukiyo, daimyo of Matsuyama and chief minister at the time] and the shogun are nowhere to be found. There are many such rumors, but it seems that in fact the shogun has offered up his authority [to the emperor]. It is also said that ships of Tosa and Satsuma are heading to the Kantō, and that hundreds of warships have been seen in the western sea. Also that no goods are being shipped by sea from Edo to Osaka.[30]

This sudden, terrifying announcement reflects the imperfect nature of communications in Japan of the 1860s. The shogun had indeed resigned his office, formally returning his authority to the emperor and bringing the 264-year-old Tokugawa shogunate to an end. Although the shogun's Kyoto palace at Nijō Castle was the setting for this dramatic event, the castle was not burned. Nor—yet—was a Satsuma navy on its way to the Kantō. However, in the weeks that followed, the western alliance of the Satsuma and Chōshū domains moved a large army into Kyoto, effectively claiming the city for themselves. On January 3, 1868, they took control of the Imperial Palace and issued in the emperor's name a rescript stripping the ex-shogun of all his lands and estates. Tokugawa Yoshinobu had not intended to fight: he had resigned his office in the interest of unifying Japan so that it could withstand the pressures of Western imperialism. But now, faced with a coup d'état and the loss of his wealth and influence, he mobilized his forces in the Kyoto area to challenge the western domains' control over the emperor. Ostensibly, Yoshinobu merely wanted to present a petition to the emperor asking him to reverse his harsh edict. But Yoshinobu accompanied the petition with a large military force, and on January 27, 1868, the forces of the ex-shogun clashed with those of the western alliance in a five-day battle at Toba-Fushimi, outside Kyoto. The battle ended in a decisive defeat for the Tokugawa shogunate.

As the crisis gathered toward its climax in Kyoto, the shogunal authorities in the Kantō area mobilized to respond to the emergency. The city commissioners imposed enormous special taxes on the Edo merchant houses, and before long the Kanagawa commissioners extended these demands to the merchants of Yokohama. The crisis playing out in Kyoto suddenly came home to Chūemon in the most painful way possible: with a ruinous special levy imposed on his landholdings. "Since the government has been incurring great expenses, it is said that land renters must pay a tax of two ryō [$5.40] for each tsubo. If that is the case, based on the one hundred fifty tsubo that I hold, my share will be three hundred ryō [$800]."[31] Although this was an enormous sum, it could have been even worse. In addition to his one-hundred-fifty-tsubo property in Honchō Nichōme (which he had leased since the port opened in 1859), Chūemon had just finished developing another one-hundred-fifty-tsubo parcel of land in the reclaimed Ōtachō district. Luckily, this land was exempted from the tax.

Nevertheless, given that his money was all frozen because of the Mitsui affair, that Chūemon himself was stuck in Edo until the affair was resolved, and that—again owing to the Mitsui affair—trade in Yokohama had come to a virtual halt, he had no idea where he would come up with this money. In spite of his recent business success, Chūemon remained cash poor. He continued to rely heavily on short-term debt to finance his business operations, and any surplus cash he had, he had put either into payment of debt or into new business investments. As he considered his options, he mulled the possibility that he would have to give up the premises he had occupied for the past decade: "At present because of the Mitsui affair I have nothing on hand. I may have no alternative but to return my land. If it comes to that, I would at least like to keep the fifty tsubo that I have been using as my living quarters . . . But even that would be [a tax of] a hundred ryō."[32]

Meanwhile, Chūemon remained stuck in Edo, required by the city commissioners to stay there until their investigation was concluded. And Edo itself was descending into chaos. In the final months of 1867, there was an unprecedented breakdown in law and order in the shogunal capital. "In Edo," wrote Chūemon,

> thieves are flooding the city and robbing the houses of the wealthy. The bands consist of a hundred or more followers, and they are forcing their way into people's homes. They tell the men in the guardhouses not to raise their voices, and if they suspect them [of trying to raise the alarm], they will cut them down. My neighbors are strengthening their security, but in places [the robbers] have been seen breaking down locked doors with axes and running riot inside. There are many instances where they have taken five hundred or a thousand ryō. At present, Mitsui and the other designated government money changers are each being guarded by twenty or thirty warriors day and night. Nabeya Jinbei of Odenmachō Sanchōme has hired fifty soldiers . . . Many of [these robbers] are said to be Satsuma rōnin who are staying on ships and coming ashore at night.[33]

Historians have speculated that the influx of samurai from Satsuma was a deliberate policy by the Satsuma authorities to foment panic in the shogunal capital. The samurai were said to be warning the townsmen to flee the city in anticipation of a coming conflict. As a handbill handed out by the Satsuma men stated, "All determined men in the nation should gather together on the fourth day of the eleventh month and form a heavenly army to burn Edo Castle and set fires throughout the city and punish evil officials. The only thing we are afraid of is that the people may suffer because of this. You should quickly move your belongings and change your residence to avoid harm. We do not intend to harm the people, only to save them."[34]

Chūemon clearly found the Satsuma men terrifying—rough, violent barbarians who barely spoke intelligible Japanese and who seemed to obey no laws but their own.

In the midst of all this trouble and uncertainty, an unprecedented wave of popular fervor swept through Japan. It began with the mysterious appearance of amulets and talismans (ofuda) bearing inscriptions and images of Shinto and Buddhist deities. The amulets were said to be falling from the sky in their thousands, landing on roads, roofs, and trees. They literally swept across Japan like a wave, starting in the west and spreading east along the major highways. They reached Odawara at the end of November, Fujisawa on December 1, and Yokohama on December 10. In Kōshū, the talismans appeared in the city of Kōfu on November 21 and spread throughout the province over the following two weeks. In one village to the west of Yokohama, a child found a talisman floating in the ocean on November 28 and brought it home to show his grandfather. A few days later he was given another talisman, by a traveler on the highway. And on the evening of December 9, a talisman fell out of the sky and lodged in the branches of a cypress tree in the family compound. On December 10, the family prepared rice, red beans, and sake for the entire village in celebration of the joyful appearance of the talismans, which they displayed in front of their household shrine. A priest came to chant Buddhist sutras in front of the talismans. On December 12, some sixty villagers, including the grandson of this family, set off on a pilgrimage to the great shrine of Ise, more than two hundred miles to the west.[35] Similar scenes played out all over the central provinces of Japan, with huge crowds converging on famous pilgrimage destinations. In many cases, the pilgrims went dancing along the highways, chanting, "Everything's good, isn't it!" ("Ee janaika") and reveling in crazy and even orgiastic behavior.

The talismans were handwritten, in ordinary Japanese, and there is no doubt that they were being spread deliberately. But there is no consensus on the agents or their motives. Some historians have suggested there was a political motive behind the wave of talismans—perhaps a desire by Satsuma and its allies to stir up revolutionary fervor. Some of the talismans did indeed contain political messages, usually antiforeign. Others have suggested the motives were commercial, since the talismans encouraged townsmen and villagers to spend more money on entertainment and celebrations.[36] Probably the motives were various: given their wide geographic distribution stretching across half of Japan, no one individual or group could have been responsible. Whatever the motives, the popular reaction was surely a response to the extraordinary upheavals that were engulfing the country, accompanied by widespread hardship and want. The talismans were perceived as signs of hope amid the darkness, and people celebrated their arrival by stopping work, giving food and drink to passersby, preparing feasts for the neighborhood, making donations to the poor, and setting off on pilgrimages. The celebrations and public demonstrations offered a kind of spiritual release from the terrible stresses of the time.

The celebratory mood infected Yokohama, too. When the talismans fell on the townsmen's houses, they displayed them in front of their homes and handed out rice cakes and sake to passersby, prompting the authorities to take measures to stop them from blocking traffic.[37] Chūemon was stuck in Edo at the time, but Naotarō was caught up in the fervor. On December 15, he wrote to his brother,

> At present around Yokohama talismans bearing divine inscriptions are falling from the clouds. Every household is filled with a spirit of celebration. Every day feels like a holy festival. On the eighteenth of this month [Keiō 3/11/18, 12/13/1867] . . . an image of the thousand-handed Kannon bodhisattva appeared on the back of a two-bu gold coin. The people were spontaneously dancing in the streets, going around the houses and announcing a festival. These things are happening daily in every house. Is it the same where you are? All around us strange things are happening.[38]

But as the end of the year approached, Chūemon faced a familiar reality. Once again, he was unable to settle his debts with his creditors. "I certainly would plan to send the money this year, but in Yokohama we are required to pay a tax of two ryō two bu on each tsubo of land . . . Because of the Mitsui affair I have no funds available. I cannot possibly repay Mr. Saijō this year. You must explain all this to him and ask for his patience. I will certainly return the money in the New Year. I am not a wrongdoer, but I must ask for an extension."[39]

By the turn of 1868, Chūemon was back in Yokohama. But rather than re-
suming trade, he spent most of his energy trying to buy more time on the
large debts he owed in both Kōshū and Yokohama. Meanwhile, "in Edo,
thieves and robbers are breaking into money-changing houses and large
merchant houses and taking three, five, or even ten thousand *ryō* before returning to their ships. The highways, too, are very disturbed. Here in Yokohama, security is very strict, so there have been no such incidents. It is very
peaceful here."[40] In one other piece of news, Chūemon mentioned in a letter that "Hyōgo [now known as Kobe] opened as a treaty port on the sixth
of this month. Many foreigners from here have gone there, and many Japanese traders accompanied the foreigners in their ships. The construction
there is still unfinished, but at present in the town of Hyōgo money is circulating and many people are able to make a living. That is what the merchants
there are saying."[41]

On January 3, 1868, Chūemon announced good news: the Mitsui affair
had been settled in principle. It is unclear what Chūemon's final losses were,
but he acknowledged that it "has cost me a great deal of money."[42] Finally,
though, Chūemon could put the affair behind him and turn his attention back
to his business.

But even as Chūemon strove to return his life to normal, events were moving quickly around him. Throughout the decade of the 1860s, Chūemon had
witnessed the slow undermining of the Tokugawa shogunate's power and
prestige as it struggled to respond to successive crises: the antiforeign insur-
gency, the rise of imperial loyalism, the campaigns of assassination and terror,
the Richardson murder and its aftermath, the imperial command to close the
ports, the Mito insurrection, the defiance of the western domains, and the
disastrous military campaign to chastise Chōshū. Ironically, the catalyst
that had set all these events in motion was the opening of the treaty ports,
the most prominent of which was Yokohama. The very place that Chūemon
had believed in so fervently for the opportunity and prosperity that it offered had undermined the political and social order on which Chūemon had
built his entire life. Now, in the course of just a few days, the long-drawn-out
crisis came to a head with the sudden and dramatic collapse of the Tokugawa
regime.

On February 11—two weeks after the decisive battle of Toba-Fushimi—
Chūemon addressed a long letter to his son, heading it "Transcription of a
Dream." The title reflects his utter disbelief at the news that had just arrived
in Edo.

Since the middle of last month, rōnin from Satsuma have been running
riot in Edo, robbing and stealing. The Edo residence of the lord of Satsuma was surrounded by the soldiers of the shogun and burned to the
ground and the rōnin arrested. Since this affair, there has been great
confusion. On the third [January 27, 1868] the lord of Aizu and others
accompanied the Kantō taikun [the ex-shogun Yoshinobu, who had
resigned three months earlier] to try to enter Kyoto. The forces of
Satsuma, Tosa, Chōshū, Owari, Echizen, Bizen, and others that had
been holding Kyoto now issued forth, and a battle followed, in which
the men of the imperial court were victorious. The surrounding towns
were burned to the ground. On the fourth, fifth, sixth, and seventh [Jan-
uary 28–31, 1868] a great battle raged, during which a prince emerged
from the palace carrying the imperial banners. The Kantō side refused
to bow to the banners and instead opened fire, while the men of Satsuma
and its allies all prostrated themselves. Now, under the leadership of the
imperial prince, a great battle followed, during which the Kantō side was
betrayed by Lord Tōdō, who was in its vanguard. After that the Kantō
taikun was thoroughly defeated. He retreated to Osaka, but the castle
there was set alight by the enemy army and burned to the ground. In
this way, the battle was lost. The lord of Aizu, together with the taikun,
retired to the south of Osaka and boarded ships. They are said to have
arrived on the twelfth of this month [February 5, 1868] in Edo . . . In
this battle, around three thousand men were killed on the spot. The
Kantō forces that remained now have nowhere to go. Around ten thousand of them went to Kishū [Wakayama]. Five officials set off from
Yokohama by ship in order to retrieve these men. They left on the fifteenth [February 8, 1868], and it is said that they are bringing the entire
army back to the Kyoto area.[43]

Chūemon is reporting on the battle of Toba-Fushimi, the decisive battle
that ended the Tokugawa shogunate. His report is generally accurate. The
shogunal forces confronted the alliance of western domains in a final attempt
to prevent the outright takeover of the country. The shogun was betrayed by
one of his key allies, Tōdō Takayuki, the daimyo of the Tsu domain. And the
shogunal alliance was thrown into confusion by the sudden and unexpected
appearance of a prince carrying the brocade banners of the imperial family.

The battle was the culmination of a decade-long confrontation between
the shogunate and the powerful domains of western Japan. Both Satsuma and

Chōshū had defied the shogunate at various points during the decade. Al-though Satsuma in particular had close ties to the Tokugawa family (in 1856 a Satsuma princess had married the reigning shogun, Iesada), both domains had gone through violent internal upheavals during the 1860s, resulting in their takeover by aggressive young samurai who were both antiforeign and anti-Tokugawa. While a part of the domains' motivation may have been gen-uine outrage over the shogunate's capitulation to foreign demands, their hostility to the Tokugawa was more deeply rooted. Both domains had been on the losing side in the Battle of Sekigahara in 1600, and it was rumored that they still held deep-rooted grudges against the shogunate.[44] Certainly, from the viewpoint of a loyal shogunal subject like Chūemon, the western domains were troublemakers at best, enemy usurpers at worst.

But the tone of Chūemon's report suggests the confusion that he and many others must have felt at the turn of events. How was a loyal subject of the shogun to respond when the shogunal forces fired on an imperial prince? Now that the shogun was apparently defeated, to whom did they owe their loyalty? Surely not to the lord of the distant Satsuma domain. But to the em-peror himself? How could they deny their loyalty to that august figure, whose family had (nominally at least) ruled Japan for more than a thousand years?

The appearance of the imperial prince on the battlefield was in fact a brilliant piece of stage management by Satsuma. The banners had been spe-cially prepared some months in advance by officials of Satsuma and had been stored by Satsuma for just such an eventuality.[45] The prince himself, Prince Komatsu, was a young man of twenty-two who had been abbot of a monas-tery until taken out of seclusion to "lead" the anti-Tokugawa alliance. That same morning, Satsuma had secured an imperial edict stating that the ex-shogun Tokugawa Yoshinobu was an enemy of the court and should be suppressed by military force. As a memo from the American consul in Yoko-hama stated, "The Mikado is now to all intents and purposes the vassal if not the prisoner of that bold and unscrupulous Daimio."[46] In this coup, the Satsuma leadership clearly demonstrated their understanding of the im-portance of controlling the person of the emperor—an understanding they were to put to extraordinary use in the following decades.

Chūemon quickly went on to reassure his son that "Yokohama is right now the safest place in all Japan. So please set your mind at rest. If anything happens, I will return to Kōshū." He reported that the defeated army was sending its wounded by ship back to the Kantō, and some of them were arriv-ing in Yokohama for treatment. "On the fourteenth, thirty-six gravely wounded men were taken to the town office here in Yokohama, where they are being treated. Those who have died have been taken away amid great disorder. Those who are unlikely to survive are being sent to Edo to their relatives."[47] A top shogunal official, Katsu Kaishū, wrote in his diary, "A succession of boats filled with the troops defeated at Toba-Fushimi is arriving in Edo . . . They are disgruntled by shortages of food and lack of shelter. Moreover, they are angered by insufficient pay. They are forming secret bands and decamping . . . The townsmen are daily more distressed and suspicious. Officials repeatedly order increases in financial contributions without specific purposes in mind . . . Even if enemy troops do not come, it will not be long before Edo collapses from within."[48]

In a vivid additional detail, Chūemon added that "since the fall of Osaka Castle, foreigners, townsmen, and peasants have been going without permission to see the site of the battle and collecting bullets and other souvenirs. Nobody is stopping them or even watching over them."[49]

Clearly, this great defeat of the shogunal forces was ominous in the extreme. For the next several days, rumors swirled around Edo and Yokohama. Katsu Kaishū wrote in his diary, "Edo is in great confusion. There are many rumors. The truth of the morning is false by night. Will the imperial army halt at Kuwana? Will it advance on Sunpu? Will it come through the Hakone Pass? As a result the people are angry and upset. They run about blindly; the situation is like a boiling cauldron."[50]

A few days later, Chūemon tried to strike a more reassuring tone: "Here there has been all sorts of confusion, but unlike the situation in the Kyoto area there are no battles in evidence. The Kyoto area is a battleground, and with the daimyo all trying to get their way, the world has become a terrible place. But here in Yokohama, no one is invading us, nor are they killing us or burning us." Chūemon went on to offer an optimistic assessment of the conflict: "At present, it is possible to stop the western army at the Oi River. And although their navy is patrolling the ocean, they have few ships, while the Kantō side has many, so it should be able to sink the entire western fleet . . . Moreover, at present the prince of Ueno has returned from Kyoto. It is said that this prince was not ordered to return here but came to be with his people. It is said that he will retire from the clergy in order to protect the east. There is also a rumor that the present shogun will retire to Kōshū."[51]

The "prince of Ueno" Chūemon refers to is the imperial prince Rinnō-jinomiya, who was the abbot of Kan'eiji, the temple in the Ueno district of Edo where six Tokugawa shoguns were buried. He was the uncle of the emperor, who had now issued a rescript calling for the destruction of the Tokugawa, but as a longtime resident of Edo, Prince Rinnōjinomiya remained loyal to the

Tokugawa faction. After the fall of Edo, he joined the remnants of the shogunal forces who retreated to northern Japan, and there was open talk about
Japan being split into two, with Rinnōjinomiya being made the "Northern
Mikado."[52] Chūemon hints at this outcome when he suggests that the prince
might "protect the east." It seems that Chūemon was willing to countenance the division of Japan into eastern and western kingdoms rather than
face the alternative, which was to see the government fall into the hands of
samurai from the western domains who, even if they were allied with the
emperor, seemed to Chūemon frightening and alien. Chūemon's attitude
was, indeed, common among Edo townsmen, who were highly distrustful
of the motivations of Satsuma and Chōshū. Cartoons and broadsheets circulating in Edo accused the western domains of exploiting the person of
the emperor for their own ends and berated the ex-shogun for his spineless-
ness. One satirical cartoon depicted Yoshinobu as a child in a schoolboy
fight: "It's better to run away," he says, as he disappears out of the top left
corner of the picture.[53]

Under the overall leadership of the Satsuma general Saigō Takamori, the
imperial army split into three columns, advancing on Edo by different routes.
One of the routes took them right through Kōshū. They occupied the city of
Kōfu in mid-March, and they defeated the battered holdouts of the shogunal
army in a second decisive battle at the post town of Katsunuma, in Kōshū, on
March 29, 1868. From there, the imperial army descended on Edo, and by May
it had surrounded the shogunal capital. After extensive negotiations aimed
at minimizing bloodshed, Edo capitulated on July 4.

Chūemon followed reports of army movements and battles from his home
in Yokohama. His sense of unreality and disbelief mounted as news came of
the fighting in his home province. "There is a rumor that Katsunuma post
station was the site of a battle and has been burned to the ground . . . It is
rumored here that Lord Iwakura [a Kyoto aristocrat who was soon to become
leader of the imperial government] has entered Kōshū. Is that true?"[54]
Chūemon passed through Katsunuma every time he traveled to and from
Higashi-Aburakawa, so the news of its destruction struck very close to home.
Nevertheless, it is remarkable that the communication routes to Kōshū continued to function. Indeed, the news of the battle of Katsunuma had taken
only two days to reach him.

Even the extraordinary dramas taking place in Chūemon's home province
paled into unimportance compared with the impending collapse of Edo itself. As the second column of the imperial forces advanced through Hakone
Pass and down into the Kantō Plain, Chūemon faced the reality that they

would soon be arriving on his own doorstep. And indeed, on March 31 Chūemon reported that some of the Satsuma troops were straggling into Yokohama.

> Yesterday six hundred Satsuma men arrived at Hodogaya, and now two hundred men have arrived at Kanagawa. Since yesterday these men have been visiting Yokohama, and today many of them came to look at the foreigners' houses. I don't understand their speech, and to be on the safe side I think it's better not to go out . . . There are reported to be very many soldiers between Hakone and Kanagawa. All the inns are keeping their doors closed. The high-ranking people and even the merchants are not going out. The Kawasaki ferry stopped running yesterday. The people of Yokohama have stored supplies and evacuated their old people and children to the official buildings. Even now I am making preparations to that effect.

Bemusedly, Chūemon added, "The common people do not seem to care at all. Everyone is walking around as carefree as usual. However, prudent people are making preparations and not taking any chances."[55]

A month later, Chūemon briefly reported the final act in the drama. "Prince Arisugawa and his army are staying tonight in Kawasaki. They will shortly enter Edo. There are around two thousand of them. Lord Hitotsubashi [the ex-shogun] was sentenced to death, but he has been pardoned and ordered to retire to Mito. He left Edo on the tenth."[56]

There were many, many changes to get accustomed to. The shogun, whom Chūemon had always known as the ultimate authority, was now a disgraced rebel (after a brief period in Mito, Yoshinobu and his retainers went into permanent exile in Shizuoka). The emperor, who had never been anything but a remote figure in Chūemon's imagination, was now to be his sovereign. Edo, the massive economic and political hub that had been the backdrop for so much of Chūemon's work and play, was a ghost town. On top of the hundred and fifty thousand or more residents who had left in the previous few years, more than three hundred thousand people fled in the months after the collapse of the shogunate, including one hundred thousand retainers who were forced to follow Tokugawa Yoshinobu into exile.[57] After losing half its population, Edo (which was shortly to be renamed Eastern Capital, or Tokyo) was a shell of its former self, inhabited by roaming thieves, bandits, and uncouth western samurai. As Katsu Kaishū wrote, "The once great castle is today overgrown with weeds. Its towers are crumbling, and its enclosures have become a den for beggars and outcasts . . . At night thieves wander about and cut down the unfortunate, the aged are left to die on the streets, and bands of young men gather in the outskirts of the city to pillage and plunder."[58]

EXPANSION

In spite of the upheavals of the Mitsui trial and the Meiji revolution—one of the most epochal moments in all Japanese history—life, and business, went on. Amid all the political turmoil and military conflict—including the advance of hostile armies into Kōshū and the Kantō Plain—the transport routes between Kōshū and Yokohama remained open, and silk egg cards and other valuable produce continued to travel down the roads. Certainly, Chūemon was concerned at times about security. Money, in particular, was a worrying commodity to transport. The Edo-based transport company Kyōya would ship money for an extra fee, but Chūemon preferred to send it with a trusted associate—if he could find one who was traveling to Kōshū. Chūemon also urged his son to stick to the main roads for both security and speed— even if the post stations were extortionate: "It is definitely not a good idea to use any other roads. If anything should happen along the road, it would not be an easy matter to take care of it."[59]

But even with armies on the move, as the season came around for the new silkworm egg supplies, Chūemon urged his partners to travel to Shinshū to buy top-quality cards (by this time his purchase needs had long outgrown the capacity of his village network).[60] By the end of April, with Edo surrounded by imperial forces and Kōshū in the hands of the enemies of the Tokugawa, Chūemon wrote, "Are you buying egg cards? I want you to try hard again this year and send many of them. The foreigners are contracting for them at one ryō two bu, and they are handing over half the money in advance. That contract can be used as security for a loan . . . According to the foreigners, they will buy double this year compared with last."[61] Chūemon's business partners scoured both Kōshū and Shinshū in search of egg cards ("Once you have the cards, as I said the other day, you must pack them in boxes or in frames to prevent damage.").[62] Chūemon reported that the prospects for the egg card market had never looked so bright. "As usual, the foreigners are coming here [to Chūemon's shop] in search of egg cards. We can certainly sell whatever you send. You should plan for a sales price of one ryō each, but people are saying that the price is likely to rise to one ryō two bu or even two ryō. But that's just speculation, it's not there yet."[63] Shōjirō responded to his father's urging and put together two large shipments totaling more than twenty-three hundred cards. By that time, prices had indeed risen. A delighted Chūemon wrote, "The foreigners' demand is not so strong and prices are declining a little, so I will hold off selling. However, the price will not go below two ryō per card."[64] And several days later, "Because of the poor silkworm egg crop throughout Japan, Yokohama is ten thousand cards short. Edo and other cities have none. The foreigners had been planning for large shipments, so now the price is likely to go up. Today there are no sellers. This is the recipe for success."[65]

The boom in the egg card market continued throughout 1868 and into the following year. Although in the early part of 1869 prices were trending lower than the previous year's peak, by June Chūemon was reporting that he could sell cards even before delivery at two ryō per sheet. On July 17, as the market prepared to receive the new crop, Chūemon reported that "recently some assistants to the foreigners have been telling us that for small batches, they are likely to pay as much as five ryō or even eight ryō per card . . . If we obtain good-quality cards, we should not rush to sell them. We should wait until the prices are clearer."[66] When trading did finally open in mid-August, prices for Kōshū cards were around two to two and a half ryō per card—not the very high price some had been anticipating but still enough to give Chūemon and his partners excellent profits.[67]

By this time, Chūemon was using the services of hikyaku (couriers) almost exclusively. He fully recognized the importance of speed in communications and transportation, and although the hikyaku services were expensive, Chūemon used them for their speed and reliability. If he could get information on market conditions to his associates a little more quickly, that could give him a crucial advantage in timing his purchases and assuring adequate supplies.

On at least one occasion, Chūemon hired a special messenger to run non-stop all the way from Yokohama to Kōshū, an ultramarathon of more than ninety miles, much of it through the mountains. The messenger made the journey in less than twenty-four hours. Chūemon wrote,

> I have now sold around half our cards, and the market is looking strong. As soon as this messenger arrives, I want you to buy that same day and send the stock, even in the middle of the night . . . One person can carry around a hundred cards and should arrive in Edo within two days. I will immediately have the cards inspected and that same evening, even at night, I will bring them [to Yokohama] . . . If you wait to check up on

the goods too closely, you won't be in time. Even if it costs extra, have the goods expedited, traveling day and night . . . No matter what you have to do, make sure they arrive in Tokyo by the evening of the nineteenth so they can be inspected on the twentieth. I will transport them even at night to Yokohama, and on the twenty-first I will sell. I am sending this on the fifteenth at the hour of the dog [around 8:00 P.M.]. It should arrive without fail on the sixteenth by the western hour [about 6:00 P.M.]. If the messenger's legs hurt, allow him to stay for up to three days. Of his wage of three ryō, I have given him one ryō two bu. Give him one ryō two bu when he arrives, provided he's on time. And if he gets there before the seventh hour [4:00 P.M.], give him another two bu.[68]

Three ryō (plus bonus) was an extraordinarily high cost for a messenger. Chūemon's willingness to pay that sum reflects his recognition of the extremely high importance of speedy information flows, as well as the large sums of money involved in his transactions. According to one recollection of these express-messenger services, "For ordinary people of course [they] were only for exceptional circumstances, but large-scale merchants and traders often used them."[69] Indeed, on one occasion Chūemon felt that he had missed an important market opportunity because he did not get the news to Kōshū quickly enough: "If only I had used an express-messenger service," he wrote, "we would have made an additional two thousand ryō in profits. It is truly a shame."[70]

As Chūemon's business continued to prosper, he turned his attention to plans for expansion and diversification. The crystal-mining venture does not seem to have gone anywhere (and anyway, the Ōshū region was the site of the bitterest fighting of the entire civil war, as the Aizu domain mounted a desperate stand against the Satsuma-Chōshū alliance), but on September 26, 1868, Chūemon wrote, "I have completed my application to open a money-exchange shop and a lending shop. This is a great joy. If I am able to open an exchange shop and trade in foreign currency, even if it's a little at a time, I will have access to large amounts of money, and there will be profit in that. Unlike interest in Kōshū, the rates here are much higher."[71] The new venture had to wait, though, until he could find the right person to manage it. A year later, on September 24, 1869, Chūemon wrote to Shōjirō: "Since the government has announced it would like to decrease the number of village officials, you should consider giving up your position in the village and taking up trade as the basis for your family's future . . . If you have time, you should come here and talk about it. If you were to run either a money-lending shop or a foreign-exchange shop, you would make far more money than you do in farming. Anyone would be able to confirm this."[72]

Meanwhile, Chūemon also undertook a project he had had in mind ever since he had first come to Yokohama. In January 1869 he broke ground on the construction of a high-class inn that would offer rooms and meals to wealthier travelers. "My inn will be mostly for Kōshū people, which makes me very happy. However, many other travelers are arriving, so we will be very busy with visitors from Kōshū and others."[73] The inn opened on March 21, and from the beginning it seems to have prospered. The inn accommodated up to fifty guests, or sixty if they were willing to crowd into the rooms. Shortly after opening, Chūemon wrote, "The construction cost around five hundred ryō. However, what I hear from the people who stay here is that my rooms are the best both on the Tōkaidō and in Yokohama."[74] In September, six months after the inn's opening, Chūemon wrote, "At present, if we only had more rooms, we could have a hundred people staying here every night."[75]

Chūemon's dreams of grandiose new ventures were not confined to his business activities. Since the abandonment of the requirement that daimyo should live in Edo every other year, the daimyo, their wives and children, and their samurai retainers had begun a long-drawn-out exodus from the city, leaving many of their huge compounds empty. In January 1865 Chūemon had raised the possibility that he might move into one such compound. Lady Tōkōin, one of the official wives of the shogun, was looking for a safe place to live amid the growing disorders in the shogunal capital. Her retainers had identified a secluded compound that was currently unoccupied.

> This place is sixty-eight hundred tsubo [more than two hundred forty thousand square feet] in size. They are looking for someone to work as the guardian [shugo] of this place, and I have secretly applied for this position. Whoever holds it would have the same rank as a senior minister. If I had this position, my status would be very different from that of a minor official in Yokohama! Moreover, this would not be a job just for the sake of appearances. I would truly provide the retired lady with peace of mind. There are roughly twenty-five rooms of up to fifty tatami mats. Inside the compound there are rice fields that produce fifty bales of rice. There is also a pine mountain, a spring, a plum garden, a cherry garden, stables, and so on. It is truly a huge place. If I moved here, your mother, the children, and others could all come. Please keep this very secret![76]

Although that plan came to nothing, in late 1869 Chūemon did buy a piece of land in another part of Edo, and he subsequently built a house there.[77] Chūemon had gone from being a humble farmer seeking permission to sell a few local goods in the new port city to a wealthy merchant with deep ties to the shogunal capital. With his large business and his widely varied business ventures, in spite of all the turmoil, his future must have seemed bright indeed.

It is remarkable, however, that after years of business success, Chūemon still had to resort to borrowing to tide him over in periods of cash shortage. For all his success and prosperity, Chūemon remained at heart a risk-taking entrepreneur. Given his lack of capital, he could never have prospered as he did without taking big risks in response to new market opportunities. In spite of his many crises, he and his business partners had achieved extraordinary success in the dynamic global marketplace of Yokohama. But Chūemon's entrepreneurial optimism also led him to continue risking his own and his associates' capital even when he might have pursued a more cautious policy of consolidation. In a hint of how overextended he was becoming, Chūemon admitted at the end of 1870 that despite his prosperity, he was still short of ready cash. "I understand that I need to send fifty ryō [to a business partner in Kōshū], but at present I have nothing on hand. When I looked into the expenses of feeding our guests in the hotel, I found that it comes to one hundred fifty ryō [per month]."[78] And indeed once again Chūemon was unable to settle his debts by the end of the year.

Modern Yokohama

On October 13, 1872, Chūemon wrote to his son of the completion of a grand new project: a railway line—Japan's first—running between Tokyo and Yokohama. The emperor himself would attend the opening ceremony the following day, and Chūemon would be present.

> Tomorrow they will hold a great ceremony, which will be attended by the Son of Heaven [Go-Tenshi-sama] . . . They are making great preparations at the railway station, preparing a pavilion for the festival. Townsmen and samurai alike will be given one tag per person, and whoever is carrying one of these tags will be allowed to enter the pavilion and pay obeisance to the emperor. Altogether there will be about five thousand people . . . On one side there will be a section for for-

eigners. Throughout the town, the railway company and others have hung around a hundred and fifty thousand paper lanterns. The towns-people have decorated the lanterns with chrysanthemums and rising-sun emblems . . . There will be theatrical performances throughout the town . . . It will cost me around twenty *ryō* in expenses. Naotarō will go too. From now on, you will be able to travel from here to . . . Edo by railway. A third-class round-trip ticket is one *bu* two *shu* [about $0.40]. There are also second and first classes. I, too, plan to try riding it. It will be so fast![79]

The opening of the railway was the symbol of a momentous period of modernization for Yokohama, announcing its arrival as one of the great cit-ies of Asia. Like many periods of great change, the transformation began with a disaster. The massive fire of 1866 destroyed much of the foreign settlement and all the Japanese official buildings, including the customs house and town hall, which had been the nerve centers of the Japanese administration. In the aftermath of the disaster, there was agreement among both foreign and Japanese officials that the city should be rebuilt on much more ambitious lines, as befitted one of Japan's major cities and its window onto the world.

Yokohama was rebuilt in the image of a modern city. The road along the waterfront was paved and widened, turning it into a fashionable promenade. The customs house was rebuilt in Western style, a grand two-story building of cut stone, its windows glassed and decorated with neoclassical pedi-ments.[80] The avenue separating the Japanese and foreign communities was widened into a "noble road . . . lined, on the one side with Japanese official buildings—the Custom-house, the Post-office, the Ken-cho [prefectural of-fice], and the Central Police office; on the other, by the British and American Consulates and other buildings, with a pretty shrubbery bounding the road in front of the edifices, throughout its entire length."[81] The avenue, which was surfaced with macadam, extended beyond the original boundaries of the set-tlement, all the way to the site of the former licensed quarter. The marsh that had separated the licensed quarter from the settlement was filled in ("thus removing a source of rheumatic and febrile complaints, then very common")[82] and turned into building lots, for foreigners on the south side and Japanese on the north. The ruins of the licensed quarter were never rebuilt. The brothel district itself was removed to a new location further from the town, while its former site was turned into a recreation ground, used for cricket matches and other leisure activities (today the site remains one of the largest parks in cen-tral Yokohama and houses the Yokohama BayStars' baseball stadium).[83]

Much of this reconstruction was carried out based on a master plan by the British engineer Henry Brunton. Brunton came to Yokohama in 1868 to build lighthouses, but he ended up playing a major role in the technological transformation of Yokohama's urban infrastructure—which in turn became a model for urban development throughout Japan. In addition to land reclamation and road improvement, Brunton also designed and built the first iron bridge in the Kantō region, and he supervised the installation of a modern drainage system, the development of gas-powered street lighting (though this project took many years to complete), the installation of flood-control barriers along the waterways, and the planning of parks and recreational spaces.[84] Another significant force in the rebuilding of Yokohama was Shimizu Kisuke. A second-generation master builder from Edo, Shimizu opened a branch in Yokohama in 1859. He was employed by the Kanagawa commissioners to build their own headquarters, as well as Yokohama's first iron foundry. After studying Western architectural models, he built the new German consulate in 1867 and worked on a variety of other reconstruction projects. After the Meiji Restoration, he took his skills in Western-style construction to Tokyo, building a number of prominent structures that blended Western designs with Japanese features. His company remains today one of Japan's largest construction firms.[85]

By the turn of the 1870s, Yokohama had become a center for much more than the textile and tea trades. The new Meiji government pursued an explicit policy of modernization and technology transfer, and Yokohama was the conduit through which a massive flow of information, knowledge, and skills was brought into Japan. Yokohama was the showcase for revolutionary transformations in mass media, financial and corporate institutions, food and drink culture, education, medicine and epidemiology, and transportation and communications.

It was in this last field, transportation and communication networks, that Yokohama had perhaps the most directly transformative impact on the Kantō region and ultimately the emerging modern nation-state. Yokohama was the starting point of Japan's first stagecoach, steamship, railway, telegraph, and postal services, not to mention the medium that revolutionized local transport throughout nineteenth-century Asia—the hand-pulled rickshaw.

We have seen in Chūemon's story the powerful business motive to accelerate the flow of information between Yokohama and Kōshū. Chūemon's on-the-spot knowledge of Yokohama market prices—which were in turn fed by news flowing into Yokohama of global market conditions—was a crucial competitive advantage. Recognizing this, Chūemon did everything he could to convey timely information to his associates in Kōshū so that they could buy or sell before the market moved. At times, he also spread misinformation in order to confuse his competitors in the Kōshū market. Chūemon was also strongly motivated to speed up the transportation of goods, since by doing so he could turn his scarce capital around more quickly. Although Chūemon would certainly have been aware of revolutionary developments in communications and transportation such as railroads, steamships, telegraph networks, and man-made water systems, he did not personally have access to any of these technologies. Instead, he invested more and more heavily in those tools that were available—packhorse and river transport and communication by *hikyaku* runners—to accelerate the flow of goods and information. But in Chūemon's experiences, it is possible to see at work a technological imperative that helps explain the rapid introduction of communication and transport technologies into Yokohama in spite of the very high costs, and that ultimately led to revolutionary change in Japan's domestic transport and communication systems as well as its global connectivity.

The first modern transport system to connect two Japanese cities was the steamship. The *Inegawa-maru*, an American-built steamer owned by Japanese entrepreneur Itō Jihei, began operating a commercial service between Yokohama and Edo in March 1868. The eighty-foot vessel was powered by a thirty-five-horsepower steam engine, but it also had five masts for wind power to help it on its way. It plied between Eidaibashi in Edo and the Yokohama docks, making the round-trip twice a day. The ship made the eighteen-mile journey in two hours and charged twenty silver *monme* (about $0.50) for a one-way ticket.[86] Early in 1869, a group of fifty-four Edo-based shipping agents grouped together to buy a small, forty-five-foot steamer they called the *Hotaru* (*Firefly*). Over the next year, another six steamships began operating the Tokyo–Yokohama route. Two of them were owned by Japanese, the other four by Yokohama-based foreign businessmen. Between them, these ships were able to carry more than one thousand passengers per day between Yokohama and Tokyo. It is unclear how profitable they were given the high cost of buying and operating a steamship, but surviving accounting records indicate that owners expected to recoup their initial investment within two to three years.[87] Although most steamships continued to be built overseas and purchased secondhand in Japan, one of them, the *Kōmei-maru*, was built in Japan's brand-new Yokosuka Shipyard, just a few miles down the coast from Yokohama. It was staffed by French-trained engineers and pilots, while its crew members were recruited mostly from the local fishing communities.[88]

The largest of the Yokohama–Tokyo steamships was the *City of Yedo*, owned by an American consortium headed by G. W. White and with a capacity of one hundred fifty passengers. Tragically, on August 1, 1870, shortly after leaving the Tokyo docks, the *City of Yedo*'s boiler exploded and the ship instantly sank. Of the 166 passengers on board, 143 were killed or injured. Five of the victims were foreigners, out of 10 foreigners who were riding the ship that morning. The Japanese passengers came from eighteen different regions of Japan, and they included merchants, government officials, and samurai. The great diversity of the passenger list indicates the magnetism of Yokohama for Japanese from throughout Japan.[89]

Passenger steamship services also began between Yokohama and other destinations in Japan and overseas. The P&O Company launched a regular service from Yokohama to Shanghai with ongoing connections to Europe in 1864. In early 1867, the Pacific Mail Steamship Company began passenger service from Yokohama to San Francisco on the *Colorado*, carrying up to a thousand passengers on each trip.[90] By the early 1870s, there were at least three ships running the Yokohama–San Francisco route (including the *America*, reputed to be the largest wooden steamer in the world), and there were daily scheduled services connecting Yokohama to Kobe, Nagasaki, Hong Kong, and Shanghai. With the opening of the Suez Canal in 1869, services from Yokohama to Europe via China also expanded.

By the turn of the 1870s there were also several horse-drawn coach services operating between Yokohama and Tokyo. In the 1860s the narrow road connecting Yokohama to Kanagawa had been unsuitable for heavy vehicles. Although this road was—with foreign tastes in mind—designed for horseback riding, it climbed several steep hills, and it had a number of bridges in the steeply humped "*taiko* drum" style, making it hard to maneuver a large vehicle. However, in 1869 a new road was laid between Yokohama and Kanagawa, the so-called Bashamichi (Carriageway). The opening of Bashamichi spelled the end of the old ferry service across the bay between Yokohama and Kanagawa, and in the following years, it became the route for coaches, telegraph lines, and the new railway.

William Rangan & Company launched a coach service on the Yokohama–Tokyo route on January 1, 1869—the same day that the Tsukiji district of Tokyo was opened to foreign residence. Rangan's coaches flew a flag emblazoned with a black horse on a red background. They held up to twelve passengers and were pulled by four horses—though a hostile newspaper report commented that the vehicles were actually "partially covered wagons," whose owners called them stagecoaches with "humorous disregard of honorable associations."[91] The one-way fare was two dollars—considerably more than the competing steamship services but with a more direct point-to-point service. At around the same time a Japanese firm, Narikomaya, opened a competing service. The firm, which operated a four-horse coach, was jointly owned by Tokyo and Yokohama merchants, the latter including the photographer Shimooka Renjō (who is discussed in chapter 3).[92]

The Japanese government permitted coach services only on the Tōkaidō route between Yokohama and Tsukiji. Government regulations dictated that when coaches encountered one another they should each pass on the left—inaugurating Japan's history of left-side driving that continues to this day. And if a coach should encounter a nobleman, regulations required that the passengers should all alight from the coach—an indication that even with the introduction of this new mode of transport, old ways of thinking had not quite died out.[93]

When the Tokyo–Yokohama railway superseded the stagecoach, the coaching companies responded by expanding services from Yokohama to points west on the Tōkaidō. Sutherland & Co. was already operating between Yokohama and Odawara, with staging posts at Fujisawa and Ōiso, at the end of the 1860s. Sutherland was bought out by Cobb & Co., which added service to Kamakura, Enoshima, Izu, and Hakone. In 1875, it added a line to the silk-trading center of Hachiōji.[94] Sutherland also operated a mail service, and it was notable for developing the first Japanese postage stamp: a perforated pink or yellow stamp depicting a galloping horse whose rider is blowing a horn. It came in denominations of a quarter bu and one bu and was printed "SUTHERLAND & Co. Postage 1 Boo."[95]

Also at the end of the 1860s, the jinrikisha (rickshaw) began appearing on the streets of Yokohama. Its origins are still unclear, although Jonathan Goble, an American Baptist missionary and adventurer, claimed to have invented it.[96] The first documentary evidence of the rickshaw's existence is from April 24, 1870, when three residents of Tokyo—Izumi Yōsuke, Suzuki Tokujirō, and Takayama Kōsuke—applied for a license to manufacture and sell the vehicles. An advertisement published by Suzuki illustrates a lady sitting at her ease in a rickshaw while being pulled along the road. A Tokyo government ruling in November 1870 gave Suzuki and his associates the sole right to manufacture the vehicles, but already many look-alikes were springing up, and it is clear that Suzuki et al. were unable to hold on to their monopoly. It has been estimated that by 1872, more than ten thousand rickshaws were plying the streets of Tokyo. In fact, the diary of the Sekiguchi family in Namamugi village outside Yokohama indicates that by the early 1870s, some of the farmers in the village were borrowing money from the Sekiguchis and building their own rickshaws to put into service on the Tōkaidō.[97] Yokohama is estimated to have had several hundred rickshaws in service by this time, and in 1871 the Kanagawa government began imposing an annual tax on rickshaws in service. In 1874, Tokyo government statistics show the manufacture of fifty eight hundred rickshaws in that year alone. The rickshaw spread like wildfire throughout Japan (and indeed throughout all Asia, where it remained a primary means of urban transportation until the mid-twentieth century), and by 1875, the number of rickshaws nationwide was already estimated at one hundred ten thousand. The cost of a vehicle in 1871 was around fourteen ryō.[98] Surprisingly, Chūemon does not once mention the rickshaw in his letters.

The rickshaw also entered the competition in transportation services between Yokohama and Tokyo. A Tokyo-based transport agent by the name of Genshichi launched a rickshaw service in June 1870. Genshichi's rickshaws were four-seaters, pulled by two runners selected from his large staff of barrow pullers and porters. Competing services quickly sprang up on this route, and when Gunma silk trader Tajima Yahei visited Yokohama in 1871, he commented that "the Tōkaidō was crowded with rickshaws going in both directions."[99]

The rapid spread of competing transport services on the Edo/Tokyo–Yokohama route illustrates the enormous importance this route had for the Kantō economy. Indeed, no other route in Japan compares in the speed of introduction of new transportation technologies. This may have been due in part to the presence of well-capitalized foreigners (as well as Japanese entrepreneurs) looking for new sources of profit. But investors were motivated primarily by the high volume of travel between the two cities. It is no coincidence that Japan's first railway was also on this route.

Eighteen years earlier, in 1854, Commodore Matthew Perry had presented the Japanese government with a miniature train and engine, together with a working telegraph system (the telegraph machine is still on display in the Communications Museum in Tokyo). Although Perry's intention was to show the Japanese the potential benefits of a policy of openness, it took almost twenty years for the promise of the railway to be realized. The problem was the enormous cost. The first plan for a Yokohama–Edo line was submitted as early as March 1867 by one of the British residents in Yokohama but quickly rejected by the government on financial grounds. Then, in January 1868—just days before the collapse of the shogunal government—a shogunal minister signed a contract with an American consortium for the construction of a railway over a three-year period. But when the new government took over, in spite of its pledge to honor the previous government's commitments, it rejected the railway contract on the grounds that the completed line would be foreign owned. In February 1869 six Japanese merchants, residents of Yokohama, submitted their own proposal, which emphasized patriotic considerations. Their proposal was vague, however, when it came to the question of financing.[100]

In December 1869, the government approved a proposal by an English businessman, N. H. Lay. Lay committed to provide financing, materials, and technical personnel for the project. The contract called for Lay himself to advance the money for the project and for payments on the loan to come from import and export taxes, as well as a percentage of the railway's revenues. The Japanese government would both own and manage the railway. The Lay proposal foundered, however, over the question of financing. Lay succeeded in floating a loan on the London exchange for one million pounds, at an interest rate of 9 percent. The Japanese government had promised to pay Lay an interest rate of 12 percent, and when it learned of the large profit he would make on the interest, it exercised its sovereign privilege and withdrew from the contract. In the end the government sent its own representative to London to negotiate a loan at 9 percent. The entire process therefore remained in the hands of the Japanese government. Nevertheless, most of the equipment, and all the key personnel, were brought to Japan from England, so the project in the end was both financed and built by the British.[101]

Construction of the eighteen-mile track began in April 1870, and for two years the construction project dominated the landscape between Yokohama and Tokyo. The complex project involved detailed surveying, the purchase of land along the route, the reclamation of coastal land to extend the line along the seashore, the grading of cuttings and embankments, the importation and construction of track, and the construction of twenty-two bridges, most notably a massive iron bridge across the Tama River.

After two years of intense effort, the trains began running on June 12, 1872. The Yokohama terminus was at what is now Sakuragichō Station, close to the center of the town. On the Tokyo end, the original line went only as far as Shinagawa, on the outskirts of Tokyo; it took another four months to extend the line to Shinbashi, just a stone's throw from the Imperial Palace in the center of Tokyo. The train took thirty-five minutes to complete the eighteen-mile route. The completed line included four intermediate stations (Kanagawa, Tsurumi, Kawasaki, and Shinagawa), forty-two railway sheds and other buildings, four engine-turning stations, four dams, ten steam engines, fifty-eight passenger cars, and seventy-eight freight cars. At the time of its completion, the railway was employing forty-four foreign specialists, including engine drivers, masons, carpenters, and clerks (this number was actually to rise to one hundred three by 1876, before dropping steeply under a new government policy of replacing foreign employees with trained Japanese specialists).[102]

In spite of his initial enthusiasm for the magnificent new transportation route, eight months after the opening ceremony Chūemon commented, "Very few people are riding the train."[103] The statistics prove him wrong. In its first three months, the Yokohama–Tokyo line had almost half a million passengers, and in the following full year (1873) the number increased to 1.4 million, or an average of almost 4,000 a day on its nine scheduled departures each way (average 220 people per train). The popularity of the railway, even at the relatively high prices charged, offered a strong confirmation of the importance of the Tokyo–Yokohama route, which by this time had become the single most-traveled route in Japan.[104]

The turn of the 1870s also saw a revolution in communications and media, starting with an explosion in newspaper publishing and extending to the laying of a national telegraph system and the inauguration of a national postal system. Once again, Yokohama was the nursery for these new services.

Three English-language newspapers opened in Yokohama during the 1860s: the Japan Times, founded in 1862; the Japan Herald, 1865; and the Japan Gazette, which was the first daily newspaper, in 1867.[105] The first Japanese-language newspaper was the Kaigai shinbun (Overseas news), founded in 1865 by Joseph Heco (see chapter 3 for more on Heco). Heco saw his newspaper as a way to inform his countrymen about overseas affairs. The material in the newspaper was translated from foreign newspapers, which arrived with each ship that docked in Yokohama.

A second Japanese-language newspaper, the Bankoku shinbun (News of many countries), was started in 1867 by an English priest, M. Buckworth Bailey. Like the Kaigai shinbun it contained summaries of foreign news, arranged country by country. Also like the Kaigai shinbun, it was published on woodblocks specially carved for each issue. Unfortunately, in spite of his good intentions, the Reverend Bailey was deeply unpopular in Yokohama. Shortly after founding the newspaper, he was forced out of his position at Christ Church, and he went home to England, leaving a relieved board of church trustees to report, "We have built a new aisle, bought an organ, and sent Mr. Bailey home. Future generations of residents should contribute their share of these expenses since they would enjoy the benefits!"[106] The newspaper, however, was forced to close.

Since these journals appeared irregularly and did not contain Japanese news or commentary, they may not qualify as true newspapers. But they clearly showed the possibilities for a regular published source of news for a wide reading public. Meanwhile the English-language newspapers, which contained local and foreign news and analysis, sometimes combative commentary including at times criticism of both the foreign and Japanese authorities, and trade reports, shipping news, advertising, and other practical items, were a model that many Japanese looked to as they considered launching their own newspapers.

Both the shogunate and the new Meiji government were intensely conscious of the utility of newspapers and of the value of controlling the news and opinions they expressed. In its final years the shogunal government sponsored several newspapers coming out of the Yōsho Shirabeshō (Center for the Investigation of Foreign Books). For the most part, like their Yokohama counterparts, they were translations of foreign news sheets. However, starting in 1870 a new and influential newspaper, the Yokohama shinbun, began publication in Yokohama. This was much more in the style of a foreign newspaper, with a mixture of advertising, news, and commentary.[107]

By the early 1870s, newspapers had become integrated into the fabric of Japanese urban life. During the 1860s, Chūemon mentioned several times that he was enclosing a copy of a letter describing some important event. Chūemon was generally well informed about major events taking place in Japan, including the turmoil in Kyoto in the mid-1860s, the actions of the restive provinces of Chōshū and Satsuma, and the doings of major daimyo whose actions might impact the Yokohama trade. He did not always indicate where he obtained this information, but we can assume it was a mixture of word of mouth from travelers along the major highways, printed broadsheets, and circulating letters, which would be copied and recopied as they made their way around the literate circles of Japan.

However, by the end of the 1860s, Chūemon was clearly supplementing his information sources with newspapers. In June 1868, he enclosed a newspaper with his letter and asked Shōjirō to give it to one of their business partners.[108] Chūemon had been faithfully reporting commodity prices by letter for years, but now Chūemon wrote, "The rest of the market conditions you can see in the newspapers."[109] The spread of newspapers was both a boon and a threat to Yokohama-based merchants like Chūemon. On the one hand, the newspapers provided comprehensive and up-to-date information on domestic and foreign events, market conditions, and shipping movements.

This information was certainly useful to merchants in both the cities and the provinces. But on the other hand, the availability of reliable and regularly printed information greatly reduced the information advantage of Yokohama-based merchants. The market information that they might previously have gleaned from talking to foreign merchant houses and then rapidly communicated to their provincial associates in order to take advantage of price differentials was now readily available to anyone with access to a newspaper.

By the early 1870s, Chūemon was also using Japan's new national postal service, one of the first branches of which was in Yokohama (the Yokohama Post Office opened on August 30, 1871). The Japanese postal service was the brainchild of Maejima Hisoka, a young samurai who had spent a year in England studying the workings of the British system. There was a particular incentive to introduce a post office in Yokohama, because several of the foreign nations already operated their own offices in the town, for international mail only and using their own systems of postage stamps. These offices served both as examples and as something of a goad to the Japanese government.

Until the opening of the postal service, Chūemon and other merchants like him used the services of private courier firms, hikyaku. The largest of these had national networks and offered sophisticated services, including the issue of bills of exchange and the discounting of notes. They sent mail and other items through a network of runners, who would operate in relays to cover the major highways of Japan in remarkably short times. These services met many of the needs of the merchants, and Chūemon was a loyal user of one in particular, the Kyōya, based in Edo but with branches in Kōshū.[110]

However, the hikyaku lacked many of the amenities of a modern postal service, and they could be extremely expensive—as much as three ryō for a single delivery in one case recounted by Chūemon. Maejima recalled in his memoirs a conversation he had with the head of the league of hikyaku firms, who had come to protest against the threat to the hikyaku business when the new postal service opened. The representative "said that for more than two hundred and fifty years the communications of our country had been excellent . . . Although one would expect the government to prize this, on the contrary, its attempt to seize this business for itself was the acme of wickedness." Maejima, however, argued that no Japanese hikyaku could offer a truly national service, including to remote areas like northern Hokkaido—let alone an international service. "I explained that communications were of the utmost importance in international trade and in the life of a society, and that throughout the world, an enlightened country had to construct a system for communications within the country and abroad. Gradually I made him understand that the house-based operations of his association, with their message delivery limited to one region or one country, could not accomplish this great purpose."[111]

However, the Japanese postal service employed many of the existing hikyaku firms, subcontracting at first and later hiring the couriers away from their former employers. The early service was quite limited: much as the hikyaku services before it, the postal service could deliver only to the post stations along the major highways, and for onward delivery the sender had to continue to rely on private services. But the system quickly expanded, and in April 1873, the Japanese post office instituted a system of standard delivery fees to any address nationwide: one sen ($0.01) within the city of origin and two sen for anywhere else in the country. This was a drastic reduction from the hikyaku fees and could be achieved only with the financial resources of the government behind it.[112]

Although Chūemon did not mention the opening of the post office, he did use the service. At least two of the five surviving letters sent in 1873 can be verified as having gone through the new postal system.

Yokohama was also a hub of Japan's rapidly developing telegraph system. While telegraph connections are much cheaper and less demanding in terms of infrastructure than railways, they nevertheless required access to advanced technology and a large amount of investment capital. They were, however, a priority for the new government, which recognized their strategic and military potential. Japan's first public telegraph line opened between Edo/Tokyo and Yokohama in December 1869. The baby steps of the Japanese system came at a momentous time in the maturation of the global telegraph network. After the development of undersea cable, massive projects were initiated to connect the world's continents. In 1866 the Atlantic telegraph connected Great Britain and Europe with the United States and Canada. In 1870, an undersea line connected India to Britain, and shortly afterward the line was extended to Singapore, Shanghai, and Hong Kong. Meanwhile, the Russian government completed an overland telegraph route across Siberia to Vladivostok. It was only a matter of time before the telegraph reached Japan, and indeed in 1871 the undersea cable was brought to Nagasaki, connecting Japan with Asia, Europe, and the United States. The spread of international cable was actually happening faster than the development of domestic telegraph lines: at the time of the opening of the undersea cable, Nagasaki was still not connected to Yokohama and Tokyo. Foreign merchant houses in Yokohama had to rely on steamship services to bring news on the last leg from Nagasaki. Nevertheless, by the end of 1871, information that a decade earlier would have taken three months to reach Yokohama from London or New York now arrived within ten days or less. In 1873 the overland telegraph route from Tokyo and Yokohama to Nagasaki was finally completed, allowing same-day communication between Yokohama, Shanghai, Hong Kong, Singapore, and the capitals of the Western world.[113]

There is no record of Chūemon using the telegraph service. Public telegraphic connections to Kōshū (which had become Yamanashi prefecture) did not open until 1879, by which time Chūemon's business career was over.[114] There is no doubt that if he had still been in business, Chūemon would have leaped at the chance to speed up his communications with his son and business associates in Kōshū and beyond. His impulse to transmit important news and instructions as quickly as possible is evident throughout his business career in Yokohama. But would he have benefited from the telegraph? Chūemon's competitive advantage in the 1860s came in part from his privileged access to information about the Yokohama market and his ability to convey that information quickly and secretly to his associates in Kōshū, enabling them to take advantage of pricing disparities between the two markets. The advent of the newspaper with its regular market reports was already chipping away at that advantage by the end of the 1860s. With the arrival of the telegraph, access to market information was instantly available to anyone with a Yokohama correspondent. Chūemon's competitive advantage would have quickly evaporated. He benefited, in fact, from a short-term window of opportunity, and the very success of his activities, and those of others like him, helped stimulate the drive to introduce new technologies that accelerated communications and transportation while drastically reducing the privileged access to information.

By the turn of the 1870s, it was also apparent that Yokohama was at the center of an emerging revolution in Japanese lifestyles. Not only new modes of transportation but also new habits of clothing, food, housing, and hygiene were taking root in the Tokyo-Yokohama area and spreading into the hinterland.

As early as June 4, 1860, Francis Hall wrote, "My servant Iwasaki came into my room this morning . . . to display his new clothes cut after the Chinese fashion with close sleeves . . . I suspect if the people were left to themselves they would readily imitate foreigners in many customs. Sadajirō, who has been wearing a shirt for several days, is an object of great curiosity whenever he appears in the Tōkaidō. He says he is envied more than laughed at."[115]

John Black reports that beginning in the mid-1860s,

gradually a custom began to show itself, of native gentlemen having one room in their houses, furnished after a foreign fashion, with a handsome square carpet or rug in the centre of the room—over their own nice mats; a table covered with a gag cloth and chairs surrounding it, in the middle of the carpet; glass windows in at least one of the sliding sashes; and, sometimes, pictures and mirrors hanging on the sides of the room. Many began to eat meat and declare that they liked it; and all would drink champagne to any extent; thus giving the best proof of their approbation. As yet none dared appear openly in foreign costume. Any who did so would certainly have been roughly handled. But it was not long before they adopted them without fear.[116]

The transformation of clothing was not only a matter of fashion. Manufactured cloth was one of the major imports into Yokohama, and its rapid spread transformed both the economics and the aesthetics of clothing. Yamakawa Kikue, a woman from the samurai class in the Mito domain (now Ibaraki prefecture), recalled how "the popularity of obi made of imported grogram [a cloth made of mixed silk and wool] spread like wildfire . . . Once the country was forced open, new goods appeared with an increasing rush, just as water, having breached a dike, floods in with ever greater force. Imported cotton yarn . . . first made an appearance about this time. Thanks to this, within a few years, both the constant sound of the spinning wheel in Mito households and the cotton fields along the banks of the Naka River had disappeared."

Yamakawa recalls the reaction of the townspeople of Mito when the largest retailer began stocking merino wool (known locally as Chinese crepe, though actually manufactured in Europe): "That smooth, soft feel, different from either silk or cotton; once one had worn it nothing else would do. People began to use Chinese crepe for obi, for the cords for fastening the kimono around the waist, for the sleeves of underrobes."[117]

Clothing was one of the many areas connected to the body that the Japanese authorities attempted to regulate in order to make their subjects more "civilized." John Black reported that beginning in 1867, all coolies in Yokohama were required to wear clothes. As the government directive stated, "Those who come from divers places to Yokohama and make their living as porters, carters, laborers, coolies and boatmen, are in the habit, especially in the summer, of plying their calling in a state bordering on nudity. This is very reprehensible; and in future no one who does not wear a shirt or tunic, properly closed by a girdle, will be allowed to remain in Yokohama. The Coolie-masters are to give liberal assistance for the suppression of such people."[118]

In 1871, the Kanagawa government supplemented these regulations with new laws against public urination. From now on, this offense would be punishable as a crime. For those with urgent need, the municipality also introduced Yokohama's first public toilets in 1871.[119]

Food culture also came under new influences, as Yokohama and the other treaty ports developed into laboratories of new lifestyles. Privileged Japanese could sample Western food at the tables of foreigners, who invited them to banquets and receptions. By 1868, there were sixteen foreign hotels and clubs in Yokohama, and it was not unknown for them to entertain Japanese guests. In 1866, the English cartoonist Charles Wirgman drew a picture of a young Japanese in the United Service Club, a cigar in one hand and a glass of champagne in the other. The top part of his body is dressed in Japanese style, but his sword is tucked into a pair of Western-style trousers. Under the caption "Young Japan at the U.S. Club (a fact)," the Japanese is saying, "I like only civilization." Wirgman's model is said to have been Hayashi Tadasu, a student at Mrs. Hepburn's school and already polished in Western manners, who would go on to be foreign minister in the Meiji government.[120] Ernest Satow, a young British diplomat in Yokohama in the 1860s, recalls in his autobiography how samurai would often visit him from Edo to discuss his views of the world, and "the two-sworded men were always happy to get a glass of wine or liqueur and a foreign cigar, and they were fond of discussion. They would sit for hours if the subject interested them."[121]

Meanwhile, the lower classes could sample Western food and drink at the many cheap drinking houses that opened along the waterfront as well as on the edge of the swamp area behind the foreign settlement. The American businessman Raphael Schoyer owned several of the waterfront properties where "grog shops" had sprung up, and one resident complained that "[on his property near the pier] is a row of Japanese-style one-story houses. In those houses, men of all nationalities are operating drinking establishments, and on Sundays and holidays there is an indescribable noise and confusion." According to a Prussian survey, Schoyer was renting to five Portuguese, four French, two English, two Americans, and one Dutchman. These bars were places where Europeans and Japanese, blacks and whites, servants and sailors could mix indiscriminately in the shared enjoyment of cheap liquor.[122]

Imported liquor was brought into Japan in large quantities, and although much of it was expensive by Japanese standards, by the turn of the 1870s it was being sold by Japanese as well as foreign retailers. The Japan Brewing Company (forerunner of Kirin Beer) began producing domestically made beer in Yokohama in 1869. In 1871 Japanese residents could buy a bottle of beer in the Fujimichō section of Yokohama for three shu three hundred mon (about $0.25). Railway engineer Kawahara Eikichi went out drinking with his friends in 1873 and drank his fill for about one yen, which was the price of twenty pounds of rice at the time.[123] There was also an increasing interest among the Japanese in the consumption of meat, and by the turn of the 1870s there were a number of restaurants in Yokohama that served the Japanese community with Western-style meat dishes.

For the most part, the Japanese government allowed food culture to develop as it would. But one issue, the question of meat eating, became embroiled in issues of national identity and national development. Many Japanese who were educated in Western medicine came to believe that the Japanese were physically smaller and more subject to disease than Westerners because of the lack of meat in their diet and that meat eating should be encouraged as a matter of national policy. To that end, in 1872 the emperor publicly announced that his household ate meat and that he himself greatly enjoyed beef and mutton. Some questioned whether it was appropriate for the emperor to eat beef when Japan's native religion, of which he was considered by many to be the high priest, abhorred any contact with death. But the emperor's handlers responded that in ancient times Japan had in fact been a vigorous meat-eating culture, and it was only with the advent of Buddhism (which was now being denigrated as an effete foreign cult) that meat eating had been proscribed.[124]

However, Sugimoto Etsu recalled that when her father brought home some beef after a doctor had told him it would make his family stronger, young Etsu found her grandmother and a maid "sitting before the black-and-gold cabinet of the family shrine. They had a large lacquer tray with rolls of white paper on it and the maid was pasting paper over the gilded doors of the shrine." When Etsu asked why, her grandmother replied, "The ox flesh is to be brought into the house in another hour and our duty is to protect the holy shrine from pollution."[125]

As a founder-resident of Yokohama, Chūemon was undoubtedly aware of many of these trends. Although neither he nor Naotarō commented in surviving letters on their own use of foreign clothing, food, or drink (and the one surviving photograph of them, taken in 1872, shows them in strictly Japanese attire), they do show an awareness of the business opportunities such new products might bring. Naotarō in particular was eager to experiment. Between 1865 and 1867 he tried shipping imported cotton thread, dyestuffs, stoves, and liquor to Kōshū.[126] None of these products seem to have caught on: after their first mention, they all disappear from the letters. However, as we will see, in the early 1870s Naotarō began regularly sending imported sugar to his brother in Kōshū, while Chūemon opened a shop specializing in the tailoring of Western clothes. Given this level of involvement, it is hard to believe that Chūemon—and more particularly Naotarō, who had spent the whole of his adult life in Yokohama—would not also have been influenced in their personal lifestyles by the new trends. Indeed, one striking feature of a family photograph of 1872 is that Naotarō is prominently holding up to the camera an imported pocket watch.

The surviving letters of another Yokohama merchant family, the Yoshidas from Gunma, do indicate a number of Western influences in the family's daily life. In November 1871, the head of the family sent home to Gunma a package of beef preserved in miso, telling his family that this was his granddaughter's favorite food in Yokohama. And in January 1872, he wrote that since his daughter-in-law was not producing enough milk to feed her baby, he was trying to persuade her to use cow's milk instead. At around the same time he writes of the spread of Western-style haircuts and comments that his own granddaughter now sported a Western hairstyle.[127]

In September 1871 the Meiji government passed a law encouraging (though not requiring) Japanese men to grow out their hair, abandoning the shaved crown and oiled topknot that had been a near-universal marker of Japanese masculinity. In the photograph of Chūemon and his family of 1872, Shōjirō and Naotarō still wear the topknot, but—perhaps because as a tailor of Western clothes he felt the need to cultivate a more Western image— Chūemon has cut off his topknot and grown out his hair. Married women's custom of blackening their teeth was also officially discouraged after the turn of the 1870s and seems to have rapidly faded from use. The symbol of new government policies in regard to bodily habits was often the imperial family. By the early 1870s, the emperor and empress both dressed in Western clothes, the emperor had styled his hair in the Western fashion, and the empress had stopped blackening her teeth.[128]

Government policies were far more intrusive when it came to new measures for the promotion of public hygiene and the prevention of disease. Again, Yokohama was a laboratory for the introduction of such measures. While the foreigners may have been responsible for introducing diseases like cholera and also for further spreading endemic diseases such as smallpox and syphilis, Western medical practitioners were also highly active in introducing facilities and regulations to control these diseases, albeit based on limited understanding of the diseases themselves (the cholera bacillus was not identified until 1883, and John Snow's theory of the relationship between cholera and drinking-water contamination was only just becoming widely known).[129]

Until the arrival of a large number of foreigners in the 1860s, health had been treated mostly as a private matter. But as Japanese doctors began to learn about foreign concepts of public health, they came to realize that, as Nagayo Sensai described it, "words such as 'sanitary' and 'health' . . . referred to a special public administrative system that was responsible for the protection of the health of all citizens of the nation."[130] New systems of sanitation, quarantine, hospitalization, and isolation were required to ensure the development of a healthy and well-regulated nation.

From the perspective of worried foreigners, there was a need for public-health measures to protect the foreign communities—if no one else—against disease. In Yokohama, foreigners advocated the creation of a municipal sanitation system in order to improve the air and water quality of the town. Through the 1860s Yokohama had no street lighting, no running water, no sewage system, and no trash-disposal system. Conditions in the Japanese town were considered particularly unsanitary—thus putting the entire community at risk of disease. As John Black described the situation, "The small canals . . . became black and offensive; and it was often as much as could be endured to pass them . . . Yet houses were not only built on their banks, but actually overhanging . . . these fetid, miasmatic canals; and it was often remarked that the rarity of any epidemic attacking the inhabitants, almost gave the lie to those who contend that stagnant pools, unripe fruit, and what foreigners would esteem low diet, are the generators of such diseases."[131]

In September 1863, the foreign community called on the Kanagawa commissioners to install proper drains in the streets of the foreign settlement, offering to pay to bring an engineer in from one of the Chinese ports. And in 1864, the foreign community organized itself to conduct a regular "scavenger hunt" "that should daily clear the streets, drains and Bund, of any offensive rubbish, and remove it to a suitable distance from the settlement; and, the formation of a corps of boats, of which one was to be at the end of each street leading to the Bund, in order to receive and convey away all the rubbish collected by the scavengers and by the coolies of private houses."[132] At the end of

1864, the Kanagawa commissioners agreed to turn over a portion of the land rents to a newly formed Municipal Council run by the foreign community. The membership of the council was apportioned according to the ratios of population among the different treaty powers, with the British, Americans, and French having the strongest representation. The council received income of about six thousand dollars a year from a 20 percent share of the land rents, together with license fees and fines that the consuls made over to the council. The council began energetically enacting measures to rid the settlement of stray dogs and forbidding the slaughter of animals and the storage of explosives within the foreign settlement. A police force was created to enforce the ordinances. However, the council soon lost its energy. By its third meeting, only eight members put in an appearance—fewer than were needed to pass a vote. The council also suffered from meddling by the consuls, who had a tendency to overrule its decisions.[133] Eventually, the management of the town's infrastructure was returned to the Japanese, with renewed pleas for them to undertake steps to improve sanitation. In 1867, the Kanagawa government finally began deepening the main canals to a depth of at least four feet at low tide so that they no longer appeared to be "hotbeds of malaria and its concomitant evils."[134]

However, in spite of all efforts, the sanitary conditions of Yokohama remained far short of what the foreign community felt was desirable. As John Black reflected in 1879, "Even now, the drainage is imperfect, the streets are requiring repairs, and the streets of the foreign settlement are dark at night," even though "the adjoining native settlement is brilliantly lighted with gas."[135]

Japanese officials took a strong interest in foreign ideas on urban infrastructure, health, and hygiene. Increasingly, Japanese elites had access to firsthand accounts of foreign cities and their sophisticated infrastructure. Japanese doctors, who had a long tradition of studying Western medical practices, were particularly interested in foreign practices relating to public health. Thus, when foreign military officials asked the Yokohama government to consider implementing compulsory medical inspections of prostitutes, with forced quarantine for those found to be infected with syphilis, the government readily agreed, even though the system would be supervised by foreign doctors and was designed primarily to improve the health of foreign soldiers, who might logically be seen as potential enemies. In February 1871, in the midst of a smallpox outbreak, the governor of Kanagawa accepted the advice of foreign doctors to begin a campaign of compulsory vaccination. In 1874, the central government extended this to the entire Japanese population. And in August 1870, the Kanagawa authorities appealed to the central government to help them create a public hospital in Yokohama. In their memorial, they pointed to the success of the foreign hospitals in both treating the sick and controlling contagious diseases through hospitalization. In the end, the large cost of construction and equipment was subscribed mostly by the Yokohama merchant community, Japanese and foreign. The hospital, which cost almost thirty thousand ryō to build and equip, was completed in 1873. It hired an American missionary doctor, Duane Simmons, as its first chief medical officer at a salary of three hundred twenty yen per month.[136]

On the surface, Chūemon was at his most conservative when it came to changes in bodily practice, particularly medicine and the treatment of disease. Chūemon mentions health and disease frequently in his letters— whether writing about his own family's struggles with scabies, or worrying about his frailer family members, or expressing his concern about regional epidemics. Chūemon clearly considered himself something of an authority on medicine and the treatment of disease: on several occasions he sent medicines to his family or advised them on medical techniques. But in spite of his connections with the foreign community and his location in Japan's main center of Western medical practice, generally Chūemon used his wealth and contact networks to provide information and medicines based on more familiar East Asian medical practices.

For example, in 1862, when measles was spreading rapidly throughout Japan and thousands were dying, Chūemon sent his son a detailed sketch showing the most effective way to prevent the disease using moxibustion— the application of burning mugwort to the skin. Chūemon clearly believed that, thanks to his access to highly educated medical practitioners in the Edo-Yokohama area, his medical knowledge was superior to that of his fellow villagers in Kōshū. After explaining how to apply burning mogusa (mugwort) in eight different places surrounding the navel, Chūemon asks his son to "tell everyone in the village about this."[137]

In 1864, hearing of a serious illness in the family of his cousin (and investor) Iemon in Nishijō village, Chūemon sent a medicine that "cures everyone without exception. When I was sick last autumn, I took three doses and I was immediately cured. There is no need for any payment for this. If they want to use it again, they should let me know and I will send more."[138] And in 1865, when Seitarō was recovering from a serious illness, Chūemon sent him "one small jar of seal." Chūemon explains, "I have been requesting this for a long time from the household of the lord of Matsumae. Now his lordship has released a small amount of his personal supply, so finally I am able to send you a little. Please give it to Seitarō. Give him three grains in the morning with hot water. Even in Edo, it is quite hard to get hold of this."[139] The use of the gallbladder and penis of the fur seal originated in Ainu medicine, and they were used by the Matsumae domain in gift exchanges and trade with the Japanese mainland. The penis was considered a potent aphrodisiac and enhancer of sexual power. Probably Chūemon obtained the gallbladder, which had more general medicinal qualities.[140]

In all these interventions, Chūemon placed a high value on known East Asian practices, spending freely and using his extensive contact network to obtain medicines with the highest reputation for effectiveness. Yet in spite of his conservatism, Chūemon's letters do hint at increasing exposure to Western medical practice, and even a reluctant acceptance of its place in his family's medical treatment. In 1864, Chūemon mentioned that his newborn granddaughter had been vaccinated against smallpox.[141] Following its introduction through Nagasaki, the practice of vaccination had spread in Japan even before the opening of the ports, with the first vaccination clinic opening in Edo in 1858. By the mid-1860s, smallpox vaccination was probably quite well established in the consciousness of educated Japanese, and it may not have appeared to Chūemon as a particularly "foreign" practice.[142] But in early 1869, Chūemon was somewhat taken aback when his relative, old Mr. Okamura, came to Yokohama and asked Chūemon's help in arranging a visit to a foreign doctor. Chūemon had been supplying Okamura with some hard-to-obtain medicine, but, "the [foreign] doctor told him he had been taking completely the wrong medicine." Chūemon added, a little resentfully, "That is a famous medicine from Edo!"[143] Nevertheless, he seemed to accept that Yokohama was a center where both foreign and Japanese practices could be tried: adherence to one method did not necessarily preclude experimentation with another. Indeed, it was this increasing comfort with imported commodities and hybridized lifestyles that set Yokohama apart as a center for the transformation of Japanese lifestyles.

Many of the changes in food, clothing, housing, hygiene, and medical practice that originated in Yokohama and eventually spread throughout Japan were intimately connected to the city's vibrant commercial marketplace. While some of the health measures were government sponsored (though with merchant financing), most of the changes in the daily lives of Yokohama residents—and, subsequently, of people throughout Japan— were stimulated by the vigorous efforts of merchants like Chūemon to import, manufacture, and sell foreign commodities such as steamships and horse-drawn carriages, food and textiles, for profit.

KŌSHŪ TRANSFORMED

In the years following the Meiji Restoration, the new government embarked
on an immensely ambitious program of administrative and social reforms,
aimed at building a powerful centralized state. The reforms included the abolition of the feudal domains and the samurai class; the introduction of a
national taxation system; the introduction of conscription and a national
military force; and the introduction of a compulsory universal education
system. These reforms, and many others in the fields of banking, finance,
commerce, law, and civil administration, can be seen as the culmination of
Japan's painful search for an effective response to the threat of foreign en-
croachment. Yokohama continued to play an important role, providing as it
did much of the knowledge base and personnel for the reform program, as
well as the foreign exchange that made possible measures (such as military
development) that required extensive imports of foreign technology. But by
this point the process had moved beyond the local. Many Japanese officials
now had direct experience of foreign travel, and the government was developing a global network of knowledge and contacts that made it less dependent on the resources that happened to be available in Yokohama.

Indeed, beginning at the turn of the 1870s, the excitement that was so
palpable in Chūemon's earlier correspondence—even amid his many trials—
seems to fade. Chūemon himself, of course, was now in his sixties, and he
was feeling his age. But there is also a sense from Chūemon's letters that the
world he had known—the world of the shogunal order and of established and
largely self-governing village elites—was fading, the old certainties gone.
While in the 1860s Chūemon often expresses his excitement at the immense
opportunities opened up by Yokohama and foreign trade, in his letters from
the early 1870s there is more of a sense of threat. Part of his concern undoubtedly came from the ongoing distress in the countryside, which continued to suffer from high taxation and additional exactions from the new
government. One village headman addressed a poem in 1869 to the governor
of Kanagawa:

The starving old and young cry out in anguish
When will the spring winds come to our desolate village?
To you I plead, take heed of the word benevolence
Make sure these people receive the imperial favor.[144]

When the government abolished the feudal domains in August 1871 and announced the termination of the feudal class system, Chūemon concluded that the samurai would now have to become either merchants or farmers. But if the samurai were to become farmers, where would they obtain land to farm? Chūemon reported a rumor that "farmers will have their excess land confiscated and distributed to the people of the villages or the country as a whole." In the light of this rumor, he advises his son, "If you have lent money by taking mortgages on property . . . you should sell them if possible. If this measure is enacted, no one will want to buy [the mortgages] from you . . . I am telling you this secretly. After you have read it, please burn this. It is said that each region will undertake a strict assessment of all rice fields, dry fields, and uncultivated land. Also of all houses and other buildings. This will certainly be perplexing and will cause many problems."[145]

In the end the government did not confiscate surplus land from farmers (that policy had to wait for the U.S.-mandated land reform of 1946). But it did undertake a comprehensive survey of village land, for the purpose of assessing a uniform tax based on land valuation. Whereas in the past villages had been assessed a village-wide tax, which they had then been left to apportion as they saw fit, the new law would introduce a cash tax based on individual landholdings. This left much less wiggle room to exert family influence to reduce one's tax burden or to hide land from the government.

In conjunction with the new system of land registration and taxation, the government introduced a new, standardized national system of household registration. During the Tokugawa period, families had been required to register with a temple, but practices were inconsistent and the information collected was very incomplete. In the new system, every household was required to register its address, property ownership, social status (nobleman, former samurai, commoner, or "new commoner," meaning former outcast), occupation, name of the family head, birth years and ages of each family member, and relationship to the family head, as well as former names and parentage for wives or adopted children.[146] This procedure clearly left many families perplexed, as family records often did not match the categories of the form they had to fill out. In Chūemon's case, he had been adopted by his older brother in order to inherit the family headship after his brother's early death. Shōjirō, filling out the forms in Higashi-Aburakawa, had to figure out all these relationships from his own point of view as family head. As Chūemon pointed out, the forms were even more complicated for residents of Yokohama, where "most people come from somewhere else, so they probably won't be able to get very full details. However," Chūemon continued, "from now on they will enforce it very strictly."[147]

Chūemon worried a great deal about the profound changes in village administration enacted by the government. During the Tokugawa era, villages under shogunal administration had generally been allowed a high degree of self-government, so long as they complied with their tax and labor obligations. Villages varied considerably in their governance: most combined a relatively inclusive village assembly with a smaller group of elite families that held hereditary (and government-sanctioned) office. The village operated as a corporation, owning communal land and other community assets.[148] Under the new regime, the central government claimed a great deal more direct oversight over village affairs. It achieved this by abolishing many autonomous village institutions, such as common lands and village assemblies, by assigning direct tax responsibility to individual families rather than to the village as a whole, and by taking greater control over and standardizing village government. In the interest of both fiscal efficiency and control, the government amalgamated small villages into larger ones and limited the number of officials who would be recognized in each village. As Chūemon described the first set of reforms, "no matter how many village officials there were, from now on there will be only one nanushi [headman] and one toshiyori [elder]. Any public works such as river levees will no longer be owned by the village . . . [This] will cause great turmoil in the villages."[149]

In another letter, Chūemon comments on the merging of villages for the sake of economic efficiency: "Many villages are to be merged into Kōfu [town], and the Isawa post station is to be abolished and its functions transferred to Kawada village. This may be profitable for the villages, but it will be a huge problem for Isawa. I feel terrible for them there. If possible, I wish they could just leave things as they were. But since these are orders from on high, there is nothing anyone can do."[150]

To make matters worse, the reforms of the 1870s varied widely from prefecture to prefecture and were punctuated by frequent about-turns and changes of policy, spreading confusion and anxiety about just how the villages were to be administered. In Kanagawa prefecture, for example, there were no fewer than eight separate reforms of the village administrative system. It was not until 1878 that systems of local government were standardized nationally.[151]

In Kōshū, while the number of officials permitted to each village was drastically reduced, the duties of those officials increased as they were required to implement a series of important reforms. These included the implementation of the land survey, the issuance of title deeds to individually owned land, the introduction of elementary schools in every village and the enforcement of compulsory education for all children between the ages of six and ten, and the implementation of a new system of military conscription. Chūemon worried about the effect of these duties on his son's health. As one of the few remaining officials in his small village, Shōjirō was responsible for the implementation of a wide range of complex and time-consuming reforms. He also had heavy farming duties, especially during the busy silkworm season. "You must be busy with the business of land deeds. It is impossible to do that and help with the farming. If the matter concerns the villagers, you have to undertake it with sincerity . . . However, if you are going to put your heart into village duty, you must not work so hard that it will affect your health. You must understand this and plan to succeed in your farming business even if you have to stop your official work for a while."[152]

Chūemon tried more than once to persuade Shōjirō to lay down his village duties and come and live in Yokohama: "Since the government has announced it would like to decrease the number of village officials, you should consider giving up your position in the village and taking up trade as the basis for your family's future. Here in Yokohama, we have been approved to start a lending and money-exchange business, but we are unable to start it because of a lack of manpower. We have forty to fifty people staying in the inn each night. In these happy circumstances, you could start up here without any anxiety."[153]

More than two years later, Chūemon again urged, "At present, here as in the villages of Kōshū . . . the number of officials in each village is to be reduced. If that is to happen in Aburakawa, I think it would be a good idea for you to resign your position and come here . . . You could let Seitarō make his living from farming."[154]

The government's reforms, particularly those relating to taxation, caused severe unrest in Kōshū (now officially Yamanashi prefecture), culminating in 1872 in some of the worst disturbances the region had seen in decades. While the central government's goal was to keep the overall burden of taxes roughly unchanged during the switchover to the new land-tax system, it singled out regions that it felt were lightly taxed—including Yamanashi—and targeted them for increases. In Yamanashi, this measure came on the heels of two consecutive years of cold summers and poor harvests. When, in 1871, prefectural governor Shigenoi Kinhisa responded to farmers' distress by distributing one hundred seventy-six thousand yen in government funds to the needy, the central government sentenced him to thirty days of house arrest. The following year the Ministry of Finance implemented its tax increase, prompting a month of protests culminating in an attack on Kōfu by more than six thousand protesters.[155]

The disturbances in Kōshū are the only time in the entire fifteen years of his residence in Yokohama when Chūemon felt the roads were too unsafe to send money and goods: "I sold 104 cards for $187.20 in silver, of which I am still owed $0.20 . . . I exchanged this money on the twenty-seventh. I will send it to you with my seal attached. However, I am getting reports from here and there of great disturbances in Kōshū . . . so I will wait till I am assured that conditions there are stable. In the meantime I am taking care of the money. Please send me your views on how things have developed to this point, and how you think they will turn out."[156] He further commented, "It will calm down in heaven's time. We must adapt ourselves to the times."[157]

While Chūemon seems to have been concerned by many of the reforms he saw enacted during these years of rapid change, his attitude was mainly that such matters were the concern of those "on high" and there was nothing people like him could do but submit. The implication, which has been well documented for the urban commoner class as a whole, is that the goings-on of the great lords were none of Chūemon's business.[158] He had watched the government that he had grown up considering more powerful than gods now being hunted down as rebels. The old certainties were all gone, and there was no telling what the future would bring. Prior to the enactment of the land reform, Chūemon even reported on a rumor that "Japan will be given to France. They say that the French flag is flying from Edo Castle. The emperor left on the twenty-third of the fifth month on a ship to go to Satsuma. From there, he will go abroad. People are saying that there is no doubt about this. Here, with the stroke of a brush, the government offices will determine the value of the land in all the villages and hand out titles. There is no knowing how it will turn out."[159]

STRUGGLING TO ADAPT

In spite of his deep misgivings about the new government and its reforms, for some time after the Meiji Restoration Chūemon's business continued to prosper. Silkworm egg cards maintained their strong demand, with prices continuing to rise. Chūemon's inn opened in March 1869, and its flourishing business seems to have met all Chūemon's expectations.

However, Chūemon's very success carried the seeds of his decline. Ever the optimist, Chūemon seized on every opportunity to expand his business, making larger and larger purchases and diversifying into a variety of additional business activities. By the early 1870s, he was severely overstretched. His borrowings increased with every new purchase and business venture. And although he had benefited from the opportunities thrown up by distant global events, he was also deeply vulnerable to sudden movements in faraway markets—perhaps more so than he himself understood.

Chūemon's vulnerability is foreshadowed by an unfortunate—and perhaps, with hindsight, ominous—incident that occurred in the middle of 1869. With the opening of Chūemon's inn, the family could no longer manage its business affairs without help. As Chūemon focused on managing the day-to-day operations of the inn, Naotarō took over more of the trading operations. By this point Chūemon seems (perhaps unwisely) to have overcome his doubts about Naotarō's business capabilities. In any case, at sixty, Chūemon had to recognize that capable or incapable, his son would need to take on more responsibilities.

In response to the expanding scale of the family business, Naotarō hired a man called Rinzō as an assistant manager. Rinzō must have come with good qualifications: unlike the young men from Kōshū who rotated in and out of positions in the business, he was given significant responsibilities from the beginning. On June 10, 1869, Rinzō wrote to Shōjirō telling him that the prospects for egg cards were looking very poor in Izu, where the firm had established suppliers. "The silkworm rearing was poor, and only a few chrysalises developed." Rinzō therefore proposed to travel to Kōshū to see if there were better prospects there.[160] Rinzō set off a day or two later with one hundred forty ryō to be used for silk card purchases and as well as for incidental expenses.

He never arrived.

On June 23, Chūemon wrote to his son Shōjirō: "Naotarō says he gave one hundred ryō to Rinzō and forty ryō to Kenzō. But it seems that Rinzō has fled with this entire amount."[161] Four days later, on June 27, Naotarō informed his brother that Rinzō had been arrested.

On the sixteenth [June 25, 1869] he visited a place called Wada village near Ōiso, and on the eighteenth he returned to his own home. There, he was apprehended and examined. He had spent thirty ryō of the money. An additional thirty-five ryō three bu three shu was found on his person. Of the remaining money, he had given seventy-five ryō to his relative

Shōhei of Iwasaki village in Ōiso. That person then handed it on to Okue-mon of Rinzō's village. Rinzō's guarantor, Shinzō, has sent a letter to the town hall via his assistant, begging that if he can raise this amount [i.e., the missing seventy-five ryō], he might be excused the rest.[162]

On July 17, Chūemon updated Shōjirō on the Rinzō affair. "Currently the affair is with the town hall, which is investigating. Apart from the thirty-five ryō we got back, we may have to write the rest off. Rinzō has been sentenced to death. I sent a letter to Rinzō's relatives by messenger service on the fourth. If his brothers can come up with the money, I will ask for mercy for Rinzō. Beyond that there is nothing I can do. If he is executed, then our money is lost."[163] The amount stolen, incidentally, had increased by fifteen ryō to a total of one hundred fifty-five ryō.

It seems that Chūemon had low expectations of the guarantor, and these turned out to be justified. On July 30, Naotarō sent a further update:

Of the 155 ryō that Rinzō stole, we have got back 35 ryō 3 bu 3 shu. More-over, when his possessions were sent to the town hall, his pockets were found to contain 3 ryō, so the total we have received is 39 ryō 3 bu 3 shu [sic]. He says that he spent the rest. The [officials at the] town hall [are] threatening him violently, but he is not saying any more. Once the offi-cial documents are complete, the matter will be sent to the court. There is a guarantor, and this man had begged for more time to raise the money. Today the guarantor came here with another man to talk to us. He is asking us to accept a loss of 55 ryō out of the original 155. Of the remaining 100 ryō, he would like us to allow him 25 ryō to cover his ex-penses in this affair. Of the remaining 75 ryō, we have already received 38 ryō 3 bu 3 shu, which leaves 36 ryō 1 shu. He said that we could realize 10 ryō of this by selling Rinzō's clothes. In addition, Rinzō's mistress would pay us 10 ryō as a fee for severing her ties with him. As for the re-maining 16 ryō 1 shu, the guarantor would pay us that by the last day of the seventh month."

Naotarō concludes, "If he would give me 100 ryō now, then I would consider calling the matter closed. However it ends up, I am going to accept it as one of this year's disasters."[164]

There is much that remains unknown or unexplained about the Rinzō affair. Unfortunately, there is no record as to whether or not Rinzō was in fact executed, nor as to whether Naotarō and Chūemon got any more of their money back, from the guarantor or from other sources. Nor is there any explanation as to why Rinzō's mistress would be willing to pay ten ryō to end a relationship that, with Rinzō sentenced to death, would seem to have had little future anyway. It seems clear, though, that Chūemon's family suffered a significant loss from this incident. Moreover, although Chūemon remains largely silent on the matter, it cannot have given Chūemon much reassurance about his son's management capabilities.

Luckily, silk egg cards were still selling well. Chūemon and Naotarō absorbed the losses from the Rinzō affair, and indeed they continued to prosper for another year or so.

Then, late in 1870, a much harsher blow struck Chūemon and his son. On September 30, Chūemon wrote of a battle that had taken place six thousand miles away and almost a month earlier: "The Prussian army has defeated the French army in a great battle and taken the French king prisoner. It is said that sixty thousand French troops were killed in the battle. Here in Yokohama, yesterday there was a fight between the nationals of the two countries and one Frenchman was killed. As a result, it is said that the market for egg cards will plummet." And indeed, "I still have not been able to sell all the egg cards and the price is falling . . . All the merchants in Yokohama are suffering. I don't know how this is going to work out, but at present the business conditions are very poor."[165]

Chūemon is referring to the Battle of Sedan, one of the climactic moments of the Franco-Prussian War. The battle was indeed a great Prussian victory, at which seventeen thousand French soldiers were killed and Napoléon III was taken prisoner. The battle took place on September 1 and 2. If it had been just a year earlier, the news would have taken three months or longer to reach Chūemon. But in November 1869, after ten years of construction, the Suez Canal had opened, drastically reducing travel time from Europe to Asia. Communications were further enhanced with the extension of telegraph service from London and Paris to Suez. The news of the defeat at Sedan reached as far as Singapore by cable. From there, it traveled to China and Japan by steamer, taking a total of twenty-eight days to reach Chūemon. Jardine, Matheson received a strong hint of the defeat as early as September 26, via a company steamer from San Francisco carrying telegraphic news up to August 31. From this source, the company's manager, Herbert Smith, concluded that "it would appear that the safety of Paris was greatly endangered."[166] The definitive news of the battle reached the Jardine, Matheson office on the twenty-eighth, giving the company a day or two to consolidate its position ahead of the rest of the market.[167]

Although Chūemon did not spell out the connection between the European war and a collapsing egg card market, he clearly understood the importance of these distant events. The vast majority of egg card exports had been going to France and Italy, which had been struggling to rebuild their silk industries after the devastating blight of the early 1860s. France, in particular, was the capital of the European luxury-clothing industry. Lyon was the greatest manufacturing center, and Paris was the continent's great center of fashion and retail sales. By January 1871, with Paris in its fifth month under siege by the Prussians, the Parisians were eating dogs, cats, and rats. They had little need for silk.

The egg card market, which had been booming for so long and had carried Chūemon and Naotarō with it to success and prosperity, went into a steep decline from which it never recovered. By June of 1871 top-quality cards that a year earlier had been selling for as much as four ryō per card were now selling for just half a ryō. The egg card market dragged other commodities down with it: top-quality silk was under five hundred dollars a picul (down from $800 a year earlier), and tea was down from a high of forty dollars to only twenty-five dollars a picul.[168] In August 1871, Chūemon wrote, "I'm relieved that you will not make any egg cards this season. They say that this year, some two to three million cards will be shipped to Yokohama. The price is sure to continue dropping. The merchants here have consulted with the authorities, and one-third of the cards will be burned or otherwise disposed of. However, the regional merchants refuse to accept this arrangement, and it remains undecided. But they are certainly not salable, and truly, this is hurting everyone's hearts. My livelihood is affected, too, and I am suffering."[169]

In the midst of all this gloom, Naotarō wrote of the forthcoming Benten Shrine festival, a lavish and expensive celebration that in better times had celebrated Yokohama's extraordinary prosperity, "We have been told that the great shrine festival will be held on the fourteenth and fifteenth of next month. Everyone is at a loss what to do. I, too, want to tell them that they should not hold it."[170]

In spite of these severe setbacks, Chūemon and Naotarō struggled on. The family production of silk—which remained a valuable commodity in spite of price declines—was a major support during these years. In 1871, Shōjirō sold all his cocoons in their raw state, but in 1872, the price of egg cards recovered a little. Although Chūemon remained cautious about trading in this commodity, he was happy to sell the cards his own family had produced. In July 1872, Chūemon wrote, "Understood that you made 103 egg cards. This year we will have a big profit. I am delighted."[171] Three months later, Chūemon reports selling the cards for $187—nothing like the large sums he had been dealing in two years earlier but a very welcome addition to the family income.[172]

At the same time, he was excited about the prospect of selling Kōshū-grown cocoons to the new Western-style silk factory that had opened in Gunma prefecture. In 1870 the government had contracted with a Frenchman, Paul Brunat, to build a state-of-the-art silk-reeling factory as a model for national development of a mechanized reeling industry. With Brunat, the government selected the village of Tomioka, near the silk-producing region of Gunma prefecture, as the site for the factory. The cost of construction was enormous, since Brunat insisted—and the government consented—to build a European-style factory in this relatively remote and mountainous location. This necessitated the import and transshipment not only of expensive and complex machinery but also of the very bricks and glass needed to build the factory. The factory opened in October 1872, with one hundred fifty silk-spinning machines operated by a staff of four hundred female workers, many of them the daughters of unemployed samurai. In anticipation of the factory's opening, Chūemon commented in a letter to Shōjirō, "I think they may want to buy Kōshū cocoons. If you have the manpower, depending on the price it might be profitable to dry the cocoons. If they are still fresh, then you have to sell through an official buyer."[173]

Meanwhile, "About forty or fifty or sixty people are staying in our inn every night. I am very happy about this. We have had some sickness in the house. I am fine right now, but since I am getting old, I feel a little weak; however, there is nothing at all to worry about. If I have any trouble, I will let you know."[174]

Entrepreneurial as ever, Chūemon and Naotarō continued to explore new business possibilities. Late in 1871, they tried their hand at dealing in imported sugar. In October 1871 Naotarō shipped twenty-eight sacks of sugar to Shōjirō, together with detailed instructions on how to distribute it to retailers in Kōshū. "In the future," said Naotarō, "I would like to send you three shipments a month. Please discuss this with possible buyers."[175] However, a sudden drop in the market the following year seems to have put them off this business.

In spite of all the setbacks, Naotarō remained optimistic about the future of his business. Indeed, in March 1872 he embarked on an ambitious new construction project, to build a much larger shop than their existing premises. The shop was opened on November 26, and two weeks later Naotarō reported, "We are offering many products. At present we have seven people working for us. Okamura Yasuke's people are also helping us. We also have four family members working here: a total of fourteen people. I am now going every day to our new shop. I am leaving Katsusuke [Naotarō's younger brother, now nineteen] to manage the Honchō shop. But of course I am available to consult in the event of any difficulties. I would love for you all to come and visit."[176] It seems that, at least in his own eyes, Naotarō was now fully in charge of the family's business affairs.

After the end of 1872, there is no longer any mention of the inn or its guests, and it seems that the operation was shut down sometime in 1873. It is not clear whether this was because of financial problems or just because Chūemon was getting older and found it hard to keep up with the work. Certainly, the financial downturn of 1871 and 1872 greatly reduced the number of merchants visiting Yokohama, and this may have impacted the business.

Beginning in 1873, Chūemon and Naotarō seem to have gone their separate ways, although they still shared a presence in the Honchō shop. From this point on, Chūemon entered a period of drifting from one new enterprise to another, none of them very successful. Again, it is unclear whether this was because of financial difficulties or because the main business had been taken over by Naotarō.

One challenge that Chūemon had always faced, and which now became harder and harder to meet, was finding and exploiting competitive advantages. During the 1860s, he had correctly identified and exploited two major advantages, his extensive network of business contacts and investors in the Kōshū region as well as in Edo and his access to firsthand information on developments in the Yokohama market. But those advantages had eroded. Seeing the enormous profits being made in egg cards, huge numbers of merchants from all over Japan had jumped into the business, sending their agents to roam the countryside in competition for new supplies. As a major player in the business Chūemon retained his advantage in egg cards, but after that market declined, it was perhaps hard to find another product where he could apply similar advantages. Indeed, once newspapers began publishing market information, timely information on market conditions became widely accessible. In the early 1870s the telegraph began spreading rapidly throughout Japan, and information that had taken days to arrive could now be transmitted instantaneously. In this increasingly technology-intensive environment, the competitive advantage tended to shift to the largest and best-capitalized companies, companies that were able to offer the most competitive pricing, outbid their rivals, buy out weaker players, and grasp new technological advantages as they became available.

By the turn of the 1870s, just three merchants—Hara Zenzaburō, Mogi Sōbei, and Yoshida Kōbei—controlled more than 50 percent of Yokohama's sales of silk thread. By the middle of the decade these men were among the wealthiest in Japan, while Chūemon was perhaps little better off than when he began in 1859.

These men came from backgrounds similar to Chūemon's. Zenzaburō was from an elite farming family in Watase village, in the mountains bordering the Kantō Plain and close to the silk-producing district of Maebashi. Like Chūemon, Zenzaburō's family were both farmers and merchants. Sōbei was a merchant from Takasaki, in present-day Gunma prefecture. As a younger son he grew up without the prospect of wealth, and he had to make his own way in the silk business through apprenticeships, talent, and luck. He was eventually adopted into the family of Ishikawaya Heiemon, a Yokohama merchant whose operations in silk, hair oil, tea, konbu seaweed, and sundries sound very similar to those of Chūemon. Of the three, perhaps Kōbei is the only one who had significant advantages of birth and background. Born into a wealthy merchant family in Ōmama town in what is now Gunma prefecture, by his late teens Kōbei was already buying up hundreds of ryō worth of silk cocoons from around the countryside, processing it and selling it as silk thread or cloth. With the opening of Yokohama, Kōbei began buying up silk thread in large quantities from throughout central and northern Japan and transporting it to Yokohama for sale. He was helped in this by the large amounts of capital to which he had access—from his family and also from members of the local community, who were eager to invest in the growing Yokohama market.[177]

Zenzaburō, Sōbei, and Kōbei had experienced many of the same challenges and weathered many of the same crises as Chūemon. It is hard to say what magic propelled them to the top among the hundreds of aspirants with similar backgrounds. All were clearly highly entrepreneurial and able to respond flexibly to new market opportunities as well as changing political and economic conditions. But the same might be said of Chūemon. What is clear, though, is that their success became self-reinforcing. By the middle of the 1860s, these three were part of a privileged elite with access to loans from the wealthy Mitsui. Through this system, Sōbei was said to be borrowing at least forty thousand ryō per year. Chūemon, too, was apparently a part of this circle thanks to his friendship with the Mitsui branch manager, Senjirō, and all the merchants had to deal with Senjirō's sudden arrest and the cutting off of Mitsui funding. But in the restructuring that followed, Mitsui—with government backing—gave privileged financial access to an elite group of silk merchants that included Zenzaburō, Sōbei, and Kōbei—but not Chūemon. Like the *ton'ya* guilds that operated in Tokugawa-era Edo, these merchants benefited from government patronage in exchange for accepting a certain amount of government influence over their business activities.

Another key difference between these men and Chūemon is that they specialized mostly in silk thread, and they tended to trade on commission and not for their own account. Their access to large supplies of silk thread from their provincial bases, and the very high value of silk shipments, enabled them to prosper even on a commission of only 2–3 percent. By contrast, Chūemon never had a large enough business to survive only on commission, and he continued to depend on risky, highly leveraged direct investments.

Whatever the causes, by the early 1870s Chūemon was struggling to find a profitable place in the Yokohama market. In October 1872, he informed Shōjirō that he intended to open a tailor's shop. "I am planning to start a shop selling foreign clothes, and I would like to take an apprentice. If you should know of someone fourteen or fifteen years old who would be willing to work from three to five years, please send him here. I will provide for his daily needs, and I will teach him a trade. Please mention this to Shiroemon, too."[178] The shop opened in the Honchō premises in November, and for a while, Chūemon could report that "the tailor's shop is prospering."[179] He even tried once more to persuade Shōjirō to abandon the family farm and come and join him in this new venture.[180] However, in June 1873 Chūemon wrote, "The number of Western-clothes tailors at present is growing. There is not enough business to go around. I, too, feel the decline. It is worrying. However, I am hoping that there will be work after August."

It also appears that Chūemon tried his hand at selling live animals from his premises. Several foreign visitors to Yokohama commented on the streets of stores devoted to this trade, so it was certainly an established business in the town. The evidence for this is only circumstantial: around the middle of 1873, Chūemon began commenting in detail on the prices of different animals. For example,

> There has lately been a craze for Nankin-Watari chickens. They are selling for three to five or even sex *ryō*. These chickens will lay from forty to as many as a hundred eggs, which sell for two *bu* each . . . Rabbits are slumping. Best quality are five *ryō* each. There are only a few buyers. Many Chinese own them, and that is a problem . . . White mice are slumping. At present a pair is selling for one *ryō*, but there are few buyers. The price will certainly keep dropping . . . Pigs are declining. Best

quality are ten *ryō*. Ordinary families are not allowed to keep them. They must be kept in the fields or mountains. The rules are strict, so I expect the price will decline.[181]

At this point, the collection of letters comes to an end, and with it the substantive record of Chūemon's life. Beyond that, only scraps of information can be found. According to the Isawa town history, in September 1873, after fourteen years of continuous business, Chūemon was forced to sell the Hon-chō premises, both buildings and land, in order to meet debt obligations.[182] According to this source, Chūemon moved to other premises that he owned in Miyozakichō. It is unclear whether this is the same premises where Naotarō was operating. Then, in 1874, Chūemon left Yokohama for good, settling in Hachiōji. For a while he was involved in relief work for the poor, then in 1878 he moved to Kami Tsuruma village in Sagamihara city, where he developed some forty-five acres of new agricultural land that, according to the Isawa town history, Naotarō managed. At the time of his death on December 24, 1891, at the age of eighty-two, Chūemon was back in his home village of Higashi-Aburakawa.[183]

What became of Chūemon and his family? The physical evidence is there to see. Fifty yards from the Shinohara home in Higashi-Aburakawa is the small temple of Senryūji. It contains the graves of perhaps twenty families, on a tiny plot of land. Many of the graves are old, although all have been set in new landscaping of concrete and gravel. Near the middle of the graveyard is the Shinohara family plot. It contains a dozen tombstones, but it is domi-nated by the large, heavily lichened monument to Chūemon, sitting atop a double plinth. At the bottom, it is deeply scored with the name 原篠 (Shino-hara) written right to left in the old-fashioned way. The monument contains an elaborate inscription, now difficult to read with the heavy discoloration and fading of 125 winters.[184] But there is no doubting the respect in which this man was held at the time of his death—nor the money his family was willing to spend to commemorate him.

The Shinohara house is standing more or less as it was during Chūemon's lifetime. It is a large, solid house, the dark wood interior softly glowing with centuries of polish and wear. The tatami mats are old and faded, and on a hot summer afternoon the screens are all wide open, allowing a little air to cir-culate through the house.

Shinohara Yukio—Chūemon's great-great-grandson—is a living witness to the history of his family. Much of what he has to tell a visiting researcher is family lore that probably resides only within the walls of his home. On a

FIGURE 4.1 Chūemon's grave, Senryūji, Higashi-Aburakawa. *Photo by author*

visit in May 2014, he tells me of the exploits of various family members—a famous scholar; an Olympic runner. He fills me in on Naotarō's children—Asa, who married and moved away, and Kōshirō, who attended Tokyo Imperial University, only to die at the age of twenty-five. He tells me that to the best of his knowledge, Naotarō's family stayed in the Yokohama area—where, he thinks, their descendants still live.

In the living room of the house, the walls are covered with portraits of deceased family members. Some died in the war—they are portrayed in their uniforms. Others have never left their childhood. In the center of the wall is a photograph, flanked by a pair of framed certificates on each side. It is clearly an old photo—the people in it are still wearing the style of the Tokugawa period: hair tied in a topknot, dressed in formal *hakama* [wide trousers] and *haori* [jacket]. One member of the group has a sword thrust in his belt.

The people in the photograph are identified by several large sheets of paper that have been stuck to the wall of the studio in which the photo was taken. It identifies them as Chūemon, Shōjirō, Naotarō, Katsusuke, and

FIGURE 4.2 Shinohara family, March 1872. On chairs from right to left: Chūemon, Shōjirō, Naotarō. On floor from right to left, Asa, Kōshirō, Katsusuke. *Studio photograph, Yokohama. Courtesy of Shinohara Yukio*

Naotarō's two children, Kōshirō and Asa. The photo was taken in March 1872, when Chūemon was sixty-three years old. How long have they been sitting quietly in that frame on the wall of the Shinohara house? Since the photo was taken? Or perhaps since Chūemon's death? In any case, for as long as Mr. Shinohara can remember—and he is well into his eighties.

The photo is a remarkable witness to Chūemon's final years in Yokohama. What does it tell us about this man, his family, and their eventful decade in Yokohama?

At first glance, the photo might seem to be a silent testimony to a world that has all but vanished—except in the fantasy universe of glamorized television dramas. These men in their formal clothes, with their Tokugawa-era topknots and stern expressions, might be living refutations of Japan's sudden embrace of modernization. The family patriarchs sit gravely in a row, their faces unsmiling, looking out in evident disapproval at this brave new world of modernization and Westernization. The children kneel in rigidly formal pose, the little girl powder faced and chignoned, the boy with head shaved and looking sullen (undoubtedly suffering through the long, still poses required by the photographic technology of the 1870s), their older brother Katsusuke in a half-kneeling pose suggesting his liminal status between childhood and full acceptance into the world of adult male privilege and responsibility. Shōjirō (the middle figure in the back row) in particular seems to embody the pride and defiance of Japan's samurai era. As he looks directly at the camera, his left hand grips his sword with casual assurance.

His carrying a sword is itself a holdover from the Edo-era status system. Farmers were not normally permitted to carry swords, but as a sign of wealth and local prestige (and often in return for a significant money payment), the samurai government of the Tokugawa granted some village leaders the special privilege. But at the time this photo was taken, the sword was in its twilight years. No longer valued as a weapon of war, it was also considered a threat to Japan's new social order. In August 1869, shortly after the abolition of the domains, the national government dissolved the former division of society into warrior, peasant, artisan, merchant, and outcast, creating instead the status categories of nobleman, former samurai (shizoku), commoner (heimin), and "new commoner" (shinheimin, meaning former outcasts). Even the status of shizoku was reserved for samurai above a certain rank, and Chūemon's family would certainly have been classified as commoners. In February 1871, commoners were explicitly prohibited from carrying swords—so Shōjirō's grasp of his weapon is indeed a small gesture of defiance. Former samurai, too, were increasingly forced to abandon the markers of their Tokugawa-era privilege. Beginning in September 1871 they were no longer required to carry swords or wear their hair in a topknot; and in March 1876, swords were outlawed even for the former samurai. Henceforth, only government officials such as policemen and army officers had the right to carry swords.

In contrast to Shōjirō, Naotarō is staring off into a corner of the room, his posture a little slouched, his *hakama*-clad legs placed wide apart. Naotarō had come to Yokohama as a young man, only too happy to escape from the limited opportunities open to a younger son in his home province. In Yokohama he had experienced many ups and downs and incurred his father's displeasure time and again. Even now, in his mid-thirties, one can sense something of the family dynamic—the upright, proud older son and his shiftless younger brother. Like his brother, Naotarō maintains the formal appearance of the Tokugawa era, but with a casual neglectfulness that suggests discomfort with its oppressive social strictures. Naotarō is, after all, a product of Japan's new era of globalization. One senses his greater comfort in the hybrid world of the Yokohama merchant district rather than with the strict formality of the Tokugawa-era status system.

And indeed, the most striking feature of Naotarō's pose is a direct reference to that hybridity: the pocket watch that he holds up to the camera with his right hand. Naotarō is holding the shiny face of the watch so that it reflects the lights of the studio, a beacon of incongruity in this otherwise traditional family portrait. What is the meaning of this gesture?

For historians of Yokohama photography, the pocket watch is a hint that the photo was taken in the studio of Shimooka Renjō (for more on Renjō, see chapter 3). Shimooka often used pocket watches in his studio photographs, apparently to emphasize the exotic location of Yokohama as a center of East-West hybridity and a place of free-flowing goods and technologies. The conspicuous display of the watch seems to make a statement about the comfort of the photographic subjects with Western technologies and lifestyles, even though they might also choose to retain many of the trappings of traditional Japanese culture. In other words, Naotarō's gesture shows his embrace of technological modernity even as he continues to live in a world bounded by traditional status hierarchies and social expectations. It is easy to see how, for this young man who had so often been upbraided for his inadequacies and failures, the watch might have represented an alternative space of freedom and opportunity.

But of course, the watch is only a part of the double message of this intriguing photograph. The entire setting—the carpeted floor, the chairs on which Chūemon and his sons are sitting, the floor-to-ceiling glass mirror or window, and indeed the photographic medium itself—speaks to the hybridity, the comfortable embrace of modernity, as well as to some extent the exoticism and novelty that the photographic studio represented. In 1872 it was still necessary to travel to Yokohama or Tokyo to have one's photograph taken. Most villagers in the Kōshū region might never have seen a photograph. For Chūemon's family and friends in Kōshū, the studio photographic portrait with its trappings of modernity may well have symbolized their extraordinary embrace of Western trade and technology and the affluence that these had brought them.

The inscriptions stuck to the wall add to the fascination and mystery of this portrait. It is almost as though the photograph is intended to memorialize its subjects—to fix them forever in their liminal pose between tradition and modernity and to label them for future generations. To the right, over Chūemon's head, a florid inscription and poem celebrate Chūemon's attaining the age of sixty-three. The cursive script, formal phrasing, and celebration of Chūemon's age suggest homage to Japan's patriarchal traditions. But the placing of these paper inscriptions also suggests an awareness of the passing of an age. The subjects of the photographic are being memorialized for the future, and the photograph itself embodies the knowledge of transformations to come.

What would Chūemon and his family think of the society they now look down upon? Chūemon's younger sons and their children came of age in Yokohama, Japan's main point of connection to global networks of trade and culture. Naotarō and his family stayed in Yokohama even after Chūemon returned to his home village. They are the products of Japan's new age of global modernity. I suspect they would look approvingly on the astounding growth and prosperity of Yokohama and Tokyo in the intervening century and a half. As for Higashi-Aburakawa, Naotarō and his family members may well look down on the Shinohara family home and be thankful that they got away!

For Chūemon and Shōjirō, there are many aspects of village life that they would not find much changed. The family still farms its five acres of land. Now, instead of wheat and cotton, the land is planted with peaches; no doubt Chūemon would have recognized the economic expediency of developing this new, high value-added crop. The house is still there, barely modernized—though two shiny cars now sit in the graveled driveway in front. Mr. Shinohara, the current occupant of the house, could probably chat happily with his great-great-grandfather about local families, about the crops and the weather, and—of course—about the failings of the government.

Chūemon had his great adventure, and for a while he transformed his fortunes and those of his fellow villagers. But in the end he came home to the land of his forebears and resumed the farming activities of his youth; and today he rests with his ancestors and descendants in the Senryūji cemetery. He has become a part of the landscape that he helped to shape.

Judging by his elaborate gravestone, Chūemon must have been celebrated in the village even in his lifetime. He had had, after all, extraordinary experiences, and in his time he had been a wealthy man. Today, he is remembered still as one of the pioneers of the Yokohama trading community. The survival of his letters has assured him a permanent place in the historical record—even the occasional foreigner now comes to his village to see what they can find out about him. Did he go to the grave unhappy, or frustrated by his failure to make a lasting fortune? I think not. Surrounded by his descendants, close to his comfortable old house amid the peach fields, Shinohara Chūemon is, I think, at peace.

CONCLUSION

THE POWER OF A PLACE

EVER SINCE I BEGAN STUDYING MODERN JAPANESE HISTORY twenty-five years ago, I have been fascinated by the overwhelming speed of change during Japan's relatively brief modern era. From the dramatic political revolution of 1868, to the sweeping Meiji reforms, to the nation's rapid modernization and industrialization, to its military adventures and imperial wars, to the all-out conflict and shattering defeat of the 1940s, to recovery and the postwar "economic miracle," just about every generation in Japan's one-hundred-fifty-year modern history has experienced dramatic social change. What can the stories of Chūemon and Yokohama teach us about the broader historical trends of Japan's tumultuous modern era?

Much of the focus of historians who study the 1860s has understandably been on the political upheavals that culminated in the Meiji Restoration. Virtually all the developments of the late-nineteenth and twentieth centuries—industrialization, militarization, imperialism, fascism, high economic growth, constitutional democracy—can be interpreted in the light of this momentous political transformation. Was the restoration a triumph—as its earliest apologists maintained—of Japanese national identity and loyalty to Japan's ancient imperial institution? Was it, as the Marxist scholars of the mid-twentieth century argued, a bourgeois revolution born of rising commercial wealth? And if so, how did this emerging democracy allow itself to be hijacked by a semifeudal, militaristic oligarchy? [1] Was it, as populist historians of the postwar period argued, a nascent people's revolution in which even farmers drafted idealistic constitutions to circulate among their village networks—until their aspirations were choked off by the iron fist of imperial autocracy? [2] Or was it, as some American academics argued, a catalyst for successful modernization—building on the legacies of the Tokugawa era, hijacked for a while by wartime militarists, and now realizing true fruition with the advent of American-style democracy? [3]

Chūemon was a child of the Tokugawa social and political order, and it treated him well. It gave him a privileged status in a relatively stable village society; it gave him opportunities for education and for advancement within the shogunal bureaucracy; it permitted agricultural and commercial expansion, from which as an elite farmer-merchant he directly benefited; and it opened up the once-in-a-lifetime opportunity of moving to the new international port of Yokohama, where Chūemon dreamed of a new and brilliant prosperity for himself and his region. Although he complained at times about the taxes imposed on him, and although there was clearly an element of fear in his relationship with the shogunate (for example, he was terrified of being arrested after the Mitsui scandal erupted in late 1867), Chūemon never expressed any sentiment implying disloyalty or dislike of the shogun or the shogunal system. And after the system collapsed, he frequently expressed concern over the reforms that were enacted one after another: "If possible, I wish they could just leave things as they were." In this sense, Chūemon's story resonates less with interpretations of the Meiji Restoration that focus on revolutionary fervor, whether of antiforeign samurai or people's rights activists, and more with those that focus on rising commercial wealth and protoindustrial antecedents to economic modernity.

Indeed, the story of Chūemon confirms the continuity, strength, and flexibility of Japan's growing commercial economy across the Tokugawa–Meiji divide. Commercial crop production had been increasing since the mid-eighteenth century to meet the growing demands of the urban centers. In particular, cotton and silk had already become vital sources of cash income to farmers in Edo's rural hinterland. Trading networks had developed to connect small- and medium-scale farmers with sources of credit for the growing season, to organize the purchase of their raw silk and cotton, to process the materials into thread or cloth in farm households or in small factories, and to transport the thread to regional markets where it was purchased by major urban wholesalers. Largely as a result of these commercial developments, a class of farmer-merchant-landlords, the gōnō, had developed in villages throughout the Kantō region—men, like Chūemon, who combined farming, village leadership, and regional commercial, financial, and even manufacturing activities. Using their advantages of local political influence, regional networking, market and product knowledge, and growing capital strength, the gōnō had by the mid-1850s become a protocapitalist class that was well placed to take advantage of the explosive growth opportunities offered by Japan's opening to foreign markets. In this sense, the opening of Yokohama highlights the underlying continuity of Japan's economic trajectory, and it helps explain Japan's rapid adaptation to the modernizing forces of capitalism and industrialization. Indeed, without the development of such sophisticated commercial and manufacturing networks, Yokohama might not have been the economic success story that it was.

The argument that Japan's commercial and industrial success in the modern era built on solid economic foundations laid in the Tokugawa era was proposed by Furushima Toshio and Thomas Smith in the 1950s and further developed by Saitō Osamu and Hayami Akira, who analyzed Japan's "industrious revolution" in the later Tokugawa period as a precursor to the industrial revolution of the 1890s and beyond.[4] More recently, Kären Wigen, David Howell, and Edward Pratt have further developed this thesis with detailed studies of economic change across the Tokugawa–Meiji divide. While these studies richly illustrate the growth of commerce and rural manufacturing during the late Tokugawa era, they also point to the radical disruptions caused by Japan's changing economic structure as well as by the sudden opening of Japan to international trade and modern economic competition. Pratt's nuanced study of the gōnō rural elite points to the destabilizing effects of Japan's rapid commercial development both before and after Japan's integration into global markets: "Japan's protoindustrial economy was far more volatile, indeed far more dynamic, than portrayed in most studies to date . . . A combination of factors—government policy, crop failures, competition, market fluctuations, and household dynamics—hurtled many rural families into decline." Wigen focuses more squarely on the impact of Japan's opening to international trade, describing how the Ina valley in Shinshū province "was slowly knit into a cohesive economic region, only to be unraveled and reworked into a very different fabric when the Japanese countryside was incorporated into a globalizing economy."[5]

Similarly, Chūemon's story illustrates both the powerful legacies of Tokugawa-era commercial expansion and the radical transformation that accompanied the opening of Yokohama and other ports to trade, over which the Japanese government had limited control. Chūemon's home province of Kōshū saw a vast increase in commercial activity after the opening of Yokohama, with silk production increasing fourfold between 1863 and 1868. The expansion brought enormous opportunities for entrepreneurial merchants and village producers, who not only expanded their income by growing, purchasing, and reselling cotton and silk but also invested in production facilities to spin thread of a high enough quality to sell in the export market. Given that prices also increased very substantially, the expansion of the silk and cotton markets also benefited countless small-scale producers. In addition to silk, cotton, and silkworm egg cards, significant shipments of charcoal, building supplies, fruit, and medicines from Kōshū to Yokohama are also evident in the course of Chūemon's letters. For many farm families, this commercial growth must have led to significantly greater prosperity. However, at the same time, the rapid transformations of the local marketplace caused disruption for both merchants and farmers. Of the established silk merchants in Kōfu at the turn of the 1860s, only one survived the decade. The others were replaced by aggressive entrepreneurial newcomers—men who, like Chūemon, were confident enough to respond quickly to new market opportunities and willing to take huge risks in order to leverage their limited capital. Looking beyond the Yokohama–Kōshū region, the radical shifts in supply and demand brought about by the opening of Yokohama initiated a long-term decline in the established textile industries of Kyoto and the Kansai region and an irrevocable shift in economic power to eastern Japan. In this context, Chūemon's story confirms and conforms to an increasingly confident historiography of economic continuity and change in nineteenth-century Japan.

More broadly, the stories of Chūemon and Yokohama suggest an approach to the study of the Meiji Restoration era that deemphasizes the role of nation-building elites and throws sharper focus on the agency of small-scale actors: farmers, merchants, entrepreneurs, and opportunists. The striking feature of many of the transformations described in this book is that they were not the result of political revolution, nor the work of the great leaders of the Meiji Restoration or their elite allies—the actors to whom scholars have credited much of the agency in Japan's transformation into a modern industrial and imperialist power.[6] Rather, they were the product of Japan's rapid integration into global flows of goods and ideas, mediated by the vibrant commercial marketplace of Yokohama and through the efforts of countless small-scale entrepreneurs like Chūemon.

Several studies of the restoration era focus on the agency of relatively unknown individuals. Anne Walthall and Laura Nenzi have written about the political activism of educated women in the final years of the Tokugawa era; Romulus Hillsborough has studied the restoration through the eyes of Katsu Kaishū, who, although a famous statesman of the Meiji era, was a relatively helpless onlooker to many of the key events of the 1860s; Neil Waters has written about the quiet adaptation of local elites to political change in the Kawasaki region, close to Yokohama; and William Steele has studied popular opinion in the late Tokugawa era through the lens of farmers' diaries and printed broadsheets.[7] While these studies offer fascinating new perspectives on the transformation of political consciousness at the grassroots level, they remain focused primarily on the political instability, ideology, intrigue, and activism that have been the subject of most scholarship on the restoration era.[8] By contrast, the story of Chūemon draws our attention to the importance of mundane profit seeking in the transformations of the late Tokugawa and early Meiji eras.

Equally important to this study is the transformative influence of the treaty port itself. Studies of nineteenth-century Japan have not generally focused on the treaty ports, other than as side actors in the political dramas of the period or as exotic (and sometimes nostalgic) outposts of European society.[9] One exception is Michael Auslin's study, which highlights the diplomatic responses of the Tokugawa regime to foreign pressure, emphasizing the relative success of the regime in negotiating the parameters of trade and sovereignty in the treaty ports.[10] Auslin's argument is a salutary response to the emphasis by W. G. Beasley and others on the agency of foreign imperialism, and it is also noteworthy for its contrast with the historiography of nineteenth-century China, which tends to analyze the semicolonial power of foreign merchant and diplomatic communities in the treaty ports as a major factor in the decline and eventual collapse of the Qing regime.[11] But Auslin has little to say about the urban spaces of the treaty ports themselves, nor on the economic, technological, and cultural impacts of the trade and interactions that took place there. In this book, I have explored some of the ways in which the new urban space of Yokohama—its layout, neighborhoods, architecture, rhythms of daily life, cultural production, commercial transactions, rituals, and physical interactions—was a catalyst for widespread social, economic, and cultural change going far beyond its own confines.[12] Beyond the economic opportunity and disruption that have been the theme of so much of this book, the dual narratives of Chūemon and Yokohama suggest a number of other vectors of transformation, each of which I have traced in the body of the book.

First, Yokohama was a conduit for technology and ideas. During the course of the 1860s and beyond, the treaty port was Japan's major point of connection with global flows of culture and technology. Novel artifacts were on display in the warehouses and homes of the foreign merchant community, and most were for sale. Steamships, silk-spinning equipment, cameras, beer and milk, Enfield and Minié rifles, manufactured cloth, telegraph equipment, railway locomotives, and a host of other goods were available to Japanese—and most found a ready market. Chūemon himself was an intermediary in some of these transactions, dabbling in foreign household equipment, food and drink, and textiles for sale in the Kōshū market. Others were on display as models for possible emulation: hospitals, pharmacies, post offices, banks, law courts, currencies, joint stock companies, churches, military organizations, newspapers, racecourses, and hotels. Again, all of these found keen students, and many were either imitated or purchased outright (including expert staff) for introduction in the Edo/Tokyo area and later throughout Japan. Others were more abstract and speculative: artistic styles, political philosophies, mathematics and physics, music and dancing.

In the eyes of the Japanese, Yokohama was a showcase of glamorous consumption. Its exciting new technologies, models of prosperity, exotic and unfamiliar lifestyles—all were on public display, much as the treasures of the modern age were exhibited in the great department stores of American and European cities. Like those department stores, Yokohama was as much about display as about consumption. Many of the goods were beyond the reach of all but a privileged few, but just seeing them—or viewing images and text about them in the guidebooks and woodblock prints that circulated widely during the 1860s—taught the viewers about the possibilities of modern life and paved the way for future changes in lifestyles.

Second, Yokohama contributed to the upending of status hierarchies in Japan of the 1860s. The East Asian treaty ports—including Yokohama—represented a unique space because they transcended national regimes. They were both global and liminal, sites where many of the normal rules and authority structures were suspended. The treaty ports were indeed in many ways places of radical equalization. Who you had been—your status in the Japanese class system or indeed your class and national identity as a foreigner—mattered less than the energy and enterprise you could bring to the economic opportunities created by the booming commercial center.

The elite Edo merchants whom the shogunal government had intended as the mainstay of the new mercantile community did not generally thrive there. The house of Mitsui, for example, opened its Yokohama branch only under strong government pressure, and although it played a major (though scandal-ridden and at times ruinous) role as customs collector and foreign-exchange broker, it never developed an important business in commodity trade. Meanwhile, the shogunal government itself spent much of the decade trying to thwart trade and restrict any further expansion of the ports—even to close the port of Yokohama itself—and found its authority undermined as it failed in most of its objectives.

By contrast, the "big three" merchants who dominated 50 percent of Yokohama's silk trade by the end of the 1860s all came from provincial or rural backgrounds. Indeed, the sometimes radically new circumstances of trade in Yokohama—unprecedented demand, uneven supply chains, market disruptions caused by distant and uncontrollable events, and the needs of aggressive foreign merchants with little respect for existing hierarchies—favored merchants who were flexible, entrepreneurial, and ambitious. Chūemon, an extremely undercapitalized merchant with few inherent competitive advantages, prospered precisely because of his neediness, determination to take advantage of any opportunity, and great appetite for risk.

The overturning of traditional elite hierarchies glimpsed in the rise of provincial silk merchants like Chūemon was mirrored in the broader undermining of the warrior-based caste hierarchy that underpinned so much of the Tokugawa political system. The multiple crises of the 1860s, many of which were directly or indirectly caused by the opening of Yokohama, led to radical responses such as the raising of commoner militias, the promotion of low-ranking warriors and even peasants to senior domainal roles, and the abandonment of the centuries-old alternate attendance system.

For men like Chūemon, the Yokohama trade nevertheless opened up hitherto undreamed-of opportunities for economic and social advancement. It is not a coincidence that while Yokohama grew during the 1860s into a thriving city, Edo itself went into a steep decline, losing half its population. Chūemon's dream of becoming guardian of a daimyo's mansion and installing his family there is emblematic of this extraordinary reversal. The immediate causes of Edo's decline included the abandonment of the alternate attendance system and the release of hostage daimyo families and their retainers back to their provincial homes; the shogunate's massive military campaigns in western Japan; and, ultimately, the collapse of the Edo-based Tokugawa regime. But in the background was the shogunate's inability to profit from the enormous opportunities generated by foreign relations and commerce. In spite of the very real threat posed by foreign imperialism, a more skillful manipulation of these opportunities might have brought solutions to the shogunate's financial problems, as well as potentially transforming its military technologies. Some of the more far-sighted shogunal administrators recognized this from the beginning and actively sought to tie Japan's opening to the fortunes of the Kantō region. But a combination of antiforeign pressure from the court and domains and the shogunate's own innate conservatism pushed the government to pursue instead antitrade policies, with the goal of closing down the port. Instead of rising with the tide of profitable foreign trade, Edo became increasingly isolated and hollowed out. When the new imperial capital of Tokyo began to reassert its dominance in the 1870s, its recovery was greatly helped by a close political and economic alliance with Yokohama and its foreign communities. Indeed, it is from this point that we can see the fusion of Yokohama and Tokyo as the mutually dependent hubs of Japan's new global political economy—a fusion that led ultimately to the Keihin megalopolis that we know today.

Third, the opening of Yokohama also brought about a complex but ultimately momentous shift in the perceptions and realities of space and time. Yokohama and the other treaty ports were unique spaces in the Japan of the 1860s. In addition to looking inward onto the domestic political and economic landscapes, they also faced outward onto global networks of commerce and power. The ships docking in the harbor brought not only foreign goods but also news, knowledge, people, and culture from every part of the globe. To be exposed to the Yokohama trade was to plug into a network in which values, power relations, priorities, and hierarchies were at times very differently structured from those prevailing domestically. Inevitably, the merchants and others who occupied the domestic space of Yokohama came to see the world—both outside Japan and within—quite differently.

One example is a new spatial perspective that often foregrounded global movements over local. The letters of Chūemon indicate an intense interest in market movements, many of which were triggered by events taking place thousands of miles away. Although Chūemon may not have reflected deeply on the causes of these distant events, nor on the inherent interconnectedness of global politics and economics, he was intensely aware that movements in the global market could have a profound impact on events and opportunities in his home province. For example, Chūemon recognized immediately that the Battle of Sedan, fought thousands of miles away, spelled the end of the boom in silkworm egg cards, which had been his most important item of trade for the past five years. By contrast, the immense drama of the Meiji Restoration—an event that reverberates to this day in Japan's history—while it alarmed and frightened Chūemon for a while, did little to disturb the tenor of commerce and daily life in Yokohama. Nor was Chūemon alone in being affected more by distant events than those nearby. Even village families living in remote mountain valleys were now—via the global node of Yokohama—vulnerable to the consequences of distant disruptions to markets they had come to depend on for their livelihood.

In the same way that we see a shifting perception of space as a result of the opening of Yokohama to global trade, we can also observe a transformation in perceptions of time. Foreign observers of the Japanese often commented on their lack of urgency: "The value of time never entered into their thoughts; and even in business operations, one of the greatest annoyances of European merchants was the difficulty, I may say the impossibility, of keeping them up to time in fulfilling their engagements."[13] But Japanese observers were fascinated by time and the role that it played in the daily lives of Westerners. Woodblock prints and guidebooks to Yokohama often portrayed clocks and pocket watches, and contemporary photographs show Japanese subjects prominently holding up pocket watches as symbols of their embrace of technological modernity.

In a family photograph taken in 1872, Chūemon's son Naotarō is indeed holding up a pocket watch. But Chūemon's interest in time, and his understanding of its value, long predates that photo. From his earliest days in the port, Chūemon was intensely aware that when it came to the transmission of information or the transport of goods, time was money. And as his business developed, he was willing to spend liberally to buy access to the fastest available services, sending runners up the Kōshū highway at ever increasing speeds.

If faster means such as horse-drawn carriages, steam trains, rickshaws, or the electric telegraph had been available during the 1860s, Chūemon would surely have embraced these new technologies and even exerted himself to introduce them into his home province. A generation later Aizawa Kikutarō, mayor of Aihara in Kanagawa prefecture, worked for a decade to bring a railway station to his home village in the belief that it would transform the local economy (which it did).[14] But during the time Chūemon was in business, neither railway nor telegraph was a realistic option, and even horse-drawn carts were forbidden on the Japanese highways. As Rutherford Alcock wrote in 1863, even "with some of the best roads in the world, they are three centuries behind the rest of the civilized world in all that concerns speed and means of communication."[15] Japan was to catch up very quickly, but by the time the telegraph was introduced between Yokohama and Kōshū, Chūemon was already retired from his trading business.

Even if he had still been in business, he may not have profited from the new communication and transport technologies. During the 1860s, Chūemon was able to gain a few days over his competitors by sending information up the highway by fast runner. But with the arrival of the telegraph, access to rapid communications became available to anyone with the money to send a wire. At that point it would have been much harder for Chūemon to steal a march on his competitors. From now on, the competitive advantage gravitated to the concerns with the greatest financial clout. They had the resources to hold on to whatever information advantage was still available—through technological investment, systems of regional agents, and international correspondents—and also to secure economies of scale that, in an otherwise equal playing field, might have made the difference between failure and lasting success.

Fourth, the treaty port created a new sense of Japanese identity, both within Japan and globally. The surviving archive of Chūemon's life indicates clearly that his main objective was to make money, both for himself and for his business network in Kōshū. Politics was relevant mostly to the extent that it contributed to economic opportunity or threat. During the course of Chūemon's first decade in Yokohama, the town and its trade were repeatedly threatened by confrontations between antiforeign agitators, the shogunal authorities, and the foreign community. Through all these dramatic events—many of which have become inscribed in Japanese historical legend—Chūemon remained stubbornly optimistic. Yes, the shogunate had promised to close the port; but trade was still flourishing, and new buildings still going up. For the most part, Chūemon took a pragmatic approach based on his direct observation of the situation on the ground. The prosperity was there in front of Chūemon's eyes, and it was impossible for him to believe that anyone would willingly dismantle such an obvious source of betterment.

To the extent that Chūemon showed a political consciousness, it was expressed in terms of loyalty to the shogunate and the system that it represented—and faith in its ability to resolve the complex problems besetting it. And yet, even as he remained loyal to the regime that, for him, represented security and privilege, there is also a sense of distance in Chūemon's letters. When events became particularly dramatic, he had a habit of shrugging his shoulders, so to speak, and leaving matters of high politics to the powers that be: "Since these are orders from on high, there is nothing anyone can do."

Chūemon generally refers to the shogun not with any particular honorifics or expressions of fervor but simply as "the person on high"—*ue-sama*. When the shogunate demanded obedience of him, he obeyed. When it demanded money, he paid. What choice, after all, did he have? As for the rest, Chūemon tended to focus on the area of his life that he could control: his quest to make money, to build a good life for himself and his family in Yokohama, and to bring prosperity to his business partners in Edo and Kōshū.

Chūemon's political consciousness was severely challenged by the overthrow of the shogunate. This epochal event forced Chūemon to examine his very identity. We can certainly see from his letters how Chūemon struggled to define his relationship to the deposed shogun. When the ex-shogun, Tokugawa Yoshinobu, raised a military force for a possible confrontation in Kyoto, Chūemon, unable to continue thinking of him as *ue-sama*, referred to him instead as the *Kantō taikun* (lord of the Kantō), delineating him as a regional rather than a national lord. For a while at least, Chūemon appeared to be willing to throw in his lot with the remains of the shogunal regime in its eastern power base, even if that meant the division of Japan into eastern and western kingdoms. For if there was one area of high politics where Chūemon did express a clear opinion, it was in his dislike for and distrust of the western domains, particularly Satsuma. Chūemon was deeply alarmed by the influx of unruly western samurai into Edo and Yokohama after the defeat of the Tokugawa. Nor at first did Chūemon buy the story that the assault on the Tokugawa was the will of the emperor. He consistently referred to the advancing army either as "the western army" (in contrast to the eastern army or the *Kantō taikun*) or simply as "Satsuma."

The western coalition, though, had an ace up its sleeve: its control over the emperor. There is no sense anywhere in Chūemon's earlier correspondence that he had any feelings of sentiment for or loyalty to this distant and rather mysterious figure. When he wrote of events at the imperial court, he usually referred simply to *kamikata*—that is, the Kyoto–Osaka area—a term that applied indiscriminately to the emperor, his retainers, and all the samurai agitators who were trying to seize control of events in the ancient capital. As a literate man, Chūemon must have been aware of the rising tide of imperial loyalism, of the school of National Learning and its emphasis on reverence for the imperial institution, and of the increasing pressure for the shogunate to subordinate itself to the imperial throne. But his letters did not address the question of loyalty to the imperial institution until his description of the battle of Toba-Fushimi in early 1868. In that description, he referred to the emergence of an imperial prince on the field of battle as a critical turning point. Although he expressed no personal opinion on the right or wrong of the shogunal army's refusal to prostrate itself in front of the imperial banners, Chūemon clearly saw the importance of this irrevocable break with the tradition of imperial loyalty.

Once the emperor assumed absolute authority, Chūemon had to learn all over again how to formulate his relationship with the "powers that be." He certainly did not resist. Although he was concerned about the influx of western samurai into Yokohama and Edo, Chūemon expressed no dissent against the new regime, nor residual loyalty to the disgraced shogun—who, he simply commented, "has been pardoned and ordered to retire to Mito." Once the emperor was installed in Edo—now Tokyo—Chūemon learned an entirely new vocabulary of loyalty and even reverence for this newly exalted figure. By the time that the emperor came to Yokohama to open the Tokyo–Yokohama railway line, Chūemon showed in his excitement and his use of reverent honorifics that he was a loyal imperial subject.

Although his loyalty to and reverence for the emperor were a late development, Chūemon did, during the course of the 1860s, show an increasing sense of national identity. While educated people undoubtedly shared a sense of "Japaneseness," the nation was only one vector of identity for subjects in the complex political and social networks of Tokugawa-era Japan. For most Japanese the idea of "Japan" was less immediate than domainal and regional identities, which demanded loyalty and tribute, and beyond the boundaries of which most people seldom strayed. In his early years in Yokohama, Chūemon identified himself primarily as a person of Kōshū. The name of his shop was Kōshūya, he described himself as representing the products of Kōshū, he hosted and represented visiting merchants from Kōshū, and when in his letters he referred to his "country" (kuni), he almost always meant Kōshū. His goal was to increase his personal wealth but also to promote the products of his region and to enrich his Kōshū business associates. Yet increasingly during his decade in Yokohama, Chūemon was forced to confront the question of national identity, particularly when Japan's sovereignty was threatened by the possibility of foreign attack. Chūemon did not even use the word "Japan" (Nippon) in his letters until 1863, but when he did, in the context of a threatened attack on Yokohama, he wrote in strongly nationalistic terms.

Chūemon's increasing sense of Japaneseness was surely related to his growing awareness of international contexts. Although generally foreigners remain undifferentiated in his letters as ijin (aliens), Chūemon certainly understood the differences between English and American, French and German.

Like the authors of the Yokohama guidebooks, he would have seen an immense diversity of race, culture, and class among the thousands of foreigners in the town, and he would have come to understand the differences between powerful and weak nations, dominant and subservient races. He understood that the French and the Italians were the major consumers of silkworm egg cards. Chūemon himself became both purveyor and to a lesser extent consumer of globally traded goods. And it was in this context of exposure to global flows that Chūemon came to see himself—perhaps for the first time— as "Japanese."

Chūemon's sense of national identity was reinforced by his expanding domestic business, which took him to many of the silk-producing domains of central Japan, as well as to the north in search of opportunities in the mining business. Chūemon's main product in the late 1860s, silkworm egg cards, was not one of Kōshū's special products. Rather, Chūemon sourced his supplies through an increasingly far-flung network. Thus, having started out selling and promoting the produce specifically of Kōshū, Chūemon became a supplier of a widely sourced product that was increasingly coming to be identified with Japanese national identity in global markets.

Indeed, Japan was more and more perceived globally as a national supplier to the world's silk and tea markets, and even more so to the collectors' markets for fine lacquer, porcelain, and "curios." The "made in Japan" brand was not yet a global phenomenon, but it is possible to see its forging in the images of Japan being created in the Japanese and foreign media. During the 1860s, Yokohama was portrayed in word, lithograph, text, woodblock print, performance art, advertising copy, and photograph to both Japanese and foreign audiences. Artists and writers from the beginning recognized that Yokohama meant far more than its small (though rapidly growing) population and trading activities might suggest. For Japanese media, Yokohama was often taken to represent the entire international community, a community in which dominant Western nations secured wealth and power through the use of advanced technologies. There was much to criticize in that international community with its uncultured technocracy, imperialist aggression, butchering of animals, evangelizing, and racial and ethnic discrimination. But there was also much to admire: useful new technologies, aggressive and profitable commercialism, comfortable lifestyles, physical health, efficient and fair-dealing institutions, and monarchical and democratic ideologies. Judgment aside, the new understandings of international institutions and international relations represented by descriptions of Yokohama also gave rise to a new awareness of "Japan" and its place in that international system. For shogunal or domainal subjects accustomed to identify primarily with local and regional loyalties, it required an aggressive but glamorous "other" such as that represented by Yokohama to formulate a new awareness and identity as "Japanese." Certainly there was no universal consensus on what "Japan" meant—or should mean. But the growing ability to articulate globally informed visions of a new national identity undoubtedly influenced initiatives to reshape Japanese political, social, economic, and cultural institutions.

And although it is tempting to think of the transformative effect of Japan's exposure to the West as a one-way street, we should not dismiss the impact of Japan on the rest of the world. Just as "Japan" was being created in the minds of Japanese through representations of Yokohama, so in the West, an imagined "Japan" was being created through news reporting, lithographed illustrations, panoramic paintings, souvenirs and curios, photograph albums, and art and craft exhibits. The "Japan" portrayed in these media was often exoticized and eroticized, an orientalist imaginary that in turn fed into political decisions predicated on Japan's supposed "weak" and "duplicitous" version of oriental despotism.

But media representations of Japan also offered competing interpretations—some influenced by Japanese artists, artisans, and performers who were operating in the same commercial spaces as the foreigners. They portrayed Japan as a nation of physical and technical prowess, a place capable of producing both unforgettable acrobatic performance and an extraordinary level of craftsmanship. And Japanese artistic traditions were held up as a model from which the rest of the world could learn. From the 1860s through the end of the nineteenth century, a craze for *japonisme* had a profound effect on the visual arts and a noticeable effect on literature, philosophy, and religion. Of course, these representations quickly came to transcend the narrow physical space of Yokohama, which was anyway seen by many as a barrier to understanding the "true" Japan. But at least in the early years, Yokohama was where "Japan" was on display.

Finally, the story of Chūemon offers intriguing glimpses into the complex relationship between personal desire and large-scale political and social transformations. There was much in Chūemon's circumstances that he could not control. The Meiji Restoration would have followed the same path whether Chūemon had been pro-shogunate or pro-emperor, whether he had moved to Yokohama or stayed in Kōshū. But there is much to be learned from the decisions Chūemon made and the actions he took in areas where he did feel that he had control.

One of the first questions raised by the story of Chūemon's life in Yoko-hama is why he decided to go there in the first place. Why do people go from one place to another, why do they risk what they have in the hope of some-thing better? Chūemon was neither poor nor desperate. He was at or close to retirement age, surrounded by family and friends. He enjoyed all the comforts and privileges that the life of an elite villager afforded. His decision to move and open a shop in Yokohama remains something of a mystery—particularly given how small a number of applicants there were from outside the Edo–Kanagawa area.

Chūemon was undoubtedly motivated by the entrepreneurial urge to seize a new opportunity to make money. Although we might justifiably label him as conservative in his political affiliations and even in his daily life, he was never conservative in the field of commerce. Whenever Chūemon saw opportunity—whether it was in a new product, a new market, or even an entirely new field of enterprise (such as mining), Chūemon seems to have been ready to jump into the fray. This urge never left him—he remained a firm believer in the possibilities of Yokohama throughout his time there.

Of course, his confidence was bolstered by the well-established commer-cial network connecting Kōshū with the Kantō Plain. But in Chūemon's case, there must have been something more—something he felt that set him apart from countless other elite villagers throughout the Edo hinterland. What was that "something"? Of course, we will never know the whole story. Was he bored with village life? Was there tension in his family? Was he frustrated by his duties as village officer? The letters unfortunately give no hint. But one thing seems sure: Chūemon did not view his project as only a personal enter-prise. He saw himself as representative of a "Kōshū Products Company," an informal collective of relatives and elite villagers throughout the region, who would use his Yokohama establishment as an outlet for their varied produce. Most of their products were agricultural, so by representing the villagers of his region, Chūemon hoped both to enrich the local farming community and to increase the wealth of his business network. That network in turn was able to provide Chūemon with investment capital, inventory, and emotional sup-port throughout his long stay in Yokohama.

As a merchant intermediary between the global market outlet of Yoko-hama and the Kōshū agricultural hinterland, Chūemon undoubtedly helped facilitate the transformations wrought by Japan's new center of international trade. But the impetus in Chūemon's case was not ideological, or political, or intellectual. Chūemon sought economic betterment for himself, his family, and his friends. Probably the same can be said of most of the thousands of people, Japanese and foreign, who flocked to Yokohama during the 1860s, turning it into one of the most dynamic centers of enterprise in Japan. This, surely, has been one of the great driving factors in social transformation throughout history.

One might well ask what anyone can learn from studying a single individual—especially a man who was not one of the movers or shakers of his time. I hope that one justification for undertaking a study like this is simply that people's lives are interesting. Why, after all, do we study history if not to try to grasp the essential humanity underlying the manifold paths of our planet's cultures and societies? Historians are—in spite of all their efforts to remodel themselves as something more scientific—still storytellers, and it is indeed the human stories of history that help us engage imaginatively with the past. While it is easy to understand the value of studying the lives of the rich and powerful, there is also much to be gained from the stories of ordinary people—people who can help us understand history as it was experienced at the time; people who did not make the history that changed our lives but who lived it.

The stories of ordinary people's lives can also inform our understanding of broader histories in unexpected ways. Historians construct narratives about the past, and by the time those narratives find their way into the textbooks, they are often understood as the "true" story, even though experience tells us that the dominant historical narratives of today will likely end up in tomorrow's historical dustbin. At the very least, the study of individual lives reminds us that, within the larger framework of historical change, there were countless variations in individual experience. By examining the ways in which Chūemon's life intersected with, and diverged from, the dominant narratives of the restoration era, I have suggested ways in which we might question or better inform those narratives. For the most part, Chūemon was not a participant in the political initiatives and modernizing fervor that are widely credited with having transformed Japan into a unified, modern, imperial nation in the second half of the nineteenth century. On the other hand, as I have shown throughout this book, Chūemon was deeply committed to the commercial potential of Japan's new global trading regime. In great part the commercial transactions of Chūemon and countless others like him took place against a background of grudging consent or even hostility from the movers and shakers of his day. And yet those transactions contributed to a radical reorientation of Japan's material, social, cultural, technological, and ideological landscapes, even before the modernizing reforms of the new Meiji government took effect.

For all the importance of analyzing Chūemon's life in the context of his historical era, we are ultimately left with the story of a human being—individual, idiosyncratic, complex, and contradictory. Who, in the end, was Shinohara Chūemon?

He was above all, I think, a man of Kōshū. This may seem a strange thing to say when Chūemon lived in Yokohama through the entire period of this study, and indeed even tried to persuade his son to leave the ancestral home and move to Yokohama to join him. But it is hard to imagine that Chūemon would ever have truly shaken off his identity as a member of the Higashi-Aburakawa village elite. Throughout his years in Yokohama, his friends, relatives, and business associates in Kōshū remained his primary community. He remained deeply concerned in village affairs, which he frequently discussed in his letters to his son Shōjirō. And, in the end, he returned to Kōshū to live out his final years and to be buried in the family plot in Senryūji temple.

And Chūemon was an extraordinary entrepreneur. This was an era in which rural entrepreneurship was a vital driver of village economies: most villagers in the Edo hinterland, if they had the means to do so, combined some level of commercial enterprise with their farming activities. But at the age of fifty, it was truly a bold step for Chūemon to risk so many of the good things he had in his life for the uncertain prospects of a new venture in Yokohama. And once he was established there, Chūemon displayed his entrepreneurial instincts again and again. Always on the lookout for competitive advantage, he jumped on opportunity when he saw it. Armed with little more than a desire to succeed, he was able to carve out a space for himself in a succession of products by making the most of his advantages. Even when his business was doing well, Chūemon never stopped to consolidate: he was always looking for the next big thing, whether it was silkworm eggs, innkeeping, or money lending. I imagine that Chūemon must have had what we now think of as the classic entrepreneurial personality—restless, hyperactive, and drawn to risk and adventure.

Related to his entrepreneurial personality was Chūemon's optimism. Even as he faced a daunting variety of challenges, including financial difficulties, heavy indebtedness, price collapses, the threat of war, heavy taxation, and bureaucratic meddling with trade, Chūemon maintained a steadfastly hopeful attitude about the future. I am particularly struck by his venture into the charcoal business in 1861. His business at this time was suffering from every kind of affliction. He had no inventory in his shop, no money to buy more, he was deep in debt to his business partners, he owed large sums of money in municipal fees and to pay for a new storehouse, his entire family was disabled with scabies, and he had mortgaged his house and pawned all his wife's kimonos just to cover his living expenses. And yet in the midst of this dark period, Chūemon's mind turned to a new opportunity. Mortgaging his last remaining piece of property, he sent his son off to Kōshū with his last forty ryō in the world, charging him with shipping charcoal to Yokohama in the hope of exploiting a market opportunity. In the same way, Chūemon seized the opportunities that he saw in raw cotton, silkworm eggs, quartz mining, innkeeping, and tailoring. In every case he fixed his gaze on the future with optimism and enthusiasm. It is one of his most appealing features.

Chūemon was also a loyal and loving family man. His letters, which dwell mostly on business affairs, give us much less than I would like of his family relationships. I do not know if he was a kind husband and father, or even a faithful one. I know that his relationship with his second son Naotarō was strained at times, but in the end Chūemon stood by his son and nurtured him as he took on a growing role in Chūemon's business affairs. In his letters to his oldest son, Shōjirō, Chūemon consistently shows affection and concern over a period of many years. He talks of his youngest son, Katsusuke, with indulgent affection. And it is also clear from the letters that Chūemon respects and admires his wife—though he reveals nothing about their relationship beyond that. We know that Chūemon had at least six surviving children, and even though he was far away from most of them, he took his responsibilities as a father seriously, worrying about the health of his daughters back in Kōshū and doing his best to ensure they were well married. And beyond his immediate family, Chūemon was deeply concerned to fulfill his filial duties toward his extended family, particularly his in-laws, the Okamura family.

Chūemon's life has become significant because the ravages of fire, earthquake, and war have left his collection of letters to his home village as one of the most important remaining archival sources on the daily life and economic activities of a member of the merchant community in Yokohama in the 1860s. In this sense, the letters are a precious historical resource, and I hope I have done them even partial justice by developing the rich insights they offer.

But it would be a shame to conclude that an individual's only significance is the coincidence that his records happen to have survived. I choose to see a more personal meaning in Chūemon's story. The collection of letters is enough to reveal Chūemon as a man with a deeply rooted personal identity, with strong family ties, incurably optimistic, but also with a restless streak that drove him constantly to undertake new ventures and take on new risks. He is a man who, though I might not be friends with him, I would recognize if I met him today. Indeed, I feel in a way that I have met him. He has left a remarkably direct line to the present day, as his great-great-grandson farms the same land, lives in the same house a stone's throw from Chūemon's grave, and is willing to share a hot early summer's afternoon with a visiting foreigner and graciously tell him the lore that has come down to him over the generations.

The most strikingly recognizable feature of Chūemon the man, as he reaches out to me across a century and a half of dramatic change, is his powerful urge to seek out opportunity and grasp it wherever he finds it. I started this book with the question, why did Shinohara Chūemon, fifty years old, affluent, respected, surrounded by family and friends, in a village where he was a recognized leader, turn his back on all those blessings to start on a completely new—and very risky—enterprise in a town that did not yet exist, trading with foreigners whom he had never before encountered? I can never know Chūemon well enough to fully answer my question. But much of the answer surely lies in Chūemon's strong urge to seek new economic opportunity, for the benefit of himself and his family. It seems to me that this urge, played out countless times on a greater or lesser scale, is one of the fundamental realities of man's historical experience. Regardless of culture, era, religion, politics, or education, men and women have thrown their energies into seeking economic opportunity in the hope of improving their daily lives. Perhaps even more than kings and generals and their wars, it is the driving force of historical change.

TABLES

Table 1

Exports and imports through Yokohama, 1859–1867 (in Mexican dollars)

Year	Exports	Imports
1859	400,000	150,000
1860	3,954,299	945,714
1861	2,682,952	14,943,154
1862	6,305,128	3,074,231
1863	10,554,022	3,701,084
1864	8,997,484	5,553,594
1865	17,467,728	13,153,024
1866	14,100,000	11,735,000
1867	9,708,907	14,908,785

Source: Yokohama Zeikan, *Yokohama zeikan hyakunijū-nenshi* (Yokohama: Yokohama Zeikan, 1981), 24.

Note: There are wide variations in estimates for these statistics. This table uses a variety of sources that reflect the debate.

Table 2

Estimates of Yokohama population, 1859–1870

	1859	1860	1861	1862	1863	1864	1865	1866	1867	1868	1869	1870
British	18			50	61	98						
American		15		43	43	97						
Dutch		10		22	28	33						
French	1			12	12	52						
Portuguese					6	9						
Prussian						19						
Chinese						100				660		1,002
Japanese		3,046		8,297	9,200	12,000					28,589	
Total	482					14,581					31,000	

Sources: Ishii Takashi, *Kōto Yokohama no tanjō* (Yokohama: Yūrindō, 1976), 225; *The China Directory*, various years. Data are very incomplete.

Notes: Blank fields indicate missing data. Women are generally excluded from the statistics of foreigners and Chinese. The 1879 census put the total population registered in Yokohama at 46,187; however, the actual population may have been greater because of the large number of transients or residents registered in their places of origin.

Table 3

Monetary values (in silver *monme*), 1859–1868

	1859	1860	1861	1862	1863	1864	1865	1866	1867	1868
Ryō/koban	73.00	73.00	72.00	75.00	84.00	89.00	101.00	115.00	127.00	216.00
Bu	18.25	18.25	18.00	18.75	21.00	22.25	25.25	28.75	31.75	54.00
Monme	1.00	1.00	1.00	1.00	1.00	1.00	1.00	1.00	1.00	1.00
Kan	6.85	6.53	6.26	6.39	6.44	6.46	6.68	7.87	8.80	13.09
Mon	0.01	0.01	0.01	0.01	0.01	0.01	0.01	0.01	0.01	0.01
Tenpō	0.69	0.65	0.63	0.64	0.64	0.65	0.67	0.79	0.88	1.31
Koku	121.00	153.00	163.00	147.00	164.00	202.00	347.00	944.00	996.00	565.00
Mexican dollars	36.00	37.00	35.00	35.00	36.00	33.00	37.00	46.00	48.00	45.00

Sources: Shinohara archive; Takeo Ono, *Edo bukka jiten* (Tokyo: Tenbōsha, 1991).

Table 4

Relative monetary values, 1865

	Ryō/koban	Bu	Monme	Kan	Mon	Tenpō	Koku	Mexican dollars
1 ryō/koban =	1.00	4.00	101.00	15.12	15,119.76	151.20	0.29	2.73
1 bu =	0.25	1.00	25.25	3.78	3,779.94	37.80	0.07	0.68
1 monme =	0.01	0.04	1.00	0.15	149.70	1.50	0.00	0.03
1 kan =	0.07	0.26	6.68	1.00	1,000.00	10.00	0.02	0.18
1 mon =	0.00	0.00	0.01	0.00	1.00	0.01	0.00	0.00
1 tenpō =	0.01	0.03	0.67	0.10	100.00	1.00	0.00	0.02
1 koku =	3.44	13.74	347.00	51.95	51,946.11	519.46	1.00	9.38
1 Mexican dollar =	0.37	1.47	37.00	5.54	5,538.92	55.39	0.11	1.00

Sources: Shinohara archive; Takeo Ono, *Edo bukka jiten* (Tokyo: Tenbōsha, 1991).

Note: Edo monetary values are notoriously complex. In the Kantō region, merchants used the ryō as the basic unit of computation. Although this was notionally equivalent to the gold koban coin, gold coins were seldom used in merchant transactions. The currencies in common circulation were the silver *bu* and the copper (or iron) *mon*. Because of recoinages, the actual specie content of these coins varied greatly. Hence, merchants used the *monme* (a weight of pure silver) as a functional standard. For a fuller explanation, see E. S. Crawcour and Kozo Yamamura, "The Tokugawa Monetary System: 1787–1868," *Economic Development and Cultural Change* 18, no. 4 (July 1970): 489–518.

WEIGHTS AND MEASURES

Table 5
Weights

	kan	kin	piculs	monme	pounds	ounces
1 kan =	1	6.25	0.0625	1,000	8.27	132.3
1 kin =	0.16	1	0.01	160	1.32	21.2
1 picul =	16	100	1	16,000	132.3	2,116
1 monme =	0.001	0.0063	0.00006	1	0.008	0.13
1 pound =	0.121	0.756	0.0076	121	1	16
1 ounce =	0.0076	0.047	0.0005	7.56	0.0625	1

Table 6
Volumes

	koku	to	shō	gō	gallons	pints
1 koku =	1	10	100	1,000	40.95	327.6
1 to =	0.1	1	10	100	4.09	32.76
1 shō =	0.01	0.1	1	10	0.409	3.28
1 gō =	0.001	0.01	0.1	1	0.041	0.328
1 gallon =	0.024	0.244	2.44	24.4	1	8
1 pint =	0.003	0.031	0.305	3.052	0.125	1

Table 7
Areas

1 tsubo =	1	35.6
1 sq. foot =	0.028	1

NOTES

1. Out of Thin Air (1859–1860)

1. 間五十年、化天のうちを比ぶれば、夢幻の如くなり. From the Noh play Atsu-mori, by Zeami.

2. Akira Shimizu, "Eating Edo, Sensing Japan: Food Branding and Market Culture in Late Tokugawa Japan, 1780–1868" (Ph.D. diss., University of Illinois at Urbana-Champaign, 2011), 109.

3. Ibid.

4. Francis Hall, *Japan Through American Eyes: The Journal of Francis Hall, Kanagawa and Yokohama, 1859–1866* (Princeton, N.J.: Princeton University Press, 1992), 594.

5. http://www.imes.boj.or.jp/cm/history/historyfaq/a5.html, accessed August 2, 2015.

6. Interview with Shinohara Yukio. This information is corroborated by the inscription on Chūemon's gravestone.

7. Isawachō Chōshi Hensan Iinkai, *Isawa chōshi*, vol. 4 (Isawachō: Isawachō Kankōkai, 1987), 913–14.

8. Yokohama-shi, *Yokohama shishi*, vol. 2 (Yokohama: Yokohama-shi, 1958), 580.

9. Memorandum by Hotta Masayoshi; see W. G. Beasley, *Select Documents on Japanese Foreign Policy, 1853–1868* (London: Oxford University Press, 1955), 165–67.

10. Quoted in W. G. Beasley, "The Foreign Threat and the Opening of the Ports," in *The Cambridge History of Japan, Volume 5: The Nineteenth Century*, ed. Marius B. Jansen (Cambridge: Cambridge University Press, 1988), 279.

11. Cited in Michael R. Auslin, *Negotiating with Imperialism: The Unequal Treaties and the Culture of Japanese Diplomacy* (Cambridge, Mass.: Harvard University Press, 2004), 38.

12. Yasuhiro Makimura, "The Silk Road at Yokohama: A History of the Economic Relationships between Yokohama, the Kantō Region, and the World Through the Japanese Silk Industry in the Nineteenth Century" (Ph.D. diss., Columbia University, 2005), 41–42.

13. Quoted ibid., 42.

14. Cited in Auslin, *Negotiating with Imperialism*, 58; translation by Auslin.

15. Ishii Takashi, *Kōto Yokohama no tanjō* (Yokohama: Yūrindō, 1976), 55.

16. Yokohama-shi, *Yokohama shishi*, 206.

17. Yokohama Zeikan, *Yokohama Zeikan hyaku nijū-nenshi* (Yokohama: Yokohama Zeikan, 1981), 74–75.

18. Kanagawa Prefectural Government, *The History of Kanagawa* (Yokohama: Kanagawa Prefectural Government, 1985), 177.

19. Quoted in Hugh Cortazzi, *Victorians in Japan: In and around the Treaty Ports* (London: Athlone Press, 1987), 55–56.

20. Abe Yasushi, "Bakumatsu no yūkaku: Kaikōjo no seiritsu ni kanren shi," *Hakodate: Chiikishi kenkyū* 25, no. 3 (1997): 18.

21. Quoted ibid., 16–17.

22. Ibid., 17.

23. Quoted ibid., 22.

24. Ibid., 23.

25. Ibid.

26. Ibid., 24.

27. Ibid.

28. Ibid., and Yoshida Tsuneyoshi, "Taigai kankei yori mitaru Yokohama kaikō no yūkaku," *Meiji Taishō shidan* 9 (1937): 3.

29. Isawachō Chōshi Hensan Iinkai, *Isawa chōshi*, 916–17.

30. Yokohama-shi, *Yokohama shishi*, 220–22.

31. Letter 9, Ansei 6/3/23 (4/25/1859), to Hatsushikano Iyokichi, in Ishii Takashi, ed., *Yokohama urikomishō Kōshūya monjo* (Yokohama: Yūrindō, 1984). Please note that all cited letters relating to Chūemon are collected in the Ishii volume.

32. Letter 10, Ansei 6/5/15 (6/15/1859), to Murata (given name unknown).

33. Ishii Takashi, "Shoki Yokohama bōeki shōnin no sonzai keitai Kōshūya Chūemon o chūshin ni shite," *Yokohama Shiritsu Daigaku kiyō*, series A, 18, no. 85 (1958): 3.

34. Letter 11, Ansei 6/5/29 (6/29/1859), to Genzaemon of Kurokoma village.

35. Aogi Michiō, "Tōkaidō Kanagawa-juku to Yokohama kaikō: Chiikiteki Shiten de miru bakumatsu Nichibei kōshōshi," *Jinbun kagaku nenpō*, no. 32 (2002): 33.

36. Yokohama-shi, *Yokohama shishi*, 214.

37. Quoted in Cortazzi, *Victorians in Japan*, 56.

38. C. T. van Assendelft de Coningh, *A Pioneer in Yokohama: A Dutchman's Adventures in the New Treaty Port*, ed. and trans. Martha Chaiklin (Indianapolis: Hackett, 2012), 35.

39. Ibid., 44.

40. Rutherford Alcock, *The Capital of the Tycoon: A Narrative of a Three Years' Residence in Japan*, 2 vols. (New York: Bradley, 1863), 1:144–45.

41. Quoted in Cortazzi, *Victorians in Japan*, 66.

42. Quoted ibid.; see also Hall, *Japan Through American Eyes*, 69.

43. November 2, 1859, in Hall, *Japan Through American Eyes*, 68.

44. December 13, 1859, ibid., 87.

45. Yokohama-shi, *Kanagawa kushi* (Yokohama: Kanagawa Kushi Hensan Kankō Jikkō Iinkai, 1977), 234–36.

46. Utagawa Sadahide, *Yokohama kaikō kenbunshi biyō*, ed. Kida Jun'ichirō (Tokyo: Meichō Kankōkai, 1967), 3, 5.

47. Ibid., 4.

48. Ibid., 10.

49. Ibid., 4.

50. Quoted in Pat Barr, *The Coming of the Barbarians: The Opening of Japan to the West, 1853–1870* (New York: Dutton, 1967), 105.

51. Assendelft de Coningh, *A Pioneer in Yokohama*, 103.

52. Jardine Matheson Archive, MS JM B10-9, reel 437, Cambridge University Library.

53. December 13, 1859, in Hall, *Japan Through American Eyes*, 87–89.

54. Ernest Mason Satow, *A Diplomat in Japan: The Inner History of the Critical Years in the Evolution of Japan When the Ports Were Opened and the Monarchy Restored* (Philadelphia: Lippincott, 1921), 29.

55. Letter dated November 22, 1859, in J. C. Hepburn, *The Letters of Dr. J. C. Hepburn*, ed. Michio Takaya (Tokyo: Toshin Shobō, 1955), 28.

56. Letter dated November 22, 1859, ibid., 21–22, 27.

57. Margaret Tate Kinnear Ballagh, *Glimpses of Old Japan, 1861–1866* (Tokyo: Methodist Publishing House, 1908), 37.

58. Letter dated November 22, 1859, in Hepburn, *Letters of Dr. J. C. Hepburn*, 21.

59. Yoshida, "Taigai kankei," 4.

60. December 13, 1859, in Hall, *Japan Through American Eyes*, 88.

61. Quoted in Hugh Cortazzi, *Collected Writings of Sir Hugh Cortazzi* (Tokyo: Edition Synapse; Richmond, Surrey, U.K.: Japan Library, 2000), 203.

62. J. E. Hoare, *Japan's Treaty Ports and Foreign Settlements: The Uninvited Guests, 1858–1899* (Folkestone, Kent, U.K.: Japan Library, 1994), 52–65.

63. For a comparative discussion of extraterritoriality in China and Japan, see Pär Kristoffer Cassel, *Grounds of Judgment: Extraterritoriality and Imperial Power in Nineteenth-Century China and Japan* (Oxford: Oxford University Press, 2012), chapter 2.

64. Quoted in Yokohama-shi, *Yokohama shishi*, 208.

65. Satow, *A Diplomat in Japan*, 22.

66. Letter 15, Ansei 6/6/21 (7/20/1859), to Amamiya Tamesuke.

67. Letter 13, Ansei 6/6/21 (7/20/1859), to eight men, including Genpei of Sakurai village and Rinzaemon of Imai village.

68. Letter 20, Ansei 6/8/12 (9/8/1859), to Yamashita Magobeimon and Shōjirō.

69. Yuki Allyson Honjo, *Japan's Early Experience of Contract Management in the Treaty Ports* (London: Japan Library, 2003), 76–81.

70. Ibid., 82–84.

71. Samuel Gower to Shanghai office, April 1, 1864, Jardine Matheson Archive, MS JM B10-9, reel 438.

72. Honjo claims that in most cases an up-front "bargain money" payment of 10 percent of the contract was paid to the seller, but I see no evidence of that in Chūemon's correspondence. If he had received such up-front payments, it would have solved many of his capital problems (*Japan's Early Experience*, 67).

73. Ishii Takashi, *Kōto Yokohama no tanjō*, 205.

74. William Keswick to Shanghai office, January 7, 1860, Jardine Matheson Archive, MS JM B10-9, reel 437.

75. Satow, *A Diplomat in Japan*, 22–23.

76. James Barber to James Whittall, October 5, 1859, Jardine Matheson Archive, MS JM B10-9, reel 437.

77. Alcock, *Capital of the Tycoon*, 2:213.

78. Letter 122, Bunkyū 3/12/30 (2/7/1864), to Shōjirō.

79. Calculated based on the following assumptions: 1 packhorse load = 1.8 piculs, Yokohama market price per picul, $500–$800, purchase in producing area at 70 percent of Yokohama price, $1 = 0.50 *ryō*.

80. Letter 53, Man'en 1/11/5 (12/16/1860), to Shōjirō.

81. William Keswick to Shanghai office, June 26, 1860, Jardine Matheson Archive, MS JM B10-9, reel 437.

82. Samuel Gower to Shanghai office, April 1, 1864, Jardine Matheson Archive, MS JM B10-9, reel 438. Jardine, Matheson continued its relationship with Seibei in the hope that he would work off his debt to them, but in 1867 they were forced to write off a large sum. See Ishii Takashi, *Kōto Yokohama no tanjō*, 208, and Honjo, *Japan's Early Experience*, 117–18.

83. Letter 24, Ansei 6/12/4 (12/27/1859), to Shōjirō.

84. Letter 21, Ansei 6/8/28 (9/22/1859), to Shōjirō.

85. Letter 14, Ansei 6/6/21 (7/20/1859), to Yamashita Kunizō.

86. Letter 17, Ansei 6/7/8 (8/6/1859), to Shōjirō.

87. Letter 23, Ansei 6/11/26 (12/19/1859), to Shōjirō.

88. Letter 31, Man'en 1/3/4 (3/25/1860), to Shōjirō.

89. See Alcock, *Capital of the Tycoon*, 1:145–46.

90. Quoted in Barr, *Coming of the Barbarians*, 87.

91. Estimates vary very widely. According to John McMaster, the total amount was no more than $300,000 at the Japanese purchase price, which would have sold for perhaps $1 million in Shanghai or Hong Kong ("The Japanese Gold Rush of 1859," *Journal of Asian Studies* 19, no. 3 [1960]: 283). However, Fujino Shōzaburō has estimated the total outflow as high as 8.2 million *ryō*, or some $16 million; see Simon James Bytheway and Martha Chaiklin, "Reconsidering the Yokohama 'Gold Rush' of 1859," *Journal of World History* 27, no. 2 (2016): 288.

92. McMaster, "Japanese Gold Rush," 276.

93. See ibid., and Peter Frost, *The Bakumatsu Currency Crisis* (Cambridge, Mass.: East Asian Research Center, Harvard University, 1970). A thorough (though inconclusive) overview of the debate can be found in Bytheway and Chaiklin, "Reconsidering the 'Gold Rush.'"

94. John M. Brooke and George M. Brooke, *John M. Brooke's Pacific Cruise and Japanese Adventure, 1858–1860* (Honolulu: University of Hawai`i Press, 1986), 179.

95. Ibid., 178.

96. Ibid., 187.

97. Ibid., 191.

98. McMaster ("Japanese Gold Rush") comes to this conclusion based on his analysis of the Jardine Matheson Archive.

99. William Keswick to James Whittall, November 16 and 17, 1859, Jardine Matheson Archive, MS JM B10-9, reel 437.

100. Keswick to Whittall, December 3, 1859, ibid.

101. Keswick to Whittall, December 10, 1859, ibid.

102. November 25, 1859, in Hall, *Japan Through American Eyes*, 80–81.

103. November 26, 1859, ibid., 81.

104. December 5, 1859, ibid., 87.

105. December 22, 1859, ibid., 92.

106. Assendelft de Coningh, *A Pioneer in Yokohama*, 82.

107. Ibid., 83.

108. Yokohama-shi, *Yokohama shishi*, 581.

2.   Years of Struggle (1860–1864)

1. July 18–19, 1860, in Francis Hall, *Japan Through American Eyes: The Journal of Francis Hall, Kanagawa and Yokohama, 1859–1866* (Princeton, N.J.: Princeton University Press, 1992), 197–98.

2. July 18–19, 1860, ibid., 203.

3. Letter 38-2, Man'en 1/5/17 (7/5/1860), to Shōjirō; letter 40, Man'en 1/6/4 (7/21/1860), to Shōjirō, in Ishii Takashi, ed., *Yokohama urikomishō Kōshūya monjo* (Yokohama: Yūrindō, 1984). Please note that all cited letters relating to Chūemon are collected in the Ishii volume.

4. Letter 40, Man'en 1/6/4 (7/21/1860), to Shōjirō.

5. Letter 38, Man'en 1/5/11 (6/29/1860), Naotarō to Shōjirō.

6. Kikuen Rōjin, *Yokohama kidan: Minato no hana* (Kinkōdō Zō, ca. 1864), 1–2.

7. Yokohama-shi, *Yokohama shishi*, vol. 2 (Yokohama: Yokohama-shi, 1958), 677.

8. Letter 95, Bunkyū 2/11/29 (1/18/1863), Chūemon and Naotarō to Shōjirō.

9. Laurence Oliphant, *Narrative of the Earl of Elgin's Mission to China and Japan in the Years 1857, '58, '59*, 2nd ed., 2 vols. (Edinburgh: Blackwood, 1860), 144. Oliphant added that in spite of the restrictions on individual freedom, "It is a singular fact that in Japan, where the individual is sacrificed to the community, he should seem perfectly happy and contented; while in America, where exactly the opposite result takes place, and the community is sacrificed to the individual, the latter is in a perpetual state of uproarious clamour for his rights."

10. Yokohama-shi, *Yokohama shishi*, 338–40. See also Kato Takashi, "Governing Edo," in *Edo and Paris: Urban Life and the State in the Early Modern Era*, ed. James L. McClain, John M. Merriman, and Ugawa Kaoru (Ithaca, N.Y.: Cornell University Press, 1994), 55–56.

11. Engelbert Kaempfer, a German doctor, writing about Nagasaki in the late seventeenth century (*Kaempfer's Japan: Tokugawa Culture Observed*, ed. Beatrice M. Bodart-Bailey [Honolulu: University of Hawai`i Press, 1999], 162).

12. May 21, 1861, in Hall, *Japan Through American Eyes*, 339.

13. Letter 40, Man'en 1/6/4 (7/21/1860), to Shōjirō.

14. Kanagawa-ken Toshokan Kyōkai, Kyōdo Shiryō Hensan Iinkai, *Mikan Yokohama kaikō shiryō* (Yokohama: Kanagawa-ken Toshokan Kyōkai, 1960), 137–217.

15. Samuel Pasfield Oliver, *On and Off Duty: Being Leaves from an Officer's Note-Book* (London: Allen, 1881), 70; Kikuen, *Yokohama kidan*, 5.

16. Gary P. Leupp, *Servants, Shophands, and Laborers in the Cities of Tokugawa Japan* (Princeton, N.J.: Princeton University Press, 1992), 127–34, 42–43.

17. April 2, 1860, in Hall, *Japan Through American Eyes*, 147.

18. Quoted in Leupp, *Servants, Shophands*, 150.

19. July 26, 1860, and January 28, 1865, in Hall, *Japan Through American Eyes*, 205–6, 589.

20. December 19, 1859, ibid., 90–91.

21. November 6, 1860, ibid., 271–74.

22. John Reddie Black, *Young Japan: Yokohama and Yedo*, 2 vols. (London: Trübner, 1880), 2:98.

23. December 19, 1859, in Hall, *Japan Through American Eyes*, 90–91.

24. January 11, 1860, ibid., 101.

25. February 1, 1860, ibid., 117.

26. Utagawa Sadahide and Kida Jun'ichirō, *Yokohama kaikō kenbunshi biyō* (Tokyo: Meichō Kankōkai, 1967), 3–4.

27. Quoted in Todd Munson, "Curiosities of the Five Nations: Nansōan Shōhaku's Yokohama Tales," *Japan Studies Review* 12 (2008): 26.

28. February 10, 1861, in Hall, *Japan Through American Eyes*, 301.

29. April 2, 1862, ibid., 410.

30. February 10, 1861, ibid., 301.

31. Kikuen, *Yokohama kidan*, 6.

32. Letter 196-1, Keiō 2/3/8 (4/22/1866), to Shōjirō.

33. Kikuen, *Yokohama kidan*, 11.

34. *The China Directory for 1862* (Hong Kong: Shortrede, 1862), 51–52.

35. "Lawless and dissolute" quoted in Harold S. Williams, *Tales of the Foreign Settlements in Japan* (Tokyo: Tuttle, 1959), 56. For the other quotes, see C. T. van Assendelft de Coningh, *A Pioneer in Yokohama: A Dutchman's Adventures in the New Treaty Port*, ed. and trans. Martha Chaiklin (Indianapolis: Hackett, 2012), 45.

36. Hugh Cortazzi, *Victorians in Japan: In and around the Treaty Ports* (London: Athlone Press, 1987), 291.

37. *The Japan Herald*, June 11, 1864, 307.

38. Quoted in Williams, *Tales of Foreign Settlements*, 60.

39. Yen-p'ing Hao, *The Comprador in Nineteenth Century China: Bridge between East and West* (Cambridge, Mass.: Harvard University Press, 1970).

40. Ishii Takashi, *Kōto Yokohama no tanjō* (Yokohama: Yūrindō, 1976), 207–8; see also Hao, *Comprador in China*. On Chinese compradors, see Marie-Claire Bergère, *Shanghai: China's Gateway to Modernity*, trans. Janet Lloyd (Stanford, Calif.: Stanford University Press, 2010), 71–74.

41. Tanaka Takeyuki, *Yokohama Chūkagai: Sekai saikyō no Chainataun* (Tokyo: Chūō Kōron Shinsha, 2009), 69.

42. Ibid., 77–80.

43. John Black, *Young Japan*, 1:362–63.

44. Chūka Kaikan and Yokohama Kaikō Shiryōkan, *Yokohama Kakyō no kioku: Yokohama kakyō kōjutsu rekishi kirokushū* (Yokohama: Chūka Kaikan, 2010), 9; Tanaka, *Yokohama Chūkagai*, 76.

45. *Japan Times* (Yokohama), April 6, 1866, 203.

46. Joseph Heco and James Murdoch, *The Narrative of a Japanese: What He Has Seen and the People He Has Met in the Course of the Last Forty Years*, 2 vols. (Yokohama: Yokohama Printing and Publishing, 1892), 62.

47. Takamura Naosuke and Yokohama-shi Furusato Rekishi Zaidan, *Yokohama rekishi to bunka: Kaikō 150-shūnen kinen* (Yokohama: Yūrindō, 2009), 193–94.

48. Gary P. Leupp, *Interracial Intimacy in Japan: Western Men and Japanese Women, 1543–1900* (London: Continuum, 2003), 83–99.

49. Utagawa and Kida, *Yokohama kaikō kenbunshi*, 22.

50. John Black, *Young Japan*, 2:99–100.

51. Quoted in diary entry of June 6, 1860, in Hall, *Japan Through American Eyes*, 180.

52. January 2, 1861, ibid., 290–91.

53. Hugh Cortazzi, *Collected Writings of Sir Hugh Cortazzi* (Tokyo: Edition Synapse; Richmond, Surrey, U.K.: Japan Library, 2000), 207.

54. John Black, *Young Japan*, 2:283.

55. Quoted in Cortazzi, *Victorians in Japan*, 277.

56. Ernest Mason Satow, *The Diaries and Letters of Sir Ernest Mason Satow (1843–1929), a Scholar-Diplomat in East Asia*, ed. Ian C. Ruxton (Lewiston, N.Y.: Mellen Press, 1998), 394–405.

57. Yoshida Tsuneyoshi, "Taigai kankei yori mitaru Yokohama kaikō no yūkaku," *Meiji Taishō shidan* 9 (1937): 5.

58. Ibid., 6.

59. Wikipedia, s.v. "Rashamen," http://ja.wikipedia.org/wiki/%E7%BE%85%E7%B4%97%E7%B7%AC.

60. Ibid.

61. Ibid.

62. Yoshida, "Taigai kankei," 5–7.

63. Ibid., 6.

64. Quoted in Leupp, Interracial Intimacy in Japan, 142.

65. Usami Misako, Shukuba to meshimorionna (Tokyo: Dōseisha, 2000), 106–8.

66. Ibid., 115.

67. Kanagawa Kenritsu Rekishi Hakubutsukan, Yokohama ukiyoe to kindai Nihon: Ikoku "Yokohama" o tabisuru (Yokohama: Kanagawa Kenritsu Rekishi Hakubutsukan, 1999), 55.

68. The report is reproduced as appendix I in Hugh Cortazzi, Dr. Willis in Japan, 1862–1877: British Medical Pioneer (London: Athlone Press, 1985), 241–46.

69. Ibid., 242.

70. Ibid., 241.

71. Letter 61, Bunkyū 1/1/5 (2/14/1861), to Shōjirō.

72. Letter 39, Man'en 1/5/18 (7/6/1860), Naotarō to Shōjirō.

73. Letter 42, Man'en 1/6/18 (8/4/1860), to Shōjirō.

74. Letter 75, Bunkyū 1/12/5 (1/4/1862), to Shōjirō.

75. Letter 57, Man'en 1/12/3 (1/13/1861), to Shōjirō.

76. Letter 75, Bunkyū 1/12/5 (1/4/1862), to Shōjirō.

77. Kanagawa-ken Toshokan Kyōkai, Mikan Yokohama kaikō shiryō, 149–52.

78. Letter 71-1, Bunkyū 1/7/24 (8/29/1861), to Shōjirō.

79. Letter 72-1, Bunkyū 1/8/5 (9/9/1861), to Shōjirō.

80. Letter 28, Man'en 1/2/20 (3/12/1860), to Shōjirō.

81. Letter 53, Man'en 1/11/5 (12/16/1860), to Shōjirō.

82. Letter 59, Man'en 1/12/21 (1/31/1861), to Shōjirō. It is not clear if Shirobei is related to the Mataemon who was reported to be selling meat from Chūemon's premises in late 1861.

83. Letter 43, Man'en 1/7/8 (8/24/1860), to Shōjirō.

84. Ibid.

85. Letter 46, Man'en 1/7/27 (9/12/1860), to Shōjirō.

86. Letter 48, Man'en 1/9/5 (10/18/1860), to Shōjirō.

87. Letter 50, Man'en 1/10/7 (11/19/1860), to Ikegami Sadaemon, Iwakura Yaheiji, and Shōjirō.

88. Letter 51, Man'en 1/10/19 (12/1/1860), to Shōjirō.

89. Ibid.

90. Kikuen, Yokohama kidan, 10–11.

91. Letter 53, Man'en 1/11/5 (12/16/1860), to Shōjirō.

92. Ibid.

93. Letter 50, Man'en 1/10/7 (11/19/1860), To Ikegami Sadaemon, Iwakura Yaheiji, and Shōjirō.

94. Letter 56, Man'en 1/11/8 (12/19/1860), to Shōjirō.

95. Letter 59, Man'en 1/12/21 (1/31/1861), to Shōjirō.

96. Letter 61, Bunkyū 1/1/5 (2/14/1861), to Shōjirō.

97. Letter 62, Bunkyū 1/1/8 (2/17/1861), to Shōjirō.

98. Ibid.

99. Letter 64, Bunkyū 1/2/14 (3/24/1861), to Shōjirō.

100. Letter 65, Bunkyū 1/3/11 (4/20/1861), to Shōjirō.

101. Letter 66, Bunkyū 1/5/9 (6/16/1861), to Shōjirō.

102. Ibid.

103. Letter 67-1, Bunkyū 1/5/17 (6/24/1861), to Shōjirō.

104. Letter 68, Bunkyū 1/7/5 (8/10/1861), to Shōjirō.

105. Letter 70, Bunkyū 1/7/18 (8/23/1861), to Shōjirō.

106. Letter 71-3, Bunkyū 1/8/5 (9/9/1861), to Shōjirō.

107. Letter 74, Bunkyū 1/11/5 (12/6/1861), to Shōjirō.

108. Letter 76, Bunkyū 1/12/11 (1/10/1862), to Shōjirō.

109. Letter 75, Bunkyū 1/12/5 (1/4/1862), to Shōjirō.

110. Letter 19, Ansei 6/7/28 (8/26/1859), to Shōjirō.

111. Wm. Theodore de Bary et al., comps., Sources of Japanese Tradition, Volume 1: From Earliest Times to 1600, 2nd ed. (New York: Columbia University Press, 2001), 621–25.

112. Ibid., 498.

113. Quoted in Cortazzi, Victorians in Japan, 68.

114. Assendelft de Coningh, A Pioneer in Yokohama, 36–38.

115. Ibid., 117–19.

116. Yokohama-shi, Yokohama shishi, 256–65.

117. Letter 57, Man'en 1/12/3 (1/13/1861), to Shōjirō.

118. Letter 59, Man'en 1/12/21 (1/31/1861), to Shōjirō.

119. Letter 80-2, Bunkyū 2/4/10 (5/8/1862), to Shōjirō and Komazawa Buzaemon.

120. Letter 82, Bunkyū 2/5/3 (5/31/1862), to Shōjirō; letter 83-1, Bunkyū 2/6/3 (6/29/1862), to Shōjirō.

121. Letter 83-1, Bunkyū 2/6/3 (6/29/1862), to Shōjirō.

122. June 24, 1862, in Hall, Japan Through American Eyes, 436–37.

123. June 27, 1862, ibid.

124. John Black, Young Japan, 1:299–300.

125. Shibusawa Eiichi, *The Autobiography of Shibusawa Eiichi: From Peasant to Entrepreneur*, trans. Teruko Craig (Tokyo: University of Tokyo Press, 1994), 20.

126. Quoted in James L. Huffman, *Politics of the Meiji Press: The Life of Fukuchi Gen'ichirō* (Honolulu: University Press of Hawaii, 1980), 29.

127. John Black, *Young Japan*, 1:156–57.

128. Letter 88, Bunkyū 2/8/22 (9/15/1862), to Shōjirō.

129. Robert Fortune, *Yedo and Peking: A Narrative of a Journey to the Capitals of Japan and China* (London: Murray, 1863), 260–61.

130. Letter 94, Bunkyū 2/10/14 (12/5/1862), to Shōjirō.

131. Letter 95, Bunkyū 2/11/29 (1/18/1863), Chūemon and Naotarō to Shōjirō.

132. Letter 94, Bunkyū 2/10/14 (12/5/1862), to Shōjirō.

133. Letter 100, Bunkyū 3/3/8 (4/25/1863), to Shōjirō.

134. May 5–6, 1863, in Hall, *Japan Through American Eyes*, 474–75.

135. Paul C. Blum, trans., "Father Mounicou's Bakumatsu Diary," *Transactions of the Asiatic Society of Japan*, 3rd ser., 13 (1976): 90.

136. May 5–6, 1863, in Hall, *Japan Through American Eyes*, 474–75.

137. Blum, "Father Mounicou's Bakumatsu Diary," 93.

138. Letter 101, Bunkyū 3/4/2 (5/19/1863), to Shōjirō.

139. John Black, *Young Japan*, 1:199.

140. *Illustrated London News*, September 12, 1863; see Terry Bennett, Hugh Cortazzi, and James Hoare, *Japan and the "Illustrated London News": Complete Record of Reported Events, 1853–1899* (Folkestone, Kent, U.K.: Global Oriental, 2006), 105.

141. Ibid., 106.

142. John McMaster, *Jardines in Japan, 1859–1867* (Groningen, Neth.: V.R.B., 1966), 111.

143. Quoted ibid., 120.

144. See, for example, Marius B. Jansen, "The Meiji Restoration," in *The Cambridge History of Japan, Volume 5: The Nineteenth Century*, edited by Marius B. Jansen (Cambridge: Cambridge University Press, 1991), 338.

145. Letter 105, Bunkyū 3/7/3 (8/16/1863), to Shōjirō.

146. Letter 109, Bunkyū 3/8/23 (10/5/1863), to Shōjirō.

147. Letter 110, Bunkyū 3/9/12 (10/24/1863), to Shōjirō.

148. Letter 98, Bunkyū 3/2/2 (3/20/1863), to Shōjirō.

149. Letter 75, Bunkyū 1/12/5 (1/4/1862), to Shōjirō.

150. Letter 99, Bunkyū 3/3/5 (4/22/1863), to Shōjirō.

151. Ishii Takashi, *Kōto Yokohama no tanjō*, 193.

152. Letter 90, Bunkyū 2/intercalary 8/8 (10/1/1862), to Shōjirō.

153. Letter 94, Bunkyū 2/10/14 (12/5/1862), to Shōjirō.

154. Letter 97, Bunkyū 3/1/9 (2/26/1863), to Komazawa Buzaemon and Shōjirō.

155. Letter 101, Bunkyū 3/4/2 (5/19/1863), to Shōjirō.

156. Letter 129, date unknown, to Shōjirō.

157. Letter 171, Keiō 1/7/22 (9/11/1865), to Shōjirō.

158. Interview with Shinohara Yukio, May 25, 2014.

3. Prosperity (1864–1866)

1.   Yokohama-shi, *Yokohama shishi*, vol. 2 (Yokohama: Yokohama-shi, 1958), 337–95; see also Wikipedia, s.v. "Gohin Edo Kaisōrei," https://ja.wikipedia.org/wiki /五品江戸廻送令.

2.   S. J. Gower to William Keswick, October 31, 1863, Jardine Matheson Archive, MS JM B10-9, reel 438, Cambridge University Library.

3.   John McMaster, *Jardines in Japan, 1859–1867* (Groningen, Neth.: V.R.B., 1966), 115.

4.   Joseph Heco and James Murdoch, *The Narrative of a Japanese: What He Has Seen and the People He Has Met in the Course of the Last Forty Years*, 2 vols. (Yokohama: Yokohama Printing and Publishing, 1892), 2:14.

5.   McMaster, *Jardines in Japan*, 115–16.

6.   Gower to Keswick, October 31, 1863, Jardine Matheson Archive, MS JM B10-9, reel 438.

7.   Ishii Takashi, *Kōto Yokohama no tanjō* (Yokohama: Yūrindō, 1976), 189.

8.   McMaster, *Jardines in Japan*, 116.

9.   Letter 133, Genji 1/7/19 (8/20/1864), to Shōjirō, in Ishii Takashi, ed., *Yokohama urikomishō Kōshūya monjo* (Yokohama: Yūrindō, 1984). Please note that all cited letters relating to Chūemon are collected in the Ishii volume.

10. Letter 135, Genji 1/8/22 (9/22/1864), to Shōjirō.

11. Heco and Murdoch, *Narrative of a Japanese*, 41.

12. William Keswick to Shanghai office, July 14, 1864, Jardine Matheson Archive, MS JM B10-9, reel 438.

13. Wikipedia, s.v. "Lancashire Cotton Famine," https://en.wikipedia.org/wiki /Lancashire_Cotton_Famine.

14. John Reddie Black, *Young Japan: Yokohama and Yedo*, 2 vols. (London: Trübner, 1880), 1:222. Black does not name the fund, but the Lancashire and Cheshire Operatives Relief Fund was the main fund open to international subscription.

15. Eugene R. Dattel, "Cotton and the Civil War," *Mississippi History Now*, July 2008, http://mshistorynow.mdah.state.ms.us/articles/291/cotton-and-the -civil-war.

16. Letter 90, Bunkyū 2/intercalary 8/8 (10/1/1862), to Shōjirō.

17. Letter 92, Bunkyū 2/intercalary 8/28 (10/31/1862), to Shōjirō.

18. Letter 111, Bunkyū 3/10/5 (11/15/1863), to Shōjirō.

19. Ibid.

20. On June 4, Chūemon reported a price of $12 per picul; letter 102, Bunkyū 3/4/18 (6/4/1862), to Shōjirō.

21. Letter 116, Bunkyū 3/11/17 (12/27/1863), to Shōjirō.

22. Letter 111, Bunkyū 3/10/5 (11/15/1863), to Shōjirō.

23. Letter 112, Bunkyū 3/10/12 (11/22/1863), to Shōjirō.

24. Letter 113, Bunkyū 3/10/26 (12/6/1863), to Shōjirō.

25. Ibid.

26. Letter 89, Bunkyū 2/8/22 (9/15/1862), to Ihei and two others. Unfortunately the other letter has not survived.

27. Letter 108, Bunkyū 3/8/10 (9/22/1863), to Shōjirō.

28. Letter 124, date unknown, to Shōjirō. For an analysis of delivery times in the collection, see Yabuuchi Yoshihiko, Nihon yūbin sōgyō shi: Hikyaku kara yūbin e (Tokyo: Yūzankaku Shuppan, 1975), 73.

29. May 3, 1860, in Francis Hall, Japan Through American Eyes: The Journal of Francis Hall, Kanagawa and Yokohama, 1859–1866 (Princeton, N.J.: Princeton University Press, 1992), 161.

30. Letter 108, Bunkyū 3/8/10 (9/22/1863), to Shōjirō.

31. Letter 113, Bunkyū 3/10/26 (12/6/1863), to Shōjirō.

32. Letter 118, Bunkyū 3/11/29 (1/8/1864), to Shimura Jizaemon, Yamashita Goroemon, and village representatives.

33. Fukuzawa Tetsuzō, "Kinsei kōki no kinai ni okeru gōnō kinyū no tenkai to chiiki," in Kinai no gōnō keiei to chiiki shakai, ed. Takashi Watanabe (Kyoto: Shibunkaku Shuppan, 2008), 250. There are many similar accounts of widespread local and regional lending. See, for example, Nakayama Tomihiro, "Kinsei kōki ni okeru kashitsuke shihon no sonzai keitai: Bingo Fuchū Nobuto-ke no jirei," Shigaku kenkyū 172 (1986): 1–20.

34. See Edward E. Pratt, Japan's Protoindustrial Elite: The Economic Foundations of the Gōnō (Cambridge, Mass.: Harvard University Asia Center, 1999).

35. Fukuzawa, "Kinsei kōki," 261.

36. Letter 119, Bunkyū 3/12/3 (1/12/1864), to Yamashita Goroemon, Komazawa Buzaemon, and Shōjirō.

37. Letter 136, Genji 1/9/4 (10/4/1864), Shōjirō to Chūemon.

38. Letter 141, Genji 1/9/23 (10/23/1864), Chūemon and Naotarō to Shōjirō.

39. Letter 148, Genji 1/10/27 (11/26/1864), to Shōjirō. See also McMaster, Jardines in Japan, 114–15.

40. Letter 137-1, Genji 1/9/7 (10/7/1864), Naotarō to Ochiai Sataro.

41. Letter 140, Genji 1/9/23 (10/23/1864), to Shōjirō.

42. Letter 155, Keiō 1/2/9 (3/6/1865), to Komazawa Buzaemon and Shōjirō.

43. Letter 156, Keiō 1/2/21 (3/18/1865), Naotarō to Shōjirō.

44. Wikipedia, s.v. "Pébrine," https://en.wikipedia.org/wiki/Pébrine.

45. Letter 159, Keiō 1/4/17 (5/11/1865), to Shōjirō.

46. For an overview of treaty negotiations with France and other countries and of the growing Japanese-French alliance that facilitated the trade liberalization, see Michael R. Auslin, *Negotiating with Imperialism: The Unequal Treaties and the Culture of Japanese Diplomacy* (Cambridge, Mass.: Harvard University Press, 2004), chapters 4 and 5.

47. Hiroshi Hasebe, "Silkworm Egg Trading and the Village in Early Modern Japan," in *Village Communities, States, and Traders: Essays in Honour of Chatthip Nartsupha*, ed. Akira Nozaki and Chris Baker (Bangkok: Thai-Japanese Seminar and Sangsan Publishing, 2003), 285–86.

48. Letter 162, Keiō 1/5/19 (6/12/1865), Chūemon and Naotarō to Shōjirō.

49. Letter 167, Keiō 1/6/21 (8/12/1865), to Yamagata Rin'emon, Yamashita Goroemon, Hanjirō, and Shōjirō.

50. Akira Shimizu, "Eating Edo, Sensing Japan: Food Branding and Market Culture in Late Tokugawa Japan, 1780–1868" (Ph.D. diss., University of Illinois at Urbana-Champaign, 2011). One of Shimizu's case studies is of Kōshū grapes, a brand that has retained its cachet right down to the present day.

51. Letter 176, Keiō 1/8/13 (10/2/1865), to Shōjirō.

52. M. Paske-Smith, *Western Barbarians in Japan and Formosa in Tokugawa Days, 1603–1868* (Kobe: Thompson, 1930), 303. Ishii Kanji has conducted a more exhaustive study of the available statistics; see Ishii, *Kōto Yokohama no tanjō*, 125–86. I have used a summary that takes both these studies into account: Yokohama Zeikan, *Yokohama Zeikan hyakunijū-nenshi* (Yokohama: Yokohama Zeikan, 1981), 24.

53. John Black, *Young Japan*, 1:55.

54. February 10, 1862, in Hall, *Japan Through American Eyes*, 398.

55. Philip Billingsley, "Bakunin in Yokohama: The Dawning of the Pacific Era," *International History Review* 20, no. 3 (1998): 550–55.

56. Shin'ichi Miyazawa, "Ernest Satow's Japan Diary, 1862–1863: An Annotated Transcript," *Saitama Joshi Tanki Daigaku kenkyū kiyō*, no. 10 (1999): 322.

57. An excellent account of a multigenerational family history in Yokohama is Leslie Helm, *Yokohama Yankee: My Family's Five Generations as Outsiders in Japan* (Seattle: Chin Music Press, 2013).

58. Yokohama Kaikō Shiryōkan, ed., *Yokohama mono no hajime kō* (Yokohama: Yokohama Kaikō Shiryō Fukyū Kyōkai, 1988), 144.

59. Ibid.

60. Ibid., 146–47.

61. Ibid., 148–49.

62. Ibid.

63. Ibid., 158.

64. Roger Mottini, "The Swiss–Japanese Treaty of Friendship and Commerce of February 6, 1864" (speech given at the city hall of Zurich, February 6, 2004), http://www.mottini.eu/articles/2004_Swiss-Japanese-Treaty.pdf.

65. Yokohama Kaikō Shiryōkan, *Yokohama mono*, 160.

66. Gonda Masumi, "Bakumatsuki kara Meiji shoki no Yokohama kaikōjo ni okeru Eigo no gakushū," *Kōwan keizai kenkyū: Nihon kōwan keizai nenpō* 50 (2013): 139–48. For Momotarō, see also Haru Matsukata Reischauer, *Samurai and Silk: A Japanese and American Heritage* (Cambridge, Mass.: Belknap Press, 1986).

67. *Wikipedia*, s.v. "Kishida Ginkō," https://ja.wikipedia.org/wiki/%E5%B2%B8%E7%94%B0%E5%90%9F%E9%A6%99.

68. A. Hamish Ion, *American Missionaries, Christian Oyatoi, and Japan, 1859–73* (Vancouver: University of British Columbia Press, 2009), 58–60.

69. John Clark, "Charles Wirgman," in *Britain and Japan, 1859–1991: Themes and Personalities*, ed. Hugh Cortazzi and Gordon Daniels (London: Routledge, 1991), 55.

70. Ernest Mason Satow, *A Diplomat in Japan: The Inner History of the Critical Years in the Evolution of Japan When the Ports Were Opened and the Monarchy Restored* (Philadelphia: Lippincott, 1921), 211.

71. Clark, "Charles Wirgman," 62.

72. *Wikipedia*, s.v. "Felice Beato," https://en.wikipedia.org/wiki/Felice_Beato.

73. Anne Lacoste, *Felice Beato: A Photographer on the Eastern Road* (Los Angeles: J. Paul Getty Museum, 2010), 13.

74. *Illustrated London News*, September 26, 1863; quoted ibid.

75. Mio Wakita, "Sites of 'Disconnectedness': The Port City of Yokohama, Souvenir Photography, and Its Audience," *Transcultural Studies* 2 (February 2013): 85.

76. Kikuen Rōjin, *Yokohama kidan: Minato no hana* (Kinkōdō Zō, ca. 1864), 20.

77. December 9, 1859, in Hall, *Japan Through American Eyes*, 85.

78. April 15, 1861, ibid., 326. American impresario Hezekiah Bateman was famous for putting four of his children on the stage.

79. Quoted in Frederik L. Schodt, *Professor Risley and the Imperial Japanese Troupe: How an American Acrobat Introduced Circus to Japan—and Japan to the West* (Berkeley, Calif.: Stone Bridge Press, 2012), 134.

80. Aya Mihara refers to a series of performances by members of the Hamaikari and Matsui families that took place as early as August 1864 ("Professional Entertainers Abroad and Theatrical Portraits in Hand," *Old Photography Study*, no. 3 [2009]: 53).

81. Schodt, *Professor Risley*, 46–47.

82. Quoted ibid., 126.

83. Hiroko Johnson, "Yokohama-e: Prints of a New Port City," in *Dreams and Diversions: Essays on Japanese Woodblock Prints from the San Diego Museum of Art*, ed. Andreas Marks and Sonya Rhie Quintanilla (San Diego: San Diego Museum of Art, 2010), 148.

84. Kikuen, *Yokohama kidan*, 5–6.

85. Ibid., 1–2.

86. Johnson, "Yokohama-e," 160.

87. Translated and quoted in Todd Munson, "Curiosities of the Five Nations: Nansōan Shōhaku's Yokohama Tales," *Japan Studies Review* 12 (2008): 24. See also Nansōan Shōhaku, *Chinji gokakoku Yokohama hanashi* (Yokohama, ca. 1862).

88. Kikuen, *Yokohama kidan*, 5–6.

89. Ibid., 22.

90. Ibid., 8–9.

91. Ibid., 19.

92. Ibid., 25–27.

93. Ibid., 10–13.

94. Ibid.

95. Ibid., 20.

96. Ibid., 22.

97. Ibid., 20.

98. Ibid.

99. Utagawa Sadahide, *Yokohama kaikō kenbunshi biyō*, ed. Kida Jun'ichirō (Tokyo: Meichō Kankōkai, 1967), 4.

100. Ibid., 2.

101. Ibid., 20.

102. Kikuen, *Yokohama kidan*, 27–28. For an extended discussion of Tokugawa-era views on race, see Gary P. Leupp, *Interracial Intimacy in Japan: Western Men and Japanese Women, 1543–1900* (London: Continuum, 2003), 83–99, 136–37.

103. Letter 164, Keiō 1/5/29 (6/22/1865), to Shōjirō; letter 186, Keiō 1/11/7 (12/24/1865), Naotarō to Shōjirō; letter 187, Keiō 1/11/9 (12/26/1865), Naotarō to Shōjirō; letter 215-1, Keiō 3/2/13 (3/18/1867), Chūemon and Naotarō to Shōjirō.

104. Letter 180, 1/8/28 (10/17/1865), Chūemon and Naotarō to Shōjirō.

105. Kären Wigen, *A Malleable Map: Geographies of Restoration in Central Japan, 1600–1912* (Berkeley: University of California Press, 2010).

106. Hiroshi Mitani, "A Protonation-State and Its 'Unforgettable Other': The Prerequisites for Meiji International Relations," in *New Directions in the*

Study of Meiji Japan, ed. Helen Hardacre and Adam L. Kern (Leiden: Brill, 1997).

107. Pat Barr, *The Coming of the Barbarians: The Opening of Japan to the West, 1853–1870* (New York: Dutton, 1967), 78.

108. "Life in Japan," August 10, 1861; see Terry Bennett, Hugh Cortazzi, and James Hoare, *Japan and the "Illustrated London News": Complete Record of Reported Events, 1853–1899* (Folkestone, Kent, U.K.: Global Oriental, 2006), 76.

109. Alan Hockley has suggested that many of the standard images of Japan portrayed in text and image actually predated the opening of the ports, reaffirming stereotypes created by earlier writers who relied mostly on Dutch accounts, some of which were centuries old ("Expectation and Authenticity in Meiji Tourist Photography," in *Challenging Past and Present: The Metamorphosis of Nineteenth-Century Japanese Art*, ed. Ellen P. Conant, 114–32 [Honolulu: University of Hawai`i Press, 2006]).

110. Lacoste, *Felice Beato*, 16–17.

111. Luke Gartlan, "Samuel Cocking and the Rise of Japanese Photography," *History of Photography* 33, no. 2 (2009): 159.

112. On *japonisme*, see Lionel Lambourne, *Japonisme: Cultural Crossings between Japan and the West* (London: Phaidon, 2005). See also Yuko Kikuchi and Toshio Watanabe, "The British Discovery of Japanese Art," in *The History of Anglo-Japanese Relations 1600–2000, Volume 5: Social and Cultural Perspectives*, ed. Gordon Daniels and Chushichi Tsuzuki, 146–70 (New York: Palgrave Macmillan, 2002). Mio Wakita discusses the agency of Kusakabe Kinbei in "Sites of 'Disconnectedness.'" I am most grateful to Mio Wakita for her valuable insights into these cross-cultural exchanges.

113. *London Times*, May 12, 1862, 12.

114. *Illustrated London News*, May 24, 1862; see Bennett, Cortazzi, and Hoare, *Japan and the "Illustrated London News,"* 97.

115. *Illustrated London News*, May 30, 1862, ibid., 100.

116. "Japanese Manufactures at the Great Exhibition," *The Friend: A Religious and Literary Journal* 36, no. 7 (October 18, 1862): 54.

117. Quoted ibid., 54.

118. [Gustave] Duchesne de Bellecour, "L'état politique et commercial de la Chine et du Japon: L'exposition chinoise et japonaise au Champ de Mars," *Revue des deux mondes*, August 1, 1867, 733.

119. Mihara, "Professional Entertainers," 49.

120. Ibid., 52.

121. Quoted in Schodt, *Professor Risley*, 194.

122. For an excellent narrative of Risley's life, the Imperial Japanese Troupe, and its performances worldwide, see ibid.

123. M. William Steele, "The Village Elite in the Restoration Drama," in *Alternative Narratives in Modern Japanese History* (London: RoutledgeCurzon, 2003), 36–38.

124. Letter 153, Genji 1/month unknown/15 (1864), to Shōjirō.

125. Yamanashi-ken, *Yamanashi kenshi: Tsūshi hen* (Kōfu: Yamanashi Nichinichi Shinbunsha, 2004), 4:816.

126. Letter 151, Genji 1/12/9 (1/6/1865), to Kino Chūkichi.

127. Letter 180, Keiō 1/8/28 (10/17/1865), Chūemon and Naotarō to Shōjirō; letter 182, Keiō 1/10/4 (11/21/1865), to Shōjirō.

128. Letter 233, Keiō 3/7/3 (8/2/1867), Chūemon to Shōjirō.

129. Letter 199-1, Keiō 2/6/17 (7/28/1866), to Shōjirō.

130. Ibid.

131. Yamanashi-ken, *Yamanashi kenshi*, 799.

132. Kären Wigen, *The Making of a Japanese Periphery, 1750–1920* (Berkeley: University of California Press, 1995).

133. Yamanashi-ken, *Yamanashi kenshi*, 799–800.

134. Yukihiko Motoyama, *Proliferating Talent: Essays on Politics, Thought, and Education in the Meiji Era*, ed. J. S. A. Elisonas and Richard Rubinger (Honolulu: University of Hawai`i Press, 1997), 22–23.

135. Peter Frost, *The Bakumatsu Currency Crisis* (Cambridge, Mass.: East Asian Research Center, Harvard University, 1970), 37–38. See also Simon James Bytheway and Martha Chaiklin, "Reconsidering the Yokohama 'Gold Rush' of 1859," *Journal of World History* 27, no. 2 (2016): 281–301. I am most grateful to Sergey Tolstoguzov (Hiroshima University) for his valuable help with the tricky topic of Edo-era currency. Dr. Tolstoguzov maintains that the third factor, government overproduction of coinage, was by far the most significant inflationary factor.

136. Mark Metzler, "Japan and the Global Conjuncture in the Summer of 1866" (paper presented at the Heidelberg History Conference on "Global History and the Meiji Restoration," Heidelberg, July 3–5, 2015), 24.

137. August 21, 1860 and May 21, 1861, in Hall, *Japan Through American Eyes*, 213, 339.

138. Takeo Ono, *Edo bukka jiten* (Tokyo: Tenbōsha, 1991).

139. Heco and Murdoch, *Narrative of a Japanese*, 14.

140. Ibid., 264–65. Wikipedia puts his death a year earlier and attributes it to his mishandling of the treaty negotiations with Prussia; *Wikipedia*, s.v. "Hori Toshihiro," https://ja.wikipedia.org/wiki/%E5%A0%80%E5%88%A9%E7%85%95.

141. Yamanashi-ken, *Yamanashi kenshi*, 810.

142. Letter 162, Keiō 1/5/19 (6/12/1865), Chūemon and Naotarō to Shōjirō.

143. Yamanashi-ken, *Yamanashi kenshi*, 820.

144. Ibid., 828.

145. Toshihiro Atsumi, "Silk, Regional Rivalry, and the Impact of the Port Openings in Nineteenth Century Japan," *Journal of the Japanese and International Economies* 24, no. 4 (December 2010): 519–39.

4. Transformation (1866–1873)

1. Letter 134, Genji 1/7/29 (7/17/1864), to Shōjirō, in Ishii Takashi, ed., *Yokohama urikomishō Kōshūya monjo* (Yokohama: Yūrindō, 1984). Please note that all cited letters relating to Chūemon are collected in the Ishii volume.

2. Letter 132, Genji 1/6/14 (7/17/1864), to Shōjirō.

3. Yamanashi Jewelry Association History, "History," http://yja.or.jp/history/.

4. Letter 164, Keiō 1/5/29 (6/22/1865), to Shōjirō. For tables of export items, see Ishii Takashi, *Kōto Yokohama no tanjō* (Yokohama: Yūrindō, 1976), 87–147.

5. Letter 209, Keiō 2/12/6 (1/11/1867), Naotarō to Shōjirō.

6. Letter 205, Keiō 2/10/7 (11/13/1866), Naotarō to Shōjirō.

7. John Reddie Black, *Young Japan: Yokohama and Yedo*, 2 vols. (London: Trübner, 1880), 2:17–24.

8. Ibid.

9. Quoted in Par Barr, *The Coming of the Barbarians: The Opening of Japan to the West, 1853–1870* (New York: Dutton, 1967), 186.

10. Letter 207, Keiō 2/11/4 (12/10/1866), Naotarō to Shōjirō.

11. Letter 209, Keiō 2/12/6 (1/11/1867), Naotarō to Shōjirō.

12. Letter 211, Keiō 2/12/23 (1/28/1867), to Shōjirō.

13. Ibid.

14. Letter 219, Keiō 3/4/2 (5/5/1867), to Shōjirō.

15. Letter 221, Keiō 3/5/3 (6/5/1867), to Shōjirō.

16. Letter 223, Keiō 3/5/13 (6/15/1867), to Shōjirō.

17. Letter 225, Keiō 3/5/19 (6/21/1867), to Shōjirō and Naotarō.

18. Letter 227-1, Keiō 3/5/25 (6/27/1867), to Shōjirō and Naotarō.

19. Letter 228-1, Keiō 3/6/6 (7/7/1867), Naotarō to Shōjirō.

20. Letter 223, Keiō 3/5/13 (6/15/1867), to Shōjirō; letter 259, Meiji 1/4/13 (5/5/1868), to Shōjirō.

21. Letter 234, Keiō 3/7/12 (8/11/1867), Naotarō to Shōjirō.

22. Letter 230, Keiō 3/6/25 (7/26/1867), Chūemon and Naotarō to Shōjirō.

23. Letter 236, Keiō 3/7/20 (8/19/1867), Chūemon and Naotarō to Shōjirō.

24. Letter 240, Keiō 3/10/9 (11/4/1867), to Shōjirō.

25. Letter 238-1, Keiō 3/7/20 (8/19/1867), to Shōjirō.
26. わるあそび之頭取いたし候, letter 199-1, Keiō 2/6/17 (7/28/1866), to Shōjirō.
27. Letter 215-1, Keiō 3/2/13 (3/18/1867), Chūemon and Naotarō to Shōjirō.
28. Letter 243-1, Keiō 3/10/24 (11/19/1867), to Tsujiya Iemon and two others.
29. Mitsui Bunko, *Mitsui jigyōshi: Honpen*, vol. 1 (Tokyo: Mitsui Bunko, 1980), 661–64.
30. Letter 244-1, Keiō 3/10/28 (11/23/1867), to Shōjirō.
31. Letter 245-1, Keiō 3/11/8 (12/3/1867), to Shōjirō.
32. Ibid.
33. Ibid.
34. Translated and quoted in M. William Steele, *Alternative Narratives in Modern Japanese History* (London: RoutledgeCurzon, 2003), 65.
35. Kanagawa Prefectural Government, *The History of Kanagawa* (Yokohama: Kanagawa Prefectural Government, 1985), 179–81.
36. George M. Wilson, *Patriots and Redeemers in Japan: Motives in the Meiji Restoration* (Chicago: University of Chicago Press, 1992), 95–99.
37. Kanagawa-ken Kenshi Henshūshitsu, *Kanagawa kenshi: Tsūshi hen*, vol. 3 (Yokohama: Kanagawa-ken, 1980), 1244–45.
38. Letter 246, Keiō 3/11/20 (12/15/1867), Naotarō to Shōjirō.
39. Letter 247, Keiō 3/11/28 (12/23/1867), to Shōjirō.
40. Letter 250, Keiō 3/12/9 (1/3/1868), to Shōjirō.
41. Ibid.
42. Ibid.
43. Letter 252, Meiji 1/1/18 (2/11/1868), to Shōjirō.
44. Albert M. Craig, *Chōshū in the Meiji Restoration* (Cambridge, Mass.: Harvard University Press, 1967), 21–22.
45. Masakazu Iwata, *Ōkubo Toshimichi, the Bismarck of Japan* (Berkeley: University of California Press, 1964), 114.
46. Quoted in Steele, *Alternative Narratives*, 95.
47. At least one grave of a dead soldier, a samurai from Aizu, has been identified in Yokohama. See Nishikawa Takeomi and Itō Izumi, *Kaikoku Nihon to Yokohama Chūkagai* (Tokyo: Taishūkan Shoten, 2002), 57.
48. Translated and quoted in Steele, *Alternative Narratives*, 67.
49. Letter 252, Meiji 1/1/18 (2/11/1868), to Shōjirō.
50. Translated and quoted in Steele, *Alternative Narratives*, 62.
51. Letter 253, Meiji 1/1/23 (2/16/1868), to Shōjirō.
52. I am indebted here to Fabian Drixler and his unpublished paper "Alternative Japanese Nations in the Meiji Restoration: The Lost History of Azuma" (paper presented at the Heidelberg History Conference on "Global History and the Meiji Restoration," Heidelberg, July 3–5, 2015).

53. Steele, *Alternative Narratives*, 68–75.

54. Letter 257, Meiji 1/3/8 (3/31/1868), to Tsuruse Seiemon, Katsunuma Chōbei, Kamisone Jōsuke, Imai Rin'emon, Saijō Matsuemon, and Kyōya Ishichi.

55. Ibid.

56. Letter 259, Meiji 1/4/13 (5/5/1868), to Shōjirō.

57. Steele, *Alternative Narratives*, 80.

58. Quoted and translated ibid., 78.

59. Letter 269-1, Meiji 1/5/20 (7/9/1868), to Shōjirō.

60. Letter 256, Meiji 1/3/2 (3/25/1868), to Shōjirō.

61. Letter 258-1, Meiji 1/4/2 (4/24/1868), to Shōjirō.

62. Letter 256, Meiji 1/3/2 (3/25/1868), to Shōjirō.

63. Letter 260-1, Meiji 1/4/21 (5/13/1868), to Shōjirō.

64. Letter 269-1, Meiji 1/5/20 (7/9/1868), to Shōjirō.

65. Letter 272-1, Meiji 1/6/1 (7/20/1868), to Shōjirō.

66. Letter 303-1, Meiji 2/6/9 (7/17/1869), to Shōjirō.

67. Letter 311-2, Meiji 2/7/11 (8/18/1869), Naotarō to Shōjirō.

68. Letter 318, Meiji 2/8/15 (9/20/1869), to Nakamura Chūjiro and Shōjirō.

69. Yabuuchi Yoshihiko, *Nihon yūbin sōgyō shi: Hikyaku kara yūbin e* (Tokyo: Yūzankaku Shuppan, 1975), 82.

70. Letter 329, Meiji 2/10/day unknown (11–12/1869), to Shōjirō.

71. Letter 282, Meiji 1/8/11 (9/26/1868), to Shōjirō.

72. Letter 319, Meiji 2/8/19 (9/24/1869), Chūemon and Naotarō to Shōjirō.

73. Letter 288, Meiji 2/1/19 (2/19/1869), to Shōjirō.

74. Letter 292, Meiji 2/2/14 (3/26/1869), to Shōjirō.

75. Letter 319, Meiji 2/8/19 (9/24/1869), Chūemon and Naotarō to Shōjirō.

76. Letter 152, Genji 1/12/29 (1/26/1865), to Shōjirō.

77. Letter 328, Meiji 2/10/29 (12/2/1869), Naotarō to Shōjirō.

78. Letter 334, Meiji 2/12/7 (1/8/1870), to Shōjirō.

79. Letter 351, Meiji 5/9/11 (10/13/1872), Chūemon to Chūemon (Shōjirō).

80. Yokohama Zeikan, *Yokohama Zeikan hyakunijū-nenshi* (Yokohama: Yokohama Zeikan, 1981), 75.

81. John Black, *Young Japan*, 2:25.

82. Ibid.

83. The site still contains a stone carved with the name Gankirō, hidden away in a Japanese garden.

84. Yūzō Katō and Yokohama Shiritsu Daigaku, *Yokohama, Past and Present: 100th Anniversary of Yokohama's Incorporation, 130th Anniversary of the Port of Yokohama* (Yokohama: Yokohama City University, 1990), 76.

85. Dallas Finn, *Meiji Revisited: The Sites of Victorian Japan* (New York: Weatherhill, 1995), 17.

86. Nishikawa Takeomi, *Yokohama kaikō to kōtsū no kindaika* (Tokyo: Nihon Keizai Hyōronsha, 2004), 55–56.

87. Ibid., 56–57.

88. Ibid., 57–58.

89. Ibid., 58–59.

90. John Black, *Young Japan*, 2:46–47.

91. Quoted in Harold S. Williams, *Foreigners in Mikadoland* (Rutland, Vt.: Tuttle, 1972), 102.

92. Nishikawa, *Yokohama kaikō*, 63–64.

93. Ibid., 67.

94. Ibid., 66.

95. Williams, *Foreigners in Mikadoland*, 127–28.

96. Ibid., 271.

97. Nishikawa, *Yokohama kaikō*, 68–71.

98. Ibid.

99. Ibid., 69–70.

100. Ibid., 73.

101. Ibid., 73–74. John Black, *Young Japan*, 2:281–82.

102. Nishikawa, *Yokohama kaikō*, 74.

103. Letter 357, Meiji 6/6/7 (6/7/1873), Chūemon to Chūemon (Shōjirō).

104. Nishikawa, *Yokohama kaikō*, 76.

105. John Black, *Young Japan*, 2:87–88.

106. Quoted in Williams, *Foreigners in Mikadoland*, 138.

107. Haruhiko Asakura, "The Origins of Newspapers and Magazines in the Bakumatsu and Meiji Periods," in *Japanese Studies*, ed. Yu-Ying Brown, 179–87 (London: British Library, 1990).

108. Letter 264, Meiji 1/5/8 (6/27/1868), to Shōjirō and Naotarō.

109. Letter 344, Meiji 5/2/4 (3/12/1872), Chūemon to Chūemon (Shōjirō).

110. Makishima Takashi, "Hikyaku ton'ya kyōya, shimaya no kinyū kinō: Mise gokantei to tegata no bunseki," *Tsūshin sōgō hakubutsukan kenkyū kiyo*, no. 4 (2012): 37–65.

111. Quoted in D. Eleanor Westney, *Imitation and Innovation: The Transfer of Western Organizational Patterns to Meiji Japan* (Cambridge, Mass.: Harvard University Press, 1987), 113–14.

112. Yabuuchi, *Nihon yūbin sōgyō shi*, 83–85. Ishii Kanji, *Jōhō tsūshin no shakaishi: Kindai Nihon no jōhōka to shijōka* (Tokyo: Yūhikaku, 1994), 8–40. See also

D. Eleanor Westney, "The Postal System," in Westney, *Imitation and Innovation*, 100–145.

113. Ishii Kanji, *Jōhō tsūshin no shakaishi*, 76–81.

114. Yamanashi Prefecture, "Yamanashi-ken no rekishi (Meiji 12 [1879]–22 [1889])," http://www.pref.yamanashi.jp/smartphone/info/98025047958.html.

115. June 4, 1860, in Francis Hall, *Japan Through American Eyes: The Journal of Francis Hall, Kanagawa and Yokohama, 1859–1866* (Princeton, N.J.: Princeton University Press, 1992), 179–80.

116. John Black, *Young Japan*, 1:400–401.

117. Kikue Yamakawa, *Women of the Mito Domain: Recollections of Samurai Family Life* (Tokyo: University of Tokyo Press, 1992), 46–48.

118. John Black, *Young Japan*, 2:62–63. See Sepp Linhart, "The Western Discovery of Nudity in Japan and Its Disappearance," in *Actes du troisième colloque d'études japonaises de l'université Marc Bloch: La rencontre du Japon et de l'Europe*, ed. Sakaé Murakami-Giroux, 157–72 (Aurillac: Publications orientalistes de France, 2007).

119. Utsumi Takashi, *Yokohama ekibyōshi: Manji Byōin no hyakujūnen* (Yokohama: Yokohama-shi Eiseikyoku, 1988), 4.

120. Kusama Shunrō, *Yokohama yōshoku bunka kotohajime* (Tokyo: Yūzankaku Shuppan, 1999), 41–42.

121. Ernest Mason Satow, *A Diplomat in Japan: The Inner History of the Critical Years in the Evolution of Japan When the Ports Were Opened and the Monarchy Restored* (Philadelphia: Lippincott, 1921), 157.

122. Kusama, *Yokohama yōshoku*, 44.

123. Ibid., 68.

124. Steele, *Alternative Narratives*, 125.

125. Etsu Inagaki Sugimoto, *A Daughter of the Samurai* (New York: Doubleday, Page, 1927), 25–27.

126. Letter 164, Keiō 1/5/29 (6/22/1865), to Shōjirō; letter 186, Keiō 1/11/7 (12/24/1865), Naotarō to Shōjirō; letter 187, Keiō 1/11/9 (12/26/1865), Naotarō to Shōjirō; letter 215-1, Keiō 3/2/13 (3/18/1867), Chūemon and Naotarō to Shōjirō.

127. Cited in Nishikawa and Itō, *Kaikoku Nihon*, 58.

128. For clothing, see Kazami Akira, *Meiji shin seifu no mofuku kaikaku* (Tōkyō: Yūzankaku, 2008), 20–31.

129. William Johnston casts some doubt on the theory that cholera was introduced to Japan on foreign ships; see his "The Shifting Epistemological Foundations of Cholera Control in Japan (1822–1900)," *Extrême-Orient, Extrême-Occident* 1, no. 37 (2014): 171–96.

130. Quoted in Susan L. Burns, "Constructing the National Body: Public Health and the Nation in Nineteenth-Century Japan," in *Nation Work: Asian Elites and National Identities*, ed. Timothy Brook and Andre Schmid (Ann Arbor: University of Michigan Press, 2000), 35.

131. John Black, *Young Japan*, 1:114–15.

132. Ibid., 295.

133. Ibid., 368–70.

134. Ibid., 2:76–77.

135. Ibid., 1:295.

136. Utsumi, *Yokohama ekibyōshi*, 12.

137. Letter 87, Bunkyū 2/8/2 (9/5/1862), to Shōjirō.

138. Letter 130, Genji 1/2/12 (3/19/1864), to Shōjirō.

139. Letter 150, Genji 1/12/9 (1/6/1865), to Shōjirō.

140. See Brett L. Walker, *The Conquest of Ainu Lands: Ecology and Culture in Japanese Expansion, 1590–1800* (Berkeley: University of California Press, 2001), 200.

141. Letter 140, Genji 1/9/23 (10/23/1864), to Shōjirō.

142. See Ann Jannetta, *The Vaccinators: Smallpox, Medical Knowledge, and the "Opening" of Japan* (Stanford, Calif.: Stanford University Press, 2007).

143. Letter 294, Meiji 2/2/26 (4/7/1869), to Shōjirō.

144. Translated and quoted in Steele, *Alternative Narratives*, 41.

145. Letter 341-1, Meiji 4/7/1 (8/16/1871), Chūemon to Chūemon (Shōjirō).

146. Osamu Saito and Masahiro Sato, "Japan's Civil Registration Systems Before and After the Meiji Restoration," in *Registration and Recognition: Documenting the Person in World History*, ed. Keith Breckenridge and Simon Szreter, 113–35 (Oxford: Oxford University Press, 2012).

147. Letter 344, Meiji 5/2/4 (3/12/1872), Chūemon to Chūemon (Shōjirō).

148. For a summary description of Tokugawa village administration, see Harumi Befu, "Village Autonomy and Articulation with the State," in *Studies in the Institutional History of Early Modern Japan*, ed. John Whitney Hall and Marius B. Jansen, 301–14 (Princeton, N.J.: Princeton University Press, 1968).

149. Letter 320, Meiji 2/8/19 (9/24/1869), to unknown recipient.

150. Letter 321, Meiji 2/8/23 (9/28/1869), to Shōjirō.

151. Kanagawa, *The History of Kanagawa*, 188–91.

152. Letter 358, Meiji 6/6/15 (6/15/1873), Chūemon to Chūemon (Shōjirō).

153. Letter 319, Meiji 2/8/19 (9/24/1869), Chūemon and Naotarō to Shōjirō.

154. Letter 353, Meiji 5/11/6 (12/6/1872), Chūemon to Chūemon (Shōjirō).

155. Yamanashi-ken, *Yamanashi kenshi: Tsūshi hen* (Kōfu: Yamanashi Nichinichi Shinbunsha, 2004), 5:18–23.

156. Letter 350, Meiji 5/9/1 (10/3/1872), Chūemon to Chūemon (Shōjirō).

157. Letter 349, Meiji 5/8/27 (9/29/1872), Chūemon to Chūemon (Shōjirō).

158. See, for example, Makihara Norio, *Kyakubun to kokumin no aida: Kindai minshū no seiji ishiki* (Tokyo: Yoshikawa Kōbunkan, 1998).

159. Letter 347, Meiji 5/6/7 (7/12/1872), Chūemon to Chūemon (Shōjirō).

160. Letter 298, Meiji 2/5/1 (6/10/1869), Rinzō to Shōjirō.

161. Letter 301, Meiji 2/5/14 (6/23/1869), to Shōjirō.

162. Letter 302, Meiji 2/5/18 (6/27/1869), Naotarō to Shōjirō.

163. Letter 303-2, Meiji 2/6/9 (7/17/1869), to Shōjirō.

164. Letter 305, Meiji 2/6/22 (7/30/1869), Naotarō to Shōjirō.

165. Letter 338, Meiji 3/9/6 (9/30/1870), Chūemon to Shōjirō.

166. Herbert Smith to Shanghai office, September 26, 1870, Jardine Matheson Archive, MS JM B10-9, reel 444, Cambridge University Library.

167. Ishii Kanji, *Jōhō tsūshin no shakaishi*, 80.

168. Letter 339-1: Meiji 4/3/24 (5/13/1871), Naotarō to Chūemon (Shōjirō); letter 340, Meiji 4/6/3 (7/20/1871), Chūemon to Chūemon (Shōjirō).

169. Letter 341-2, Meiji 4/7/1 (8/16/1871), Chūemon to Chūemon (Shōjirō).

170. Letter 339-1: Meiji 4/3/24 (5/13/1871), Naotarō to Chūemon (Shōjirō).

171. Letter 347, Meiji 5/6/7 (7/12/1872), Chūemon to Chūemon (Shōjirō).

172. Letter 350, Meiji 5/9/1 (10/3/1872), Chūemon to Chūemon (Shōjirō).

173. Letter 346, Meiji 5/5/2 (6/7/1872), Chūemon to Chūemon (Shōjirō).

174. Letter 349, Meiji 5/8/27 (9/29/1872), Chūemon to Chūemon (Shōjirō).

175. Letter 342, Meiji 4/8/20 (10/4/1871), Naotarō to Chūemon (Shōjirō).

176. Letter 352, Meiji 5/11/5 (12/5/1872), Naotarō to Chūemon (Shōjirō).

177. For biographical portraits of all three merchants, see Yokohama Kaikō Shiryōkan, ed., *Yokohama shōnin to sono jidai* (Yokohama: Yūrindō, 1995).

178. Letter 351, Meiji 5/9/11 (10/13/1872), Chūemon to Chūemon (Shōjirō).

179. Letter 354, Meiji 5/11/25 (12/25/1872), Chūemon to Chūemon (Shōjirō).

180. Letter 353, Meiji 5/11/6 (12/6/1872), Chūemon to Chūemon (Shōjirō).

181. Letter 357, Meiji 6/6/7 (6/7/1873), Chūemon to Chūemon (Shōjirō).

182. Isawachō Chōshi Hensan Iinkai, *Isawa chōshi*, vol. 4 (Isawachō: Isawachō Kankōkai, 1987), 941.

183. Ibid.

184. The inscription on the stone is transcribed in full in Kanagawa-ken Toshokan Kyōkai, Kyōdo Shiryō Hensan Iinkai, *Mikan Yokohama kaikō shiryō* (Yokohama: Kanagawa-ken Toshokan Kyōkai, 1960), 148.

Conclusion: The Power of a Place

1. The classic text on this question is *Nihon shihonshugi hattatsu-shi kōza* (Tokyo: Iwanami Shoten, 1932).

2. See, for example, Daikichi Irokawa, *The Culture of the Meiji Period* (Princeton, N.J.: Princeton University Press, 1985). For a detailed analysis of this "people's history" movement, see Carol Gluck, "The People in History: Recent Trends in Japanese Historiography," *Journal of Asian Studies* 38, no. 1 (November 1978): 25–50.

3. The classic statement is Edwin O. Reischauer, *Japan: The Story of a Nation* (New York: Knopf, 1970). See also Cyril Edwin Black, *The Modernization of Japan and Russia: A Comparative Study* (New York: Free Press, 1975). For a broader treatment of modernization issues, see Sheldon Garon, "Rethinking Modernization and Modernity in Japanese History: A Focus on State-Society Relations," *Journal of Asian Studies* 53, no. 2 (May 1994): 346–66. For more recent work, see Kären Wigen, *The Making of a Japanese Periphery, 1750–1920* (Berkeley: University of California Press, 1995); Edward E. Pratt, *Japan's Protoindustrial Elite: The Economic Foundations of the Gōnō* (Cambridge, Mass.: Harvard University Asia Center, 1999); D. L. Howell, "Hard Times in the Kantō: Economic Change and Village Life in Late Tokugawa Japan," *Modern Asian Studies* 23, no. 2 (May 1989): 349–71.

4. Thomas C. Smith, *The Agrarian Origins of Modern Japan* (Stanford, Calif.: Stanford University Press, 1959); Furushima Toshio, *Edo jidai no shōhin ryūtsū to kōtsū: Shinshū Nakauma no kenkyū* (Tokyo: Ochanomizu Shobō, 1951). For Saitō and Hayami, see Ōshima Mario, ed., *Tochi kishōka to kinben kakumei no hikakushi: Keizaishijō no kinsei* (Kyoto: Mineruva Shobō, 2009). See also D. L. Howell, "Proto-Industrial Origins of Japanese Capitalism," *Journal of Asian Studies* 51, no. 2 (May 1992): 269–86.

5. Wigen, *Making of a Japanese Periphery*, 267. Pratt, *Japan's Protoindustrial Elite*, 183. See also Howell, "Hard Times."

6. Much of the Japanese scholarship on the Meiji era and beyond focuses on the emergence of an "emperor system," in which a small group of oligarchs harnessed the legal and symbolic power of the emperor in pursuit of a capitalist and imperialist agenda. See, for example, Ōe Shinobu, *Meiji kokka no seiritsu: Tennōsei seiritsushi kenkyū* (Kyoto: Mineruva Shobō, 1998). A representative work in English translation is Irokawa, *Culture of the Meiji Period*. In English-language scholarship, a similar focus on the use of the emperor in the assertion of elite power can be found in, for example, Takashi Fujitani, *Splendid Monarchy: Power and Pageantry in Modern Japan* (Berkeley: University

of California Press, 1996). On Meiji-era industrial growth and institutional modernization, many works similarly focus on top-down initiatives. See, for example, D. Eleanor Westney, *Imitation and Innovation: The Transfer of Western Organizational Patterns to Meiji Japan* (Cambridge, Mass.: Harvard University Press, 1987); Richard J. Samuels, *"Rich Nation, Strong Army": National Security and the Technological Transformation of Japan* (Ithaca, N.Y.: Cornell University Press, 1994).

7. Anne Walthall, *The Weak Body of a Useless Woman: Matsuo Taseko and the Meiji Restoration* (Chicago: University of Chicago Press, 1998); Laura Nenzi, *The Chaos and Cosmos of Kurosawa Tokiko: One Woman's Transit from Tokugawa to Meiji Japan* (Honolulu: University of Hawai`i Press, 2015); Laura Nenzi, "Portents and Politics: Two Women Activists on the Verge of the Meiji Restoration," *Journal of Japanese Studies* 38, no. 1 (2012): 1–23; Romulus Hillsborough, *Samurai Revolution: The Dawn of Modern Japan Seen Through the Eyes of the Shogun's Last Samurai* (Tokyo: Tuttle, 2014); Neil L. Waters, *Japan's Local Pragmatists: The Transition from Bakumatsu to Meiji in the Kawasaki Region* (Cambridge, Mass.: Harvard University Asia Center, 1983); M. William Steele, *Alternative Narratives in Modern Japanese History* (London: RoutledgeCurzon, 2003).

8. The major works on the restoration in English all focus (albeit in different ways) on the political, diplomatic, and ideological maneuverings that led to the collapse of the Tokugawa regime. See W. G. Beasley, *The Meiji Restoration* (Stanford, Calif.: Stanford University Press, 1972); Conrad D. Totman, *The Collapse of the Tokugawa Bakufu, 1862–1868* (Honolulu: University Press of Hawaii, 1980); Paul Akamatsu, *Meiji 1868: Revolution and Counter-Revolution in Japan*, trans. Miriam Kochan (New York: Harper and Row, 1972); Harry D. Harootunian, *Toward Restoration: The Growth of Political Consciousness in Tokugawa Japan* (Berkeley: University of California Press, 1970).

9. See, for example, J. E. Hoare, *Japan's Treaty Ports and Foreign Settlements: The Uninvited Guests, 1858–1899* (Folkestone, Kent, U.K.: Japan Library, 1994); Peter Ennals, *Opening a Window to the West: The Foreign Concession at Kōbe, Japan, 1868–1899* (Toronto: University of Toronto Press, 2014); M. Paske-Smith, *Western Barbarians in Japan and Formosa in Tokugawa Days, 1603–1868* (Kobe: Thompson, 1930); Brian Burke-Gaffney, *Nagasaki: The British Experience, 1854–1945* (Folkestone, Kent, U.K.: Global Oriental, 2009); Hugh Cortazzi, *Victorians in Japan: In and around the Treaty Ports* (London: Athlone Press, 1987); Harold S. Williams, *Foreigners in Mikadoland* (Rutland, Vt.: Tuttle, 1972).

10. Michael R. Auslin, *Negotiating with Imperialism: The Unequal Treaties and the Culture of Japanese Diplomacy* (Cambridge, Mass.: Harvard University Press, 2004).

11. For a review essay on the Chinese historiography, see Bryna Goodman and David S. G. Goodman, introduction to *Twentieth-Century Colonialism and China: Localities, the Everyday and the World* (Milton Park, Abingdon, U.K.: Routledge, 2012). Rhoads Murphey is one of the few scholars to study the impact of the Chinese ports beyond politics and ideology, though his analysis is limited mostly to the economic impact, which in any case he finds was minimal (*The Treaty Ports and China's Modernization: What Went Wrong?* Michigan Papers in Chinese Studies, no. 7 [Ann Arbor: University of Michigan, Center for Chinese Studies, 1970]).

12. My approach here has something in common with that of Catherine Phipps, although her fascinating work on Moji focuses on the emergence of Japanese imperialism in a later period, and Moji itself was not a formal treaty port (*Empires on the Waterfront: Japan's Ports and Power, 1858–1899*, Harvard East Asian Monographs 373 [Cambridge, Mass.: Harvard University Asia Center, 2015]).

13. John Reddie Black, *Young Japan: Yokohama and Yedo*, 2 vols. (London: Trübner, 1880), 1:163–64. For a more historically informed examination of time consciousness in Japan, see Nishimoto Ikuko, *Jikan ishiki no kindai: "Toki wa kane nari" no shakaishi* (Tokyo: Hōsei Daigaku Shuppankyoku, 2006).

14. Simon Partner, *The Mayor of Aihara: A Japanese Villager and His Community, 1865–1925* (Berkeley: University of California Press, 2009), chapter 3.

15. Rutherford Alcock, *The Capital of the Tycoon: A Narrative of a Three Years' Residence in Japan*, 2 vols. (New York: Bradley, 1863), 2:240.

BIBLIOGRAPHY

Abe Yasushi. "Bakumatsu no yūkaku: Kaikōjo no seiritsu ni kanren shi." *Hako-date: Chiikishi kenkyū* 25, no. 3 (1997): 12–32.

Akamatsu, Paul. *Meiji 1868: Revolution and Counter-Revolution in Japan*. Trans. Miriam Kochan. Great Revolutions. New York: Harper and Row, 1972.

Alcock, Rutherford. *The Capital of the Tycoon: A Narrative of a Three Years' Residence in Japan*. 2 vols. New York: Bradley, 1863.

Aogi Michio. "Tōkaidō Kanagawa-juku to Yokohama kaikō: Chiikiteki shiten de miru bakumatsu Nichibei kōshōshi." *Jinbun kagaku nenpō*, no. 32 (2002): 1–42.

Asakura, Haruhiko. "The Origins of Newspapers and Magazines in the Bakumatsu and Meiji Periods." In *Japanese Studies*, ed. Yu-Ying Brown, 179–87. London: British Library, 1990.

Assendelft de Coningh, C. T. van. *A Pioneer in Yokohama: A Dutchman's Adventures in the New Treaty Port*. Edited and trans. Martha Chaiklin. Indianapolis: Hackett, 2012.

Atsumi, Toshihiro. "Silk, Regional Rivalry, and the Impact of the Port Openings in Nineteenth Century Japan." *Journal of the Japanese and International Economies* 24, no. 4 (December 2010): 519–39.

Auslin, Michael R. *Negotiating with Imperialism: The Unequal Treaties and the Culture of Japanese Diplomacy.* Cambridge, Mass.: Harvard University Press, 2004.

Ballagh, Margaret Tate Kinnear. *Glimpses of Old Japan, 1861–1866.* Tokyo: Methodist Publishing House, 1908.

Barr, Pat. *The Coming of the Barbarians: The Opening of Japan to the West, 1853–1870.* New York: Dutton, 1967.

Beasley, W. G. "The Foreign Threat and the Opening of the Ports." In *The Cambridge History of Japan, Volume 5: The Nineteenth Century,* ed. Marius B. Jansen, 259–307. Cambridge: Cambridge University Press, 1988.

———. *The Meiji Restoration.* Stanford, Calif.: Stanford University Press, 1972.

———. *Select Documents on Japanese Foreign Policy, 1853–1868.* London: Oxford University Press, 1955.

Befu, Harumi. "Village Autonomy and Articulation with the State." In *Studies in the Institutional History of Early Modern Japan,* ed. John Whitney Hall and Marius B. Jansen, 301–14. Princeton, N.J.: Princeton University Press, 1968.

Bennett, Terry, Hugh Cortazzi, and James Hoare. *Japan and the "Illustrated London News": Complete Record of Reported Events, 1853–1899.* Folkestone, Kent, U.K.: Global Oriental, 2006.

Bergère, Marie-Claire. *Shanghai: China's Gateway to Modernity.* Trans. Janet Lloyd. Stanford, Calif.: Stanford University Press, 2010.

Billingsley, Philip. "Bakunin in Yokohama: The Dawning of the Pacific Era." *International History Review* 20, no. 3 (1998): 532–70.

Black, Cyril Edwin. *The Modernization of Japan and Russia: A Comparative Study.* New York: Free Press, 1975.

Black, John Reddie. *Young Japan: Yokohama and Yedo.* 2 vols. London: Trübner, 1880.

Blum, Paul C., trans. "Father Mounicou's Bakumatsu Diary." *Transactions of the Asiatic Society of Japan,* 3rd ser., 13 (1976): 5–103.

Brooke, John M., and George M. Brooke. *John M. Brooke's Pacific Cruise and Japanese Adventure, 1858–1860.* Honolulu: University of Hawai'i Press, 1986.

Burke-Gaffney, Brian. *Nagasaki: The British Experience, 1854–1945.* Folkestone, Kent, U.K.: Global Oriental, 2009.

Burns, Susan L. "Constructing the National Body: Public Health and the Nation in Nineteenth-Century Japan." In *Nation Work: Asian Elites and National Identities,* ed. Timothy Brook and Andre Schmid, 17–50. Ann Arbor: University of Michigan Press, 2000.

Bytheway, Simon James, and Martha Chaiklin. "Reconsidering the Yokohama 'Gold Rush' of 1859." *Journal of World History* 27, no. 2 (2016): 281–301.

Cassel, Pär Kristoffer. *Grounds of Judgment: Extraterritoriality and Imperial Power in Nineteenth-Century China and Japan*. Oxford: Oxford University Press, 2012.

The China Directory for 1862. Hong Kong: Shortrede, 1862.

Chūka Kaikan and Yokohama Kaikō Shiryōkan. *Yokohama kakyō no kioku: Yokohama kakyō kōjutsu rekishi kirokushū*. Yokohama: Chūka Kaikan, 2010.

Clark, John. "Charles Wirgman." In *Britain and Japan, 1859–1991: Themes and Personalities*, ed. Hugh Cortazzi and Gordon Daniels, 54–63. London: Routledge, 1991.

Cortazzi, Hugh. *Collected Writings of Sir Hugh Cortazzi*. Tokyo: Edition Synapse; Richmond, Surrey, U.K.: Japan Library, 2000.

——. *Dr. Willis in Japan, 1862–1877: British Medical Pioneer*. London: Athlone Press, 1985.

——. *Victorians in Japan: In and around the Treaty Ports*. London: Athlone Press, 1987.

Cortazzi, Hugh, and Gordon Daniels, eds. *Britain and Japan, 1859–1991: Themes and Personalities*. London: Routledge, 1991.

Craig, Albert M. *Chōshū in the Meiji Restoration*. Cambridge, Mass.: Harvard University Press, 1967.

Crawcour, E. S., and Kozo Yamamura. "The Tokugawa Monetary System: 1787–1868." *Economic Development and Cultural Change* 18, no. 4 (1970): 489–518.

Dattel, Eugene R. "Cotton and the Civil War." *Mississippi History Now*, July 2008. http://mshistorynow.mdah.state.ms.us/articles/291/cotton-and-the-civil -war.

de Bary, Wm. Theodore, et al., comps. *Sources of Japanese Tradition, Volume 1: From Earliest Times to 1600*. 2nd ed. New York: Columbia University Press, 2001.

Drixler, Fabian. "Alternative Japanese Nations in the Meiji Restoration: The Lost History of Azuma." Paper presented at the Heidelberg History Conference on "Global History and the Meiji Restoration," Heidelberg, July 3–5, 2015.

Duchesne de Bellecour, [Gustave]. "L'état politique et commercial de la Chine et du Japon: L'exposition chinoise et japonaise au Champ de Mars." *Revue des deux mondes*, August 1, 1867, 710–43.

Ennals, Peter. *Opening a Window to the West: The Foreign Concession at Kōbe, Japan, 1868–1899*. Toronto: University of Toronto Press, 2014.

Finn, Dallas. *Meiji Revisited: The Sites of Victorian Japan*. New York: Weatherhill, 1995.

Fortune, Robert. *Yedo and Peking. A Narrative of a Journey to the Capitals of Japan and China*. London: Murray, 1863.

Frost, Peter. *The Bakumatsu Currency Crisis*. Cambridge, Mass.: East Asian Research Center, Harvard University, 1970.

Fujitani, Takashi. *Splendid Monarchy: Power and Pageantry in Modern Japan*. Berkeley: University of California Press, 1996.

Fukuzawa Tetsuzō. "Kinsei kōki no kinai ni okeru gōnō kinyū no tenkai to chiiki." In *Kinai no gōnō keiei to chiiki shakai*, ed. Takashi Watanabe, 227–91. Kyoto: Shibunkaku Shuppan, 2008.

Furushima Toshio. *Edo jidai no shōhin ryūtsū to kōtsū: Shinshū Nakauma no kenkyū*. Tokyo: Ochanomizu Shobō, 1951.

Garon, Sheldon. "Rethinking Modernization and Modernity in Japanese History: A Focus on State-Society Relations." *Journal of Asian Studies* 53, no. 2 (May 1994): 346–66.

Gartlan, Luke. "Samuel Cocking and the Rise of Japanese Photography." *History of Photography* 33, no. 2 (2009): 145–64.

Gluck, Carol. "The People in History: Recent Trends in Japanese Historiography." *Journal of Asian Studies* 38, no. 1 (November 1978): 25–50.

Gonda Masumi. "Bakumatsuki kara Meiji shoki no Yokohama kaikōjo ni okeru Eigo no gakushū." *Kōwan keizai kenkyū: Nihon kōwan keizai nenpō* 50 (2013): 139–48.

Goodman, Bryna, and David S. G. Goodman. Introduction to *Twentieth-Century Colonialism and China: Localities, the Everyday and the World*. Milton Park, Abingdon, U.K.: Routledge, 2012.

Hall, Francis. *Japan Through American Eyes: The Journal of Francis Hall, Kanagawa and Yokohama, 1859–1866*. Princeton, N.J.: Princeton University Press, 1992.

Hao, Yen-p'ing. *The Comprador in Nineteenth Century China: Bridge between East and West*. Cambridge, Mass.: Harvard University Press, 1970.

Harootunian, Harry D. *Toward Restoration: The Growth of Political Consciousness in Tokugawa Japan*. Berkeley: University of California Press, 1970.

Hasebe, Hiroshi. "Silkworm Egg Trading and the Village in Early Modern Japan." In *Village Communities, States, and Traders: Essays in Honour of Chatthip Nartsupha*, ed. Akira Nozaki and Chris Baker, 282–91. Bangkok: Thai-Japanese Seminar and Sangsan Publishing, 2003.

Heco, Joseph, and James Murdoch. *The Narrative of a Japanese: What He Has Seen and the People He Has Met in the Course of the Last Forty Years*. 2 vols. Yokohama: Yokohama Printing and Publishing, 1892.

Helm, Leslie. *Yokohama Yankee: My Family's Five Generations as Outsiders in Japan*. Seattle: Chin Music Press, 2013.

Hepburn, J. C. *The Letters of Dr. J. C. Hepburn*. Ed. Michio Takaya. Tokyo: Toshin Shobō, 1955.

Hillsborough, Romulus. *Samurai Revolution: The Dawn of Modern Japan Seen Through the Eyes of the Shogun's Last Samurai*. Tokyo: Tuttle, 2014.

Hoare, J. E. *Japan's Treaty Ports and Foreign Settlements: The Uninvited Guests, 1858–1899*. Folkestone, Kent, U.K.: Japan Library, 1994.

Hockley, Alan. "Expectation and Authenticity in Meiji Tourist Photography." In *Challenging Past and Present: The Metamorphosis of Nineteenth-Century Japanese Art*, ed. Ellen P. Conant, 114–32. Honolulu: University of Hawai`i Press, 2006.

Honjo, Yuki Allyson. *Japan's Early Experience of Contract Management in the Treaty Ports*. London: Japan Library, 2003.

Howell, David L. "Hard Times in the Kantō: Economic Change and Village Life in Late Tokugawa Japan." *Modern Asian Studies* 23, no. 2 (May 1989): 349–71.

——. "Proto-Industrial Origins of Japanese Capitalism." *Journal of Asian Studies* 51, no. 2 (May 1992): 269–86.

Huffman, James L. *Politics of the Meiji Press: The Life of Fukuchi Gen`ichirō*. Honolulu: University Press of Hawaii, 1980.

Ion, A. Hamish. *American Missionaries, Christian Oyatoi, and Japan, 1859–73*. Vancouver: University of British Columbia Press, 2009.

Irokawa, Daikichi. *The Culture of the Meiji Period*. Princeton, N.J.: Princeton University Press, 1985.

Isawachō Chōshi Hensan Iinkai. *Isawa chōshi*. Vol. 4. Isawachō: Isawachō Kankōkai, 1987.

Ishii Kanji. *Jōhō tsūshin no shakaishi: Kindai Nihon no jōhōka to shijōka*. Tokyo: Yūhikaku, 1994.

Ishii Takashi. *Kōto Yokohama no tanjō*. Yokohama: Yūrindō, 1976.

——. "Shoki Yokohama bōeki shōnin no sonzai keitai: Kōshūya Chūemon o chūshin ni shite." *Yokohama Shiritsu Daigaku kiyō*, ser. A, 18, no. 85 (1958): 1–33.

——, ed. *Yokohama urikomishō Kōshūya monjo*. Yokohama: Yūrindō, 1984.

Iwata, Masakazu. *Ōkubo Toshimichi, the Bismarck of Japan*. Berkeley: University of California Press, 1964.

Jannetta, Ann. *The Vaccinators: Smallpox, Medical Knowledge, and the "Opening" of Japan*. Stanford, Calif.: Stanford University Press, 2007.

Jansen, Marius B. "The Meiji Restoration." In *The Cambridge History of Japan, Volume 5: The Nineteenth Century*, ed. Marius B. Jansen, 308–66. Cambridge: Cambridge University Press, 1991.

"Japanese Manufactures at the Great Exhibition." *The Friend: A Religious and Literary Journal* 36, no. 7 (October 18, 1862): 54.

Jardine Matheson Archive. Cambridge University Library.

Johnson, Hiroko. "Yokohama-e: Prints of a New Port City." In *Dreams and Diversions: Essays on Japanese Woodblock Prints from the San Diego Museum of Art*, ed.

Andreas Marks and Sonya Rhie Quintanilla, 145–73. San Diego: San Diego Museum of Art, 2010.

Johnston, William. "The Shifting Epistemological Foundations of Cholera Control in Japan (1822–1900)." *Extrême-Orient, Extrême-Occident* 1, no. 37 (2014): 171–96.

Jones, H. J. *Live Machines: Hired Foreigners and Meiji Japan*. Vancouver: University of British Columbia Press, 1980.

Kaempfer, Engelbert. *Kaempfer's Japan: Tokugawa Culture Observed*. Edited and trans. Beatrice M. Bodart-Bailey. Honolulu: University of Hawai`i Press, 1999.

Kanagawa-ken Kenshi Henshūshitsu. *Kanagawa kenshi: Tsūshi hen*. Vol. 3. Yokohama: Kanagawa-ken, 1980.

Kanagawa Kenritsu Rekishi Hakubutsukan. *Yokohama ukiyoe to kindai Nihon: Ikoku "Yokohama" o tabisuru*. Yokohama: Kanagawa Kenritsu Rekishi Hakubutsukan, 1999.

Kanagawa-ken Toshokan Kyōkai, Kyōdo Shiryō Hensan Iinkai. *Mikan Yokohama kaikō shiryō*. Yokohama: Kanagawa-ken Toshokan Kyōkai, 1960.

Kanagawa Prefectural Government. *The History of Kanagawa*. Yokohama: Kanagawa Prefectural Government, 1985.

Kato Takashi. "Governing Edo." In *Edo and Paris: Urban Life and the State in the Early Modern Era*, ed. James L. McClain, John M. Merriman, and Ugawa Kaoru, 41–68. Ithaca, N.Y.: Cornell University Press, 1994.

Katō, Yūzō, and Yokohama Shiritsu Daigaku. *Yokohama, Past and Present: 100th Anniversary of Yokohama's Incorporation, 130th Anniversary of the Port of Yokohama*. Yokohama: Yokohama City University, 1990.

Kazami Akira. *Meiji shin seifu no mofuku kaikaku*. Tokyo: Yūzankaku Shuppan, 2008.

Kikuchi, Yuko, and Toshio Watanabe. "The British Discovery of Japanese Art." In *The History of Anglo-Japanese Relations 1600–2000, Volume 5: Social and Cultural Perspectives*, ed. Gordon Daniels and Chushichi Tsuzuki, 146–70. New York: Palgrave Macmillan, 2002.

Kikuen Rōjin. *Yokohama kidan: Minato no hana*. Kinkōdō Zō, ca. 1864.

Kusama Shunrō. *Yokohama yōshoku bunka kotohajime*. Tokyo: Yūzankaku Shuppan, 1999.

Lacoste, Anne. *Felice Beato: A Photographer on the Eastern Road*. Los Angeles: J. Paul Getty Museum, 2010.

Lambourne, Lionel. *Japonisme: Cultural Crossings between Japan and the West*. London: Phaidon, 2005.

Leupp, Gary P. *Interracial Intimacy in Japan: Western Men and Japanese Women, 1543–1900*. London: Continuum, 2003.

———. *Servants, Shophands, and Laborers in the Cities of Tokugawa Japan*. Princeton, N.J.: Princeton University Press, 1992.

Linhart, Sepp. "The Western Discovery of Nudity in Japan and Its Disappearance." In *Actes du troisième colloque d'études japonaises de l'université Marc Bloch: La rencontre du Japon et de l'Europe*, ed. Sakaé Murakami-Giroux, 157–72. Aurillac: Publications orientalistes de France, 2007.

Makihara Norio. *Kyakubun to kokumin no aida: Kindai minshū no seiji ishiki*. Tokyo: Yoshikawa Kōbunkan, 1998.

Makimura, Yasuhiro. "The Silk Road at Yokohama: A History of the Economic Relationships between Yokohama, the Kantō Region, and the World Through the Japanese Silk Industry in the Nineteenth Century." Ph.D. diss., Columbia University, 2005.

Makishima Takashi. "Hikyaku ton'ya Kyōya, Shimaya no kinyū kinō: Mise gokantei to tegata no bunseki." *Tsūshin Sōgō Hakubutsukan kenkyū kiyō*, no. 4 (2013): 37–65.

McMaster, John. "The Japanese Gold Rush of 1859." *Journal of Asian Studies* 19, no. 3 (1960): 273–87.

———. *Jardines in Japan, 1859–1867*. Groningen, Neth.: V.R.B., 1966.

Metzler, Mark. "Japan and the Global Conjuncture in the Summer of 1866." Paper presented at the Heidelberg History Conference on "Global History and the Meiji Restoration," Heidelberg, July 3–5, 2015.

Mihara, Aya. "Professional Entertainers Abroad and Theatrical Portraits in Hand." *Old Photography Study*, no. 3 (2009): 45–54.

Mitani, Hiroshi. "A Protonation-State and Its 'Unforgettable Other': The Prerequisites for Meiji International Relations." In *New Directions in the Study of Meiji Japan*, ed. Helen Hardacre and Adam L. Kern, 293–310. Leiden: Brill, 1997.

Mitsui Bunko. *Mitsui jigyōshi: Honpen*. Vol. 1. Tokyo: Mitsui Bunko, 1980.

Miyazawa, Shin'ichi. "Ernest Satow's Japan Diary, 1862–1863: An Annotated Transcript." *Saitama Joshi Tanki Daigaku kenkyū kiyō*, no. 10 (1999): 317–46.

Motoyama Yukihiko. *Proliferating Talent: Essays on Politics, Thought, and Education in the Meiji Era*. Ed. J. S. A. Elisonas and Richard Rubinger. Honolulu: University of Hawai`i Press, 1997.

Mottini, Roger. "The Swiss–Japanese Treaty of Friendship and Commerce of February 6, 1864." Speech given at the city hall of Zurich, February 6, 2004. http://www.mottini.eu/articles/2004_Swiss-Japanese-Treaty.pdf.

Munson, Todd. "Curiosities of the Five Nations: Nansōan Shōhaku's Yokohama Tales." *Japan Studies Review* 12 (2008): 23–36.

Murphey, Rhoads. *The Treaty Ports and China's Modernization: What Went Wrong?* Michigan Papers in Chinese Studies, no. 7. Ann Arbor: University of Michigan, Center for Chinese Studies, 1970.

Nakayama Tomihiro. "Kinsei kōki ni okeru kashitsuke shihon no sonzai keitai: Bingo Fuchū Nobuto-ke no jirei." *Shigaku kenkyū* 172 (1986): 1–20.

Nansōan Shōhaku. *Chinji gokakoku Yokohama hanashi.* Yokohama, ca. 1862.

Nenzi, Laura. *The Chaos and Cosmos of Kurosawa Tokiko: One Woman's Transit from Tokugawa to Meiji Japan.* Honolulu: University of Hawai`i Press, 2015.

———. "Portents and Politics: Two Women Activists on the Verge of the Meiji Restoration." *Journal of Japanese Studies* 38, no. 1 (2012): 1–23.

Nihon shihonshugi hattatsu-shi kōza. Tokyo: Iwanami Shoten, 1932.

Nishikawa Takeomi. *Yokohama kaikō to kōtsū no kindaika.* Tokyo: Nihon Keizai Hyōronsha, 2004.

Nishikawa Takeomi and Itō Izumi. *Kaikoku Nihon to Yokohama Chūkagai.* Tokyo: Taishūkan Shoten, 2002.

Nishimoto Ikuko. *Jikan ishiki no kindai: "Toki wa kane nari" no shakaishi.* Tokyo: Hōsei Daigaku Shuppankyoku, 2006.

Ōe Shinobu. *Meiji kokka no seiritsu: Tennōsei seiritsushi kenkyū.* Kyoto: Mineruva Shobō, 1998.

Okura, Takehiko, and Hiroshi Shinbo. "The Tokugawa Monetary Policy in the Eighteenth and Nineteenth Centuries." *Explorations in Economic History* 15, no. 1 (1978): 101–24.

Oliphant, Laurence. *Narrative of the Earl of Elgin's Mission to China and Japan in the Years 1857, '58, '59.* 2nd ed. 2 vols. Edinburgh: Blackwood, 1860.

Oliver, Samuel Pasfield. *On and Off Duty: Being Leaves from an Officer's Note-Book.* London: Allen, 1881.

Ono Takeo. *Edo bukka jiten.* Tokyo: Tenbōsha, 1991.

Ōshima Mario, ed. *Tochi kishōka to kinben kakumei no hikakushi: Keizaishijō no kinsei.* Kyoto: Mineruva Shobō, 2009.

Partner, Simon. *The Mayor of Aihara: A Japanese Villager and His Community, 1865–1925.* Berkeley: University of California Press, 2009.

———. *Toshié: A Story of Village Life in Twentieth-Century Japan.* Berkeley: University of California Press, 2004.

Paske-Smith, M. *Western Barbarians in Japan and Formosa in Tokugawa Days, 1603–1868.* Kobe: Thompson, 1930.

Phipps, Catherine L. *Empires on the Waterfront: Japan's Ports and Power, 1858–1899.* Harvard East Asian Monographs 373. Cambridge, Mass.: Harvard University Asia Center, 2015.

Pratt, Edward E. *Japan's Protoindustrial Elite: The Economic Foundations of the Gōnō.* Cambridge, Mass.: Harvard University Asia Center, 1999.

Reischauer, Edwin O. *Japan: The Story of a Nation.* New York: Knopf, 1970.

Reischauer, Haru Matsukata. *Samurai and Silk: A Japanese and American Heritage.* Cambridge, Mass.: Belknap Press, 1986.

Saito, Osamu, and Masahiro Sato. "Japan's Civil Registration Systems Before and After the Meiji Restoration." In *Registration and Recognition: Documenting the Person in World History,* ed. Keith Breckenridge and Simon Szreter, 113–35. Oxford: Oxford University Press, 2012.

Samuels, Richard J. *"Rich Nation, Strong Army": National Security and the Technological Transformation of Japan.* Ithaca, N.Y.: Cornell University Press, 1994.

Satow, Ernest Mason. *The Diaries and Letters of Sir Ernest Mason Satow (1843–1929), a Scholar-Diplomat in East Asia.* Ed. Ian C. Ruxton. Lewiston, N.Y.: Mellen Press, 1998.

——. *A Diplomat in Japan: The Inner History of the Critical Years in the Evolution of Japan When the Ports Were Opened and the Monarchy Restored.* Philadelphia: Lippincott, 1921.

Schodt, Frederik L. *Professor Risley and the Imperial Japanese Troupe: How an American Acrobat Introduced Circus to Japan—and Japan to the West.* Berkeley, Calif.: Stone Bridge Press, 2012.

Shibusawa Eiichi. *The Autobiography of Shibusawa Eiichi: From Peasant to Entrepreneur.* Trans. Teruko Craig Tokyo: University of Tokyo Press, 1994.

Shimizu, Akira. "Eating Edo, Sensing Japan: Food Branding and Market Culture in Late Tokugawa Japan, 1780–1868." Ph.D. diss., University of Illinois at Urbana-Champaign, 2011.

Smith, Thomas C. *The Agrarian Origins of Modern Japan.* Stanford, Calif.: Stanford University Press, 1959.

Steele, M. William. *Alternative Narratives in Modern Japanese History.* London: RoutledgeCurzon, 2003.

——. "The Emperor's New Food." In *Alternative Narratives in Modern Japanese History,* 110–32. London: RoutledgeCurzon, 2003.

Takamura Naosuke and Yokohama-shi Furusato Rekishi Zaidan. *Yokohama rekishi to bunka: Kaikō 150-shūnen kinen.* Yokohama: Yūrindō, 2009.

Tanaka Takeyuki. *Yokohama Chūkagai: Sekai saikyō no Chainataun.* Tokyo: Chūō Kōron Shinsha, 2009.

Totman, Conrad D. *The Collapse of the Tokugawa Bakufu, 1862–1868.* Honolulu: University Press of Hawaii, 1980.

Usami Misako. *Shukuba to meshimorionna.* Tokyo: Dōseisha, 2000.

Utagawa Sadahide. *Yokohama kaikō kenbunshi biyō*. Ed. Kida Jun'ichirō. Tokyo: Meichō Kankōkai, 1967.

Utsumi Takashi. *Yokohama ekibyōshi: Manji Byōin no hyakujūnen*. Yokohama: Yokohama-shi Eiseikyoku, 1988.

Wakita, Mio. "Sites of 'Disconnectedness': The Port City of Yokohama, Souvenir Photography, and Its Audience." *Transcultural Studies* 2 (February 2013): 77–129.

Walker, Brett L. *The Conquest of Ainu Lands: Ecology and Culture in Japanese Expansion, 1590–1800*. Berkeley: University of California Press, 2001.

Walthall, Anne. *The Weak Body of a Useless Woman: Matsuo Taseko and the Meiji Restoration*. Chicago: University of Chicago Press, 1998.

Waters, Neil L. *Japan's Local Pragmatists: The Transition from Bakumatsu to Meiji in the Kawasaki Region*. Cambridge, Mass.: Harvard University Asia Center, 1983.

Westney, D. Eleanor. *Imitation and Innovation: The Transfer of Western Organizational Patterns to Meiji Japan*. Cambridge, Mass.: Harvard University Press, 1987.

Wigen, Kären. *The Making of a Japanese Periphery, 1750–1920*. Berkeley: University of California Press, 1995.

———. *A Malleable Map: Geographies of Restoration in Central Japan, 1600–1912*. Berkeley: University of California Press, 2010.

Williams, Harold S. *Foreigners in Mikadoland*. Rutland, Vt.: Tuttle, 1972.

———. *Tales of the Foreign Settlements in Japan*. Tokyo: Tuttle, 1959.

Wilson, George M. *Patriots and Redeemers in Japan: Motives in the Meiji Restoration*. Chicago: University of Chicago Press, 1992.

Yabuuchi Yoshihiko. *Nihon yūbin sōgyō shi: Hikyaku kara yūbin e*. Tokyo: Yūzankaku Shuppan, 1975.

Yamakawa, Kikue. *Women of the Mito Domain: Recollections of Samurai Family Life*. Tokyo: University of Tokyo Press, 1992.

Yamanashi Jewelry Association. "History." http://yja.or.jp/history/.

Yamanashi-ken. *Yamanashi kenshi: Tsūshi hen*. Vols. 4, 5. Kōfu: Yamanashi Nichinichi Shinbunsha, 2004.

Yamanashi Prefecture. "Yamanashi-ken no rekishi (Meiji 12 [1879]–22 [1889])." http://www.pref.yamanashi.jp/smartphone/info/98025047958.html.

Yokohama Kaikō Shiryōkan. *Yokohama mono no hajime kō*. Yokohama: Yokohama Kaikō Shiryō Fukyū Kyōkai, 1988.

———, ed. *Yokohama shōnin to sono jidai*. Yokohama: Yūrindō, 1995.

Yokohama-shi. *Kanagawa kushi*. Yokohama: Kanagawa Kushi Hensan Kankō Jikkō Iinkai, 1977.

———. *Yokohama shishi*. Vol. 2. Yokohama: Yokohama-shi, 1958.

Yokohama Zeikan. *Yokohama Zeikan hyakunijū-nenshi.* Yokohama: Yokohama Zeikan, 1981.

Yoshida Tsuneyoshi. "Taigai kankei yori mitaru Yokohama kaikō no yūkaku." *Meiji Taishō shidan* 9 (1937): 1–7.

INDEX

Note: *Italic* page numbers refer to tables and figures.